Paraguay and the Triple Alliance:
The Postwar Decade, 1869–1878

Latin American Monographs, No. 44
Institute of Latin American Studies
The University of Texas at Austin

Paraguay and the Triple Alliance
The Postwar Decade, 1869–1878

by Harris Gaylord Warren
with the assistance of
Katherine F. Warren

Institute of Latin American Studies
The University of Texas at Austin

International Standard Book Number 0-292-76444-8 (paper)
0-292-76445-6 (cloth)
Library of Congress Catalog Card Number 77-075824

The Latin American Monographs Series
is distributed for the Institute of
Latin American Studies by:
  University of Texas Press
  P. O. Box 7819
  Austin, Texas 78712

To the memory of
two great Paraguayan scholars
Efraím Cardozo
and
Pablo Max Ynsfrán

Contents

Figures

Paraguay and the Triple Alliance:
The Postwar Decade, 1869–1878

Preface

Francisco Solano López made a momentous decision in November, 1864, when he precipitated the War of the Triple Alliance. This war, the most terrible conflict in South American history, had far reaching effects on the four countries involved. Paraguay, crushed by the armed forces of Brazil, Argentina, and Uruguay, was all but annihilated. Allied armies occupied the capital for more than seven years, and for the entire postwar decade the Argentine flag flew over Villa Occidental, capital of the Chaco Boreal. Although the war did not end until López was killed on March 1, 1870, the Allies occupied Asunción during the first week of January, 1869, and at once began the process of creating a Paraguayan government with which they could deal. The decade 1869–1878 ended with the arbitral award by which Argentina was eliminated as a claimant to the Chaco Boreal, and in that year the election of Cándido Bareiro as president of Paraguay marked the ascendancy of that political group that was already being called the Colorado party.

There have been no studies in depth of this critical period in Paraguayan history. Gomes Freire Esteves, Héctor Francisco Decoud, Justo Pastor Benítez, F. Arturo Borbón, and Efraím Cardozo have made valuable contributions, as have authors of numerous articles. Augusto Tasso Fragoso of Brazil, Ramón J. Cárcano of Argentina, and Luís G. Benítez and Cecilio Báez of Paraguay have written extensively on the complex diplomatic issues but without benefit of multiarchival research. Archives in Buenos Aires, Rio de Janeiro, London, and Washington are rich in source material to which the scholar finds ready access. Unfortunately, the same is not true of Asunción. The Paraguayan Archivo Nacional has practically no manuscripts relating to the last hundred years—at least, this was true as of July, 1973. There are incomplete files of published documents, and the Biblioteca Enrique Solano López, which was a section of the Archivo, contains some rare books, pamphlets, and newspapers. Persistent efforts to obtain access

3

to ministerial archives in Asunción met with ingenious excuses that simply meant refusal, but this is a condition with which Paraguayan scholars themselves must cope. One suspects that the materials are not organized for research and may indeed have been purloined by office holders long ago. Consequently, major dependence has been placed on reports of foreign diplomats and travelers for much of the information indispensable to an understanding of the postwar decade. Fortunately, the Brazilians were especially productive, much more so than the Argentines, whose diplomatic representation in Asunción was very inadequate.

Many institutions and individuals have aided me in this project. The American Philosophical Society was generous in awarding grants from the Penrose Fund. The Faculty Research Committee of Miami University, the Social Science Research Council, and the American Council of Learned Societies all provided financial assistance. Señor Carlos Alberto Pusineri Scala, scholarly and genial director of the Casa de La Independencia in Asunción, with rare generosity gave me access to his invaluable collection of manuscripts and newspapers. Dr. Nettie Lee Benson gave me carte blanche to use the magnificent resources of the Latin American Collection in the University of Texas Library. The staffs of these many libraries and archives in the United States, England, Argentina, Paraguay, and Brazil were always courteous and helpful: the Library of Congress, Columbus Memorial Library of the Pan American Union, and the National Archives in Washington, D. C.; the British Museum, Public Record Office, and Somerset House in London; the Archivo General de la Nación, Biblioteca Nacional, Biblioteca del Congreso, Biblioteca del Ministerio de Relaciones Exteriores, and Museo Mitre in Buenos Aires; the Archivo Nacional and Biblioteca Nacional in Asunción; the Biblioteca Nacional, Arquivo Nacional, and Instituto Histórico e Geográfico Brasileiro in Rio de Janeiro. I am especially indebted to Dr. Marta Gonçalves, Chief of the Arquivo Histórico, Ministério das Relações Exteriores, Itamaraty, and her former assistant, Senhor Affonso de Almeida. Mrs. Jean Barman, principal organizer of the Coleção Cotegipe, introduced me to that indispensable collection. Professor Stanley E. Hilton, for two years director of the Contemporary History Project of the Arquivo Nacional in Rio de Janeiro, was particularly helpful. I have profited greatly from the many studies by Professor John Hoyt Williams, former director of the Georgetown University Project of the Universidad Católica Nuestra Señora de la Asunción, whose reasearch in early nineteenth-century Paraguayan history has provided new insights into the Paraguayan character. To Professors Lewis U. Hanke, John E. Fagg, Donald E. Worcester, and C. Harvey Gardiner, my gratitude for their long-continuing interest and encouragement.

Carlsbad, New Mexico

There is an infinite, rending sorrow that weighs heavily on the heart of our people; there is bitterness for the injustice consummated with such impunity on the live embers of suffering and misery. The Paraguayan people are tired and sad; night has fallen on their destiny after a magnificent sunset of glorious crimsons; and that weariness and that sorrow, which are not dissipated with the first convulsion of a skin-deep democracy, explain and define much of the sickly process of our political development from then until now.

Arturo Bray, *Hombres y épocas del Paraguay*

1. End of the Paraguayan War

Facing each other beside a flaming torch at the entrance to the National Pantheon of Heroes in Asunción, two soldiers stand at attention throughout the daylight hours, rifles on their shoulders, ignoring the stifling heat of summer and the raw cold of winter. Within this shrine, in a casket at the bottom of a well-like mausoleum, lies Paraguay's Unknown Soldier. Crypts around the circular wall hold smaller caskets. Here with other heroes are the remains of Carlos Antonio López, of Marshal Francisco Solano López, and of the great leader in the Chaco War, Marshal José Félix Estigarribia.

War is inseparable from the will to wage it, from the willingness to accept whatever sacrifice it demands. This willingness was imbedded in the Paraguayan character. Carlos Antonio López emblazoned on his banner the rousing slogan "Independence or Death!" And Francisco Solano López ordered his people to "Conquer or Die!" A frontier people, forced to be self-reliant, forced to accept adversity and severe hardship as a common experience, Paraguayans had always been ready to fight. Threats from marauding Indians had subsided in the nineteenth century, but ambitious neighbors coveted much of Paraguay's domain.

The two marshals in the National Pantheon symbolize the death and resurrection of a heroic nation. Carlos Antonio raised Paraguay to a level of prosperity never before reached in its long history. His son, the Marshal-President, plunged the nation into a catastrophic war in whose horrors at least one-half of the population perished. Then began the slow, agonizing process of reconstruction, of creating a political system, of peopling an empty land. Six decades later came the Chaco War, a long and exhausting conflict in which Marshal Estigarribia led Paraguay to victory. But an observer in 1869, viewing the shambles of a shattered nation, would have had small basis for predicting a hopeful future.

Historians continue to speculate about the motives that led Francisco Solano López into the War of the Triple Alliance. There were good reasons, viewed from Asunción. Territorial disputes with Argentina and Brazil were still far from solution. Argentina claimed title to Misiones, the center of the former Jesuit "empire" of Indian settle-;ments, which flanked southeastern Paraguay across the Paraná River. West of the Paraguay River, between the rivers Bermejo and Pilcomayo, lay the potentially rich Chaco Central, which Argentina also claimed. Brazil insisted on confining northern and northeastern Paraguay behind the Apa River and two low mountain ranges. The area between the Apa and Branco rivers was rich in *yerbales*, where leaves from a low bushy tree were processed into yerba maté, or Paraguayan tea, which was widely used in Brazil and the Platine countries.

To these territorial and boundary disputes was added the issue of free navigation of the rivers. Lacking both railroads and highways to its vast interior province of Mato Grosso, Brazil depended on the rivers for communication with such interior towns as Corumbá and Coimbra. Although he had grudgingly granted freedom of navigation, Carlos Antonio López had built the seemingly formidable fortress of Humaitá on the left bank of the Paraguay River. This fortress was a constant threat to foreign shipping.

A third issue deserves at least some consideration. López probably thought that Argentina would not permit Brazil to absorb Uruguay, but there was a remote possibility that Argentina might withdraw its opposition in exchange for a free hand in Paraguay. There was more than just a lingering desire among Argentine politicians to reincorporate Paraguay into Argentine territory. Both Uruguay and Paraguay had been parts of the Viceroyalty of La Plata and both had broken away from Buenos Aires early in the nineteenth century.

Finally, López was convinced that the independence of Uruguay was necessary to maintain political equilibrium in the Plata. Argentina and Brazil had fought over the country, both wanted it, and both had intervened in its politics. A peculiar combination of circumstances found them supporting the same Uruguayan party in 1864, and the Uruguayan government sought aid from Paraguay.

The War to 1869

López moved cautiously while the Uruguayan situation was building to a climax. He increased the army, intensified military training at Cerro León, attempted to hasten the shipment of arms from Europe, and sought to augment the navy. Early in 1864 he warned Brazil against military intervention in Uruguay, a warning that the Empire rejected brusquely. Although Edward Thornton, British minister to Argentina, led other diplomats in a futile attempt to mediate between Brazil and Uruguay, Brazilian forces invaded the Banda Oriental in October, 1864, and units of the Brazilian fleet steamed up the Uruguay River to besiege the port of Paysandú. A month later López seized the Brazilian *Marqués de Olinda* after it had cleared Asunción for Corumbá. This act of November 12, 1864, began the war against Brazil.

Uruguayans hoped that López would immediately send his armies to their aid. Instead, the Paraguayan dictator at the end of 1864 struck swiftly against Brazilian posts in Mato Grosso. A combined naval and land expedition captured Brazilian positions and large quantities of military supplies. Leaving a small occupation force, López recalled his victorious troops and prepared to attack southern Brazil. Denied permission to cross Argentine territory to attack Rio Grande do Sul, López seized the small river port of Corrientes in April, 1865. This invasion of Argentine territory brought Argentina, Brazil, and the victorious Uruguayan rebels into a triple alliance in May, 1865, and began a new phase of the war.

López sent strong columns to the south in a two-pronged attack that ended in the destruction of the best part of his army. One Paraguayan force under General Wenceslao Robles marched southward from Corrientes. Brazilians then sent 4,000 men on ten ships to attack the city on May 25. The Paraguayan garrison withdrew after resisting valiantly. A rumor that Paraguayan reenforcements were enroute from Humaitá caused the Brazilians to reembark the next day. The ships dropped down to the Riachuelo a short distance below Corrientes. López then prepared a very daring attack. He sent nine vessels, each towing a flat-bottomed *chata*, or raft, armed with one gun, against the Brazilian fleet. In the ensuing battle of Riachuelo on June 16, 1865, the Brazilians destroyed half of the Paraguayan *chatas* and vessels. With luck, better timing, and expert command, what appeared to have been a mad escapade might well have resulted in a Paraguayan victory. While Robles did practically nothing along the left bank of the Paraná, Lt. Col. Antonio de la Cruz Estigarribia advanced with 10,000 men to the Uruguay River. The main force continued to Uruguayana, where Estigarribia was compelled to surrender on September 19, 1865.

These two defeats of Riachuelo and Uruguayana forced López to change his plans. Now on the defensive, he ordered the remaining troops to abandon Corrientes at the end of October, 1865, and replaced Robles with General Isidoro Resquín. Despite the presence of Brazilian ships, which did nothing to impede the movement, Resquín recrossed the Paraná. López made the most of Allied slowness in moving to the attack. Col. George Thompson, an Englishman who had entered Paraguayan service before the war, directed the development of strong defenses in the swampy, difficult terrain of southwestern Paraguay. When the Allies finally crossed the Paraná, Paraguayan forces attacked ferociously, suffering and inflicting heavy losses. During these early months of 1866, the Allies were slowly building their strength under the command of General Bartolomé Mitre, president of Argentina. Mitre made a grave error on September 22, 1866, when he ordered an attack against Curupaity, one of the strongest points in the Paraguayan defenses. Commanded by General José Eduvigis Díaz, the entrenched Paraguayans inflicted terrible losses on the Allies.

The war entered a quiet period after Paraguay's great victory at Curupaity. Ten days earlier, Marshal López and General Mitre had met in the famous interview of Yataity-Corá. Here López realized that a major objective of the Allies was to drive him out of Paraguay—there would be no peace so long as he remained.[1] The relative inactivity after Mitre's crushing defeat at Curupaity lasted until November, 1867. It was a period that drained Paraguay's resources through attrition while the Allies improved their positions and refused all offers of mediation. The most promising of these efforts was made by Mr. C. Z. Gould, a secretary in the British legation in Buenos Aires, in August, 1867. His failure delighted the Brazilian government, which had been undergoing harsh criticism at home.[2] Argentina, to be sure, was anxious for peace. The country was politically unstable, rebellious caudillos had not been subdued, and the new foreign minister, Marcelino Ugarte, understood clearly the danger of a Brazilian-Argentine clash after the war.[3] Brazil's General Luis Alves de Lima e Silva, Marquês de Caxias, agreed that peace was necessary and that López should be allowed to retire honorably; but Dom Pedro II was determined to drive López out of Paraguay at any cost, and to guarantee this objective he made significant changes in his high command.[4]

Slowly the Allies moved to isolate the greatly feared river fortress of Humaitá. Mitre, impatient with the plodding Brazilians, ordered the fleet to run the batteries; but Admiral Inácio, who was under the orders of Caxias, refused to obey. Forced to return to Buenos Aires by the death of his vice president, Mitre left the field to Caxias as supreme commander in January, 1868. A month later the Brazilian fleet passed Humaitá without loss. With two ironclads and a monitor, Captain Delfin Carlos de Carvalho steamed up the Paraguay toward Asunción, shelling the telegraph line, river craft, and military positions.[5]

Paraguayans had placed such great faith in the supposedly impregnable Humaitá that news of the Brazilian river advance caused consternation and near panic, except among the foreigners who were waiting impatiently in Asunción for the Brazilians to free them from the López terror. López had become convinced that General Robles had dealt with the enemy at Corrientes and eventually executed him. All relatives of persons suspected of treason were subject to imprisonment and torture, and foreigners were not exempt. Vice President Francisco Sánchez called a council of war at the urging of Col. Venancio López, brother of the Marshal and military commander of Asunción. The capital was practically defenseless. There were few projectiles for its battery of seven cannons. The two infantry battalions and one cavalry squadron, augmented by 200 poorly armed police, were under strength and desperately short of munitions, and no one knew for sure where López was at the moment. Gloomily the council anticipated that Asunción would be reduced to rubble. Nevertheless, at its second session, on February 22, the council decided that Asunción must be defended. Sánchez ordered Asunción to be evacuated within forty-eight hours and designated Luque, some ten kilometers to the east, as the provisional capital.[6] The American minister, Charles Ames Washburn, refused to go, arguing that Asunción was the legal capital and it was his duty to remain.

Feverishly Asunción awaited the expected bombardment while people streamed out of the city, which probably had fewer than 15,000 inhabitants. Many Paraguayans and foreigners, including Elisa Alicia Lynch, the notorious mistress of López, hastened to deposit their valuables in the American legation. So many foreigners sought refuge under his flag that Washburn enlarged his domestic staff and rented an adjacent house. The three Brazilian vessels entered the harbor on February 24, fired a few shells wildly, then steamed away, leaving the foreign colony bitterly disappointed. A landing force could easily have taken the capital then, but Caxias had no such plans, although Asunción lay open to attack whenever the Allies chose to assault the old and helpless Mother of Cities.[7] During the next ten months Asunción was a ghost city. Day after day the few remaining inhabitants expected a large force of Brazilians to come, but not until January 1, 1869, were their hopes or fears realized.

After the fall of Humaitá, López established a new base at San Fernando on the Tebicuary River a few kilometers from its mouth. Here occurred the worst atrocities of an atrocious war. Convinced that the meetings of the council of war in Asunción demonstrated the existence of a conspiracy against him, López ordered first the council members and then scores of prominent Paraguayans and many foreigners to be arrested and brought to San Fernando, where they were tortured into confessing to non-existent crimes. At least 368 "conspirators" are known to have been executed or to have succumbed to torture by the end of the year. Among them were the dictator's brother Benigno López and his foreign minister, José Berges, the latter one of Paraguay's most distinguished statesmen. As Efraím Cardozo writes, "San Fernando was the theater of horrible scenes." [8] During the slaughter at San Fernando, López subjected Washburn to severe pressure. The American minister supposedly was a key conspirator who harbored other López enemies.[9]

López moved from San Fernando at the end of August, 1868, and took up positions near Villeta, a little river port some twenty-five kilometers downstream from Asunción. A fortified line from the mouth of the Pykysyry protected his headquarters at Itá-Ybaté in Lomas Valentinas, low hills southeast of Villeta. Here López made his last serious resistance of the war and prepared as best he could to meet the overwhelming force that Caxias could throw against his pitiful army of 10,000, most of them old men and young boys. This remnant of the Paraguayan forces could still inflict grievous losses on the enemy, as Caxias discovered at the battle of Ytororó. The Brazilian commander executed a flanking movement through the Chaco to avoid the Angostura-Pykysyry line and came down from the north with 19,000 men. López sent General Bernardino Caballero with fewer than 5,000 men to defend the narrow bridge across the Ytororó and so protect Lomas Valentinas. The forces clashed on December 6, a Sunday. Fighting with magnificent courage, the small Paraguayan force withstood three charges before finally giving way when Caxias himself, brandishing his sword, led his troops with the famous battle cry: "Follow me, those of you who are Brazilians!" [10]

Still the way was not open to Villeta and Lomas Valentinas. Caballero, with about 4,000 men and boys, fell back to the Arroyo Avahy and its high ground overlooking Villeta. On December 11, a hot and rainy day, Caxias attacked with some 18,000 men. After five hours of extremely vicious fighting, Caballero's force was nearly annihilated. The Brazilians buried 3,000 Paraguayans and captured 800, most of them wounded; but Caballero escaped, as he did from every battle, without a scratch.[11]

López awaited the final Brazilian assault in what appeared to be a strong position. His rear, however, was unprotected, and the most elementary reconnaissance would have revealed this weakness to Caxias. His army had been reduced to about 7,000 men and boys, of whom 3,000 under Col. George H. Thompson were cut off at Angostura, a small fortified spot on the Paraguay River four miles away. Another

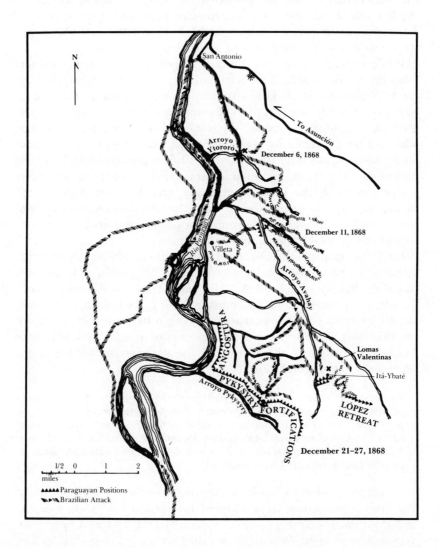

Map 1. Pykysyry – Itá-Ybaté Campaign, November-December 1868
(After Tasso Fragoso, História da Guerra entre a Tríplice Aliança e o Paraguai,
IV, 106)

1,500 manned the Pykysyry line, leaving no more than 2,500 to hold the semicircular trench that protected the Marshal's headquarters on the low hill of Itá-Ybaté. The unprotected rear opened toward Cerro León, site of the prewar training camp and, at 2,295 feet above sea level, one of the highest points in the country.[12]

While waiting for the Allied attack, López received a new minister from the United States. Washburn had been rescued in September by the U. S. gunboat *Wasp*. His succcessor, General Martin T. McMahon, was determined to stay out of Washburn's quarrels. He reached Paraguay on December 9, obtained the release of two controversial figures who had been claimed by Washburn as part of his legation, and presented his credentials on December 14.[13] López greeted McMahon cordially, and the latter, quite in contrast with Washburn, was very sympathetic with the Paraguayan cause. The American minister remained at the López headquarters until the situation became hopeless and so had an unrivaled opportunity to observe the final battle that should have ended Paraguayan resistance.

Caxias developed a three-pronged attack with 25,000 men against the Paraguayan positions. One force contained Angostura, a second reduced the Pykysyry line, and the third and largest assaulted the trench guarding Itá-Ybaté. After preliminary shelling and skirmishing, the Brazilians struck with a frontal attack by two columns at mid-afternoon on December 21. For three hours the troops fought furiously. McMahon, fascinated by the bravery of the Paraguayan defenders, described the action graphically:

> Twice the Brazilian cavalry penetrated the Paraguayan lines in heavy force, advancing quite to the Head Quarters. But the Paraguayans although in greatly inferior numbers, swarmed around them, officers and soldiers, men and children on horseback and on foot, in absolute confusion, but all dashing against the heavy column with the most admirable gallantry until at last the enemy retreated in confusion.[14]

Brazilians used their artillery very inefficiently, while the clumsy Paraguayan pieces had to be dragged into position by men, women, and children. Fourteen guns fell to the attackers, leaving López with very little armament. When Caxias called off the attack both sides had suffered heavy losses, and López certainly had fewer than 2,000 troops to withstand a renewed attack. McMahon, hardened veteran of the American Civil War, was appalled:

> I regret to say that more than one half of the Paraguayan Army is composed of children from ten to fourteen years of age. This circumstance rendered the battle of the 21st and the ensuing days peculiarly dreadful

and heart rending. These little ones in most cases absolutely naked, came crawling back in great numbers, mangled in every conceivable way. There seemed to be no place for them to go and they wandered helplessly towards the Head Quarters without tear or groan.[15]

In the López camp, McMahon observed, were "several thousand women," many of whom were killed or wounded during the attack. They served by moving artillery, "dragging the ammunition wagons," and bringing in the wounded.

There was little that López could do as he awaited the final blow. A few troops came in from Cerro León, but no other reenforcements were available. López had left the Pykysyry line manned too long and so lost the men, guns, and munitions that could have been very important in the battle of Itá-Ybaté. No troops could come from Angostura, where Colonel Thompson held the enemy off. With Brazilians holding the outer trench, a more helpless situation for López would be difficult to imagine. Caxias, too, had been badly hurt, with some of his finest officers among the dead and wounded.

There was no hurry to complete the destruction of López. While Brazilian artillery and infantry kept up a sporadic fire on December 22 and 23, Caxias prepared for the *coup de grâce*. López expected the worst. He entrusted four of his children to McMahon, whose quarters were protected by "thick matrasses [sic] to save them from the bullets which constantly pierced the walls." The dictator made his will, a simple document in which he bequeathed all of his property to his mistress, Elisa Alicia Lynch, and gave it to McMahon, who left for Piribebuy on December 23.[16] Madame Lynch sought no opportunity to escape or to accompany McMahon to the safety of Piribebuy. In these presumably last hours she was extremely busy, although her role probably has been grossly exaggerated. One report credits her with actually taking over command, "frequently 'running' the lines in her showy garb." [17]

Early on December 24, Caxias sent a flag of truce with the demand that López surrender. On his head alone, the Allies sternly charged, rested responsibility for past and future bloodshed. López rejected the demand, bitterly reminding the Allied generals that he had vainly sought peace at Yataity-Corá. He would treat on honorable terms but never surrender unconditionally.[18]

Small Argentine and Uruguayan elements arrived and Caxias regrouped. A Paraguayan deserter reported that López had some 600 men and eleven cannons left, and that his rear was open to attack. To celebrate Christmas day, the Allies fired 2,300 rounds of artillery into the Paraguayan position. This terrific bombardment caused such heavy losses that López desperately ordered a cavalry attack, but it accomplished nothing and caused further losses. When the Allies attacked on December 27, Caxias had 23,000 men to throw against the tiny group of defenders. The handful of Paraguayans fought with their customary bravery, but the issue was quickly decided. In the terrible confusion that resulted, López and a few officers escaped on horseback, as did Madame Lynch. The chief surgeon, Dr. William Stewart, providentially fled into the Brazilian lines, although he could have accompanied Madame Lynch, who frantically sought for López. All of the dictator's baggage and personal papers fell to the enemy.[19]

López established temporary headquarters at Cerro León, and there McMahon went on December 29 to propose mediation. If López would leave the country, McMahon assured him that he would find "a hospitable welcome in the United States." The dictator was willing to make any sacrifice for his country but would never agree to a dishonorable peace and rejected the proffered mediation. The Marshal had hopes of resisting the Allies and counted on the continued resistance of Angostura; but Thompson, with no choice if he wished to prevent the destruction of his troops, surrendered on December 30.[20]

Occupation of Asunción

The Allies prepared to enter Asunción in triumph instead of pursuing López relentlessly. This decision gave the Marshal several months to rebuild an army, to cast new artillery pieces at Caacupé, where contracted English experts continued to work faithfully, and to assemble what remained of munitions and supplies. The remnant of the population had taken refuge in the Cordillera: "They have abandoned their growing crops, their houses and all their possessions," McMahon observed. "They are now almost unclothed, thousands without shelter, many without food or the means of obtaining it, including this [Piribebuy] and other villages of the mountains where the cholera is already appearing." Despite these conditions, "if the Allied commanders insist upon the unconditional surrender of the President and his little army . . . the war will only cease when the Paraguayan race is wholly exterminated."[21] This gloomy prediction did not come true, partly because many thousands of Paraguayans lived in the small area around Asunción and so came under protection of the Allied forces. Many did indeed take refuge in the Cordillera with López, but far more of the remaining people sought safety in and near Asunción.

Caxias has been criticized severely for his decision to mark time after the December victories. None of the reasons he gave at first justified his inaction: he did not know where López had gone, there was still an armed force at Angostura (but not for long), and his men were tired. Occupation of the enemy's capital, generally a major objective in every war, signified an approaching end to hostilities, and Caxias really did think that the war was over. Following orders from Caxias, Colonel Hermes Ernesto da Fonseca with 1,700 men landed from Brazilian ships during the night of January 1, 1869, to take possession of Asunción. The few Paraguayan troops in the city, observers rather than defenders, withdrew at once. Caxias came in with the bulk of the army on January 5, having taken the precaution of stationing a strong force at Luque to ward off any danger from the east. The Argentines, 4,000 strong under General Emilio Mitre, occupied the old military area of Campo Grande on the outskirts; some 200 Uruguayans and a few Argentines shared the city with Brazilians. Caxias found quarters in the sumptuous home of Vicente Barrios across the street from the Cathedral, while lesser officers appropriated public buildings and homes, most of them deserted, and even used dwellings as stables for their horses.[22] Soon there was not a vacant home in the city.

Utmost confusion prevailed in the fallen capital. With the victorious Allies came a heterogeneous assortment of camp followers, sutlers, tourists, official and unofficial observers, Paraguayan exiles returning home after many years, about 800 officers and men of the Paraguayan Legion—a group of Paraguayan exiles who served the Allies—and hundreds of starving Paraguayans, many of them wounded, maimed, diseased, and all of them objects of the deepest pity. Hastily improvised businesses served the great influx of people: "Hotels, inns, restaurants, cafes, gambling places, public dance halls, shops, stores, coffee shops were supported profitably by the 30,000 Allied soldiers and innumerable tourists, speculators and curiosity seekers who hurried to visit the ruins of the once powerful conquered nation."[23] There was no government except that imposed by the indifferent military commanders. Asunción, Mother of Cities, was a mother without comfort for children who had wept so long they could weep no more.

The first wave of troops ran wild through the city, sacking homes and warehouses and setting many fires. Brazilians insisted that they had placed guards over identifiable consulates and legations, but one eyewitness reported that the troops "pillaged the city thoroughly, leaving not a pane of glass, nor mirror, nor lock untouched."[24] Another who arrived early in January "found the Brazilian officers & seamen breaking open the doors, plundering the furniture, and with axe & hammer breaking the chests and taking all the valuables, throwing the papers, books & documents to the wind." Among the ravaged buildings were the American legation and the French and Italian consulates. General

Enrique Castro, commander of the Uruguayan contingent, and his officers loaded plundered hides and tobacco on a steamer bound for Buenos Aires. Given the chance, Argentines might have been just as avaricious, although General Emilio Mitre seems to have prevented his troops from engaging in the plunder.[25] Marauding troops and adventurers ripped houses apart, violated tombs in the cemeteries, and dug up gardens in a wild search for hidden treasure. Caxias refused to be bothered with formal protests presented by Lorenzo Chapperon, the Italian consul, and his French counterpart, Aimé Paul de Cuverville.[26]

Many boats loaded with booty soon disgorged their stolen wealth on the docks at Buenos Aires. Military commanders made little if any effort to impede this traffic, which continued for several months, although they did establish an ineffective Allied Mixed Claims Commission on March 6 to which complaints could be brought. With three Brazilians, three Argentines, and one Uruguayan on this commission, a Paraguayan complaint had small chance for a sympathetic hearing. People in Buenos Aires were astounded by the quality of booty that came from a land generally held to be inhabited by barbarians. Not until June did the Argentine government act to end the traffic and to sell former shipments at auction, much of it in the sales room of a prominent merchant-auctioneer, Mariano Billinghurst. Some items found their way into the office of President Domingo Faustino Sarmiento.[27]

Very sensitive to the charges that Brazilian officers failed to prevent the pillage of Asunción and Luque, and even participated in looting them, the Brazilian minister of foreign affairs later published an impassioned but unconvincing defense. He asserted that all identifiable buildings containing valuable goods were guarded and Brazil could not be held responsible for damages that occurred between Paraguayan evacuation and Allied occupation. López himself had ordered the removal of all moveable goods. Moreover, Brazilians had fed and clothed foreigners saved from the López tyranny and had delivered to the Provisional Government valuables captured at various places as well as goods found in Asunción. This, he protested, was quite in contrast with the atrocities committed by Paraguayan forces in their sneak attack on Mato Grosso.[28] Despite this defense, there is no doubt about the plundering of Asunción and Luque.

Caxias, ill and unhappy, let the situation get completely out of hand. Several of his close friends had died in the last battles, there was criticism in Rio de Janeiro, the Argentine press was increasingly caustic and hostile, and he longed for a rest. On January 14, 1869, he issued his famous Order of the Day No. 272 which closed with the assurance: "The war has come to its end, and the Brazilian army and fleet may take pride in having fought for the most just and holy of all causes."[29] While attending Mass in the Cathedral on January 17, Caxias fainted. On the next day he relinquished his command to Marshal Guilherme Xavier de Sousa and left for Montevideo on January 19.[30]

The departure of Caxias marked an intensification of the looting that left Asunción and Luque stripped of their wealth. The Brazilian army, the French minister in Buenos Aires reported, "was in a thoroughly disorganized state."[31] The commission, which supposedly was to protect property in warehouses, aided in the spoliation. Sutlers for the Brazilian army had a good thing going: "The Brazilian army is almost without horses, and those that remain are dying fast; and no wonder, for the poor animal receives half of his rations and 'someone' receives the other half in pounds sterling!"[32]

Unfriendly observers, and especially Paraguayans, charged that Allied troops were a licentious, undisciplined lot who created scenes of horror in the occupied capital. The few women were fair game for all ranks: "Free love reigned in the streets and plazas, the 300 Paraguayan women who had fallen into the enemy's power after Itá-Ybaté being victims of this vandalism."[33] Granted his anti-Allied bias, still one cannot discount entirely the testimony of an indignant eyewitness, General McMahon, who reported that "the prevailing unnatural crime in the Brazilian army, destroying as it does the authority of the guilty officers, converts the army into a licentious and lawless horde, who disgrace alike humanity and the name of soldier." The Argentine army was better disciplined but nevertheless shared the blame for "the barbarities which are practiced by its allies upon the helpless women and children in Paraguay."[34]

There was more money to be made in profiteering and graft than in the ludicrous scramble for buried treasure in which natives, foreign adventurers, and Allied soldiers joined. The López will, understandably, did not mention buried treasure. This oversight did not discourage the mythmakers who spun fantastic tales about how López in his flight buried the treasure he was thought to have with him. He did, indeed, leave treasure along the route of his retreat to Cerro Corá—the lives of hundreds of Paraguayans, loyal followers or prisoners, who died of wounds, disease, hunger, and the lance thrusts of executioners. This was not the treasure sought by those who spent their time digging in the once beautiful gardens of Madame Lynch's country home at Patiño-cué. Other areas became pock-marked by gullible diggers. "Some explorers came to Paraguaty [Caraguatay?] and dug by day and night, so that the whole town and district, overgrown as it is, is full of deep holes in the ground dangerous for the incautious traveler who ventures from the beaten path." [35] López did have treasure, the £16,000 sent out of Paraguay in 1868 and the £12,000 taken out by General McMahon in 1869. When the Brazilians captured Madame Lynch on March 1, 1870, she had $8,000 in gold and jewelry valued at 25,000 *pesos fuertes*, roughly equivalent to dollars. [36] That either López or Madame Lynch would have been so stupid as to bury significant treasure does great injustice to their foresight, although one cannot ignore the possibility that something remained after the shipments of 1868 and 1869. The gold possessed by Madame Lynch may well have been all that was left.

The Last of López

Organized resistance to the Allied attack ended in August, 1869, when the Allies crushed López at Piribebuy and Campo Grande (Acosta Ñu). [37] In the meantime there were several bloody encounters, and even after the decisive battles of August, López kept alive his hopeless resistance for another six months.

López worked a miracle in the early months of 1869 while the Allied troops rested and slowly regrouped in Asunción, their morale steadily deteriorating. Although the dictator had escaped with but a handful of followers into the hills that form a low cordillera some 50 kilometers east of Asunción, the Allies had very poor information as to the size of his "army." One report placed it at 5,000, of which 3,000 or more were wounded. [38] López made Piribebuy his capital, established an arsenal at Caacupé with equipment moved from the Asunción arsenal, and called for the people to rally behind him. Some of the rallying was anything but voluntary as small patrols scoured the countryside to drive people into the dictator's camp. A motley but valiant army of regular troops, escaped prisoners, old men, boys, and women was assembled and held the fortified Azcurra pass that guarded Caacupé. López spent much of his time with this makeshift force at Azcurra. This was a very strong position, and here López could have inflicted heavy damage on an enemy foolish enough to launch a frontal assault, despite his woeful inadequacy in small arms, cannons, and ammunition. At Caacupé, John Nesbitt and Charles H. Thompson, English armorers, cast eighteen howitzers and two rifled pieces from church bells and Brazilian artillery balls. [39]

Living conditions deteriorated swiftly in Piribebuy and Caacupé. Piribebuy normally was a village of 800 people, but more than 10,000 persons crowded into it. Food was so scarce that survivors reported having "subsisted principally on the roots of cocoa trees, orange leaves, and such substance for some time." Flour made from the macaíba palm was a food that barely kept people alive. Nevertheless, for the more valuable members of his party, such as Percy Burrell, Henry Valpy, Charles Twyte, and other Englishmen and his own favorites, López managed to find better food, including plenty of wine.[40]

López forced as many Paraguayans as possible to take refuge behind his nebulous lines at Caacupé, Piribebuy, and Villa Rica until the latter was overrun by Brazilians. Small patrols constantly went out to round up stragglers, and often these patrols committed horrible atrocities. On one occasion, after an Argentine cavalry regiment had returned from patrol, its commander reported having found

> about 1000 Paraguayan women & children in a most wretched state of destitution, as well as about 10 prisoners, 5 of them it appears gave themselves up but the others in trying to make their escape through the woods were captured.
>
> They state that President López sent an ensign out with about 15 men with orders to kill all the families they came across between the Paraguayan line & Angostura and to bring back a report of the position of the Allies.
>
> The officer and other 5 scouts succeeded in making their escape by knowing the different paths through the woods . . . [The Argentine colonel] who was in command of the Cavalry reports that he saw on the road about 40 or 50 women & children from 2 years upwards with their throats cut, having been recently done as their bodies were quite warm.[41]

Another eyewitness, a Swiss who deserted after having been forced to serve in the Argentine army, recalled that the fleeing dictator sent squads of executioners, clad in red ponchos, to cut the throats of all who refused his order to abandon their homes. Thus scores of villages were deserted in this brutal scorched-earth policy.[42]

López was able to assemble the pitiful remnants of his resources because the Allies lolled around Asunción, scarcely maintaining adequate patrols. However, near Luque Brazilians captured three roughly clad Indians from a five-man Paraguayan patrol. None of them spoke Spanish. Interrogated in Guaraní, they asserted that López would make a stand at Azcurra. Had the Marshal been able to equip and mount as many as 5,000 cavalry, he could have caused severe damage to the Allies sweating through the summer. As it was, he gave them a little scare on March 10 when he mounted small guns on a railroad car and fired on an advanced Brazilian post near Luque. Alarmed, the Brazilians sent several hundred cavalry and "some thousands of infantry marching out of town."[43]

The ability of López to arouse support seems phenomenal. Part of the explanation surely lies in Article 16 of the Treaty of Alliance, which provided for the division of much Paraguayan territory among the Allies. This well publicized provision convinced the people that they were fighting for their country's existence. Fear and hatred of Brazil and Argentina could be aroused easily because both were widely regarded as traditional enemies. General McMahon, a few days before the Allies began their last crushing offensive, reported that "the Paraguayan army has greatly improved in numbers and enthusiasm and looks forward with extraordinary confidence to the next encounter with the enemy, which there is good reason to believe, will be the decisive battle of the war."[44] Thus the awful tragedy continued as Paraguayans exposed their diseased, mutilated, and starving bodies to the relentless Allied attack.

While López was mobilizing and equipping his last army, Marshal Guilherme Xavier de Sousa reorganized his in Asunción. The Paraguayan Legion, under Colonel Federico Báez, and an Argentine regiment reconnoitered the environs without encountering resistance, while engineers restored the railway and telegraph line as far as Pirayú. Since López had removed all of the rolling stock except one old engine, a sutler brought up what passed for a locomotive and four cars from Buenos Aires, equipment that became known as the Brazilian Train, and on March 7, 1869, the whistle of a locomotive announced that the railway was again operative.[45] Although López, as on March 10, occasionally made quick raids against bridges, he failed to deny limited use of the railway to the Allies.

For the most part, there were only minor patrol clashes for more than six months as the Allies prepared for the Cordillera campaign. Leaving Col. Hermes da Fonseca in command of the Asunción garrison of 2,800 men, Sousa grouped the Argentine and Brazilian forces near Luque. José Maria da Silva Paranhos, one of Brazil's great statesmen, who was soon to become the Visconde of Rio Branco, arrived in Asunción to take charge of civil affairs. His immediate problems were to form a provisional government and to report on the military situation. He urged the Emperor to continue the war until López had been eliminated, and he decided to remain in Asunción until the Allies resumed the offensive. To replace the ailing Sousa, Dom Pedro II sent his young son-in-law, Luiz Felipe Maria Fernando Gastão de Orleans, the Conde d'Eu, to take over supreme command. The count arrived on April 14,

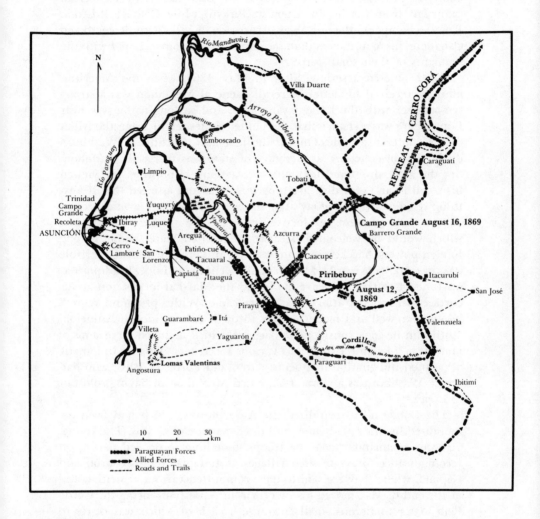

Map 2. Piribebuy, or Cordillera, Campaign, August 1869
(After Tasso Fragoso, História da Guerra entre a Tríplice Aliança e o Paraguai,
IV, 256)

took command two days later at Luque, and began preparations to crush López. General Bernardino Caballero, who figured so prominently in postwar Paraguay, annoyed the Brazilians with a guerrilla campaign from his headquarters at Pirayú, while Colonel Rosendo Romero hampered them in their occupation of Villa Rica. Romero and Caballero, more nuisances than serious threats, rejoined López with the remnants of their small forces.[46]

López suffered a serious blow in May, 1869, when the American minister received his letter of recall. General McMahon was a strong sympathizer with the Paraguayan cause, and so long as he was near López there was a chance that the United States might bring the Allies to the conference table. One of the first acts of Elihu B. Washburn during his brief tenure as secretary of state was to recall McMahon, but the general delayed his departure as long as possible. He viewed his recall as an event disheartening to López, and asserted that if anything remained of Paraguay after the war, the country would present "a vast field of most productive industry" for American enterprise, which would be welcomed because the United States, alone among foreign powers, had kept a representative in Paraguay during "terrible days of trial."[47] When McMahon finally went to the López headquarters on June 24 to take his leave, he found the Marshal in position at Azcurra expecting the attack that never came. With "profound regret" he said farewell and made his way through Allied lines to Asunción. With him he took considerable baggage, which included large sums of money for Madame Lynch and various foreigners. This undiplomatic act caused indignation in Buenos Aires, and Porter C. Bliss, who had served Washburn as a secretary, accused McMahon of having sold out to López.[48]

The Conde d'Eu revitalized the Allied forces, which had been demoralized by disease, idleness, and the departure of Caxias. The young, vigorous commander gave the troops something to do, led parties on reconnaissance forays to such villages as Itauguá, Itá, Yaguarón and Capiatá, where they are said to have committed various atrocities, and at the end of May moved his two corps into positions facing the Cordillera. After numerous small encounters, each of which was costly to López,[49] the count ordered a flanking movement around the left of the Paraguayan line that avoided the Azcurra strongpoint. This tactic surprised López, who had been accustomed to frontal assaults. Advancing methodically with an overwhelming force of more than 21,000 men, well balanced among artillery, cavalry, and infantry, the Allies swept through the Paraguayan positions.[50]

The plan of attack was a classic envelopment. While artillery bombarded Azcurra, General Emilio Mitre turned the Paraguayan right flank; the large Brazilian army in two corps skirted the Cordillera to the southeast, turned east, and then struck swiftly northward through Valenzuela to attack Piribebuy. All units executed their assignments admirably, overcoming slight resistance. López, whose army was in a miserable condition, reacted very sluggishly and failed to evacuate Azcurra until it was too late. Under the circumstances, there was little he could do. After a heavy bombardment on August 12, the Allies threw 21,000 men against the 1,800 men, boys, and women who manned the trenches around Piribebuy. The battle was over quickly. Seven hundred Paraguayan dead testified to the bravery of the hopelessly outnumbered defenders. The Conde d'Eu took 1,000 prisoners and one small portion of Paraguayan archives that López had with him, supplies of flour and yerba, "a great quantity of European wines," chests of clothes, silver objects, a quantity of foreign coins, Brazilian paper money, and assorted booty. The Allies lost only 53 killed, among them General João Manuel Mena Barreto.[51] The soldier-historian Alfredo d'Escragnolle Taunay celebrated the taking of Piribebuy by playing on Madame Lynch's piano for more than two hours after first removing the "body of an unfortunate Paraguayan, killed during the morning bombardment by a grenade that penetrated the roof of the house and struck him from above."[52]

López finally realized his danger. He abandoned Azcurra and Caacupé on August 13. Two days later the Allies entered Caacupé, where they found more than 600 wounded and sick in a hospital, "breathing the air infected by the putrefaction of 30 unburied corpses." The Allies also seized many sacred vessels taken from five churches, parcels of jewelry, and numerous other valuables, which they delivered to the Provisional Government in Asunción.[53] The Allies took up the chase of Paraguayan troops commanded by Generals Caballero and Resquín. Caballero gave battle at Campo Grande, a small plain near the village of Barrero Grande, where the issue was never in doubt. Caballero escaped into the woods, again unscathed, leaving behind 2,000 dead, most of them boys who had disguised themselves with false beards. The Allies captured 2,300 prisoners and all of the Paraguayan artillery.[54] With Resquín and the few who survived the mid-August disasters, López fled to Caraguatay and on through the wilderness of northeastern Paraguay.

A pitiful contingent, more than 2,500 strong in September, 1869, started with the Marshal on this last flight but steadily dwindled away. Along the route Brazilian pursuers found the bodies of hundreds of Paraguayans, mostly women and children, who had died of starvation, succumbed to wounds, or been executed brutally. Still the Brazilians rescued hundreds of emaciated, nearly naked survivors of this tragic retreat, among whom were surviving members of Paraguay's leading families.[55]

General José Antônio Correia da Câmara easily destroyed detachments left by López as the Conde d'Eu pressed the pursuit. López halted his much diminished column, reduced to about 500, on February 8, 1870, at Cerro Corá in the foothills of the Amambay cordillera, which he had crossed twice, and in this wildly beautiful natural bowl he waited for death to end his tortured career. The Marshal stationed guards, sent two parties out to forage, and spent some time fishing in the Aquidabán-niguí, a small tributary of the Aquidabán River. Whatever he intended to do, the enemy gave him very little time.[56]

The task of running down the fugitive fell to General Câmara. Paraguayan deserters and his own patrols kept track of his quarry's movements. Câmara divided his forces. While he led one group toward Cerro Corá, another swept around to cut off a possible retreat toward Bolivia.[57] To Lt. Col. Francisco Antônio Martins fell the honor of delivering the final blow. He attacked the López outpost at Paso Tacuaras with cavalry at 7:00 a.m. on March 1. The fleeing defenders barely had time to reach the camp and sound the alarm when Brazilian cavalry galloped in to end the long war in a brief but furious action during which Vice President Francisco Sánchez and Foreign Minister Luis Caminos were killed. Badly wounded, the Marshal made his way on horseback toward the Aquidabán-niguí. After falling from his horse, he staggered across the stream and fell against the bank, knee-deep in water. General Câmara hurried to the stream, identified himself, and demanded that López surrender. The dying dictator brandished his sword feebly and cried: "I die with my country!" Câmara ordered a soldier to disarm López, who attempted feebly to defend himself. The soldier shot him in the heart.[58] So ended in dramatic gestures the life of Paraguay's most controversial ruler.

News from Cerra Corá caused rejoicing in Asunción. Celebrants serenaded Paranhos and General Julio de Vedia, the new Argentine commander, on Saturday night, March 5. The Provisional Government marked the war's end with a Te Deum in the Cathedral on Sunday morning and a magnificent dance in the evening. La Regeneración, journalistic voice of the Paraguayan Legion and the Provisional Government, exulted in the tyrant's death as it proclaimed:

Glory to General Cámara . . .
Glory to His Highness, the Conde d'Eu!

> Long live the Allied arms!
> Long live the Paraguayan nation! [59]

The Provisional Government's proclamation on March 6 acknowledged that Paraguay had learned a bitter lesson. Hereafter the country must cherish liberty, promote human rights, safeguard the free exercise of political liberties, protect commerce, suppress crime, and promote immigration. A free election would be held. Pending this happy event, the chief of police released all prisoners held for minor crimes and removed the irons from others. In gloomy but extravagant prose *La Regeneración* declared that "The 1st of March of 1870 must always be the anniversary of the liberty of Paraguay, sealed with the ignominious death of a monster who ruled it with blood and exterminated its sons in martyrdom." [60] A much saner and more valid epitaph came from the Buenos Aires *Standard*, which found López unwise, incompetent, indiscreet, and unpatriotic for having refused to end the war by leaving the country, but "He died sword in hand, and having lived like a tyrant, died like a soldier." [61] Judiciously surveying the horrible catastrophe, the *Standard*'s editor provided a judgment upon which a century of research has not improved:

> If vanity and ambition provoked the war which has terminated at Aquidaban, imbecility and intrigue prolonged it. We make room for every demonstration of triumphant rejoicing, yet it cannot conceal the secret mortification we must all feel that to overthrow one man in a rude isolated South American State fully two hundred and fifty thousand of our fellow beings have perished—a sacrifice so awful—a victory so dearly bought suggests reflections which in a measure rob victory of its glory and defeat of its humiliation.
>
> The stranger who attempts to study this memorable war will in spite of all the atrocities laid at the door of López find it more difficult to appreciate the brilliant tactics of the allies than the unswerving resolution of Solano López . . . In the consideration of this subject, which we can now calmly examine with impartiality, but not with indifference, a difficulty arises— that of ascertaining the precise object of López in inviting a struggle which proved his own and his country's ruin. Mere personal ambition and vanity are urged by political writers, but it seems on closer examination of the position of affairs at the breaking out of the war, that López after all was less the victim of a lust of conquest than of circumstances which drew him into the final vortex.[62]

During the immediate postwar period in occupied Paraguay, few voices were raised in defense of the fallen López. But even before the last Brazilian troops had left the country, Lopiztas appeared who found in the martyr of Aquidabán a symbol around which to rebuild a strong sense of nationalism. Many who were to become Colorados had served the Marshal long and faithfully. They could not, without severe damage to their own egos, accept the image of López as a monster. Even before 1878, the Lopiztas began the movement to rehabilitate the Marshal's reputation, a movement that in half a century was to result in the apotheosis of the man who in 1870 was being excoriated as a bloody tyrant.

2. The Stricken Nation

Too many Paraguayans of the postwar decade had little sense of patriotism, of nationalism. If we accept Renan's dictum that a nation is a daily plebiscite, a renewal of striving in common toward a national goal, Paraguay was not even a nation. Instinctively, perhaps, some Paraguayans sought to put the past behind them, sensing that, as Ortega y Gasset insists controversially, a past is not necessary for a nation to exist. The strangling grasp of the past must be broken, by violence if necessary. Revolution and conquest by a foreign enemy may be that cathartic violence. For Paraguay, the War of the Triple Alliance shattered much of the past and destroyed the stranglehold of the López family, but there·were Paraguayans who sought to revive some of the basic relationships that had all but disappeared with the near annihilation of their nation. Theirs was the wiser course. A nation is an entity with a past, for it is born in time and retains its identity only so long as the past lives vigorously in the continuing present.

La Regeneración, a newspaper begun by returned exiles, desperately sought to arouse a spirit of patriotism. Its audience was small, but those who read this unique paper and its later rival, *La Voz del Pueblo*, provided the leaders who carried Paraguay through the Allied occupation and Colorado era that ended in 1904. The foreigner—soldier, sutler, adventurer, diplomat, immigrant, curiosity seeker, journalist—dominated so much of Asunción's life in 1869 that the *asunceno* was thrust into the background. Perhaps the appeals of such *legionarios* as Adolfo Decoud were received resentfully by survivors who had fought with López or who had simply managed miraculously to stay alive. A new spirit must be instilled in the remnant of the Paraguayan people. Those who sought to accomplish this Herculean task could not but be dismayed as they surveyed the wreckage of their country.

Francisco Solano López had inherited a fairly prosperous nation in 1862. The railway built by Carlos Antonio López had made a promis-

29

ing beginning, and Paraguay had forty sailing vessels, some displacing as much as 200 tons, plying its rivers, and eleven major steam warships. River trade was increasing, with more and more ships making the run from Montevideo and Buenos Aires. Under the guidance of foreign technicians employed by the elder López, Paraguay had completed an arsenal, a foundry, and a shipyard. An iron smelter at Ibicuy, with a capacity of 500 kilos in twelve hours, partially relieved the country's dependence on imports. Charcoal from seemingly boundless forests provided fuel to smelt small deposits of high-grade ore. Asunción had a furniture factory and brick kilns. Much concerned with developing agriculture, Carlos Antonio had imported cotton seeds from the United States and tobacco from Cuba. Sugar cane, corn, rice, cotton, coffee, mandioca, orange, and tobacco crops flourished. In 1860 alone, Paraguay produced 6,900,000 kilos of tobacco. Forest products, especially yerba maté, yielded a steady income in foreign trade. The cattle industry, although lacking the best breeds, had some 3,000,000 head in 1864. Prices were good: a cow brought the equivalent of £2 sterling, or about $10 in gold, and a good ox fetched $18. Horses, also numerous, were less expensive. Paraguay had no foreign or domestic debt. Tariff revenues and income from state monopolies and properties yielded enough to provide a surplus and at the same time to pay for needed imports.

Although largely an unknown land, despite the thriving trade at Pilar and Itapúa that had become significant under Francia, Paraguay's contacts with foreign countries had increased steadily under Carlos Antonio. *El Semanario*, the official paper, provided news of a sort that could be read widely since there were some 20,000 pupils in 500 free schools before 1860. Although Paraguayan literacy has been exaggerated, there is no doubt about the government's interest in furthering education. In transportation, industry, and agriculture, Paraguay had made great progress under the first López. The war destroyed Paraguay's manpower, left its industry in a shambles, and inflicted wounds still unhealed many decades later.

The Price of Victory and Defeat

Any attempt to cast up the costs of the war must end in confusion. Brazil bore the largest burden for the Allies and so could expect to play the most important role in postwar settlements. The Empire's sacrifice in manpower was certainly well over 100,000 dead and probably another 65,000 wounded. An incredibly low estimate gives the total Brazilian combat dead, wounded, and missing as 23,917, and the same writer fixes the cost to Brazil at about $199,000,000.[1] R. C. Kirk,

American minister to Argentina, estimated the Brazilian losses as 168,000, Argentine as 20,000, and Uruguayan as 3,000; he placed costs at $281,400,000 for Brazil, $50,000,000 for Argentina, and $6,000,000 for Uruguay. He further reported the belief that Brazil would be crippled for years, while Argentina would suffer less because Brazil had spent so much in that country. "But to Paraguay," he continued, "this war has been a death blow, almost final distruction [sic] . . ." And all because of López. As to McMahon's pleas for intervention in Paraguay, Kirk could see no benefit to the United States, which "had never had a dollar of commerce with it." The United States, Kirk observed, had no interests to protect, and therefore should have no further relations with the country.[2]

Paraguayan monetary and property losses are impossible to measure. That the country had suffered grievously cannot be doubted, but its condition was by no means hopeless. Argentine-Brazilian rivalries would prevent excessive losses of territory or absorption by either country. Although there was no money in the treasury and almost no base for taxation, the country had no debt, a happy situation that shady characters in London and Asunción would quickly remedy. López had paid his troops almost nothing, and he had shipped enough gold to England to satisfy his creditors there. The soil was fertile but not as rich as ecstatic immigration promoters would advertise. A large proportion of the best land belonged to the state, as did the railway and much real estate in Asunción.[3] There was hope that foreign enterprisers—small businessmen who opened shops in Asunción, bankers from London and Buenos Aires, ranchers who would come from Argentina and Europe—would provide needed capital and "give their influence to good government and to successful methods of developing the valuable resources with which nature has so abundantly favored Paraguay." Recovery was slow in coming. Paraguay needed time "for the grass to grow over its four hundred thousand graves. It desires time for its thousands of orphan boys to attain the strength of manhood."[4]

One of the most controversial matters concerns Paraguay's population, its nature as well as its numbers. That there were several thousand uncivilized Indians in the Chaco and even east of the Río Paraguay cannot be disputed. Indeed, Paraguay was still very much a frontier country in 1864. Indian forays reached close to Asunción, and widely separated estancias depended upon their own resources for protection against Indians and wild beasts, primarily the jaguar. No one knows how many Indians there were, nor the degree of miscegenation that had occurred since the sixteenth century. Guaraní blood ran freely in Paraguayan veins and the majority of Paraguayans were more at home speaking Guaraní than Spanish. The Negro population, including slaves and freedmen (*libertos* or *pardos*), may have exceeded 40,000: "At the beginning of the Paraguayan War . . . as many as 20,000 Paraguayans were slaves and perhaps another 25,000 were blacks of other classifications."[5] But how many Paraguayans, exclusive of Indians, were there in 1864? Estimates vary from about 400,000 to more than triple that number. A Paraguayan writer on political economy stated soon after the war: "During the last war it is well known that in 5 years of continuous blockade and siege nothing was introduced into this country from abroad, and nevertheless it maintained an army of one hundred thousand men and a population of 500 thousand people with its own resources."[6] The most authoritative source of information on the Plata countries was the *Handbook of the River Plate*, published for years by the brothers Michael George Mulhall and Edward Thomas Mulhall, owners and publishers of the Buenos Aires *Standard* and *The Weekly Standard*. There is no good reason to question their summary of 1875:

> The inhabited and cultivated portion never exceeded 20,000 square miles; and although a census taken in 1857 pretended to give 1,337,449 inhabitants, the real population never could have reached more than 500,000 souls, and at present hardly exceeds 100,000. The number of male inhabitants who perished in the war is computed at 100,000, and a still larger number of women and children died of exposure and starvation in the woods, the survivors in many cases having lived for months on bitter oranges.[7]

George G. Petre, a British minister to Argentina, insisted that the population was "reduced from nearly a million (not as Mr. West was informed, half a million) under the rule of the elder López, to no more than three hundred thousand, of whom more than three-fourths were women."[8] Whatever figure one accepts as the prewar population—and 450,000 is probably very close to being correct—more than one-half perished during the war. Disease and starvation certainly killed more people than enemy bullets. Always suspicious of conspiracies and quick to inflict the death penalty for the most minor transgressions, López either ordered or permitted the execution of several hundred soldiers and civilians—how many, no one knows.[9] The question as to how many survived the war is also difficult to answer with any degree of certainty. The American minister to Paraguay and Uruguay made a quick trip to Asunción in August, 1870, and reported that "There is left alive of the original population a larger proportion than has been represented."[10] The Allies made some sort of count in eastern Paraguay in 1872 and reported a total of 176,000 natives and 55,796 foreigners.[11] Most of the foreigners were Argentines, Brazilians, Uruguayans, and Italians who served the Allied forces or were merchant adventurers who had hurried upriver in an effort to make a quick fortune. In Asunción were 6,284 males and 11,066 females, excluding foreigners.[12] Most of the Paraguayan males were children.

The Prostrated Capital

Asunción enjoyed a very favorable location on low hills that overlooked a small bay, but the city was not built to take advantage of the site, and visitors found the capital more rustic than they had expected. There were no paved streets, almost no sidewalks, no sewers, · ..d no street lights other than an occasional lantern. Torrential storms left the streets thick with mud and sand and pitted with holes, and often brought all business to a standstill. Coming from the harbor, one encountered an unlighted and rough street bordered by a brick walk that was a "veritable death trap."[13] To keep horseback riders off the few sidewalks, the Provisional Government threatened a fine of five pesos or twenty-four hours in jail.[14] A branch of the railway, still to be seen, ran from the central station to the Plaza San Francisco (today Plaza Uruguay), south to the customs house, and out to what had been the arsenal.

From the harbor, where various kinds of river craft mingled with foreign gunboats, one saw the white pillars of the customs house, which from a distance looked like a cloister. To the left was the López Palace, its damaged tower outlined against the sky. To the right, the buildings of the arsenal served as barracks for Brazilian troops, while close by were the red tiles of the unfinished tramway station. The hull of an iron ship lay on the river bank, "its warped ribs resembling the skeleton of some gigantic animal." A small quebracho pier served as the wharf, while steam-powered cranes installed by Carlos Antonio López still operated. On the whole, Asunción was drab, with only the remnants of an industry once unsurpassed in the Plata area. Some walls had been smashed by cannon fire and a few ranchos had been burned by the invaders. Even in 1872 there were no signs of repair work.[15]

As one landed and went toward the Cathedral, the "old palace" was on the left. This had been the seat of government, and here on the ground floor died General José Joaquim de Andrade Neves, Barão do Triunfo, on January 9, 1869.[16] Francia's home across the plaza and the military barracks were somber reminders of dictatorship, "of tyranny surrounded by bayonets" that was eased if not ended by the death of José Gaspar Rodríguez de Francia in 1840. The old home of Carlos Antonio López was across the railway track from the Cathedral. An elegant veranda extended along the front, its fifteen Tuscan pillars supporting another veranda. The columns and wall were painted in brilliant colors; the walls of the front rooms were covered with rich paper and the splendid furniture had not been stolen. Behind this house was the magnificent home of Vicente Barrios, who had been executed by his brother-in-law, Francisco Solano López. In these palatial surroundings, Caxias and then Marshal Guilherme Xavier de Sousa found comfortable lodgings,[17] a circumstance that prevented them from being looted.

The Cathedral, a spacious temple with two tall towers, dominated the city. Architecturally uninteresting, the brick-paved interior provided a grand altar and four side altars, all decorated sparingly. An extensive veranda formed by octagonal columns ran along the sides and back. To the left of the Cathedral was a building that served as the seminary for the diocese. Massive walls pierced by small openings with iron grilles made it look like a prison, which indeed it had been in Francia's days. Here lived the Brazilian chaplains, supervised by the Capuchin José Fidelis Maria d'Avola Meza, familiarly called Padre Fidelis. The Paraguayan priests Claudio Arrúa and Policarpo Páez lived here temporarily.[18]

Asunción was not ready for an influx of entrepreneurs, and many who came in 1869 and 1870 soon regretted the move. Nevertheless, reports in the Argentine press usually exaggerated the severity of conditions in the city. The Provisional Government provided for free introduction of cattle and free exploitation of yerba; to raise revenue, it decreed license fees for engaging in business, a decree that caused much grumbling and a proposal from merchants that a tariff would be better. The government replied that tariff duties would discourage imports; anyway, the license fees were not onerous. The ubiquitous Edward Augustus Hopkins, who knew Paraguay well from his prewar experiences, established a sawmill at Villa Occidental, and his agent in Asunción, Antonio Decoud, solicited business. The mill, established in October, 1869, apparently proved unprofitable. In May, 1870, Hopkins advertised a "magnificent sawmill" for sale, together with the steamer *Gamo*, built in the United States especially for the river trade. Advertisements in *La Regeneración* in October, 1869, show a steady increase in business. More ships arrived with goods, Hopkins was soliciting logs for his sawmill, and the Empresa Brasilera del Ferro-Carril (Brazilian Railway Enterprise) managed to run two trains daily to Pirayú. It was hoped that Paraguay was "destined to be one of the principal commercial centers of the Río de la Plata" because of its position and natural riches.[19]

Economic activity was hampered by the lack of a genuine monetary system until well after 1880. There was no stock of gold to use as a reserve or backing for paper, and no central bank to act as a financial agent and exchange office. During the period of occupation, foreign coins circulated freely, their value ineffectively regulated by laws and decrees. The official monetary unit was the peso fuerte (strong or hard peso), a term commonly used in Argentina and Spain, its sign being a capital *F* superimposed on a capital *S*, with the *F* being larger than the *S*. Less frequently the peso fuerte was indicated by the sign $f. This peso fuerte was referred to as moneda nacional (national money) or curso legal (legal tender), abbreviated respectively as m/n and c/l. In theory the peso fuerte was a gold or silver peso, but there were no Paraguayan hard pesos, neither of silver nor of gold. The patacón, either an Argentine or a Brazilian coin roughly equivalent to the United States silver dollar, was in very short supply after the war.

There was also reference to gold pesos, designated by the dollar sign, which were pesos of account. In general practice, a sum written $1,000 could mean paper, silver, or gold pesos, although if gold were meant it would more properly be written $1,000 oro, or o/s for oro sellado, which meant coined gold nine-tenths fine. When the peso fuerte sign was used, it might mean actual paper pesos, hard pesos, or pesos of account. A decree of February 14, 1871, defined five pesos fuertes as equal to the pound sterling, and four pesos fuertes equal to twenty French francs.[20] It would be logical, therefore, to use the peso fuerte sign only for gold or silver pesos, but frequent issues of paper money were designated as pesos fuertes, and just as frequently they were depreciated drastically in terms of gold. Therefore, when the law of January 20, 1875, and subsequent measures fixed the value of foreign coins circulating as legal tender in Paraguay, the equivalents were stated in pesos fuertes. Silver pesos of some countries were valued at 20¢, the Spanish gold ounce at $16.50, the Colombian, Mexican, and United States gold ounces at $16.30, the United States gold eagle at $5.10, and the English pound sterling at $5.00. The Chilean silver peso, Peruvian sol, and new Bolivian peso were valued at $1.00, and the United States silver dollar at $1.03.[21]

Paraguay began its experience with paper money on March 1, 1847, during the regime of Carlos Antonio López. His son, Francisco Solano, greatly increased the amount of paper, which became worthless when the war ended. Congress, by law of July 31, 1871, demonetized the López paper retroactively to March 1, 1870, the day López was killed. Laws and presidential decrees during the postwar decade authorized many issues of paper money and certificates of indebtedness, which fluctuated so widely in terms of gold that business transactions suffered severely. The first postwar coinage in Paraguay came in 1871 when Congress authorized $f100,000 in copper pieces of 1¢, 2¢, and 4¢. In less than a year these coins, which contained very little copper, had depreciated so rapidly that merchants refused to accept them in ordinary trade. Importers would buy the coins by weight since they could pay 10 percent of customs duties with them at face value. Bolivian silver, despite wide fluctuations in value, continued to be the principal circulating medium for commercial transactions. Almost all of the other hard money came from the occupation forces and from Argentine merchants who sent unwelcome debased coins to Paraguay.[22]

Paraguayan commerce, hampered by monetary confusion, recovered slowly despite journalistic enthusiasm. By far the greater part of imported goods were for the account of sutlers supplying occupation forces. Some of the merchandise drifted into the interior. At Paraguarí one could buy cheap cottons and inferior hardware made in England, boots from Argentina, linen from Europe, and "cheap wines of horrible quality, a little sugar, tallow, frightful gin from Hamburg, potato alcohol whose odor alone suffices to put one to flight, some boxes of candles, oil, and soap."[23] Fireworks from China were in good supply for the many fiestas. Exports passing through Asunción were almost entirely of yerba, tobacco, hardwoods, hides, and casks of caña, a native firewater seemingly 200 proof to the uninitiated. Smuggling of these products through other river ports was extensive. Cattle and other animals came in primarily through Encarnación or Paso de la Patria. Asunción was a poor port for importing cattle unless for quick slaughter. Pastures were good back of Encarnación but transport to the Asunción area, where population was concentrated, would have to be on the hoof.

Food was so scarce that one could make a small fortune with a little imagination and fewer scruples. One enterprising Frenchman came to Paraguay right after the war with three milk cows. He added water to the milk and sold the bluish mixture for one dollar per liter. For a period of three months he took in about $60 a day, but by 1872 this business was ruined and the dairyman planned to return to France with his small fortune and Paraguayan wife and child.[24] Women and children sold vegetables in the Asunción market "at famine prices, mandioca in small parcels, or poultry dearer than in London." There was no butter "except salt Cork or Bordeaux, forwarded from Buenos Ayres."[25]

To take advantage of what was expected to be a lucrative commerce, five shipping agencies serviced twenty-two boats in regular service between Asunción and Buenos Aires and Montevideo,[26] but there was not enough trade to keep this fleet in profitable operation. Most of the 750 or more merchants were Argentines who depended primarily on the Allied armies for their trade. Since they had invested a capital of about $£7,000,000, prospective losses were large for these merchants in the Asunción "deserts."[27] Other dismal reports came from Paraguay early in 1870. One writer wailed that many business houses were in liquidation and the government must do something to promote commerce, or Paraguay would remain "a desert with ruins and nothing more."[28] The Mulhalls, usually cautiously optimistic about Paraguay's future, gave way to pessimism:

> The few traders who had settled in Asunción are winding up their affairs to leave the country, business and trade being utterly out of the question in such a land. . . . The future of Paraguay is so dark that none can read it. As regards its trade, people in the Plate have at last opened their eyes to the fact that the land has exhausted all its elements of production, and as regards consumption, it has nothing wherewith to pay.[29]

Many businessmen, native and foreign, refused to accept this requiem. Paraguay had abundant supplies of products scarce in other countries, and production of tobacco, woods, yerba, cereals, coffee, cotton, and minerals could be promoted by the government. That everything was not hopeless was shown by a meeting of merchants, members of the Sociedad Protección Mútua (Mutual Protection Society), to explore the possibilities of forming a commercial bank.[30] The government, however, had no resources with which to promote business, and, as will be shown later, proceeds from two London loans floated in 1871 and 1872 brought almost no benefits to Paraguay.

Despite some improvement, business languished during all the years of occupation. Halfway through this period, and in the midst of a revolution, a keen observer placed the blame where it belonged:

> Listless, sick, or mutilated men, impoverished and miserable, appeared with unfortunate women in the same or worse condition, as the only remnants of the old Paraguayan population; for the wealth that was formerly taken from the Paraguayan soil was substituted a complete desolation, the result of war and the consequent loss of population, with the result that if the Allies at that time had left the country to its own resources, hunger would have done with the few Paraguayans who escaped the lead, illnesses, and privations of the López camps and vengeance.[31]

Toward the end of the eight-year occupation, another editor wrote in despair: "Poverty that today afflicts Paraguay is frightful, commerce being confined only to the capital, people from the country do not come and the lack of principal articles of consumption is beginning to be felt." [32]

The story might well have been different had that group of politicasters who fought one another for control of the puppet government turned their attention instead to working for the good of Paraguay. "Manos a la obra!" Hands to the task, to be sure; but the task was political for altogether too many, with the result that Paraguay became an Argentine economic satellite, and this commercial bondage had by no means been completely broken nearly a century after the last Brazilian troops gladly embarked for their homeland.

The Back Country

The heart of Paraguay was Asunción and the towns that lay within fifty leagues of the capital. Most of the country south of Pilar was sparsely settled, as was true of the much better land lying between Villa Rica and Encarnación. North of Asunción there were no large villages. Rosario and San Pedro, some 130 and 180 kilometers to the north, had only a few hundred citizens. Concepción, the river port 250 kilometers upstream, was a languishing village. There were, in the Asunción–Villa Rica axis, isolated villages, estancias, and ranchos that escaped the devastation of war; but rarely did one find a property of any significance that retained its prewar prosperity. Whether it was Paraguarí, terminus of the railway, or Villa Rica, or Encarnación, the war had taken a terrible toll in manpower.

Among the many travelers who came to Paraguay after the war, the French journalist-artist Laurentian Forgues was most perceptive. He confined his attention primarily to interior towns easily reached and to Villa Occidental across the Río Paraguay on the edge of the Chaco. Other travelers, while adding details, verified his reports. Some of them were representatives of Buenos Aires papers and others were Allied officers who preceded Forgues by a year or more.

Rural areas immediately around Asunción showed how fiercely the Four Horsemen had ridden through the country. Trinidad, Itá, Itauguá, and Luque, all small towns near Asunción, were practically deserted. Rural poverty defied description. A visit to these villages was so depressing that one traveler saw Paraguay as "one vast ruin. Not for several generations will the country recover itself." [33] The Argentine surgeon Dr. Miguel Gallegos traveled extensively in the interior in 1869–1870. The road between two small villages about 250 kilometers northeast of Asunción—Panadero and Igatimí, close to the mountainous border with Brazil—had been found "covered with bodies of women, especially girls, dead from weariness and weakness, and others by lance and knife." Still the survivors uttered no complaint against López. "Foreigners who hear such tales say at times that the Paraguayan women have no heart and that their eyes have no tears; but no, such an idea is false; it is that those women have lost everything in the struggle, and today live only in response to natural law and without passion."[34] Another traveler at about the same time saw nothing but ruin and desolation around Asunción:

> Berges' delightful quinta, famed for its "chorro," [fountain] has been withered by the blighting soldiers barrack; the old tannery establishment, which in former days was worked by the "Estado," belies the saying that "There is nothing like leather." . . . Is there a thinking Paraguayan left in the Land? If there is, let him come forward and tell the world his country's future—explain the crimes of his native land that demanded such awful expiation. . . . I can compare Paraguay to nothing save a tree withered, scorched, blighted by a flash of lightning, . . . I fear, for the unutterable woes of these unfortunate people; the land is cursed, and its future is a blank.[35]

Conditions improved very slowly. Travelers in 1872 reported that the "rural districts are waste; without men to till them, the few male survivors of the war being mostly invalids who have lost a leg or arm. Brushwood and scrub are growing up where sugar-cane, maize and mandioca formerly grew, and the forest is beginning to invade even the suburbs."[36] At Ibicuy, site of the iron foundry, Forgues visited the estancia of Margarita Rivarola, cousin of the former President Cirilo Antonio Rivarola, and found her almost dead of hunger. "We lunched on a macaw which I had the unfortunate idea of killing . . . That admirable bird is horrible game!"[37] Villa Rica, spared destruction by the arrival of Brazilian forces, suffered primarily from lack of people to till the fields. The area appeared to be a fine spot for a foreign colony. The military post of Humaitá, once so important in keeping the Brazilian fleet from ascending to Asunción, was deserted except for a contingent of Brazilian troops.[38]

For more than three centuries Paraguay had been dependent upon agriculture, animal husbandry, and silviculture. Its mineral production was insignificant and confined almost entirely to the quarrying of stone and, under the López, to some iron smelting that could not meet domestic demands. Economic recovery in the postwar period would come only as the fields, pastures, and forests once more sent their produce into the markets. Agricultural activity at best limped along after the war. A few very enterprising persons did well. Some farmers continued to raise sugar cane and to distill caña from cane and oranges; still Asunción imported sugar from Europe and Brazil.[39]

One of the estancias to survive destruction was owned by Vicente Fleytas near Capilla Borja, a few kilometers south of Villa Rica. Fleytas was rich in land but lacked labor to work his fields and build up his herds. When Forgues attended a dance at the Fleytas estancia in October, 1872, his host occasionally fired shots to frighten jaguars, explaining that once a jaguar had seized a dog in that very ballroom. Jaguars were common, frequently attacked people, and were as constant a menace as they had been when Indians first came to Paraguay. To catch the beasts, huge snares baited with meat were constructed along forest paths. No part of an estancia, a forest, or a village was safe from these predators. A particularly bold jaguar had eaten three of his dogs, so Señor Fleytas decided to lie in wait in the shed, which was filled with drying tobacco:

> His loaded gun at hand, our man waited. "While I was thinking of something else," he said, "the tobacco leaves parted silently, and a certain snout, covered by two well known carbuncles, made its panting appearance within two feet of my figure . . ." Leaping from his hammock, giving a cry of terror and without remembering for a moment to use his firearm, it was a matter of an instant for the gentleman; to make a leap and disappear was also a quick thing for the beast; so that the host ended his story by adding: "Having been badly frightened, the jaguar fled!" Ah! if jaguars knew how to talk! [40]

Six leagues beyond the Fleytas estancia, by a terrible road through beautiful country, lay the estancia of Matías Ramírez, "another Paraguayan of the old race." Forgues and his host rode for six hours through a forest of thorny thickets, masses of dead tree trunks, and webs of twisted vines while swarms of vicious bees stung the horses. Yerba, quebracho, lapacho, and orange trees were abundant.[41] This was typical of Paraguayan forests, where large stands of a single variety were rare, thus increasing the difficulty of profitable exploitation. The exuberance of insect life further compounded the trials of farmer, rancher, and forester and was a factor in discouraging settlement of much of the country for more than another century.

Paraguarí, terminus of the railway, had fifty or sixty houses grouped around the plaza and numerous ranchos scattered in the vicinity. Probably 3,000 people were in the town and surrounding area, which offered a haven for brigands: "This is the place," Forgues observed, "where people gather who are no longer able to live in Asunción, where the reach of the central power and of the metropolitan police permits them to live at other people's expense with complete freedom." In the town's dismal market, vendors offered meager supplies of eggs and corn. A fifth of the buildings were shops that had small quantities of English cottons and other imports to trade for hides, tobacco, and maté. The two gambling houses drew many patrons, "since the Paraguayan is always a gambler in the fullest sense of the word. It is not rare for these people to risk a stake of five cents or a thousand francs on the throw of the dice." Probably most of the larger sums came from Italian, Argentine, and Brazilian adventurers.[42]

From the railroad at Paraguarí, Forgues continued by horse to reconnoiter the rail route to Villa Rica. Ibimití, a village about two-thirds of the way to Villa Rica, was practically deserted, except for a few naked inhabitants who gathered at dusk to watch Forgues sketch the plaza. Itapé, site of the "Lincolnshire farmers" fiasco (see chapter 8), was probably more interesting, although Forgues refrained from commenting on that quixotic adventure. As the Frenchman approached Villa Rica, he met more people and found a colorful trader in Hippolite Colón, who bought native produce. The Villa Rica area was relatively rich in cotton, indigo, tobacco, and yerba. By buying a house, Forgues became an important person and was considered a capitalist, the vanguard of an expected flood. At the moment the observant Frenchman was strongly impressed by the women "enveloped in white veils, with short white skirts that revealed their beautiful bronze legs."[43] One of the prosperous merchants of Villa Rica was Lucas Papaluca, a cigar manufacturer and dealer in general merchandise who had a "rich stock of ponchos, hats, boots, and shoes of all sizes and prices." But his trade was carried on by barter. There was almost no livestock in the area, and people came from points two or three days' travel away "to obtain a little piece of meat, offering in exchange tobacco, oranges, lemons, bananas, palm nuts and other products."[44]

Forgues returned to Asunción and turned his attention to the Chaco's eastern fringe. Across the Río Paraguay and north a few kilometers from Asunción was Villa Occidental, now Villa Hayes, a crude hamlet despite its role as capital of the temporarily Argentine province of Chaco. A few scattered places large enough to be named clustered around Villa Occidental before the war, but their inhabitants lived in constant fear of Indian and jaguar attacks. The Chaco, eventually to be 60 percent of the country's area, was largely unexplored and almost entirely unsettled. The few rash or hardy people who defied its dangers could expect no aid from Asunción, from whose low hills could be seen the camp fires of marauding bands. Apparently friendly Indians murdered the French owner of Quinta Misère, a small establishment four kilometers inland, and three of his workers. A white woman captured there escaped and made her way back to Villa Occidental. Some seven or eight kilometers south of the town, at the mouth of the Río Confuso, an Italian veteran of Giuseppe Garibaldi's Uruguayan adventure in 1845, one Perucchino, operated an indifferent sawmill. Bearded, with long curly hair, Perucchino wore a red shirt embroidered with gold ornaments. He greeted his visitors, Forgues and General Julio de Vedia, with proper exuberance. One can understand why Indians let him alone. Three pieces of cannon guarded his door, "His bedroom was an arsenal: there were guns no more than half serviceable, rusted pieces from the war of independence, sabers without scabbards, pikes corroded by rust, with which to arm fifteen fighters."[45]

Indians often raided villages and captured Paraguayans whom they held for ransom. Most of the captives were women and children. Hearing reports that a Brazilian deserter with the Guaycurús had kidnapped Paraguayans in order to sell them in Corumbá, the Brazilian minister ordered an investigation. The military detachment sent to the north late in 1872 encountered more than a score of Paraguayan women fleeing from a Guaycurú village that was later found to have more than thirty captives still living there, but no Brazilians were involved. A steamer from Concepción brought to Asunción a few released captives who reported that many others were in Indian villages, naked and living under the most miserable conditions. An Asunción paper urged that relief be sent to the captives and that a rescue expedition be sent out under competent command—it might have better success than "the celebrated expedition of Rivarola's administration, which, after many expenses and gifts, ended with everything in the hands of one or two persons." That expedition made no effort to reach the Indian camps, and its mules, oxen, and horses enriched a ranch in the country.[46]

Allied occupation, which did little for eastern Paraguay, revived Villa Occidental. Brazilian troops pushed the Indians back and the Argentine Military Legion, Vedia's occupation force, protected the few sugar and tobacco plantations that survived the war. By the end of 1870, the streets had been improved, many buildings were under construction, small industries to process local crops were thriving, and the lumber industry employed 100 men.[47]

Refugees, Foreign and Native

Well before the war was over, the Allies had reason to regret that Carlos Antonio López had had the foresight to employ scores of foreign engineers, armorers, artisans, technicans, and doctors, most of them British. Among the best known were the surgeons Drs. William Stewart,[48] Frederick Skinner, and James Rhind; the engineers George

Thompson, George Paddison, John William K. Whitehead, Percy Burrell, and Henry V. F. Valpy; the armorers William Newton, George Miles, William Eden, and George Higginbotham; the pharmacist George Frederick Masterman; and the military engineers Francisco Wisner von Morgenstern and Charles Henry Thompson.

The fate of these foreigners, including a number of Portuguese, many Italians, and other neutrals, became a matter of great concern to their governments, especially when reports of imprisonment, torture, and executions reached the outside. Commanders of American, British, French, and Italian gunboats were particularly solicitous after the USS *Wasp* took off Charles Ames Washburn and his legation in September, 1868. Two months later, French and Italian gunboats carried 27 refugees to Buenos Aires.[49] After Allied victories at the end of 1868, anxious neutrals discovered that a surprisingly large number of foreigners had survived the war. As early as January, 1869, some 70 English, 140 Italians, 140 French, 30 Spaniards, and about 30 of other nationalities were identified among the destitute and starving population of Asunción.[50] The Allies were very reluctant to aid other countries in rescuing their nationals early in 1869. Only with ill grace did they finally permit foreign gunboats to anchor at Asunción; in the meantime, wild rumors circulated about the fate of foreigners behind the López lines. Even General McMahon, it was widely believed, was being detained against his will.[51]

Prominent among the Englishmen rescued at the end of 1868 were Colonel George Thompson and Dr. William Stewart, both of whom surrendered to the Brazilians after having served Paraguay for many years, and who both returned to participate in the country's reconstruction. Alonzo Taylor, master builder of several of Asunción's finest buildings, also escaped after very cruel treatment.[52] The next opportunity to rescue a fairly large group came in August, 1869, after López had been routed at Piribebuy. The Allies found Dr. Diego Domingo Parodi, an Italian, and 70 other Europeans, most of them English, in Caacupé on August 15. Among them were Percy Burrell and Henry Valpy, two of the principal engineers who had directed construction of the Paraguay Central Railway.[53]

Very few foreigners remained with López after August, 1869. Dr. Frederick Skinner continued faithful to the end and reached Asunción safely one month after Cerro Corá. He was more fortunate than Everhard Monck, a Swedish naturalist, who was executed by López in March, 1869, after twenty-five years of service to Paraguay and the López family.[54] Among other notable foreigners who died or were executed during the war were Dr. James Rhind, staff surgeon; John

Watts, master mechanic; Charles Cutler, engineer; the Portuguese consul, José Maria Leite Pereira, who had once been given asylum by Washburn; and the once powerful Uruguayan statesman, Dr. Antonio de las Carreras. More fortunate was Col. Francisco Wisner von Morgenstern, principal military adviser to the López, whom Brazilians found hiding in the forest at Lomas Valentinas with his wife, daughter, and eleven slaves.[55]

Probably nine-tenths or more of the surviving Paraguayans had been displaced during the war and became refugees seeking to renew their lives in familiar surroundings or looking for aid in Asunción. Slowly the towns were partly repopulated, especially those along the Río Paraguay, although the people were in abject poverty and many were literally naked. Justices of the peace constantly implored aid from Asunción, but that city could not meet the demands of thousands of refugees, almost all of them women and children, who "poured out of the hills and forests, flowing in endless caravans leading to the city."[56] Refugees from rural areas continued to drift into Asunción during the Allied occupation. With no housing at all available, some found shelter in army tents erected on the outskirts. Survivors of many families discovered that their homes were occupied by strangers, their clothing and furnishings pillaged, floors and patios dug up by greedy fortune hunters. Brazilian officers had given long-term leases to many of the occupants, some showed fake bills of sale, and in some cases camp followers had taken possession, claiming to be mistresses of soldiers or officers. Feeble efforts by the Allies to untangle the housing mess were entirely ineffective.[57]

Journalists who went among the refugees graphically described their horrible plight. Going from door to door, begging for food and clothing, these miserable people faced at best a bleak future: "they seem living skeletons, and some of them are boys of 10 or 12 years old, for the most part shockingly mutilated with bullet & sabre wounds."[58] During the hot, sticky Christmas season of 1869, "more than four thousand women almost nude, since clothing they wore hardly covered their bodies," wandered in the city.[59] A short time later, another report showed little improvement:

The gaunt forms of the owners of the soil stalk through the streets of Asunción, living proofs of a mendicancy of which the world in its eventful history can paint no parallel. We witnessed scenes in Paraguay last July which no pen can describe—too shocking, too repulsive to think of. Better, far better, that the whole Paraguayan race had gone down into one common grave at Lomas Valentinas than to survive such afflictions.[60]

Widespread starvation caused an estimated thirty or more deaths daily in Asunción and nearly as many in San Pedro, a small village some 190 kilometers to the north.

Allied commanders, not indifferent to the problem, provided some aid. The Provisional Government, formally inaugurated in August, 1869, had few resources, and private efforts to provide relief were woefully inadequate. As it did in so many civic projects, *La Regeneración* took the lead in relief efforts. The Decouds were responsible for forming the Comisión Beneficencia (Charity Commission) on December 10, 1869, to aid the destitute. Continuing its efforts for several months with very limited resources, this commission had received only $f335 by January, 1870. Directors of *La Regeneración* also set up relief stations, a work in which the two budding political groups, El Gran Club del Pueblo and the Club del Pueblo, cooperated.[61] The Provisional Government created a Comisión Protectora de los Paraguayos Desválidos y Huérfanos (Commission for the Protection of Destitute and Orphaned Paraguayans) on December 19, 1869, whose instructions were to establish asylums, provide work, create schools, and perform other good works. Of course, it had practically no resources. The country house formerly belonging to Carlos Antonio López in Trinidad was designated as one asylum, but it had no medicines, poor food, and no doctor. Vagrancy inevitably resulted from postwar confusion, adding to the problem of administering the very few relief funds available.[62]

Appeals for aid did not go unheeded in Buenos Aires, where subscription followed subscription to meet needs of Argentine soldiers and Paraguay's starving thousands. The response understandably became increasingly parsimonious:

> The charity of Buenos Ayres has been taxed to the very utmost both by the conquerors and the conquered. We have subscribed to raise soldiers, to heal invalids, and to feed Paraguayans until we may almost say charity has ceased to be a virtue; in fact the subscription business on account of this war has been pushed to such an extreme that the last appeal for the asylum opened in Asunción for the houseless met with scarcely any response save from the Masons, although the most deserving charity, since this charitable war began.[63]

The poor gathered daily before the homes of Anarcasis Lanus and Carlos Loizaga to receive food and clothing sent up from Buenos Aires. General Justo José Urquiza, the great Argentine caudillo, offered to lend the Provisional Government 1,000 head of cattle; from Corrientes in Argentina went appeals to President Domingo Faustino

Sarmiento for aid in caring for the "pauper Paraguayan families who flooded the city." [64]

Considering the immediate postwar conditions, one can but wonder that any sort of order could be maintained in Asunción and the rural areas. The old order had been destroyed; new social relationships had to be established on the ruins. Paraguay had paid a terrible price for challenging the power of Brazil and Argentina, and many decades must pass before the new nation could emerge.

3. Politics and Diplomacy, 1869–1870

Paraguayan exiles, especially in Buenos Aires, had dreamed for years of the day when at last they could return to Asunción as free men and construct a democratic republic. They came home to an appalling task. Economic ruin, destroyed institutions, a decimated population, and Allied occupation forces were enough to dismay even the gods from Olympus had they deigned to sojourn in Paraguay. The returning exiles, whether civilians or soldiers of the Paraguayan Legion, and the pitiful refugees who crowded into the chaos that was Asunción, were not from that ancient pantheon, but their efforts to create the foundations of a new Paraguay were heroic, even though at times their struggles were so pathetic as to elicit compassion from the neutral observer.

Among all of the loosely formed groups that sought to gain ascendancy in forming a provisional government, officers and men of the Paraguayan Legion, which exiles had organized in Buenos Aires, were the strongest nucleus. Returned prisoners of war, López officials coming back from foreign posts, and miscellaneous expatriates had to find some political role, some magnet to serve as the cohesive force. Rival leaders had to emerge, to form alliances, to bow to the immediate needs that pressed in from all sides demanding solution. In all of this process, the politicians who obtained support from Brazilian commanders and diplomats obviously would emerge supreme. This was a truism grasped most firmly by those who led a coalition of some legionnaires and the Lopiztas, who distrusted intellectuals with their liberalism and to whom politics was the art of the militarily possible. The Allies had to create a government that could enter into treaties. This they did, but bitter rivalry between Argentina and Brazil cropped up repeatedly and caused the failure of every effort to negotiate a general treaty.

One might well wonder how exiles in Argentina were able to support themselves. Some had relatives with whom they lived, others found employment in various capacities. Many Paraguayans who had left to seek employment in neighboring Corrientes or other Argentine provinces obviously belonged to a class different from that of those who had fled to escape the wrath of dictators or who were representatives of commercial houses that handled the semi-processed products of Paraguay's fields and forests. The mere fact that certain Paraguayans were exiles, or were caught abroad when war came, by no means assured their cooperation with one another. They were not, moreover, uniform in their political beliefs or their economic outlook. They quarreled among themselves in Argentine cities, primarily Buenos Aires. On one matter they were more united: dislike, even hatred, of Brazil. While staunch in their resistance to any Argentine effort to reincorporate Paraguay into the Argentine political sphere, their long-standing territorial disputes with Brazil and much closer cultural ties with Argentina gave the latter a great advantage initially in the struggle with Brazil for control over postwar Paraguay. Argentine leaders, unequal to the task of making use of these natural and historical advantages, bungled the opportunity. When the Allies attempted to make peace with Paraguay they had to use Paraguayan exiles who had fought with them, prisoners of war released for the purpose, and young men returning from education abroad. Very quickly Allied leaders discovered that Paraguayans could take advantage of disagreements among their enemies, and that while these arguments continued it was advantageous to support various Paraguayan factions that could be used to their benefit.

Legionnaires and Lopiztas

The Legion was intended to be the fighting arm of the Asociación Paraguaya, which originated among exiles who had gathered in Buenos Aires. All of them were enemies of López, although the degree of their animosity varied widely. A few were survivors of the Francia regime, some had suffered grievously at the hands of the López, others had fled to escape just punishment, some were young men whose foreign education included a heady dose of French liberalism. Not all of them were patriotic Paraguayans. As early as September, 1851, a small group of exiles favored incorporation of Paraguay into the Argentine Republic. Some of them signed a manifesto in 1858 that called for the overthrow of Carlos Antonio López, and on August 2, 1858, organized the Sociedad Libertadora de la República del Paraguay. Among the editors of its short-lived publicity organ, *El Grito Paraguayo*, was the Chilean *enfant terrible*, Francisco Bilbao. Most of the founders of this "liberation front" were among organizers of the Asociación Paraguaya in November, 1864.[1] Members of the Association, as well as those who later enlisted in the Legion, soothed their consciences for taking up arms with Paraguay's enemies by protesting that their only objective was to overthrow the López tyranny. To avoid the charge of treason, they desperately wanted to organize a Paraguayan Legion that, bearing the Paraguayan flag, would fight with the Allies as a separate unit. The exiles expected Paraguayan resistance to crumble quickly, after which they would be in a position to control the postwar government.

The Association as such had a short existence. Internal wrangling prevented adoption of a charter or constitution, although an executive committee (comisión directiva) did have some influence in persuading the Argentines to characterize the war as a fight against López and not as a war of conquest against Paraguay.[2] Upon informing the Brazilian and Argentine governments of its existence, the Association proposed to raise an armed force of 2,000 Paraguayans to fight with the Allies, a figure that affords a rough measure of the number of exiles. When first formed, the Association wanted to be recognized as the legitimate government of Paraguay and to sign a treaty of alliance with Brazil. The Brazilian minister in Buenos Aires, Felippe José Pereira Leal, Barão de Maracajú, encouraged the Paraguayans, who named Fernando Iturburu as commander of the proposed Legion, with Juan Francisco Decoud second in command. Seeking funds and recognition, the executive committee sent envoys to Rio de Janeiro, where they met with complete failure. The Empire would accept Paraguayan volunteers but wanted no Paraguayan Legion to complicate matters during and after the war.[3]

Rebuffed by Brazil, the Association turned to Argentina, which had maintained its neutrality until April, 1865. When López began his invasion of Argentina, the Association immediately offered "to raise a legion of Paraguayans which, flying their own flag, will ask the Commanding General of the Army that it be permitted to lead the attack." President Bartolomé Mitre and his minister of war, Juan A. Gelly y Obes, gladly accepted the Paraguayan offer and authorized the Association to organize a legion that would fight with the Argentine army.[4] An irreparable schism quickly appeared among Paraguayan leaders. Lt. Col. Juan Francisco Decoud refused to take orders from Iturburu and resigned in July, 1865. His sons, José Segundo and Juan José, and several others followed in October. This schism among the exiles had a profound effect on reconstruction politics and marked the formation of the Decoudista faction. Members of this group aided in persuading Lt. Col. Antonio Estigarribia to surrender at Uruguayana in September, 1865.[5] The loss of Estigarribia's army was a severe blow to López.

Despite Iturburu's urging, Mitre delayed in formally organizing the Legion, although many Paraguayan prisoners were forced to fight in Allied ranks. Brazilian opposition and the Decoud-Iturburu quarrel gave Mitre an excellent opportunity to procrastinate, but Iturburu did manage to create a shadowy Legion by drawing upon Paraguayan prisoners,[6] then waited long and impatiently for recognition as a separate unit. Not until March 20, 1869, did the Allies agree to give the Legion a Paraguayan flag. General Emilio Mitre formally presented their national banner to the Legion with a florid, impassioned proclamation on May 25. Thereafter, the Legion symbolized the new Paraguay that continued the fight against López.[7]

The Paraguayan Legion, or its continuing influence, was a divisive factor in Paraguayan politics for nearly a century. Lopiztas naturally regarded legionnaires as traitors, although schisms in their own ranks led to the incorporation of legionnaires in governments they dominated. Brazilians generally distrusted the Legion because it was nurtured in Argentina and its more vociferous members were strongly nationalistic. Brazilian hostility gave liberal legionnaires little opportunity to establish themselves firmly in government. The few who did, like José Segundo Decoud, crossed over to the political enemy.

Legionnaires took the lead in numerous moves preliminary to the formation of a provisional government. They could see nothing wrong in this cooperation with Paraguay's enemies since they, like the Allies, advanced the untenable sophistry of having fought against López, not against the Paraguayan people.[8] Serapio Machaín, a member of the old Revolutionary Committee, drafted a proposal for a provisional government that was the subject of discussion by thirty-two men who met in Felipe Recalde's home on January 24 and 25, 1869. Dissension appeared at once. Some wanted to organize a corps of volunteers to continue in pursuit of the pitiful remnants of the López army; others argued against any more sacrifices by a people exhausted by the terrible war. Prominent among the latter was José Segundo Decoud, who, despite the fact that he was only twenty-one years of age, was a prominent member of the Decoudista faction, which centered around Juan Francisco Decoud, and with which the Machaíns were closely associated. The Decouds insisted that any government should be the result of a free vote by the people, a somewhat unrealistic proposal as the arrival of more refugees and returning exiles led to a very fluid situation.[9]

Notably absent from the January meeting was Col. Fernando Itur-

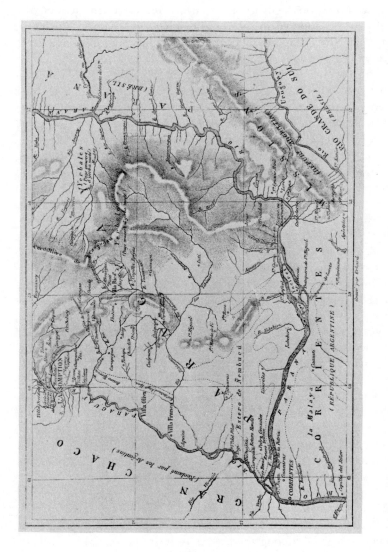

Map 3. Southern Paraguay
From L. Forgues, "Le Paraguay," Le Tour du Monde: Nouvelle Journal des Voyages
27, no. 700 (June 1874): 387

buru, commander of the Legion, whose troops found quarters in the government palace. Ambitious for his own advancement, he had made too many enemies and made still more by proposing General Juan Andrés Gelly y Obes, Argentine commander whose father was a Paraguayan, as provisional governor of Asunción. Iturburu became the focus of a group opposed to the Decoudistas. The Decouds, Machaíns, Recaldes, Haedos, Benigno Ferreira, and Jaime Sosa Escalada were prominent Decoudistas, or Liberals, pro-Argentine in sympathy.

Cándido Bareiro arrived from Europe in February, 1869. This capable, urbane, experienced, and ambitious López agent was a ruthless and cynical politician charged by his enemies with having no scruples whatever. At once he became the center of a Lopizta group that came to include General Bernardino Caballero and Colonel Patricio Escobar, both great war heroes. Lopiztas, too few to dominate the situation, found allies in the Iturburu faction and among such intellectuals·as Cayo and Fulgencio Miltos and Juan Bautista Gill, men who made no effort to conceal their jealousy of José Segundo Decoud. The Bareiro and Iturburu groups formed a coalition and soon counted the Taboadas among them. Rufino Taboada, a great favorite among the ladies, was a rakish, dapper, slender young fellow whose political career surely would have been interesting and fiery had he survived.[10]

Bareiro was the nemesis of the Liberals until his death on September 4, 1880, midway in his term as president. He was the center of numerous shifting alliances. Occasionally an equally skillful politician, like Juan Bautista Gill, could supplant him in power. With good reason the Brazilians never trusted Bareiro and his faithful cronies, Caballero and Escobar. His principal enemies met violent deaths: Gill, Rivarola, and Facundo Machaín fell to assassins. Bareiro's complicity in Gill's murder is highly unlikely, and there is much reason to question that he gave orders for the brutal murders of Machaín, Rivarola, and other annoying men. Although General Caballero is now honored and even revered as the founder of the Colorado Party, if any one politician deserves that honor it is Cándido Bareiro, although that group was not formally organized during his lifetime.

Formation of the Provisional Government

The Allies were not letting matters drift aimlessly while Paraguayan politicians struggled among themselves to seize the shadowy substance of power. Dom Pedro sent his most skillful diplomat and minister of foreign affairs, José Maria da Silva Paranhos, to arrange matters with Uruguay and Argentina. Silva Paranhos reached Buenos Aires on February 10, 1869, and, after a conference with President Sarmiento, went on to Asunción, where he arrived on February 20 in the midst of the Bareirista-Decoudista feuding. The Allies, meaning Brazilians for the most part, had to take these rival groups into account since they needed a provisional government through which to rule, but it must be amenable to Allied demands. The five or six thousand Paraguayans in Asunción, observed Her Majesty's minister in Buenos Aires, were "composed entirely of refugees, emigrants, and prisoners." Rivalries and jealousies hampered the formation of a national government, although Silva Paranhos, already being called the "Viceroy of Paraguay," did succeed in a temporary reconciliation.[11] Many people in Asunción believed that the delay in forming the Provisional Government was caused by the intrigues of López agents, who stirred up dissension and played on the fear that the Allies intended "to abolish the Paraguayan Republic and to enslave its people."[12] However, the apparent reconciliation of warring factions led to a popular meeting on March 31 at which 335 citizens signed a petition asking for a provisional government, and selected four delegates to carry the request to Buenos Aires.[13]

The emissaries sailed with Silva Paranhos to Buenos Aires at the end of April to confer with Dr. Mariano Varela, Argentine minister of foreign affairs, who in turn consulted the Uruguayans. Immediately there arose the question of interpreting the Treaty of Alliance of May 1, 1865. Brazilians knew well their territorial demands; the Argentines, vague as to their own aims, grew suspicious of the Empire, and for nearly a decade these suspicions threatened to cause war. Silva Paranhos wanted the Provisional Government to accept the "secret" treaty as a basis for peace; but Varela, in a notable memorandum of May 8, insisted that since the Allies had pledged to respect Paraguayan sovereignty—to allow Paraguayans freedom to organize their own government—the Provisional Government must not be compelled to compromise major issues.[14] When Silva Paranhos insisted on his views, Varela and the Uruguayan representative, Dr. Adolfo Rodríguez, stood firm. The Brazilian appeared to agree with Varela's categorical statement that "victory did not give the Allied nations the right to consider as theirs the limits stated in the treaty."[15]

The Allied representatives, putting aside controversial points, met on June 2 and drafted protocols that were to result in the Provisional Government for Paraguay. The Paraguayans, who signed on June 11, agreed "to proceed in entire accord with the Allies until the termination of the war, without ceasing to have full liberty in the exercise of national sovereignty." The Provisional Government would have no control over the Allies, their troops, vessels, or supplies. A junta of three, with one to serve as president, was to hold the executive power. The Provisional Government, therefore, was a triumvirate. The Allies, on their part, promised moral and material aid. One provision in the protocols guaranteed smuggling on a large scale: "All individuals, ships, provisions, forage and other material of whatever species, belonging to the Allied armies or to its contractors shall have ingress into and egress from the Republic, free of all and every onus or search, the same as granted to the generals and diplomatic representatives of the Allied Governments."[16] Back to Asunción went the delegates with the protocols, and with them were Silva Paranhos and José Roque Pérez for the principal Allies, determined to keep the Paraguayans in line.[17] These moves to establish a Paraguayan government caused General McMahon, in Buenos Aires enroute to London, to call the proceedings a farce:

> [The Allies] are aiming to collect from all parts of the country such of the unhappy people of Paraguay whom famine and suffering compel to abandon the national cause, for the purpose of furnishing a constituency to this pretended government. These people, for the most part women and children, are often collected with threats and whips [,] marched to Asunción [,] paraded mercilessly through the streets for days naked and footsore to be exhibited to the army of traders, sutlers and camp followers who throng that city occupying the very homes of the poor unfortunates who are thus so publicly exhibited. . . . All this is done to prove that President López is a monster of cruelty and that the Allies are the human regenerators of the land. When these exhibitions are closed the unfortunate victims are turned loose to live or rather to die as best they may, subject to the brutal caprices of a debauched soldiery who are almost absolutely beyond the restraints of discipline.[18]

Other foreign observers in Buenos Aires, particularly British and French diplomats, were also skeptical of the whole business. The British minister considered the negotiations and protocols mere window dressing, since the Provisional Government could not possibly have any power but would be "a shadow behind which the allied governments will seek to elude some of their most serious & embarrassing responsibilities without dispossessing themselves of any material power." The French minister planned to withdraw his consul from Asunción, but the Italian minister decided to await developments. The British minister finally concluded that the Allies had signed a secret protocol promising not to conclude any treaty with the puppet regime, that the Paraguayans did not want such a government at all, and that José Roque Pérez had found conditions far different than Silva Paranhos had reported.[19]

Plaintively, Gregorio Benites, the López representative in Paris, warned the United States and Great Britain that the Allies were treating Paraguay as the French had Mexico. Paraguay was not conquered and Brazil was simply out to spread its empire. Clarendon replied that the British had not recognized the Provisional Government. From his distant post in Rio de Janeiro, Her Majesty's minister wondered if this non-recognition policy was encouraging López to continue his hopeless resistance.[20]

With a government about to be organized, the politically ambitious Paraguayans intensified the activity begun early in 1869 and formed Paraguay's first political clubs. The Decoudistas on June 26 organized the Club del Pueblo, with Facundo Machaín as president, which had on its first governing body young men imbued with the century-old ideas of the French Revolution. This group, which changed its name to Gran Club del Pueblo in March, 1870, published *La Regeneración*, the first issue of which appeared on October 1, 1869. Rival Bareiristas, or Lopiztas, formed the Club Unión, occasionally referred to as the Partido Popular, with Cayo Miltos as president. Here in embryo were the foundations of Paraguay's two principal traditional parties, Liberals and Colorados, although the situation was too fluid to have either name affixed permanently to any group. The Club del Pueblo favored ex-sergeant Cirilo Antonio Rivarola as president of the Triumvirate. Rivarola, son of a deputy who had opposed the coup of Carlos Antonio López in 1844, had suffered torture at Cerro León. The Club Unión opposed him with Félix Egusquiza, a former López agent in Buenos Aires. This division annoyed the Allied ministers, who resented the failure of Paraguayans to agree on a candidate.[21]

For the time being, Silva Paranhos and the Decoudistas seemed to be backing the same man. Actually, José Segundo Decoud had more support from the Club del Pueblo than did Rivarola, since Decoudistas strongly resented Brazilian influence. Come what might, Silva Paranhos would have Rivarola and went through an elaborate process to get him. Roque Pérez and Silva Paranhos called for a grand assembly to meet at the National Theater on July 22, but they met a day earlier to agree on how to handle the meeting. Dutifully, 129 citizens assembled with Roque Pérez in the chair and the Brazilian minister in control. The assembly first elected its officers, then a Junta Nacional of twenty-one members. This junta, presided over by Rivarola with Benigno Ferreira as secretary, in turn selected five of its members to be an electoral committee to name the three triumvirs. The electoral committee displeased Silva Paranhos on August 5 by naming Carlos Loizaga, Juan Francisco Decoud, and José Díaz de Bedoya. The Allied agents refused to accept Decoud because one of his sons, Juan José, was writing scathing articles in a Corrientes paper. In Decoud's place they named Rivarola, thus plunging a very mediocre man into a maelstrom that eventually engulfed him. The Triumvirate appeared to please the people, such as they were, for on the night of August 6 the "populace" demonstrated before the houses of the Allied ministers.[22]

Putting on a show of ceremony, the Allies chose August 15, traditionally observed as the day of Our Lady of Asunción, for installation of the Triumvirate. Idlers and curiosity seekers, foreigners and natives, gathered in the Plaza 14 de Mayo before the Cathedral to listen to proclamations. The people then filed into the Cathedral, where men in the nave and women in the aisles welcomed Silva Paranhos and Roque Pérez, their entrance heralded by a flourish of trumpets. Another flourish greeted the triumvirs, who advanced to the high altar, where the chief Argentine military chaplain administered the oath. After a Te Deum, notables lunched at the government palace, where the Allied ministers protested their good intentions and Rivarola promised full cooperation.[23]

Cirilo Antonio Rivarola, President of the Provisional Government, added very little luster to a distinguished Paraguayan family. A contemporary who obviously disliked him characterized Rivarola as a "splenetic spirit, devoted to legal forms and with arbitrary and despotic instincts; a mixture of good and bad, of truth and falsehood. He himself did not know what he was nor what he wanted; . . . he was, in short, a man without character."[24] Rivarola had passed as a lawyer before the war and fell into disfavor with Solano López for daring to advocate liberal ideas and a democratic government. Although many were executed for less cause, Rivarola escaped with imprisonment and forced military service. Captured by the Allies on May 25, 1869, the barefooted Sergeant Rivarola was taken before the Conde d'Eu, who gave him clothes and sent him to Asunción with a note commending him to the Brazilian minister, who found in Rivarola a man he could trust. Haughty, crude, and pretentious, Rivarola was a genius in his ability to antagonize those who would work with him for the good of the country. Carlos Loizaga and José Díaz de Bedoya, former members of the Asociación Paraguaya, were mediocrities with no particular talents.[25] Loizaga was an elderly intellectual worn out by the struggle to survive abroad. Tired of controversy, he could be counted on for nothing but to follow the easiest course. Bedoya was a coarse, uneducated merchant whose older brother, Saturnino, had served López as minister of hacienda (finance).[26]

Rivarola, more to be pitied than censured, made an earnest effort to provide substance to the shadowy position he held. Descendant of a revolutionary hero, his antecedents were impeccable, but antecedents were of little value. At first supported by Brazilians who expected him to be their supine creature, he aroused their antagonism by a show of independence.[27] While Rivarola was widely regarded as a Brazilian puppet and a leader of the Brazilian faction, his leading Lopizta rival, Cándido Bareiro, headed the pro-Argentine group.

Bareiro, an experienced diplomat, appeared to his friends as talented, refined, simple and dignified in bearing, discreet in speech, and faithful to Paraguay. A contemporary who knew both men compared Rivarola with Francia. He would ride up to a group, dismount, throw the reins to the highest official present, "ask for a jar of water, and daintily folding the sleeves of his black frock coat, would wash his hands in the midst of the gathering; Bareiro, his shiny coat clinging to his body from perspiration, would fraternize with the most rustic peasant who would want him to fill the highest post in the nation."[28] This contrast simply does not fit the characters of the two men. An Argentine critic regarded Rivarola as the only popular candidate who was a native of Asunción.[29] To increase this popularity, Rivarola made several trips into the country. On one of these excursions to Pirayú, he took "a numerous escort and a band of music."[30]

Argentines in Asunción resented Brazilian influence in the Provisional Government. The Triumvirate, one sarcastic observer wrote, knew no more about government than he did of Greek. Silva Paranhos was the real ruler, and things would not be bad if Rivarola and Bedoya did what he told them. But while the Triumvirate wanted to reform everything, they spent their time frivolously. Argentina's best hope was the corps of youth educated in the country and adamant in opposing Brazil. Suspecting that Brazilians also controlled La Regeneración, Dr. Miguel Gallegos, who held the rank of colonel as a military surgeon, planned a rival paper. He complained that La Regeneración attacked foreigners, and Rivarola would have to be shown that he could not rule like López. However, La Regeneración was independent and so critical of the Provisional Government that observers in Asunción expected Rivarola to take drastic measures unless the paper moderated its attacks.[31]

The Preliminary Treaty of June 20, 1870

Long before the war was over, the Brazilian Council of State considered terms of peace. In its early discussions, the Council was concerned primarily about five matters: the fate of López, his family, and supporters; territorial arrangements; formation of a provisional government; Brazilian influence in postwar Paraguay; and Bolivia's claim to the Chaco. An overriding concern was interpretation of the Treaty of Alliance of May 1, 1865. As early as May, 1867, Caxias was authorized to sign a provisional treaty with a Paraguayan government friendly to Brazil. Salient provisions were to be the expulsion of López and recognition of Bolivia's right to dispute possession of the Chaco Boreal with Paraguay and Argentina.[32] By offering a degree of support in its claim to the Chaco, Brazil might find Bolivia less adamant in their own boundary dispute.

Discussions in the Council late in September, 1867, arrived at positions that were to be modified only slightly in following years. The session of September 30 considered a draft treaty presented by Argentina that followed closely provisions of the Treaty of Alliance. The Argentines favored proscription of the entire López family, and the Visconde e Marquês de Olinda, Pedro de Araújo Lima, proposed a policy that would bar all of the dictator's relatives but would permit Paraguay to use the services of prominent Lopiztas not odious to Brazil. The Visconde de São Vicente, José Antônio Pimenta Bueno, opposed dealing with any representative of the López family, and Conselheiro Francisco de Salles Torres Homem made clear the Council's position: "The Government of López must disappear; not a single member may be permitted to remain in the Republic without making a farce of the Allied victory, considering how the dictator has injured his fellow citizens." However, an exile of ten years instead of perpetual banishment would be enough punishment. Benigno and Venancio must not be permitted to restore Francisco's influence, although Benigno had always been favorable to Brazil, and must be banished for at least five years. This concern with the López brothers and brothers-in-law was settled by López himself, who executed all of them before his own death. Argentina's desire for the early formation of a provisional government in Paraguay met with a cool reception in the Council. São Vicente insisted that only when most of Paraguay was under Allied (meaning Brazilian) control should a government be formed; and after Brazil had occupied the capital, strenuous efforts must be made to establish Brazilian influence.[33] There was no opposition in the Council to this view.

Territorial arrangements quickly emerged as the most difficult problem. Paraguay's prewar boundary disputes with Argentina included ownership of Misiones and the Chaco Central between the Bermejo and Pilcomayo rivers. Francia had actually held Misiones, but Carlos Antonio López had allowed Argentina to establish a nebulous control over the area before 1865, and Paraguay did not contest its possession after the war. The Chaco Boreal, north of the Pilcomayo and beyond

the insignificant port of Bahía Negra, was an area that had been
partially explored both from eastern Paraguay and Bolivia, and had a
few fringe settlements along the Paraguay River. Bolivia had good
claims to at least some of this Indian-infested region, but Argentina
had scarcely the shadow of a claim. Possession of major islands was
also disputed. A large swampy island cut off from the west shore of
the Paraguay by a shallow channel lay at the confluence of the Paraguay and Paraná rivers. It was variously known as Atajo or Cerrito.
Argentina claimed title, but Brazil had set up a naval station on it
during the war. In the Paraná River, downstream from Encarnación
and Posadas, were the large islands of Yacyretá and Apipé. Argentina
claimed the latter. Article 16 of the Treaty of Alliance provided that
the Chaco and Misiones, but not the islands, were to be Argentine.
Brazil's boundary dispute with Paraguay involved much less territory.
On the north, the yerba-rich area between the rivers Apa and Blanco
(also Branco) extended eastward toward low hills. A range of mountains, the Sierra Maracayú or Maracajú, extends westward from the
Paraná and then turns north to form the Sierra Amambay. Paraguay
claimed the area north of the Maracayú and east of the Amambay
ranges, although Brazil had held the region for many years. Article 16
awarded these territories to Brazil and the Chaco Boreal to Argentina:

> In order to avoid the dissensions and wars that boundary disputes cause,
> it is agreed that the Allies will demand of the Government of Paraguay that
> it conclude definitive treaties of limits with the respective governments on
> the following bases:
> The Empire of Brazil will be divided from the Republic of Paraguay:
> On the side of the Paraná by the first river below the cataract of the Seven
> Falls, which, according to the recent map by Mouchez, is the Igurei, and
> from the mouth of the Igurei upstream until reaching its source; On the
> left bank of the Paraguay, by the river Apa, from its mouth to its source;
> In the interior, by the heights of the sierra Maracaju, the streams running
> eastward belonging to Brazil and those running westward to Paraguay, and
> following the same range along a line as straight as possible between the
> sources of the Igurei and the Apa.
> The Argentine Republic will be divided from the Republic of Paraguay
> by the rivers Paraná and Paraguay to the boundaries of the Empire of
> Brazil, which on the right bank of the Río Paraguay is Bahía Negra.[34]

It would seem that these provisions were perfectly clear, but in futile
negotiations for a definitive treaty of peace, the Allies quarreled bitterly over the introductory sentence. Argentina insisted that Article 16
determined boundaries; Brazil maintained that the phrase "on the
following bases" meant that the boundary claims were to be bases for
discussion only. A so-called secret protocol agreed that Humaitá would

be demolished, no fortifications would be permitted on the river, and all military supplies and loot would be divided equally among the Allies.

Although not unanimous, the Brazilian Council of State, consistent with its actions in 1866, was determined to hold Argentina at the Pilcomayo and to gain a hearing for Bolivia's claims to the Chaco. The Visconde de Abaetê, Antônio Paulino Limpo de Abreu, insisted that the delineation of boundaries between Argentina and Paraguay would "influence the future destiny of the Empire." Article 16 of the Treaty of Alliance clearly stated that Argentina was to have Misiones and the Chaco as far north as Bahía Negra. He was also willing that Argentina have the islands of Apipé and Atajo. Abaetê read the future accurately: "I fear that this stipulation of limits between the Argentine Confederation and Paraguay would facilitate the absorption of Paraguay by the Argentine Confederation, would strengthen the latter through an expansion most dangerous for all the neighboring states and fatal to Brazil." Paraguay, therefore, must be given a chance to advance its own interests. Abaetê, too, insisted that Bolivia's claim to the Chaco must be considered. São Vicente was willing to modify Brazil's claims along the Paraná near Sete Quedas (Seven Falls), hoping to persuade Argentina to recede from its extreme Chaco claims, which were prejudicial to Brazil: "They mean disequilibrium [!] and Argentine preponderance, a stronger enemy on Brazil's frontiers, [Argentine] preponderance and our own subordination on the Paraguay and Paraná rivers, with the consequent loss in importance of our river fleet." Paraguay would be completely dependent on Argentina, and war between Argentina and the Empire would be inevitable. The Chaco should be divided: Argentina to stop at the Pilcomayo, Paraguay to extend from the Pilcomayo north to a point opposite the Río Apa, and Bolivia to have the area from there to Bahía Negra. Conselheiro José Tomas Nabuco de Araújo summed up what was to be the Empire's position: territorial disputes caused the war but allocation of territory was not a condition of the Alliance. Limits defined in the Treaty of Alliance were merely bases for negotiation, and both Bolivia and Paraguay must participate in signing treaties of limits.[35] Throughout the Council's consideration ran a current of distrust of Argentina, a determination to limit her territorial gains even at the risk of war.

The Council continued to consider the treaty question from time to time, and before formation of the Provisional Government had worked out provisions it would seek in a general treaty. Its instructions to Silva Paranhos for a preliminary treaty were to provide the framework for a general treaty. The principal provisions would be declaration of peace between the Alliance and Paraguay, insistence that the Provisional Government accept the conditions of peace stated in the Treaty of Alliance, freedom of navigation of Paraguay's territorial waters and a ban on river fortifications, a pledge by the Allies not to interfere in any way with the free election of a permanent government, the provision of moral and material aid to maintain public order and to support the legal government of Paraguay as long as Allied troops were in the country, and the stipulation that some of the principal Lopizta officers might be judged dangerous to the internal peace of Paraguay and to the Allies. The Council added that the Allies must retain freedom of action in the matter of aid, guarantee of Paraguay's independence to be left to the final treaty, and a definite time for Allied evacuation could not be fixed. There would be no separate negotiation with the Provisional Government unless the Allies absolutely refused to come to a reasonable agreement, in which case the Imperial Government reserved freedom of action. It was natural to suppose that these provisions would not be objectionable.[36]

Silva Paranhos took the lead in negotiations and persuaded Argentina and Uruguay to send representatives to Asunción early in April, 1870. There was no disagreement between the Uruguayan representative, Adolfo Rodríguez, and Silva Paranhos; but the Argentine Mariano Varela did not like the proposed draft. Asserting that the Provisional Government, being the creation of the Allies, lacked authority to sign a preliminary treaty, he returned to Buenos Aires on April 13.[37]

Varela's actions caused the Brazilian Council of State to face major questions. Should Brazil proceed with signing a treaty and should the Alliance be considered broken if Argentina refused to negotiate? Abaeté held that a definitive treaty could not be signed with the Provisional Government and that Argentina's refusal to sign a preliminary treaty could not be considered as breaking the Alliance. São Vicente advised patience and a course that would permit Brazil to consolidate its influence in Paraguay: Brazil would face the same problem of containing Argentine influence with or without a preliminary treaty, so nothing could be gained by treating separately with Paraguay. Brazil could afford to wait. A definitive peace, not merely an end to hostilities, must be the objective, and Brazil could always maintain ample forces in Mato Grosso. But if Argentina refused to adopt a reasonable stance, Brazil should proceed to negotiate alone or jointly with Uruguay. In the meantime, Brazil could keep in Paraguay whatever forces it might judge necessary "to give moral or material aid to the Paraguayan Government."[38] The Council's consensus was that Brazil had the right to negotiate a treaty with the Provisional Government and should do so.

Fortunately, the Argentines reconsidered their position and authorized General Julio de Vedia to proceed with negotiations. In view of the political confusion prevailing in Asunción, one may well wonder that any kind of treaty could have been signed in 1870. Nevertheless, Silva Paranhos, Vedia, Loizaga, and Rivarola did sign a treaty on June 20 that declared the war over, guaranteed freedom of river navigation, reserved to Paraguay the right to propose modifications in the Treaty of the Triple Alliance, promised non-intervention in Paraguayan politics, and provided for elections within three months. Argentina promised to evacuate Villa Occidental, a promise not carried out until the end of the decade.[39]

One cannot take exception to the sentiments expressed in this treaty. The preamble begins: "Considering that the termination, de facto, of the war imposes on the Allied Powers the duty of leaving [to Paraguay] entire liberty of action in the political organization of the Republic of Paraguay, as also in the election of their permanent authorities . . ."[40] Behind this favorable statement may have been some clever maneuvering by Rivarola, who, a contemporary observed, "was a Brazilian with Paranhos and an Argentine with Varela."[41]

The Preliminary Treaty of June 20, 1870, met with hearty approval from Bartolomé Mitre's enemies in Buenos Aires. *La República* was pleased that territorial discussions were to be left for a later time and considered the treaty a triumph over Brazil: "In that treaty Paraguayan independence has been saved; the right of conquest has disappeared." Now it was up to Paraguay to make the best use of documentary evidence to defend its territorial claims.[42] *La Nación*, Mitre's paper, had nothing good to say about the treaty. The victors gained no rights, although they had been vindicated by the sword: "The war was not made only to repel the López invasion. Paraguay had usurped our territories in the Chaco and on the Paraná."[43] Silva Paranhos, in defending the treaty before the Brazilian Senate on September 6, 1870, protested that it was not an attempt to break up the Triple Alliance and that the Provisional Government was competent to make peace. Moreover, since the Treaty of Alliance had recognized as Argentine territory the right bank of the Paraguay River as far as Bahía Negra, he could not oppose Argentina's occupation of Villa Occidental.[44] Neither Argentina nor Brazil was willing to risk a break at this juncture.

4. The Provisional Government in Power

Neither Paraguayans nor the Allies were ready for a genuinely independent government in Asunción. Since the war continued for more than six months after the triumvirs were installed, the Allies obviously were not going to give them any real power. Confronting them were the immediate tasks of finding relief for the famished, diseased, and homeless, creating elements of national and local government, maintaining order, promoting agriculture, and meeting an endlessly growing number of problems. The Allies, anxious to wind up the Paraguayan business as soon as possible, could agree on the need for a permanent government and so promoted the calling of a constituent assembly. With their eyes on a permanent treaty, they sought to control the Provisional Government for their own purposes and to transfer that control to the first constitutional regime. Argentines naturally expected the legionnaires to be more favorably inclined toward them, although their exaggerated claim to the Chaco alienated many who would have been pro-Argentine. Suspicious of legionnaires, Brazilians preferred Lopiztas but trusted none of the ambitious survivors of the war, nor the equally ambitious agents and exiles returning from abroad. Paraguayans quickly aligned themselves with two loosely organized political groups that launched what was to become the traditional Liberal-Colorado struggle for power. Through these embryonic parties the Allies would continue their feuding until the last of their troops had left the conquered country. The welfare of Paraguayans and the speedy recovery of Paraguay were of minor concern to the victors.

A more frustrating task than that of the Triumvirate never confronted a Paraguayan government. None of the many efforts made to meet and solve a host of overwhelming problems received any real aid from the Allies. To be sure, the war continued for fourteen months after the occupation of Asunción, and during more than six months of this period a truncated Triumvirate attempted to function as a government. Allied soldiers and Paraguayans alike generally ignored the dedicated efforts of Rivarola and his aides, and there was no military government. Under the circumstances, Rivarola deserves far more respect than he has received from students of Paraguayan history.

Brave Deeds

The Triumvirate was the Paraguayan government in theory from August 15, 1869, to September 1, 1870. With Rivarola in charge, the triumvirs divided the embryonic ministries among themselves and recruited bright young men for key positions. The secretary-general was Serapio Machaín, who also served as secretary to Carlos Loízaga; José Segundo Decoud and Miguel Palacios were secretaries to Rivarola and Bedoya, respectively. Rivarola, aided by Decoud, completely overshadowed his associates. Bedoya soon departed for Buenos Aires to seek a loan, bearing with him "some boxes of worked silver" that he was to sell for the government. Bedoya stayed in Buenos Aires and so did the silver.[1]

Overwhelming tasks faced the Provisional Government, but the triumvirs—more properly the duumvirs—struggled to act like a responsible body. Promptly they issued decrees on August 17 to name themselves the Provisional Government and to declare López an outlaw, "a blot on our civilization and patriotism." Another decree branded as traitors all who continued in the Marshal's service.[2] "Rivarola was obviously obsessed with López," the brilliant but erratic Juan Silvano Godoy observed. Although always talking disparagingly about López, Godoy wrote, Rivarola tried to act like the tyrant by riding a white horse, wearing grenadier boots, and conducting public business on horseback.[3]

After the Marshal's death, the Provisional Government continued its persecution of the López family. Decrees on March 19 and May 4, 1870, confiscated all property belonging to López and embargoed all property claimed by Madame Lynch, who had acquired, through gift and purchase, extensive land holdings. Attempting to obtain the gold López and Madame Lynch had sent to Great Britain, the Rivarola government became entangled in a series of legal actions in British courts. Paraguay recovered none of the treasure.[4]

Persecution of the López family was not a Brazilian policy. Rio Branco assured Dom Pedro II that he had done what he could for the surviving relatives of the dictator and would continue to give them his attention, but Brazil's efforts would not suffice to suppress all obstacles that the family would encounter, nor to kill the avarice aroused by their ownership of extensive properties.[5] Lopiztas or not, individual Paraguayans would seize everything they could.

Paraguayans there were who still regarded López with admiration and even adoration. Despite the terrible calamities for which he was in large measure responsible, despite the savage and vicious cruelties he had inflicted upon his most faithful followers, López was still the symbol of Paraguay, still the Marshal-President. Even before Cerro Corá, the controversial priest Gerónimo Becchis (also called Becchi) dared to praise López from the pulpit early in 1870; a French traveler found in 1872 that many people admired López;[6] and a correspondent from Buenos Aires reported in amazement: "It is wonderful what respect many people cherish for the name of López. I have heard many say they would die for López, and those not of the ignorant and poor, but men of some education and position."[7] Ten years later a British minister unerringly explained this phenomenal support:

> López, in spite of his selfish ambition, his grinding tyranny, and his relentless cruelty, was identified by the Paraguayans who fought with him until the last with such extraordinary devotion and heroism with the national cause, and even now, the name of the man who almost depopulated the country, and who ruined it for generations to come, is not execrated as it should be.[8]

One might expect that a prime order of business for the triumvirs would be ratification of the June 2 protocols by which the Provisional Government had been created. But the triumvirs were in no hurry until, prodded by the Allies, they issued the ratifying decree on August 18. More important to Rivarola was consolidating his position with the Club del Pueblo. He appointed Col. Juan Francisco Decoud as chief of police of Asunción, Trinidad, and Lambaré. Benigno Ferreira, who was to figure so prominently in politics during the occupation and again at the turn of the century, became captain-general of ports. Dr. Facundo Machaín, a brilliant and highly respected young lawyer, headed the Superior (or Supreme) Court, charged with organizing the judicial branch. Juan Silvano Godoy, home from foreign study in September, 1869, was Machaín's secretary and later became senior judge of the civil court. Sinforiano Alcorta, president of the municipality of Asunción, had Jaime Sosa Escalada as secretary and vice-mayor. These appointments, of course, infuriated the Bareiro-led Lopiztas, although they had been offered a few minor posts.[9]

Lopiztas could take little comfort from Rivarola's impassioned manifesto of September 10, 1869, probably written by José Segundo Decoud, in which the Triumvirate defended the Paraguayan Legion and promised aid to the Paraguayan people, who, naked and hungry, beset by epidemics and destroyed by misfortune, were returning to their homes only to be met at their own doors by foreigners. Rivarola's double-edged expression of gratitude to the Allies must have made Rio Branco realize that his puppet could tighten the strings. Paraguay's tyrants, the manifesto declared, had kept the country from participating in the glorious triumphs of the "classic land of liberty, equality, and fraternity." Tyrants had "closed Paraguay to immigration, the harbinger, the pacific vanguard that civilization sends like an exploring party to the land that it wishes to favor with its gifts, its arts and its glories." Tyrants stifled commerce and filled the jails with enterprisers; tyrants stifled liberties and every liberal sentiment; they destroyed the family, promoted polygamy, maintained slavery, made espionage a fine art, weakened religion, militarized the entire country. No liberty went unsuppressed, no right unviolated, no guaranty unbetrayed, and no asylum unviolated. Defeated in battle, they converted a promising land into a vast cemetery "where silence of the tomb guards the secret of crimes, where the most sacred feelings of humanity have been trampled, violated, ridiculed." Paraguayans must be reborn to avoid again falling into slavery: "Through public instruction and liberal institutions, the creation and elevation of a tyrant must be made impossible." Paraguayans must have the great freedoms of democracy.[10]

This manifesto, while not a fully accurate analysis of Paraguay's troubles, was a ringing call for democratic institutions. The Triumvirate had little enough to work with, existing as it did in the shadow of foreign troops and desperately trying to establish a semblance of authority in a chaotic city and country. Moreover, followers of Bareiro felt left out of things and refused to cooperate.[11]

Decree followed decree in rapid order as the triumvirs sought to organize a government, place people on deserted land, introduce livestock, promote the exploitation of abandoned yerbales, provide for relief, create schools, maintain order, attract commerce, and raise revenue by the sale of stamped paper. The organization of government to provide essential services should have been a concern of the Allies, and their indifference is difficult to explain, especially when the Triumvirate, with no resources at all, sought by decree to exorcise the devils crowding around. The decree of August 26, 1869, created ministries of interior, justice, and finance.[12] A decree of September 30, 1869, is eloquent of conditions in Asunción: to prevent congestion during the coming summer, the triumvirs ordered homeless persons to be assigned quarters in Trinidad; others with homes anywhere must go to them; people unable to work must report to the railway station for removal to Luque. Burial, so often ceremonial, was perfunctory in the extreme, and a human body received little more attention than that of a stray dog. Since men were lacking to carry bodies to public cemeteries and women were too weak to do the work, the sergeant of each local police company was required to be a burial supervisor. A commission created in December was to provide care, work, and education for the destitute, but no provision was made for financing their efforts.[13]

The Provisional Government named jefes políticos (political leaders), justices of the peace, military commandants, and priests or chaplains for the departments. To provide revenue, the municipality of Asunción could collect license fees for retail trade, burial permits, and weights and measures. The city also reassumed title to the meat market, the unfinished National Theater, and all abandoned lands.[14]

The first efforts to promote agriculture and animal husbandry failed to bring immediate results to a country still in chaos. Anyone could import cattle and pasture them free for one year on public lands. Another decree created the Department of Agriculture, Industry, and Commerce within the Ministry of Hacienda. All branches of yerba and timber production, formerly government monopolies, now were open to private exploitation. Since many vagrants roamed the country and crimes of violence increased, the triumvirs required passports for travel between departments, a regulation reminiscent of travel restrictions in the Francia and López eras. Attempting to employ these wanderers, the busy Triumvirate decreed compulsory labor groups to work in agriculture, but no successes were recorded. Another interesting experiment, also without notable success, was an attempt to abolish the siesta! This daily interruption of work, a decree of November 17, 1869, solemnly declared, "is prejudicial to the activity that commerce, which is increasing notably, demands." The work day would be from 9:00 in the morning to 3:00 in the afternoon,[15] surely not a heavy burden but very impractical in the hottest part of the day.

Several Paraguayan slaves asked the Conde d'Eu for their liberty. The count, surprised that slavery still existed in Paraguay, intimated to the Provisional Government that it should end. The result was the decree of October 2, 1869, that abolished slavery throughout the republic. Any person would be free six months after setting foot on Paraguayan soil. Owners would be compensated, but what the triumvirs would use for money was not clear.[16] Two weeks later another decree abolished forced exile to any part of the republic. Pending adoption of a constitution, the Triumvirate promulgated a bill of rights that included freedom of religion, although Roman Catholicism was established as the state religion. For its judicial system, Paraguay adopted the Siete Partidas and other Spanish codes, and the Argentine commercial code.[17]

These various decrees amazed the Argentines. Col. Miguel Gallegos, head of the Argentine hospital, complained that the Allies had intended to establish a government for Asunción only, "a municipal authority, charged with regulating imports, to attend to cleaning up the town, and to supervise the health and life of the unfortunate women who then as now were perishing and will go on perishing from hunger in the streets of the town unless some charitable hand does not provide them with the necessities of life." Rivarola had a mania for decrees and "spent the greater part of his time in dictating or writing them in his own hand."[18] Many were shelved for future reference.

Finance

The people of Moses, ordered to make bricks without straw, were in no greater plight than the Triumvirate, which attempted to govern with no sure source of income. There was no coinage, no issue of bills, under the Provisional Government. Among the many kinds of foreign money in circulation, the Brazilian patacón, roughly equal to $1.00 in gold, predominated for a while.[19] The Provisional Government could issue all kinds of decrees except a very necessary one to levy duties on all imports. Customs could not be collected on goods introduced by sutlers for the Allies; other merchants, with or without aid of sutlers, "introduced their goods as destined for the army of occupation."[20] One source of income was the ubiquitous stamped paper required for all public acts, contracts, and petitions. License fees, levied at the end of 1869 to raise money, ran from three pesos monthly for *pulperías* (saloons) to 150 pesos for banks[21]—but there were no banks. There was no tax system that could be reactivated, since the López had met expenses primarily from customs and the sale of produce belonging to the state. The only favorable aspect of this gloomy financial picture was a complete lack of foreign debt, a blissful state that the Triumvirate hoped to end promptly. The Brazilian and Argentine armies each operated a train on the short railway that they soon placed in uncertain operation, but the traffic yielded nothing for the public treasury. For the period from August 12, 1869, to the end of the year, the Triumvirate was able to collect $f205,786.40, nearly all of which it spent.[22]

Desperate for more money than the pittance doled out by Brazil, the Triumvirate decided to seek a loan in Buenos Aires and to sell what was left of the church ornaments turned over by the Allies. To accomplish this mission, Rivarola and Loizaga sent their fellow triumvir, José Díaz de Bedoya, who had a wide acquaintance in Buenos Aires. Bedoya's instructions of December 20, 1869, authorized him to borrow 2,000,000 pesos in gold, offering the railway and government property in Asunción as collateral.[23] Bedoya left promptly, never to return, in an effort to carry out the impossible mission.

Severely critical of Brazil, the Argentine press scoffed at the Triumvirate's efforts. An Argentine in Asunción charged that the whole thing was a Bedoya speculation, that the Provisional Government had no power to borrow, or sell national property. Paraguay was poverty-stricken, with no resources. One editor held Silva Paranhos to be author of the ridiculous scheme: since he knew that Paraguay could not borrow one peso in Buenos Aires, Silva Paranhos in Machiavellian style wanted to emphasize Paraguay's dependence on the Empire.[24] A more friendly editor thought the loan might have had possible success two months earlier, but the very tight money situation in Buenos Aires made it impossible in 1870. Nor was the proffered collateral impressive: the railway would produce nothing after the army withdrew, and then "the only passengers will be the engine driver and the guard." Judging by the money market, the editor concluded, "we doubt if all Paraguay were put up at auction it would fetch even one half the amount of the mooted Paraguayan 'emprestito.' "[25]

Try as he might, Bedoya could borrow nothing for Paraguay, and news of his failure reached Asunción quickly. Without funds, the government could last not more than three months unless it retrenched by firing needless employees and disbanding the Paraguayan Legion. Income could be increased by renting government houses, putting vagabonds to work, attracting immigrants, protecting commerce, enacting a good tax system, and exploiting the country's natural wealth. Bedoya did realize $11,000 from the sale of church ornaments to Mariano Billinghurst in Buenos Aires, but none of the money reached Asunción. Pleading illness, the emissary resigned[26] and never seemed to recover enough strength to send the money to Asunción.

Decoudistas bitterly assailed Bedoya, who was said to be retiring "to Europe without leaving any memory in Paraguay other than that of having exploited what little he could exploit in this country. He rose to the government by chance, or perhaps through the bad faith and perversity of those who then wanted to do no good for Paraguay."

Fearing that Brazil might insist on Bareiro as a replacement, *La Regeneración* warned: "Bareiro will be thousands of times worse than Don José de Bedoya."[27]

Origins of Party Warfare

Political and journalistic activity continued while the Triumvirate busied itself with decrees laudable in purpose but impossible to enforce. The first issue of *La Regeneración*, which was also the first free newspaper in Paraguay, came from the press on October 1, 1869. Col. Juan Francisco Decoud bought the press with his own funds, and his son Juan José was the first principal editor. Contributors were all Decoudista Liberals, all prominent in the Club del Pueblo, all fiercely independent and champions of liberalism. Decrees of the Triumvirate were closely integrated with articles in *La Regeneración*, although it is impossible to say how many of them originated with the paper's personnel.

A major objective of the Decoudistas and their rivals, the Bareiristas, was control of the Constitutional Convention that was to meet late in 1870. Juan José Decoud on October 10, 1869, published the first in a series on a constitutional project and concluded: "The constitution marks the degree of civilization of a people, is the barometer of its progress, and more or less outlines on the horizon its adverse or happy future."[28] These articles, completed on November 21, 1869, were the guide for the Convention of 1870. Decoudistas, obviously, intended to lead in the reconstruction of Paraguay. A correspondent of the Buenos Aires *La Tribuna* charged that the Decouds ran the Provisional Government. Adolfo Decoud hotly denied the accusation, named others who were in positions of responsibility, and asserted the government's need for a thousand citizens to help.[29]

In order to broaden support for a new fundamental charter, the Club del Pueblo in January, 1870, organized the Asociación Constitucional. The way had been prepared a month earlier with the announcement that various Paraguayans wanted a political association and that a nonpartisan group should result: "The thought could not be more noble and opportune, the more so since the program that is to be championed is the union and fraternity of all Paraguayans without regard for the party colors that today unfortunately divide Paraguayan society so deeply."[30] The first meeting of the group assembled in Jaime Sosa Escalada's home and welcomed everyone.[31]

The Triumvirate decreed civil and political guarantees on February 5, 1870, and a month later announced impending elections for a constitutional convention. An idealist rhapsodized: "For the first time the Paraguayan citizen is to go to the polls to deposit his ballot in the balance of suffrage, free and without coercion, to contribute to the welfare of his country." [32] In preparation for this important event, the Club del Pueblo held an important meeting on March 23 to widen party structure and to guarantee that delegates to the convention would truly represent the people—meaning the liberal Decoudistas. At this meeting they changed the name of their group to Gran Club del Pueblo.[33] The rival Bareiristas countered this move with two steps on March 24. They organized the Club del Pueblo, dropping their former name of Club Unión and assuming the name abandoned by the opposition, with Col. Fernando Iturburu as president.[34] Their second move was to start publication of *La Voz del Pueblo*, with the strong support of Col. Miguel Gallegos, who sought a way to counteract Brazilian influence and to oppose Rivarola. One of the first clashes between the rival papers was over the presence of Allied troops. *La Regeneración* feared they would prevent free elections, but *La Voz del Pueblo* urged their retention until the formation of the constitutional government.[35]

The leadership of opposing political groupings in 1870 anticipated fairly accurately divisions that existed in the 1880s when political parties formally took shape. The terms Azules (Blues) and Colorados (Reds), used as early as 1869, corresponded to Liberals and Colorados, the only parties that amounted to anything until the Febreristas exploded on the Paraguayan scene in 1936. The Lopiztas were responsible for the successful campaign, begun even before the death of the Marshal-President at Cerro Corá, to rehabilitate the reputation of Francisco Solano López. Just as Republicans in the United States waved the "bloody shirt" long after the Civil War in order to arouse political antagonism toward Democrats, so did the Paraguayan Colorados constantly accuse their Liberal opponents with the crime of *legionarismo*. In the Colorado lexicon, *legionario* and *traidor* (traitor) were synonymous.[36] The ease with which Liberals and Colorados changed sides should be taken for granted. The distinguished statesman and academician Prof. Pablo Max Ynsfrán observed at the height of Liberal power that the two parties were very similar, with no special solutions for national problems and no fundamental differences. "So strong is the power of tradition in these parties," he wrote in 1929, "that it is very rare to find a member of one deserting to the other." [37] But this was not true in the 1870s when the two parties were being formed. Factions appeared constantly, and intra-party disagreement found an outlet in this feuding. The rival groups of 1870 did represent real differences. As the Liberal writer Adolfo Decoud saw it:

> Some represent the reaction of the past that is bloodstained by the murders of the tyrant who finally perished, who had exploited the wealth of the people; others represent the cause of the victims, the cause of the Yegros and Caballeros who died rather than submit to the tyrants of their Fatherland.
>
> Some represent what in the Argentine Republic is given the name *mazorca*; others are like the *unitarios*.
>
> Some are motivated only by their personal interests and by their purses; others, the Liberal party, one that loves neither Francia nor the López, but worthy and honored citizens who have been sacrificed for their Fatherland. . . .
>
> We shall always oppose that party, or, better said, that gang that is motivated by desire to seize control in order to raise from its black tomb the figure of the past that symbolizes the martydom of the Fatherland.
>
> We shall fight it because of the ideal it represents, since its motives are well known to all who read *La Voz del Pueblo*.[38]

Decoud could have said it more simply by declaring that the Liberals strove for democracy while the Lopiztas wanted to return to dictatorship.

This atmosphere was hardly conducive to a union of the two clubs, a fact clearly demonstrated by events of May 5, 1870. Hoping to present a united front to contest foreign influence in Paraguayan affairs, the Gran Club del Pueblo invited its rival to meet in the national theater. By enlisting foreigners and Argentine soldiers in civilian dress, the Bareiristas filled the theater well before the meeting was to start. Many were armed with revolvers and knives. When Dr. Facundo Machaín and his friends appeared, their voices were drowned in the uproar raised by their rivals.[39]

After the disrupted meeting had ended in turmoil, Lopiztas poured into the streets, firing into the air, shouting vivas for Cándido Bareiro. This *mazhorcado*, or criminal tumult, *La Regeneración* claimed, caused great alarm, and the people were warned not to forget that "El Petit Club López" represented tyranny. The Gran Club del Pueblo, if we can believe "Otelo," staged a counter-demonstration, with more than 2,000 people and two bands parading through the streets shouting vivas for Rivarola, themselves, the foreigners, and the Allies and death to the Lopiztas. Benigno Ferreira solemnly proclaimed that they were lighting the sacred fire. At Bernardo Recalde's house, the Gran Club saluted Carlos Loizaga and, after a speech by Juan José Decoud, went to the harbor master's to repeat their cheers for the Allies, the Paraguayan people, and Rivarola.[40] There was to be no quarter in this political warfare, and the Gran Club del Pueblo elected Benigno Ferreira as their leader to direct the combat.

While the two political clubs were squaring off in the Paraguayan arena, the Bareiristas were accused of trying to bribe Rivarola. Col. Fernando Iturburu, secretary of the Ministry of Interior, promised Rivarola that he could be constitutional president if he would desert the Liberals. At the same time, early in May, Rufino Taboada and Juan Bautista Gill were accused of trying to bribe the police. This matter was turned over to the courts, but the Liberals dropped the charges at Rivarola's urging.[41] Blinded by ambition, Rivarola was trying to play both sides and as a result lost the confidence of both.

If Liberals had hoped for cooperation from Bareiristas, their various journalistic attacks gave no room for accommodation. Ferreira exercised no restraint:

> The savage cry of future tyranny has been heard. Do not be deceived by his false words—they are the futile pretexts of the hungry wolf that wants to devour the weak lamb. Bareiro represents tyranny—his past is black—his antecedents perfidious. . . . In Bareiro is incarnated the most hateful despotism; raised and educated by López, besides being his relative [a nephew], he defends in our country and has defended abroad the death and extermination of Paraguay.[42]

The satirist "Casi-miro" in his "Mosaico" column addressed Bareiro's supporters first in Italian and sneered: "The palace of your relative López has been made ready and there you may await the arrival of Mdme Lyme [Lynch]." With heavy sarcasm, "Casi-miro" continued in Spanish: "Poor Cándido! How candid you are, how candid your ambition, how candid the air castles you build day and night, what candid illusions! Poor fellow, I sympathize with you! What candor—Oh, Cándido, candidate ad hoc! Your constant obsession is the presidency of the land to whose extermination you have contributed."[43] The editor summarized Bareiro's career with less than sympathy. He had been a spy in the customs who reported daily to López, who, confident of his fidelity, sent him as a secretary to spy on the Paraguayan legation in France. After that mission, he wanted to be minister to France and England. López left him in France, where he lived sumptuously; placed in charge of Paraguayan students abroad, he used the money sent for their support in orgies and banquets, and let fourteen students die while he consorted with prostitutes. He returned to Asunción after the Allies entered the city and vainly attempted to name the Provisional Government. Although he fawned before the Allies, his intrigues were in vain since good Paraguayans, both Liberals and Lopiztas, were appointed. He refused an offer to head the commercial court. Paraguayans should forget Bareiro and make Rivarola president.[44] Some of these charges are obviously false, especially those concerning the students in France.

Journalistic restraint has existed in Paraguay only when imposed by censorship, and certainly some sort of control was needed in 1870. There was nothing subtle in attacks launched by rival groups through their newspapers, attacks of which the following is a good example:

> Blood! Blood! Blood!
> Listen, Paraguayans!
> The members of the Petit Club López, seeing themselves impotent and defeated, today threaten that they will make blood flow in Paraguay if they do not win in the elections.
> Here are the new executioners![45]

Foreigners could not ignore the political ferment, did not need the warning to be on guard, and could find mutual support in various clubs. Italians and Spaniards each had a club, and a European club was organized on May 8, 1870, two days after the formation of the Asociación Estrangera de Protección Mútua (Foreigners' Mutual Protective Association), which was open to all foreigners.[46] Many Argentines and some Brazilians supported Bareiro, but while Argentina officially pretended neutrality, it was no secret that Brazil's representatives backed Rivarola. Their preferences were based on personalities, not on party differences, since the rival clubs had not yet achieved the status of formally recognized political organizations. Jaime Sosa Escalada, a charter member of the Gran Club del Pueblo, clearly showed this emphasis in his attack on Bareiro: "Paraguayans—eternal reproach for us and eternal ignominy for all civil citizens, if a man from the López family comes once more to rule the destinies of our beloved Fatherland."[47] Adolfo Decoud pleaded in vain for an end to political agitation that could do nothing except to increase antagonism.[48]

In the midst of this journalistic warfare and vicious recrimination, General Julio de Vedia arrived as Argentine commander. A French traveler described him as "a big man, with a long grey beard, whose black eyes are very sharp and intelligent. Very friendly, a man of the world to his fingertips, he speaks the French language fluently." Well versed in the classics, Vedia had a broad if not deep education and appeared to be well qualified for his difficult role.[49] He sized up the situation after visits from José Segundo Decoud, Cándido Bareiro, and

Fernando Iturburu, all of whom he had probably met in Argentina. Although he felt neutrality to be the best course, Vedia favored Iturburu for the presidency.[50] The Argentine commander, who divided his time between Asunción and Villa Occidental, was an excellent choice by the Argentine president at a very critical time, a diplomat who gained the respect of all parties while not neglecting intrigue as a means of advancing his country's interests.

5. The Convention of 1870

The Paraguayans who formed the Constituent Assembly of 1870 were inexperienced in government and poorly prepared in political theory. There were a few exceptions, especially among those who had been educated abroad. Drafting a constitution that could serve Paraguay was a tremendous task, one whose final result must reflect Paraguayan experience if it were to endure.

Meeting after a tumultuous election in an atmosphere charged with passion, the convention gave more of its time to politics than to statesmanship. The members were aware of advantages to be gained from controlling the government, and the Allies, especially the Brazilians, recognized the imperative to control the convention. Deliberations of the convention met with little if any interference from the Allies as long as constitutional matters were under discussion; once the convention turned to politics, Allied influence was overwhelming.

The principal models followed by the convention were the Argentine charter of 1853, the United States Constitution of 1787 and the Federalist essays, and the French Constitution of 1789. There were changes, of course, but of a minor character. The constitution that emerged rested on a foundation of liberal ideas that had never taken root in Paraguay. Unfortunately, the Paraguayan experience had been with ruthless dictatorship for more than five decades and with a colonial authoritarianism that, while not without democratic aspects, could not be called rule by the people. Authoritarianism was as deeply ingrained among the people as the use of the Guaraní language, and any effort to deviate from it entailed serious dangers that could be overcome only by an ideological revolution in which Paraguayans would agree to observe democratic political principles. Paraguay, therefore, did not achieve democratic government under the Constitution of 1870. This fundamental charter made such basic assumptions as freedom for political action, willingness to abide by the results of genuinely free elections, and the ability of voters to understand basic political issues. These assumptions were not valid in the Paraguay of 1870. Even if they had been, the Allies would not have allowed Paraguayans the political freedom necessary to make a constitution workable. As the Liberals themselves discovered after coming to power in 1904, frequent states of siege, press censorship, and controlled elections were necessary for political stability. Bluntly put, Paraguayans had far more faith in the cartridge pouch than in the ballot box. The relative peace that prevailed during the Colorado era to 1904 was secured largely by ignoring the imposed aberration of 1870.

Election of the Convencionales

While the preliminary treaty of 1870 was being negotiated, plans to hold elections for the Constituent Assembly, which would double as a congress, matured rapidly. The Provisional Government on April 1, 1870, ordered the election of delegates by various districts. To register voters, rolls would be open for fifteen days in May, and all males aged 17 and over were eligible to vote. When he registered, each voter received a numbered ticket to be surrendered at the polls, where voting would be by voice before an electoral board in each district. The Provisional Government on May 3 set the following June 12 for what were supposed to be the first free elections in Paraguay's history.[1] There was some fear that violence would attend the voting, but the Brazilians had 3,000 troops in Asunción and a reserve of 5,000 at Humaitá. To police the city, the Provisional Government had a force of 150.[2] This would make very little difference in rural areas unless a respectable body of troops guarded each polling place.

The June 12 date proved to be too early, so the election was moved back to July 3. This would give more time for prospective convencionales (convention delegates) to study the essays of Juan José Decoud "on the bases and principles of a constitution for Paraguay." These Paraguayan "Federalist Papers," primarily the product of one thinker, began with some excellent advice: a constitution must reflect the needs of the people, must be fifty years ahead of its time in order to be a guide for progress, and must be founded on a sound knowledge of the past and of the future possibilities of the country.[3] The delay also increased opportunities for Bareiristas and Decoudistas to campaign vigorously. The former, fearing defeat at the polls, attempted a coup to oust Rivarola on June 29 but failed miserably.[4] An overwhelming victory at the polls on July 3 gave the Gran Club del Pueblo, or Decoudistas, a large majority in the convention. Forty-four delegates won undisputed election, while the returns from one district were disputed and in another the electoral board could not certify the election of anyone.[5] Although disorders were mild, there was some violence that had a tragicomic outcome.

Rufino Taboada, a Bareirista, led an attack against Dr. Facundo Macháin, who, with José Segundo Decoud, was elected from the Encarnación parish in Asunción. Macháin suffered a wound; Taboada suffered imprisonment, but not before he had attacked the election board in San Roque parish, where he tore up the list of electors. There was a duplicate list.[6] News of Taboada's imprisonment spread rapidly and caused a "march of the women" to free him. In man-short Asunción, the rakish Taboada was a great favorite. Ten to fifteen prominent women led a mob of 3,000 to 4,000 creoles and mestizas, *quiguaberás y placeras*,[7] to demand Taboada's freedom. A Brazilian military band was in front of its barracks across from the government palace. The band leader signaled for the *palomita*, a habanera modified by Paraguayan footwork, which delighted the Paraguayans. The mob of women marchers became a mob of dancers as they approached the palace. Although the leaders failed to win Taboada's release from Rivarola, the Brazilians had found a new way to control a feminine mob![8] More serious was the violence against *La Voz del Pueblo* when an officer led a score of Brazilian soldiers in an attack against the pro-Argentine paper on July 15. The chief of police, Col. Juan Francisco Decoud, protested in vain to General José Auto da Silva Guimarães, who commanded Brazil's forces.[9]

Rio Branco, as Silva Paranhos was generally called, was too sophisticated to believe that Asunción was politically safe, but he and General Câmara left for Brazil on August 10, 1870, leaving General Guimarães, Barão de Jaguarão, in command. He also left a watchdog, Colonel Felipe Neri, who would provide Jaguarão and Admiral Pereira Pinto with advice. Neri, by means of articles in *El Derecho*, a Brazilian paper published in Spanish, kept Paraguayan officials informed as to how they were doing. Jaguarão referred to Neri as "the Filipino," indicating a degree of dislike. To this agent has been ascribed complete domination of Rivarola and a change in direction of the newspaper *El Pueblo* at the end of 1871. Neri mixed freely with the Paraguayans, determined who were friends and who were enemies of the Empire, brought about Rivarola's fall, and protected the Empire's favorite, Juan Bautista Gill, through all vicissitudes.[10]

The Liberals, having won the election, made no effort toward reconciliation with their enemies. *La Regeneración* continued its virulent attacks, and one of its columnists, "Hassan," bemoaned the fate of Paraguay "if unfortunately the Lópizta party supported by 'La Voz del Pueblo' and led by Bareiro had triumphed! Proscription, innocent bloodshed in the jails would have been the result. 'La Regeneración' and the young Paraguayans who support it have won, and that victory will inaugurate happy days of peace and prosperity for this poor country."[11] The shedding of blood in jails was an accurate prophecy, for the Liberals soon overreached themselves. Days of peace and prosperity were not to come for many years.

Convention Maneuverings

Liberals appeared to be firmly in control when the Constituent Assembly met in the main salon of the Cabildo at noon on August 15, 1870. A strong majority of the forty-nine members present professed attachment to the Gran Club del Pueblo and showed their power by electing Col. Federico Guillermo Báez as acting president and José Segundo Decoud and Jaime Sosa Escalada as acting secretaries.[12] This done, they sent a committee to inform the triumvirs that the assembly was in session. The Argentine General Vedia and his Brazilian counterpart, General Guimarães, accompanied Rivarola and Loizaga to the hall. Loizaga, speaking first, roundly condemned past tyrannies in florid figures that anticipated a better future for Paraguay. Previous assemblies had been abject creatures of dictators that delivered the people to "the criminal passions of their tyrants." The Provisional Government, itself a piece of driftwood on a "deep ocean of blood and tears," existed in a time of anguish and desolation.[13]

After their oratorical flourishes, the triumvirs withdrew, leaving the delegates to elect their permanent officials. Colonel Báez appointed three leading Liberals to form a committee that would elect a permanent president of the convention. While this committee was deliberating, Colonel Báez took the floor to observe that a new era was dawning for the Paraguayan people with this, the first freely elected assembly in Paraguayan history. Thus began the first of eighty-three sessions of the Constituent Assembly, whose labors would not end until December 10, 1870. The second session, on August 16, was a portent of things to come. Tumultuous debate and impassioned polemics on the floor and shouts from the gallery kept the convention in an uproar that required frequent police intervention. Cayo Miltos from Concepción, Pedro Recalde representing Paraguarí, and Cirilo Solalinde, delegate from Rosario, were the principal Colorado troublemakers and appeared bent on disrupting the convention.[14]

Events of the next fortnight convinced Liberal leaders that they must take drastic measures if democracy was to survive in the wreckage that was Paraguay. In the background were the Allied generals, Vedia and Guimarães, themselves drifting but determined not to lose control over the convention. Bareiristas from the start did everything possible to disrupt proceedings, even resorting to bribery in an effort to transform their minority position. Of forty-two eligible members, only thirty attended the stormy session of August 17, during which guards were posted to exclude non-members and Cayo Miltos led twelve other delegates in a short walkout.[15] In the face of Allied machinations and Bareirista intransigence, Liberals closed ranks to elect José Segundo Decoud as president of the convention on August 18 and authorized the Rivarola government to restrain the foul tirades that appeared in *La Voz del Pueblo*.[16]

The convention, of course, was far from being free. Events of August 31 and September 1 amply demonstrated this fatal weakness, brought Liberals and Bareiristas into a fateful clash, and revealed how very, very far Paraguayan leaders were from being ready to entrust their political fortunes to genuinely democratic processes, and how unwilling the Allies were to tolerate a genuine exercise of sovereignty.

Many of the Liberals were very young men whose fiery eloquence was a poor substitute for experience. Such a one was Juan Silvano Godoy (or Godoi), who was born in Asunción on November 22, 1851, and who had studied in Uruguay and Argentina.[17] Clever and brilliant, this young delegate conceived the plan whose short-lived success inspired Cándido Bareiro to strike swiftly with a countercoup that within hours completely reversed the political fortunes of the rival clubs and set a pattern of conflict that was to endure for more than a century. Godoy's plan was logical and, to the Decoudistas, entirely sensible, although it had the characteristics of a coup minus the military sanctions so necessary for continued success. Godoy, Dr. Facundo Machaín, and Bernardo Recalde decided that they could not depend upon Rivarola's liberalism to match the idealism of Machaín, who was anti-Brazilian and "the living incarnation of those burning desires of the first Paraguayan liberalism."[18] Very little persuasion was needed to convince Dr. Machaín that he was Paraguay's best hope in that uncertain hour.

Facundo Machaín, tragic victim of Lopizta vengeance, was the most intellectual of the Liberals.[19] Born in Asunción on November 29, 1845, he received a good education that culminated in the study of law with Andrés Bello at the University of Chile, from which he received the Doctor of Jurisprudence degree. He returned to Asunción early in 1869, became president of the Gran Club del Pueblo, and served honorably in the convention, where "he was the most persuasive and eloquent orator."[20] Juan Bautista Gill, a political enemy, nevertheless made him minister of foreign affairs and entrusted to him the very important missions to Brazil and Argentina in 1875 and 1876. A professor and director of the first Colegio Nacional, he was teaching a class when notified of President Gill's assassination, an event that was to lead to his own murder.[21] Godoy calls him Paraguay's foremost humanist. Aristocratic in manner and temperament, he was arrogant but at the same time a champion of the common people. A very handsome man, Machaín was just under six feet. With curly blonde hair, a full beard, and intensely blue eyes, he made a striking appearance. His frank, courteous manner and almost childlike simplicity inspired confidence, respect, and affection.[22]

Godoy's plan to catapult Machaín into power was simple: The Liberal leaders would have the convention declare the Triumvirate ended and replace it with Machaín as provisional president. They needed an opportune time to put the scheme into operation. When Rivarola recommended arbitrary punishment if an unwelcome Uruguayan officer entered the country, Godoy moved. He persuaded Loizaga to resign, leaving Rivarola the surviving triumvir. With both Bedoya and Loizaga gone, there was no Triumvirate, a fact the convention would recognize. The Decoud brothers, José Segundo and Juan José, urged the impetuous Godoy to go slowly, pleading that the time was not opportune; nevertheless, the plot matured under Godoy's leadership. Not desiring to alienate Rivarola, the Liberals invited the Bareirista minority to participate in the scheme, "offering inducements and special guarantees that might stimulate their determination."[23]

The Bareirista leader in the convention was Cayo Miltos, a young man whom Liberals would have liked to claim as their own. Born in Concepción in 1842, he had studied in Buenos Aires and Paris before attending the University of Brussels.[24] Miltos accepted the promise of a prominent role in the new administration and on August 31, when Loizaga's resignation was read, moved acceptance and followed with another motion declaring an end to the Triumvirate. Godoy then presented the constitutional argument that the Constituent Assembly, like its predecessors in other countries, was invested with sovereign power, entitled to take whatever measures appeared best for the nation. He proposed that the assembly designate a provisional president of the republic and moved the election of Dr. Machaín. The assembly, with near unanimity, voted Rivarola out and Machaín in.[25] To inform Rivarola, a committee made up of Miltos, Jaime Sosa, and Agustín Cañete crossed over to the Government House with the message.

Rivarola, with no choice apparently, agreed to turn the executive authority over to Machaín, leaving his own fortunes to the Brazilians.

News of what was going on obviously got around, since a crowd of 200 was present when the assembly went en masse to the Government House with the provisional president at 5:00 p.m. There Rivarola spoke briefly, regretting that he had been unable to do much for his unfortunate country but accepting the convention's decision. "The gathering dispersed, and a half hour later a public crier, accompanied by a musical band and the notary public, traveled through the principal streets of the city, announcing the event to the public in the midst of unanimous manifestations of public rejoicing."[26] But Godoy was worried because things had gone too smoothly. He advised Dr. Machaín to seek safety in the police station that night, but Machaín went to his home while followers spread the news. Miltos, in the meantime, conferred belatedly with Cándido Bareiro to get his reactions.

Bareiro was very much displeased with Miltos as he learned the details. The Liberal coup, he realized, would put his party into permanent eclipse. Quickly analyzing the stiuation, he saw in the attitude of the Allies his major support. Rivarola was still the favorite of Vedia and Guimarães, who were displeased with the upstart assembly. So Bareiro and Miltos, with the approval of Juan Bautista Gill, hastened to the Argentine hospital to confer with their adviser, Dr. Miguel Gallegos, who agreed with Bareiro's analysis and on the need to act quickly. The plan was as simple as the one executed by the Liberals: Bareiro, in conference with Rivarola, would propose that he renounce his resignation immediately; in the assembly on the next day, while Brazilian troops occupied the Cabildo, Miltos would move a reconsideration and nominate Rivarola as provisional president. In the meantime, Liberal partisans of Rivarola would be won over, Dr. Gallegos would gain the approval of Generals Vedia and Guimarães, the Bareiristas would assemble in the Argentine hospital, and the capital police and the Paraguayan Legion would be enlisted.[27]

There were no unexpected barriers to the smooth execution of Bareiro's countercoup. At the interview with Rivarola, the deposed triumvir agreed to being reimposed, with Bareiro a partner in power. Together they issued a proclamation that condemned the attempted revolution and gave assurance that the convention was in order and would occupy itself henceforth in drafting the constitution for which it was called.[28] Rufino Taboada, the Bareirista who had tried to prevent a peaceful election and was still in jail, had a friend in the French merchant Juan Balirán, who persuaded the police captain Zacarías Jara to release the troublemaker and join the coup. The chief of police, Col. Juan Francisco Decoud, was ill in bed. Jara set Taboada free; then, with Lt. Col. Pedro Fernández of the Legion, they went to the Argentine hospital, where they learned that the Allied generals were agreeable to the coup. Rivarola declared himself back in power, appointed Bareiro as secretary-general, ordered Colonel Decoud under house arrest, and made Rufino Taboada chief of the capital police! All of the leading Liberals lost their jobs in this amazing reversal of fortune: Dr. Facundo Machaín as president of the Superior Court, Juan Silvano Godoy as judge of the Civil Court, Juan José Decoud as attorney general, Jaime Sosa as inspector general of schools, and Bernigno Ferreira as captain-general of ports.[29]

Unable to believe what had happened, Dr. Machaín was dumbfounded when he faced reality on the morning of September 1. He sent a note to the Allies with the decree that had made him provisional president, wrote to Rivarola a gentlemanly reprimand, and issued a proclamation inviting Paraguayans to help him rebuild the country. The Allied generals saw in the Bareiristas willing tools and fully endorsed Rivarola's assumption of authority, thus making Machaín's activity completely useless. The spectacle of Bareiro and Rivarola, widely recognized as deadly enemies, working together caused one observer to remark: "The union has been shameful; every Paraguayan knowing the ideas of those men will cross himself, so incomprehensible is that which has occurred."[30]

Bareiro, in reporting on the coup and countercoup to foreign diplomats, insisted that the convention had exceeded its powers in substituting Machaín for Rivarola, who, "animated by the highest patriotic sentiments," made no resistance. But the people, aware of the dangers that threatened them, urged Rivarola to resume his office, and the convention, realizing its error, reversed itself the following day. Informed of these events, the Allied commanders were most pleased and offered their support. So "the Government and the country are to be congratulated on the triumph of justice and the moral reestablishment of public tranquility and harmony among the powers in discord." He closed this pious version with a bit of flowery nonsense: "Today the country, traveling the path of civilization, culture, and progress, moves swiftly and surely, supported by justice and the people, to win the position that without doubt it will reach among the great Nations in the era of reorganization that awaits it under the permanent government."[31]

Liberals found no help in the convention, where the Bareiristas had suborned enough delegates to change their party into a majority position through support of the Rivarolistas. Only thirteen Liberals voted against the motion to reconsider the decree that had declared the Triumvirate abolished.[32] When Miltos moved Rivarola's nomination as provisional president, the thirteen Liberals withdrew in protest and so were not present when the convention expelled Dr. Machaín and declared Rivarola elected unanimously. Well might the Liberal historian Gomes Freire Esteves conclude: "Since that day the Liberal Party was disrupted and there began the period of bloody anarchy, of endless convulsions, in which fell, one after another, the principal actors in the drama of our constitutional organization."[33]

One may, according to partisan leanings, condemn one or the other of the parties to the coup and countercoup of August 31 and September 1. The Liberals, led by rash young men, were audacious but naïve. They neglected to obtain Allied approval and they had no military strength whatever. A recent writer, obviously with strong Colorado bias, saw the Rivarola-Machaín fracas as an Argentine effort to displace Brazilian influence: "Brazilian arms restored the order of their preference and the Constituent Assembly . . . abandoned Machaín to name Rivarola. The latter was, by this free and spontaneous pronouncement, first constitutional president of the Republic (October 1, 1870)."[34] The chronology is wrong but the sarcasm is obvious. When the convention returned to its major task there was a new set of officers: José del Rosario Miranda, delegate from Curaguatay and vice-president of the convention, replaced José Segundo Decoud as the presiding officer.[35] The drafting committee remained unchanged, but the Bareiristas appointed an elections review committee (comisión revisadora de las elecciones) to review members' credentials. As a result there were several changes in personnel as eleven new members were added between September 7 and October 12 to replace those who had resigned or had been expelled.[36]

Probably few contemporary Paraguayans realized the significance of these events. Government by military coup (that Brazilian troops were the military did not matter), unseating of fairly elected delegates, and controlled elections had become established as political processes. Liberals were just as guilty as their opponents. The counterplot succeeded only because it had Brazilian approval. Guimarães had no liking for Machaín nor for any attempt by the convencionales to show signs of independence. "The Convention . . . to avoid dissolution had to approve the coup d'etat" that restored Rivarola and resulted in Machaín's expulsion.[37] The time had not come in 1870, nor would it come in the next century, when any party could survive on a foundation of legalism alone. Godoy knew the history of the French Revolution and hoped to emulate the role of the famous Assembly; Bareiro preferred the role of Carlos Antonio López, and in this he was well within the mainstream of Paraguayan history.

There was little left for the discomfited Liberals except literary protests in *La Regeneración* and secret plotting. Bareiristas attacked so shrilly in *La Voz del Pueblo* that Liberals feared violence. The first retaliation came in the convention, which expelled Machaín on September 2, refused to seat Benigno Ferreira on the 13th, and then expelled Jaime Sosa, Ramón Babañoli, Juan Silvano Godoy, León Machaín, and Serapio Machaín. Bareiro wanted to expel all Liberals who had been elected by the capital parishes, charging fraud in their election. He was, of course, using *La Voz del Pueblo* for its propaganda value to build up his own claims to the presidency; but the Allies still favored Rivarola. José Segundo Decoud became editor of *La Regeneración*,[38] but his tenure was to be short since, unwittingly, he gave the Bareiristas a perfect opportunity to destroy the Liberal organ.

Bareiro's attacks had begun before Decoud took over as editor. Some "30 men of the police" assaulted the paper's office after dark on September 3 but the attack was repulsed.[39] Three days later the editor announced suspension of the paper because of harassment: "Freedom of the press has disappeared as well as the individual security that protects the citizen in the free and independent expression of his ideas and principles." The government, in power as the result of a coup, had overthrown the president elected by the convention and so could not be trusted by either the citizens or the Allies. Gloomily but with great accuracy, José Segundo Decoud predicted that the country must be prepared for anarchy or perpetual dictatorship. This premature farewell praised *La Regeneración* lavishly: "It was the first light that shone full of splendor over Paraguay to lead it to the door of happiness." Constantly defending justice, its young and patriotic editors steadfastly fought evil and sought only the country's welfare. When the Triumvirate took over, two were members of the "liberal party" although all citizens were asked to serve. Enemies of freedom refused; the Machaíns and Decouds, who then assumed leadership, "are now the most vilified . . . It is forgotten that they accompanied the Allied Army from the first day until the Government was established, thus contributing to the overthrow of tyranny." In the coup and counter-coup, Brazil was the greatest loser.[40]

This recriminating editorial, which upbraided the Brazilians for their failure to support the Liberals, revealed the confusion existing in a very fluid situation. The interesting reference to the "liberal party," while meaning only a group with liberal ideas, clearly recognized the two poles of political thought. Rivarola, deposed and reimposed, obviously was merely a pawn in a game he understood only vaguely. As to the September 3 attack, police definitely were in the mob, thinking that a political meeting was under way. Actually, the Esperanza Society was meeting in the paper's office.[41]

Bareiro used *La Voz del Pueblo* to answer the charges. In a circular he asserted that a few misguided and deluded persons, heeding only their own ambition, tried to overthrow the government. These foolish men were the ones who "compose that narrow circle, the same ones who, posing as liberals and good Paraguayans, seek only to entrench themselves in the high offices in order to take possession of the country without giving a single thought to our beloved fatherland."[42] Rivarola, too, protested his lofty motives. He, "a patriotic, humble, and obedient citizen," had not sought office but acceded to popular demand. He had not been imposed by foreign influence but was elected freely and spontaneously. Although the Triumvirate was a dictatorship, the loyalty of its members had created a healthy government that had rendered great services under the most difficult circumstances. There had been a governmental crisis long before the events of August 31, and Rivarola had offered his resignation. Then, in a remarkably accurate confession, he presented himself as a very humble servant without any special political capacity to counter evil moves against him. However much he had erred, his intentions were always good if misunderstood, and he had endured the most tenacious opposition without loss of heart or exasperation of his spirit.[43]

When José Segundo Decoud succeeded his brother as editor of *La Regeneración*, he launched a furious attack against Bareiro and *La Voz del Pueblo*. Bareiro, he charged, was a Lopizta who had worked violently against the Allies and had thus helped to prolong the martyrdom of Paraguay. *La Voz del Pueblo* had insulted Rio Branco, Brazilians generally, and the Empire. Rivarola, so recently praised, was ignorant and arrogant, but one who, having reached Asunción "in the most frightful state of misery, was a meritorious, loyal, and patriotic man." Somberly he predicted that the convention had committed suicide: the best of its members had been expelled, and the government had won by force. Rivarola had became a tyrant and the days of López were come again. Nevertheless, he insisted that the convention was revolutionary and hence had sovereign powers, even though it had misused those powers and had resorted again to tyranny.[44]

A number of Italians were in Asunción. Some were survivors of the war; others had come with the Allies, particularly the Argentines, as sutlers. In the tense atmosphere of the capital, where law enforcement was haphazard, there was a growing resentment against foreigners. Much of this resentment centered on the Italians, perhaps because some of them were profiteering merchants. Some two weeks after José Segundo Decoud had taken over as editor of *La Regeneración*, a Paraguayan servant woman, according to one version, committed suicide with an Argentine's gun. *La Regeneración*, in a violent article on September 18, accused an Italian woman of beating the servant to death because she had asked for wages! Unnamed leaders of the Italians, perhaps encouraged by Bareiro, demanded a retraction. Decoud apologized on September 21 but added further insult with a strong anti-Italian editorial. The Italians then conferred with Taboada, the newly appointed chief of police. The Decouds at the same time asked for police protection, and Taboada tried in vain to bring the two parties together. Italians held a mass meeting on September 23 at which they heard inflammatory speeches, after which they attacked *La Regeneración*'s offices, destroyed the press, and sent the brothers Decoud fleeing for their lives. The police arrived belatedly; Brazilian and Argentine troops, under pretense of seeking rioters, sacked several houses. Rioting continued as Paraguayans retaliated. An eyewitness reported that "the City was a battle-field." Police were rumored to have arrested some 500 Italians and on September 24 ordered all Italians to register at police headquarters.[45]

The Decouds refused to give up. Somehow they obtained another press, or repaired the old one, and began to publish *La Opinión Pública* on November 6. This ephemeral organ published seven numbers in which José Segundo Decoud attacked Rivarola with unrestrained venom, even accusing the provisional president with having stolen Madame Lynch's furniture. Rivarola had not stolen the furniture— he was only using it! Nevertheless, the outraged executive ordered the paper closed on November 21, the first press censorship in the post-López era.[46] Thus ended Paraguay's brief experiment with freedom of the press.

The Constitution of 1870

Despite the distractions of riots and party warfare, the convention proceeded with its work. Since most of the intellectuals were young Liberals, the Bareiristas had to enlist their aid. Sinforiano Alcorta, in giving advice on how to draft a constitution, demonstrated familiarity with the Philadelphia Convention of 1787 and various state conventions in the United States.[47] Juan José Decoud played a leading role in the work and he, if anyone, was the father of the Paraguayan Constitution of 1870.[48] Most of the text he had already published in *La Regeneración*, so the convention should not have been surprised by the draft he presented on October 6. Intellectuals debated at length but made few changes. The convention adopted the document on November 18, and fifty-eight members, including two secretaries, signed on November 24.

The next business was to elect a president and vice-president. Cándido Bareiro had been hopeful that the convention would elect him to the presidency, but his circle was very fluid, made up of young men anxious for preferment. Guimarães and other Brazilians distrusted Bareiro, and rumors circulated that if he became president he would name to office such Bareiristas as Juan B. Egusquiza and Adolfo Saguier.[49] Rivarola, not without some political skill, promised positions to Bareiristas. When confronted bluntly by his followers, Bareiro loftily replied that he would deal with the appointments problem only after he became president. By the middle of November it was clear that Rivarola was the Brazilian choice; there was no objection to Bareiro as vice-president but he refused the position, which fell to Cayo Miltos.[50]

After electing Rivarola and Miltos on November 25, the convention adjourned to the Cathedral for a Te Deum attended by a large number of natives and foreigners, who continued the celebration with a street dance in the evening. Two days earlier the Brazilians had returned some 500 Paraguayan prisoners of war, among whom was Colonel Antonio de la Cruz Estigarribia, who had surrendered his army at Uruguayana early in the war. The convention had completed its work, and even to this day Paraguayans consider it an honor to be descended from one of the convencionales.

The principal model for Paraguay's Constitution of 1870 was the Argentine Constitution of 1853, which in turn had incorporated many ideas from the French and United States constitutions. The preamble follows closely these models, although it was hardly true that the convention had met "by the free and spontaneous will of the Paraguayan people." More truthful would have been an acknowledgement of close Brazilian and Argentine supervision, but the beautiful sentiments and unfilled promises were there: "to establish justice, assure domestic tranquility, provide for the common defense, promote the general welfare, and secure the blessings of liberty for ourselves, for our posterity, and for all people of the world who may come to inhabit Paraguayan soil, invoking All Powerful God, Supreme Legislator of the Universe . . ." There can be no quarrel with the definition of democratic liberties in this second Paraguayan constitution except that there were insufficient safeguards for labor. Roman Catholicism was the established religion but Congress could not prohibit the practice of any other religion. The national government was to promote immigration, and this it was to do in the belief that therein lay a major hope for the future. A state of siege, or martial law, could be declared in case of internal turmoil or foreign attack, a provision that was to be abused frequently in the future. Congress could never grant dictatorial powers to the president, and anyone who promoted dictatorship would be guilty of treason. Ratifying the decree of October 2, 1869, the constitution outlawed slavery.[51]

Provisions for a bicameral congress contained no surprises, although a unicameral body would have been more feasible for such a small country. The first congress was to be composed of thirteen senators and twenty-six deputies, serving terms of six and four years respectively. The permanent· commission, composed of two deputies and four senators, served as a guardian of the constitutional system and as an electoral committee. Congress enjoyed the customary legislative powers.

The president, too, had powers customary in a republic. He could declare a state of siege only when Congress was not in session, since the power to do so was a legislative attribute. In administration, the president had the aid of five ministries whose duties were to be defined by Congress. Eventually, the Ministry of Interior, in control of the capital and rural police, mails and telegraph, hygiene and public welfare, dominated the cabinet. The Ministry of Foreign Affairs was concerned only with relations with other countries. The Ministry of Hacienda (Finance) eventually became the depository of many agencies, including customs, taxes, statistics, ports, exchange, public works, agriculture, animal husbandry, lands and colonies, and banking. The Ministry of Justice, Religion, and Public Instruction also had a variety of duties before the turn of the century. In addition to supervising education, church-state relations, and the administration of justice, this ministry was in charge of the Natural History Park and Museum, National Library, National Museum and Archives, the official register, and the Government Printing Office. The duties of the Ministry of War and Marine were not exceptional.[52]

The constitution was also very brief in treating of the judicial system. A Superior Tribunal of Justice (Supreme Court), composed of three members, headed the court system that Congress was to create.[53] Eventually two appellate courts were created, one with civil and the other with commercial and criminal jurisdiction. Appeals to these courts came from six civil, two commercial, and nine criminal courts.

Seven justices of the peace served Asunción, ten were in interior cities, and twenty-five in rural areas.[54] The constitution provided for universal manhood suffrage, with the voting age lowered to eighteen, although the law made young men subject to parental authority until they reached the age of twenty-two.[55]

Apparently the charter of 1870 contained nearly everything needed to serve as the basis for a sound government. However, one analyst has observed that "there wasn't a government that could rule without violating it." Large areas of social concern were not recognized, and prohibition of dictatorship was a useless gesture. Many laws, not prohibited by the constitution, proved to be very harmful, especially those that granted pensions to public officials. There was no statement regulating the clergy except to prohibit them from serving in Congress, yet seven clerics were in the convention![56]

This constitution was too elaborate for a country with but a handful of people who knew anything beyond how to read and write, and the war left a large proportion of functional illiterates in the population.[57] The judgment of a twentieth-century critic is sound:

> The ideologues who, at the point of Allied bayonets, imposed their hegemony on a Paraguay in ruins, had to show quickly their desire to fulfill the signed agreements. To do so, it was necessary to provide legal wraps for the system of power they represented. The nation had died on the battlefields; the people had been annihilated; the wealth consumed. Over the scorched and barren land it was necessary to shape a fictitious body: the caricature of a State. But of a State traced on exotic models, which by foreign and artificial institutions would restrain forever the inevitable rebirth of the Paraguayan soul. It was necessary to place in a strait-jacket the natural and original tendencies of a people who had not been left deluded by the illusion of abstract principles, those "laws of progress" that in neighboring countries manifested themselves through civil wars, servitude, and anarchy. That was the mirror in which the "legionnaires" saw themselves; that was the model they proposed to follow.[58]

For a country under military occupation, with no dependable source of income, no party system, and no regularized economic life to adopt such a difficult form of government demonstrated an almost childlike faith in some divine providence that had never been very noticeable in Paraguay. The democratic revolution had touched Paraguay but lightly, and the dictatorial regimes of Francia and the López had continued the Spanish oligarchical system. The efforts of Carlos Antonio López to lead Paraguay into the modern world had ended in the cataclysm that engulfed the Río de la Plata countries. For orderly development under national auspices there was substituted, after the war, foreign economic control and political adventurism.

6. Politics and Diplomacy, 1870–1871

Rivarola's hold on the presidency was very tenuous, a fact that should have occurred to him when he took the oath of office on November 25, 1870. He had very little support among the major political factions, and Brazilians would use him so long as it suited their purposes but considered him expendable. Bareiristas could not be depended upon, although they had been forced to support him. Struggling valiantly to be president, Rivarola mistakenly placed his trust in men who would betray him with crass cynicism.

Not even the press charged Brazil with the deliberate policy of destroying the Liberals, promoting anarchy, and eliminating patriotic leaders. Brazil's policy was to keep a rein on internal politics until a satisfactory treaty could be signed, and by "satisfactory" was meant one that would hold Argentine territorial gains to a minimum while Brazil gained all of its objectives. The gross political mistakes of 1871 and 1872 would not have occurred had Brazil been controlling everything in Paraguay.

Throughout the period of occupation, Brazil's major attention was focused on its recent ally and old enemy, Argentina, and Paraguay was of secondary importance to the Empire. Geography had made that unfortunate country the victim of Argentine-Brazilian rivalries. Historians susceptible to conspiratorial interpretations might see the Machiavellian hands of British financiers behind everything, as indeed some do, but this is too wild a fancy to merit serious consideration. Brazilian statesmen sincerely wished to end the Paraguayan business, to get their troops home, to turn their considerable talents to solving the great problems overhanging the Empire. They hoped to sign definitive treaties in Buenos Aires and Asunción, but neither Rio Branco nor Cotegipe, the Empire's greatest statesmen, could bring Argentina to terms.

As one reviews the swiftly changing political patterns during the first constitutional period of 1870–1874, it is apparent that neither Argentina nor Brazil was exercising complete control in Paraguay. Dr. Benigno Ferreira and José Segundo Decoud participated in the cabinets of Rivarola and his successor, Salvador Jovellanos, when Rivarola fell from power. Juan Bautista Gill and Ferreira feared and hated each other but they were allies temporarily. Then Gill was impeached, but Rivarola defied Congress to support him. Gill won control of Congress and double-crossed Rivarola. Revolutions promoted by Lopiztas finally succeeded in 1874 in driving Ferreira out of power. Still, to ascribe all of this to Brazilian or Argentine manipulation is to underrate Paraguayan capacity for intrigue and to deny patriotic motives to men whose loyalty to Paraguay cannot be doubted, even if they were determined to make that loyalty pay handsomely.

The Trials of President Rivarola

Paraguay's political factions understood the power of the press. After destroying *La Regeneración* and closing *La Opinión Pública*, the Lopiztas had no rival to *Él Pueblo*, a paper subsidized by Rivarola and edited by Miguel Macías. By advocating the release of General Bernardino Caballero, who had been captured at Cerro Corá, *El Pueblo* clearly revealed its sympathies. Rivarola, the editor admitted, had been a mystery; but by the end of October "the mystery has disappeared—he and the people are one." Rivarola and Bareiro—this was the combination that Paraguay needed. Indeed, the government and the people's party had been fused in September, and any effort by "that bad group" would be met with proper measures. The Liberal conspirators had threatened to kill anyone who betrayed the August plot, Macías charged, and now that little cabal of ten young men could do nothing but scream "Tyrant!"[1]

One of the young Liberals, pro-Argentine in sympathy, insisted that Paraguay was entirely dominated by Brazil and that "its government neither wants nor thinks other than what Brazil wants and thinks through its more or less competent agents."[2] This gratuitous slap at Brazilian ministers was by no means unwarranted, but it could not apply to João Maurício Wanderley, Barão de Cotegipe, and Rio Branco.

Rivarola had enough political acumen to know that he would need support from Brazil and all major domestic factions to remain in power. Reported "as a man of energy and integrity, but . . . altogether uneducated and inexperienced in state matters,"[3] his first moves were conciliatory. *El Pueblo* called for an end to factionalism and for a responsible opposition press,[4] and Rivarola selected capable men for the cabinet and other high positions. All but two had served in the convention of 1870. Principal leaders in the cabinet as first constituted were Bareiristas, Rufino Taboada as minister of interior and Juan Bautista Gill as minister of hacienda.[5] This group had as good a chance as any to work together, but it was necessarily temporary while more permanent political groupings were forming. Rivarola made many changes in the cabinet within a year, and he made a fatal mistake in putting his trust in Gill, a very clever politician who enjoyed strong support from the Brazilians.

Shortly after his inauguration, Rivarola issued a florid proclamation to the people. Paraguay, which under three tyrants had been a blot on the map of America, had at last broken its chains: "Today the Paraguayan nation . . . [has come] to the end of its past misfortunes, and it is in this glorious epoch that I have been called to the post as First Magistrate to pilot the ship on the unfathomable sea of its destiny . . . [being charged with] the reconstruction of our almost extinguished nationality."[6] Proceeding with governmental organization, the president assigned duties to the various ministries and proclaimed creation of the permanent commission as elected by Congress.[7] Before adjourning, the convention had authorized the sale of government property and the floating of a loan for $f2,000,000. A commission was to be created to study the feasibility of coining copper, a census was to be taken, and an election law was approved. Elections for the first Congress under the constitution were held on January 25, 1871, and the Congress met in February.[8]

This first session of Congress was extremely busy with problems of finance, governmental organization and, above all, politics. Laws to collect duties on imports, to provide for sale of the railway, to authorize a loan of £1,000,000 in London, to clarify the tangle of land claims and counterclaims, to create a government for Asunción, to encourage immigration, to establish a schedule of fees for religious services—these and many more were dutifully recorded in the *Registro Oficial,*[9] an important organ that began publication in 1869. The most important of these measures were those relating to finance. The major source of revenue should have been customs duties, but sutlers continued large-scale smuggling. Gill attempted to stop this leak by requesting that the Brazilians require sutlers to deliver to Hacienda detailed lists of imports destined for the Allied armies.[10] Nothing came of this attempt. Having failed to obtain needed financial support through the Bedoya mission, Rivarola's government adopted three measures that were to plague Paraguay for a century and whose effects would be felt for an even longer period: the sale of public lands and other property, issuance of fiat money, and negotiation of foreign loans. The first issue of fiat money, for 100,000 pesos on December 29, 1870, was followed by an issue of 300,000 pesos on July 15, 1871. The first issue was secured by government property in Asunción, the second by the railway. Strictly speaking, therefore, these issues were not fiat money; but the Paraguayan Congress generally forgot what property had been pledged as collateral. In addition to the paper money, the government had various drafts and other obligations, which together with the paper issues, were consolidated on September 28, 1871, into national public credit bonds in the amount of $fl,648,301, all of which was to be retired with proceeds from the 1871 English bond issue.[11]

Rivarola, of course, was anxious to obtain recognition by world powers as soon as possible. Expecting a Rivarola-Bareiro slate to be elected, the British envoy in Buenos Aires asked the Foreign Office if he should recognize the government and reported that the Italian minister had been instructed to extend recognition at once. Granville noted indifferently: "I should think we might recommend an unpaid v. consul."[12] So much for the charge that Britain wanted to make Paraguay an economic satellite! The minister of foreign affairs, Miguel Palacios, sought recognition in a note that pictured Paraguay as a haven where "men of sound disposition from the whole world" could gain success from their labors while being protected by a constitution "in which not a single right inherent in man is not proclaimed, nor a single franchise, the legitimate offspring of those rights, is not recognized."[13] The British Foreign Office was in no hurry and rather offhandedly recognized the Rivarola regime by acknowledging receipt of the Palacios dispatch.[14] In the meantime, Rivarola decided to appoint as his confidential agent in Great Britain Dr. William Stewart, who was then in England to protect his interest in various funds deposited in the Royal Bank of Scotland, to interest financiers in floating a Paraguayan loan, and probably to promote other ways to profit Paraguay and himself. But when Stewart sought to present his credentials, he was informed that no British subject could serve in a diplomatic capacity for a foreign country. He could, however, become the Paraguayan consul.[15]

Stewart had attempted to persuade Gregorio Benites, the López minister to Great Britain and France, to surrender the legation's archives to him; but Benites refused to do so, knowing full well that Stewart would not be received in a diplomatic capacity.[16] Rumors of Stewart's appointment had raised strong protests from other sources. Madame Lynch, in the United Kingdom trying to recover more than

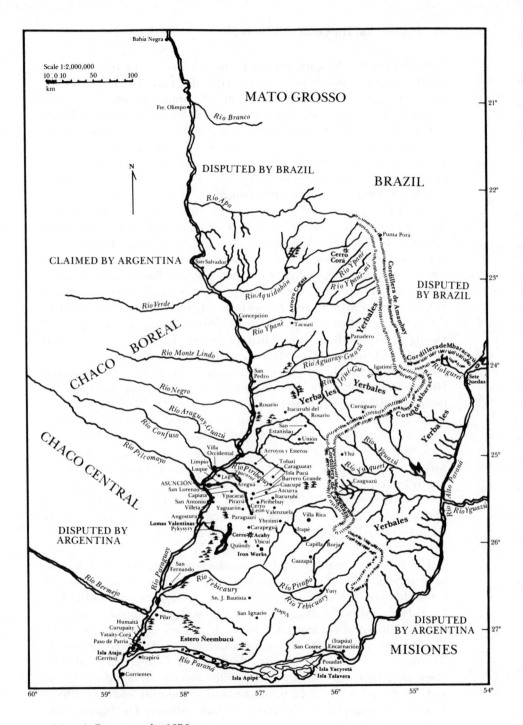

Bahía Negra

Scale 1:2,000,000
10 0 10   50   100
km

MATO GROSSO

Fte. Olimpo   *Río Branco*

N

DISPUTED BY BRAZIL

BRAZIL

21°

22°

Río Apa

Punta Porá

CLAIMED BY ARGENTINA   San Salvador

Cerro Corá   *Río Ypané*

Río Verde

Arroyo Corá

Río Aquidabán

Río Ypané-mi

Cordillera de Amambay

DISPUTED BY BRAZIL

23°

Concepción   *Río Ypané*   Tacuatí

Panadero   **Yerbales**

CordilleradeMbaracayú

Río Monte Lindo

Río Aguaray-Guazú

Igatimí   *Río Igurei*   Sete Quedas

CHACO BOREAL

San Pedro   *Río Jejui-Gu*   **Yerbales**   **Yerbales**

24°

Río Negro

Rosario   Itacurubí del Rosario   **Yerbales**

Curuguaty   **Cordillera de Mbaracayú**   **Yerbales**

Río Araguay-Guazú

San Estanislao   Unión

Río Yguazú

Río Confuso

Río Pilcomayo

Villa Occidental   Arroyos y Esteros

Yhú   *Río Yuqueri*

25°

CHACO CENTRAL

Limpio   Luque   *Río Piribebuy*   Tobatí   Caaguatás   Isla Pucú   Barrero Grande   Caacupé

Caaguazú   *Río Alto Paraná*   *Río Yguazú*

ASUNCIÓN   San Lorenzo   Lago   Pacarai   Azcurra

Capiatá   Aregua   Ypacarai   Itacurubí

San Antonio   Pirayú   Piribebuy

Villeta   Yaguarón   Cerro León   Valenzuela

Angostura   Paraguari   Ybytimi   Villa Rica

Yerbales

Lomas Valentinas
Pykysyry   Carapeguá   Itapé

Cerro **Acahy**   Capilla Borja

DISPUTED BY ARGENTINA   Quiindy   Ybicuí

26°

San Fernando   Caazapá

Río Tebicuary   Yuty

Río Paraguay   *Río Bermejo*   *Río Tebicuary*   Sn. J. Bautista   *Río Pirapó*   *Río Tebicuary*

Iron Works

San Ignacio   *Vtera*

DISPUTED BY ARGENTINA

27°

Humaitá   Pilar
Curupaity
Yataity-Corá
Paso de Patria

Estero Ñeembucú

San Cosme   (Itapúa) Encarnación

MISIONES

Isla Atajo (Cerrito)   Itapirú

Corrientes   *Río Paraná*   Posadas

Isla Yacyretá
Isla Talavera

Isla Apipé

60°   59°   58°   57°   56°   55°   54°

Map 4. Paraguay in 1870
(*After Alberto da Ponte*)

£30,000 from Dr. Stewart, protested and referred to the trial in Edinburgh that had established Stewart's liability. Emiliano López, eldest son of Francisco Solano López by another mistress, also protested, asserting that Stewart owed more than £37,400 of Paraguayan funds entrusted to him.[17] Stewart did not become Paraguayan agent in London, but he did perform many services for the country and later was British consul in Asunción while carrying on his medical practice and enlarging his already large holdings.

Many Paraguayan leaders felt hopelessly isolated as they struggled to establish a government and to prepare for the approaching negotiations with the Allies. They could depend on a schism between Argentina and Brazil, but what advantage could they derive from such a rift? To gain the favor of either country it would be necessary to become its protectorate, and here the choice was decidedly limited. Only Brazil had the power to dominate the situation, and there were many Paraguayans who not only recognized this but were willing to play the Empire's game in return for its support in domestic politics. Chief among these pro-Brazilian politicians were Juan Bautista Gill and Juan José Brizuela. Rivarola, whose faults overwhelmed the good qualities he undoubtedly possessed, instinctively sought aid from the United States and Great Britain—instinctively or at the urging of his ministers of foreign affairs.[18]

Turning first to Great Britain, Palacios praised the country lavishly. Paraguay, having been extricated from "the abyss into which she had been hurled by the barbarous madness of her last tyrant . . . desires to follow the footsteps of England as far as she possibly can, and by these means to attain the prosperity that is desired and the high and sincere moral consideration of all nations that, like the English, are bulwarks of the world's liberty and guides for its civilization." [19] Palacios, making no attempt to dissemble, asked for British aid in negotiations with the Allies.

The British were much cooler than the Americans. On his first visit to Asunción, John Lloyd Stevens had done little more than to present his credentials. His next trip was more leisurely. Leaving Montevideo on July 5, 1871, the *Wasp* took nineteen days to make Asunción. Stevens stopped at various ports for little purpose other than to show the flag. On July 25, the day after his arrival in Asunción, President Rivarola, the cabinet, members of the Superior Court, leaders of Congress, and other prominent persons visited Stevens on board the *Wasp*, and the next day Rivarola accompanied his guest on what must have been a revealing ride on the forty-five–mile railway. The Paraguayans were very grateful for American recognition, and Stevens observed that the American federal and state constitutions had served as a guide for Paraguay's Constitution of 1870. The Paraguayan promise was encouraging, but fear of the Allies still hung over the country. Specifically, Rivarola expected the Allies to demand large territorial cessions and payment of some $400,000,000—more than the entire country was worth—and he asked the United States to proffer its good offices. Stevens, careful not to commit himself, promised to relay the request to President Grant and observed to his government that the time was ripe for such representation. All that came of this was the promise that the United States would informally ask Argentina and Brazil to be moderate in their demands.[20] Not even the wildest critic could accuse the United States of having made a strong effort on Paraguay's behalf. Close relations with Brazil were far more important to the northern republic.

There may have been more than cordiality behind Rivarola's treatment of Stevens. Brazil's envoy had grown cool toward Rivarola and would have a major role in replacing him with Jovellanos later in the year. No matter what political currents were flowing in Asunción, Stevens was impressed by the sumptuous ball given in his honor on the eve of his departure.[21] If Rivarola thought that he himself was secure or that his attentions to the American minister had strengthened his position, he failed to read the political tea leaves correctly.

The Fall of Rivarola

Rivarola faced a Congress unfriendly if not openly hostile. Cándido Bareiro's followers were strong and still resented what they termed Brazilian machinations in the political devil duster of August 31–September 1, 1870, that had resulted in the imposition of Rivarola as provisional president and had assured his election as president in November. The vice-president, Cayo Miltos, fell victim to the plague on January 7, 1871; therefore, when Congress met, the president of the Senate, León Corvalán, served as acting president during Rivarola's absences from the capital. This in itself was a dangerous situation, but Rivarola believed that he had appointed faithful men to key military and police positions both in Asunción and the country districts. Believing that his enemies were plotting a revolt, Rivarola on March 23 sent out patrols that made several arrests, but there was no conspiracy.[22] Rivarola had reason to be uneasy, since the Brazilians were turning to Gill as their man, and Gill was willing to undergo the sneers of his countrymen in order to reach the high office he craved. Gill and Brizuela were Brazil's loyal supporters, although Cotegipe never trusted them completely.[23]

Rivarola might have been fairly popular, despite his being widely known as Brazil's puppet, had he possessed more finesse. He entered the government poverty stricken, but in a few months he had stocked an hacienda and acquired a house that López had given to Madame Lynch. Rivarola appreciated the relatively luxurious quarters, and his fondness for playing Madame Lynch's piano came close to ending his career:

> [Rivarola] was living at the time [May, 1871] at Madame Lynch's far-famed quinta, once the sweetest place in all Paraguay. It was in the afternoon; the President was sitting in the "sala" playing on Madame Lynch's piano. Dr. Muniz Barreta was sitting listening to the music when all of a sudden a man galloped by and fired through the window at His Excellency. The ball passed close to the President's head and lodged in the wall opposite. This stopped the music. The President rushed out, accompanied by the Doctor, but the would be assassin galloped off in the direction of the Recoleta. It is supposed that he belonged to the opposite party, but his name is not known.[24]

President Rivarola placed an inordinate amount of trust in Gill and for a time his confidence appeared to be justified. Rufino Taboada, minister of interior, was briefly the cabinet's strong man, Lopizta and Bareirista in sympathy. Gill obviously wanted to be rid of Taboada. An excuse appeared when Taboada refused to admit a vessel that was bringing repatriated prisoners of war to Asunción. Yellow fever was in Platine ports and Taboada was simply doing his duty; but the president, probably urged on by Gill, demanded Taboada's resignation. This act increased opposition in Congress, and Rivarola made several cabinet changes in an attempt to strengthen his support in that hostile body. He sought to woo the Liberals by bringing José Segundo Decoud into the cabinet as *ad interim* minister of foreign affairs, and to mollify the Lópiztas by making General Caballero his minister of war and marine.[25] Caballero had been released by the Brazilians and sent back to Asunción in May, 1871.

The reconstructed cabinet had no one's confidence. Not even Rivarola trusted Decoud and Caballero, both of whom were actually the President's enemies. The Brazilian commander, Guimarães, was on good terms with Rivarola but had no faith in the government. The Congress, having opposed him strongly, feared that Rivarola would dissolve it, counting on Brazilian armed support. Congress was more concerned with its own than the country's welfare, having voted two-thirds of the government's revenue to its own use. Paraguay wished to resume control over the Church, the domination of foreign priests was deeply resented, and Padre Fidel Maíz was causing considerable trouble. This constituted the "religious question," which was becoming more difficult. Economic conditions were worsening steadily, and the Argentine merchant Gumercindo Coll was trying to obtain the railway and other government property to satisfy his claims.[26]

Congress was preparing to convict Gill of malfeasance in office, the Allied representatives were soon to arrive in an effort to negotiate a definitive treaty, and elections were to be held on October 1 to fill vacancies from San Roque and Cathedral parishes in Asunción. Rivarola and Gill left nothing to chance in these elections, since they needed all the support they could get. Although the president stayed aloof from the electoral combat, Gill and Jovellanos were very active. For the opposition, Jaime Sosa was a "turbulent character, who always figures in all the brawls, and who is one of the most esteemed of the present opposition leaders."[27] Government candidates won, but there was disorder and bloodshed in Asunción, where "the streets were filled with strange men, mostly drunk, shouting vivas for the Ministers Gill and Jovellanos, and keeping the city in a state of alarm." By use of force at the polls, Rivarola's enemies were denied the vote. Decoud and Caballero worked actively for the opposition, while Carlos Loizaga definitely favored Rivarola's enemies.[28] In the afternoon of election day, Gill sent "carts loaded with drinks for distribution to the people, as well as bread, fruits, etc., and at night there were many disorders which caused serious injuries to the Argentines."[29]

Rivarola's enemies in Congress concentrated their fire on Gill. The Chamber of Deputies in August, 1871, had accused him of exceeding his authority. Gill appeared before the Chamber late in the month and began a strong defense that was interrupted by rowdy scenes on the floor and planned turmoil in the galleries. Gill retired from the scene, humiliated by this scornful treatment. Accusing Gill of peculation, the Chamber impeached the unpopular minister, and on October 12 the Senate convicted him and ordered him removed from office. These actions caused another cabinet crisis, during which Gill discovered that he had few friends among his colleagues. When Rivarola insisted upon protecting Gill, three ministers resigned from the cabinet.[30] Their brief service together apparently convinced Decoud that Caballero was the man of the future, and thereafter his swing away from the Liberals proceeded until he was a stalwart of what became the Colorado Party. Among those whom Rivarola appointed to replace the disgruntled ministers was Benigno Ferreira, a move that marked his brief ascendancy. The president, refusing to replace Gill, summoned several lawyers and Padre Fidel Maíz to his home, probably to tell them what he was going to do rather than to ask for advice. This meeting took place on October 13, the day he had reprimanded the Senate and asked for reconsideration of Gill's conviction. The Senate, controlled by Gill's enemies, stood fast. Rivarola then moved swiftly. He dissolved Congress on October 15 and ordered new elections to be held on December 20 for a Congress to assemble on January 1, 1872. The decree of dissolution, in itself unconstitutional, charged the Congress with having proceeded unconstitutionally.[31]

Rivarola, to justify his actions, issued another of his flowery manifestoes. The constitution had been his guide, he protested, but there were intransigent spirits who would destroy what was left of Paraguay and "bury it among the dark ruins of our devastated fields." Congress, he charged, had sought to usurp total power and to arouse the people through incendiary polemics in *La Voz del Pueblo*. Congress had even asked Brazilian troops to surround the palace! In the face of this vicious plotting, he had thought of resigning but this would be cowardly. The constitution, he admitted, gave him no power to dissolve Congress, but his act was in the spirit of the constitution and in the name of the people, in whom ultimate sovereignty lay. Complicating the situation was the imminent arrival of Allied representatives who hoped to negotiate a general treaty. Rivarola thought it best to move the elections ahead and issued a decree setting November 19 for the elections and December 8 for opening of the new Congress. Very much in the dark about what was going on, observers in Buenos Aires deplored Rivarola's actions. *La Prensa* looked to a new generation to free Paraguay from its anarchy, and the British minister erroneously reported the recall of envoys appointed to negotiate a treaty.[32]

While preparations were hurried for the elections, Gill and his friends repeated their previous performance. His enemies accused Gill of organizing a group of *raidos*, or thugs, to terrorize the voters and to assault his opponents. Gill's enemies launched two revolutionary plots in November. Bareiro had sought Argentine aid, promising if successful that Paraguay would renounce its claims to the Chaco,[33] but Manuel Quintana, the Argentine envoy, had nothing but moral support to offer and that was not enough. Bareiro, Caballero, and Germán Serrano were unable to make any headway before Gill had them jailed. Far more serious but equally ineffective was the so-called Revolt of Tacuaral, which came to a head after Gill and his circle had won the election of November 19. The government knew about the scheme, and Brazilian forces were on guard to help suppress the revolt if needed.[34] Prime movers in this plot were Col. Patricio Escobar, Col. José del Carmen Pérez, Capt. José María Concha, Juan Silvano Godoy, Bernardino Caballero, and Juan Antonio Jara. Here were Godoy and

Decoud, Liberal stalwarts, cooperating with the most notorious Lopiztas! Their purpose was to keep the old Congress. Various conspirators were assigned to towns close by Asunción to raise recruits who
would meet at Jara's quinta in Tacuaral, board the train, and attack
Asunción. But the plan went awry. Unable to take the train, the eighty
men who assembled at Tacuaral on November 25 rode to Luque,
where they learned that the plot had been discovered. Escobar, Godoy,
and Decoud made good their escape to Villa Occidental, where the
Argentines provided asylum. Captain Concha, believing himself safe,
returned to his home at Pirayú, where he was seized, questioned, and
then shot.[35] Gill, with the approval of Rivarola and the Brazilians, organized his raídos into the Batallón Guarará, which instituted a reign
of terror in Asunción. Several prominent men joined Bareiro and
Caballero in jail and others died from injuries inflicted by the raídos.[36]

When the new Congress met on December 8, Juan Bautista Gill was
in control. Instead of suffering disgrace as an impeached minister convicted of misusing national funds, he had been elected to the Senate!
Three other members of the Senate had also served under Rivarola:
Palacios, Loizaga, and Falcón. Benigno Ferreira, also a cabinet member, was a deputy. To fill the vice-presidency left vacant by the death
of Cayo Miltos, Congress elected Salvador Jovellanos,[37] one of the
bright young men whom López had sent to France to be educated and
who was apparently a faithful member of the Rivarola circle. When
the two houses of Congress completed their organization, Gill emerged
as president of the Senate and his cousin, Higinio Uriarte, as president of the Chamber of Deputies. Believing that his control of Congress was assured, Rivarola defended his acts in a special message,
named Vice-President Jovellanos as acting president, tendered his resignation, and prepared to leave the capital for what he thought would
be a brief visit to his estancia in Barrero Grande. Entirely unaware of
any plot against him, Rivarola boarded the train on December 16, com-
forted by cheers of the "loyal" followers who were on hand to see him
off. Rivarola did take the precaution of telling two friends to warn
him if Congress accepted his resignation and left his best horse for a
messenger. Two days later, Congress accepted Rivarola's resignation
and named Jovellanos to complete the term![38] In Congress Gill had
the temporary cooperation of Ferreira, the man who later proved such
a staunch defender of the Jovellanos regime and an implacable opponent of Brazil.

With so much plotting and double-crossing going on among Paraguayan politicians, rumors and speculations were as thick as mosquitoes. Shrewd observers guessed that Brazil's Cotegipe had tired of

Rivarola and so had turned to Gill as the Empire's man.[39] Their speculation was correct. Gill conferred frequently with Cotegipe and on the day of Rivarola's resignation had informed his mentor about what would happen:

> You know the pressures that were coming from men of my party to hasten the resignation question.
> In accordance with what I had told you, I called a meeting of the most influential persons to see if I could delay the matter a few days.
> They opposed my proposal with arguments that I could not reasonably reject, and seeing their determination that the matter be resolved today, I felt obliged to agree.
> At three this afternoon Congress will meet and the unity of purpose of the members, almost without exception, causes me to be very confident that we shall have no dissent.[40]

Cotegipe replied that he was glad that the question was settled and that things would go quickly. He would stop by to see Gill after the session adjourned. Rio Branco approved Cotegipe's intrigue with Gill and, although he himself had put Rivarola in power, admitted that "Rivarola lacks qualities to be a good chief of state, but I do not see there anyone his equal in good will, intelligence, and courage"[41]

Dismayed by the turn of events, General Vedia found the situation growing worse every day. Dr. Manuel Quintana, the Argentine representative in treaty negotiations, had aroused Paraguayan animosity and was being falsely accused of aiding the plot against Rivarola. Quintana advised Vedia to support the government, but Vedia feared that such a course would involve his small forces in domestic politics. And, he asked, what if Brazil should support Rivarola? Should he break the alliance? Before Vedia could conclude his dispatch, Jovellanos sent Sinforiano Alcorta to determine the Argentine attitude if Congress accepted Rivarola's resignation. Vedia decided to confer with Jovellanos on December 18, but Congress had acted before the meeting took place. No one had believed that there would not be a single vote for Rivarola, which led Vedia to observe that "the unexpected is the only thing that one can reasonably expect to happen in this country. Congress should have met yesterday morning, but it didn't do so because . . . it rained—"[42]

After his unexpected reversal, Rivarola complained to Cotegipe that the pro-Argentine party had been strengthened by his ouster. Gumercindo Coll, a personal friend but political opponent of Rivarola, insisted that the only way for Paraguay to escape Brazilian control was through political union with Argentina. Moreover, Coll had an intrigue going with Gill and Jovellanos: the principal buildings owned by the state would be sold at a fraction of their value to pay Coll's accounts. Rivarola opposed this deal, so it was necessary for him to be removed. Congress, he complained bitterly, had unexpectedly accepted his resignation and without a vote of appreciation for his sacrifices. Now he would retire and raise cattle.[43] Rivarola's future might have been more tranquil had he persisted in animal husbandry, but his ego had been badly wounded and he was willing to combine forces with any group that offered him a way back to power. All of his efforts, all of his intrigues, were to fail because of his own exaggerated claims and the megalomania that possessed him.

Failure of the General Treaty

Brazilian diplomacy put the highest priority on signing general and definitive treaties with Paraguay. According to the Treaty of Alliance, the Allies agreed not to make peace separately, and the Preliminary Treaty of June 20, 1870, provided that negotiations were to commence within three months. The stipulated time passed and not until the end of the year was Argentina willing to talk. There was now a legitimate government in Paraguay, one created by the Constitution of 1870, and Argentina's former objections to dealing with the Provisional Government no longer held.

Two conferences, one in Buenos Aires and the other in Asunción, failed to produce a general treaty. To the Buenos Aires conference, Brazil sent Silva Paranhos, now the Visconde do Rio Branco. In his instructions to Rio Branco on October 12, 1870, the Visconde e Marquês de São Vicente, José Antônio Pimenta Bueno, generally followed instructions drafted on February 1, 1869.[44] The Treaty of Alliance of May 1, 1865, would serve as the guide. Aside from the usual general treaties of friendship, commerce, and navigation, Brazil must be guaranteed freedom of transit and Paraguay must not construct fortifications that could impede river traffic. São Vicente realized that this proviso might play into Argentine hands and arouse Paraguayan hostility, since Argentina would be free to erect fortifications on her side of the Río Paraguay. As a last resort, Brazil would yield the point, since it would be easy for Paraguay to install batteries very quickly if she had the means.

Argentina was certain to make a big issue of waiving war indemnities, thus gaining favor with Paraguay. São Vicente observed, with poorly concealed sarcasm, that "the generosity of our Ally explains itself naturally by the advantages that it derives from the war with the ownership of the territory of the Missions and of a great part of the Chaco, while Brazil gains nothing in territory and the major bur-

den of the war rests on the Empire." Politically Brazil could not surrender the right to indemnities, although Paraguay was ruined and
could not even pay interest on a debt for many years. Nevertheless,
reparations must be admitted and provision made for paying. On this
matter the Allies could treat separately. Aside from the general indemnity, mixed commissions would determine the sums due private
claimants, which would be paid in bonds bearing interest varying
from 3 to 6 percent.

In view of Argentine suspicions that Brazil sought to absorb Paraguay, it is especially interesting to note that Brazil entertained the
same suspicions as to Argentine intentions. If Argentina refused to
guarantee Paraguayan independence and sovereignty beyond the five-
year period stipulated in the Treaty of May 1, then Brazil would
undertake the task alone.

The Treaty of Alliance recognized Argentine claims to Misiones and
to the Chaco as far north as Bahía Negra. Argentina had no legal
title to these lands, and São Vicente found it fortunate indeed that
Dr. Mariano Varela had generously stated that military victory conferred no special rights. São Vicente had informed Silva Paranhos in
1869 "that it does not seek to cross the Pilcomayo. It is in truth the
most that it can claim, without committing a great violation of Paraguay. This is the point on which Your Excellency must employ all of
your efforts." Argentina should stay south of the Pilcomayo, leaving
ownership of the rest of the Chaco to be decided between Bolivia and
Paraguay. In this latter dispute, as well as Bolivia's claim to the Chaco
Central, Brazil would be neutral; however, should Bolivia press her
claims, Brazil would urge Paraguay to accept a point opposite the
mouth of the Río Apa, leaving all to the north to Bolivia. The island
of Atajo, or Cerrito, at the mouth of the Río Paraguay, was recognized
as really belonging to the Argentine bank, but Rio Branco should try
to get it for Paraguay. At any event, it should be neutralized. As to
her own boundaries, Brazil would insist upon the Apa and it would
hope to acquire some high ground to the south where depots could
serve the ranches of Mato Grosso. Brazil had no desire to occupy Paraguay, and all forces, naval and land, would be withdrawn upon conclusion of the definitive treaties.

These instructions, which set Brazilian policy toward Paraguay and
Argentina, indicated that fears of Brazilian ambition to absorb Paraguay were unfounded. In succeeding years, Brazil remained firmly
committed to the policy enunciated in the instructions to Rio Branco.
For itself, the Empire wanted recognition of boundary claims advanced when Carlos Antonio López ruled Paraguay. Although Brazil

had some basis for its claims to the disputed territory it occupied on the north and northeast of Paraguay, its alleged title certainly was no better than Paraguay's. Free transit of the rivers was vital for communication with Mato Grosso, neutralization of Paraguay was nothing but a gesture, and Paraguayan acknowledgement of its liability for reparations and indemnities, recognized as of no pecuniary value, was primarily a political ploy that might calm criticism at home. Brazil was willing that Argentina should have Misiones and the Chaco Central, handsome winnings to which her suspicious and reluctant ally had dubious title, but Argentina must be held south of the Pilcomayo. Armed with these instructions, Rio Branco went to Buenos Aires, where on December 9, 1870, he began discussions with Dr. Carlos Tejedor and Dr. Adolfo Rodríguez, representing Argentina and Uruguay, respectively.[45]

Even before the Buenos Aires conference began, the Brazilian Council of State was summoned for further consultation. São Vicente, president of the council, had reason to believe that Argentina, despite having indicated a willingness to be content with the Pilcomayo, had changed its position and now would insist on extending to Bahía Negra, according to the provisions of Article 16 of the Treaty of Alliance, and would insist on having the island of Atajo. The council was asked to decide what Brazil should do in various cases: if Argentina would agree on the Pilcomayo line but insist on having Atajo, if Argentina would insist on the Bahía Negra limits and Atajo, if each of the Allies should be free to negotiate separately, if there was any other course of action. The council decided that Rio Branco should be instructed to yield on the island and other questions if Argentina would agree to the Pilcomayo line; otherwise, he was to notify Argentina that the Treaty of Alliance was compromised by Argentina's actions and he must seek further instructions. Rio Branco believed that Brazil should open negotiations with Paraguay to give that country a chance to be heard if Argentina proved to be stubborn on the limits question.[46]

Tejedor, opening the conference on December 9, 1870, stated his preference that all negotiations be held in Buenos Aires, but he was willing to discuss basic provisions to be incorporated in a general treaty that would be signed in Asunción. Rio Branco would have preferred to have the conference moved to Asunción, where all parties could be present and thus avoid delay. In order that something might be accomplished, the envoys decided to draft treaty provisions upon which agreement could be reached, leaving boundaries, war debts, and indemnification for separate acts; but the final general treaty with

Paraguay must include a definition of boundaries.[47] During the discussions, Tejedor revealed that the Argentine Congress in secret session had insisted that the protocol to the Treaty of Alliance that guaranteed the independence, territorial integrity, and neutrality of Paraguay be subjected to its approval. Rio Branco protested that the protocol was an integral part of the treaty. This point was therefore left over without agreement. Altogether, the Buenos Aires conference, which ended on January 25, 1871, agreed upon ten protocols, but vital decisions had been postponed to another conference to be held in Asunción.[48]

Rio Branco was looking forward confidently to negotiation of the definitive treaty in Asunción, where his good relations with Rivarola and influential Paraguayans, based on "experience, friendship, and personal confidence," would be very advantageous to Brazil. Imperial politics dictated that Rio Branco was to be spared another visit to Asunción. The emperor insisted on recalling him to Rio de Janeiro, where he became president of the council and minister of finance on March 7, 1871.[49] His good friend, the Barão de Cotegipe, would have the honor of negotiating in Asunción.

Carlos Tejedor and President Sarmiento realized that the Asunción conference would be critical. Cotegipe was a politician of consummate skill, a veteran of provincial and national battles, extraordinarily capable and ruthless, a diplomat who knew how to use to full advantage every artifice of language and procedure to gain his point. To oppose this formidable champion, Tejedor turned to Bartolomé Mitre, "the friend of the Empire and enemy of the rejected policy of victory without rights."[50] But Mitre had various reasons for refusing the mission. Tejedor then proposed Dr. Manuel Quintana, a brilliant if pedantic lawyer and professor who had held many public positions, an enemy of the Alliance, advocate of preparedness against Brazil, and strong opponent of Sarmiento's government. Sarmiento, naturally, demurred; but Tejedor insisted and the president gave way. Unfortunately, Quintana accepted the appointment.[51]

Cotegipe sailed for Paraguay on September 2, 1871, and stopped in Montevideo and Buenos Aires to confer with Uruguayan and Argentine leaders. In Buenos Aires he saw Tejedor, Sarmiento, Quintana, and Mitre without obtaining a clear understanding of Argentine policy. So far as he could tell, Argentina wanted the Chaco to Bahía Negra but recognized that Bolivia must be heard in the matter. If Argentina recognized that Bolivia had a claim to the area, Cotegipe could not agree to support a treaty provision awarding it to Argentina.[52] Rio Branco knew the Argentine position thoroughly and had no illusions about the outcome of negotiations in Asunción. Quintana he recognized as a very capable opponent, one who would use his Paraguayan connections to the utmost in an effort to checkmate Brazil; but in Cotegipe the Empire had a man capable of outwitting Quintana. Rio Branco believed it would probably be necessary for Brazil to resort to unilateral negotiations with Paraguay, was confident that the Council of State would sanction such a course, and did not believe that Argentina would go to war with Brazil as a result.[53]

The Allied ministers arrived in Asunción during the political crisis of October, 1871. Rivarola had just dissolved the Congress and ordered new elections, but he met the envoys with all the pomp Paraguay could muster and gave them a dignified formal reception. If one could believe the exchanged courtesies, a just treaty would emerge from the conference. Again President Rivarola reminded the envoys that the war had been against López, not against the Paraguayan people, and now was the time to show mercy to a prostrated country and to recognize its sacred rights.[54] Rivarola probably had in mind Sarmiento's message to the Argentine Congress in the previous July that accused Paraguay of having taken advantage of anarchy in Argentina to usurp part of the Chaco.[55]

In the midst of Paraguay's political confusion, the three delegates began their sparring on November 3, although they were not received officially until a day later. As discussions proceeded, two major points of disagreement emerged. Cotegipe insisted that Paraguay be forbidden to erect fortifications on the Paraguay and Paraná rivers; Quintana objected on the grounds that such a prohibition would be meaningless. Argentina's claim to the Chaco to Bahía Negra was the second obstacle. Since the Allies had agreed in Buenos Aires to negotiate separately on the question of limits, this would have presented no problem had Brazil been willing to support Argentina, but Paraguay would never agree to an Argentine claim that had no Brazilian support.[56]

The draft treaty that Quintana had brought with him to Asunción provided for Argentine ownership of the Chaco to Bahía Negra and the islands of Atajo and Apipé. Paraguay would have Yacyretá. All of Paraguay's property and revenues would be pledged to pay the war debt; there would be freedom of navigation of all major rivers; the Allies would guarantee Paraguay's independence, sovereignty, and territorial integrity for five years. With the exception of boundaries, including Argentina's claim to the Chaco, these points were not basically controversial, so the negotiators had agreed on November 6 to twenty articles of the proposed treaty, leaving boundaries and the fortification question for further negotiation. Here the conference fell apart. Quintana deeply resented Brazilian influence in Paraguay. Reluctant to deal with Rivarola, he had suggested that the envoys support the dissolved Congress and that Rivarola resign. Steadfastly Cotegipe insisted that the Allies should not interfere in Paraguay's internal affairs![57] This hypocritical attitude fooled no one, since it was common knowledge that Juan Bautista Gill had become the strong man temporarily and that he was doing Cotegipe's bidding.

Quintana knew what was going on about him and correctly assessed Brazilian strength. The Empire had armed forces to guarantee its control over politics, a medical corps and many Catholic priests who could report accurately on "the most sensitive pulsations of Paraguayan life," and a secret police that penetrated all parts of the republic, and Rivarola had some 300 well armed urban police at his command. Argentina's influence was as weak as its occupation forces, which did not exceed 300 poorly armed men in Asunción and Villa Occidental, and two decrepit boats. After Rivarola's dissolution of the Congress, the pro-Argentine party plotted to overthrow Rivarola. Quintana thought of asking the deposed Congress to request Allied intervention and he protested to Rivarola, who replied with specious excuses. The Argentine envoy then hoped "to restore the constitutional government without breaking the Alliance, without spending a peso, and perhaps without firing a shot." Tejedor approved Quintana's course while waiting for better times to promote Argentine interests.[58] Quintana's hopes were empty dreams in the face of Brazilian power and the Argentine tendency to look toward a future when Brazil would be contained by an alliance of the Platine countries and Bolivia, and Tejedor did not know how deeply Cotegipe was involved in manipulating Paraguayan politics.

Paraguay was ready to treat with the envoys, but Quintana demanded that the Allies be in complete agreement. The Argentine maintained that Cotegipe had attempted to modify the Buenos Aires protocols by proposing continued occupation of Paraguay after the definitive treaty, and had introduced the fortifications question to force Argentina to give up its Chaco claim.[59] The envoys continued to meet informally while Quintana received many dispatches from Buenos Aires and Rodríguez moved over to support Cotegipe. Quintana continued to delay until November 30, when he recapitulated Argentina's position. Nothing in previous conferences had impaired the Treaty of Alliance. Paraguay had the right to be heard on the matter of limits, but the validity of its arguments would not concern the other allies, and "if any of the Allies does not obtain from Paraguay recognition of the limits it rightly claims, the others may not negotiate on any matters embraced by the Alliance." Paraguay's refusal to recognize limits as stated in the Treaty of Alliance left everything as it was at the end of hostilities, and the Allies must decide what to do. If the Allies would not support Argentina's claim, then the Alliance might as well be considered broken.[60] Cotegipe reviewed previous negotiations and protested that Uruguay and Brazil were not required to support Argentina's claims. This exchange ended the Asunción conference. Quintana informed Tejedor that Brazil's grip on Paraguay was firm and he could not undo the work of Rio Branco in a single day. Cotegipe refused to resume negotiations in Buenos Aires and announced his intention of treating directly with Paraguay, leaving Quintana no choice but to prepare his departure, while Cotegipe sent out invitations to a grand ball to honor the Emperor's birthday on December 2.[61]

Uruguay's Rodríguez left Asunción the day after the ball, disgusted with Quintana's actions, and in complete agreement with Cotegipe. Quintana was delayed until December 15, when he embarked on the decrepit *Espora*, despite assurances by President Jovellanos that the new ministry then being formed would promote the success of his mission. The *Espora* called at Villa Occidental to pick up Paraguayan refugees from the Tacuaral revolt and on the way downstream ran ashore in the dark. When all efforts to free the vessel failed, Brazilians offered to take the Argentine party to Buenos Aires on the commodious *Vizconde Rio Branco*, an offer Quintana politely refused. The Brazilian vessel stood by while futile efforts continued to free the *Espora*, whose passengers suffered severe discomfort from the blazing sun, clouds of mosquitoes, and quarters so cramped that many slept on the deck. Ill from liver trouble, Quintana gave up after three days and accepted Brazilian hospitality. With the Argentine flag flying from its masthead, the *Vizconde Rio Branco* returned Quintana to Buenos Aires.[62]

7. Crises of 1872

The entire postwar decade was a crisis for Paraguay, seminal years in which enduring social and political patterns were being formed in the midst of what appeared to be hopeless confusion. Had the 1871 conferences in Buenos Aires and Asunción resulted in a general treaty, Paraguay would have recovered its sovereignty. Brazil's decision to ignore the Treaty of Alliance and negotiate unilaterally with Paraguay brought prompt retaliatory moves by Argentina. Unable to risk a war with the Empire, Argentine statesmen engaged in a kind of brinksmanship intended to cause a reversal of Brazilian opposition to their Chaco claims. Argentine newspapers shrilly condemned the Empire's perfidy, the minister of foreign affairs all but threatened war, Paraguayan rebels found safe refuge on Argentine soil and sympathy for their revolutionary plans.

Control of Paraguayan politics was so important that the contending factions were labeled according to their orientation toward Argentina or Brazil. Porteños enjoyed the advantages of a common cultural heritage and many family ties with prominent Paraguayan families, advantages neutralized by the presence of overwhelming Brazilian forces. Argentine agents placed great faith in Benigno Ferreira and helped to disgrace Juan Bautista Gill in 1872. Believing conditions more favorable to its position, the Sarmiento government persuaded Bartolomé Mitre to undertake a difficult mission to Rio de Janeiro in an effort to restore the Alliance. Mitre succeeded and then agreed to resume negotiations in Asunción, where Ferreira was thought to be agreeable; but exiles were preparing a revolt to overthrow the Jovellanos-Ferreira regime, a development whose ramifications probably were unknown to Mitre.

The crises of 1872 were of paramount importance to the Allies and Paraguay, and also to Bolivia. By negotiating separately with Paraguay, Brazil took a calculated risk in offending Argentina. These ne-

113

gotiations were inextricably entangled with Paraguayan politics, and the anti-Brazilian party succeeded in consolidating its power after the departure of Brazil's minister. The fall of Juan Bautista Gill marked the brief ascendancy of his pro-Argentine rival, Benigno Ferreira. However, as will be seen in a later chapter, Argentina permitted rebels to use its territory as a base from which to attack Ferreira. The Cotegipe-Loizaga treaties temporarily destroyed the Argentine-Brazilian alliance. Recognizing the realities of the situation, Argentine officials knew that they could not fight the Empire with any hope of success, so they sent Mitre to Rio de Janeiro to salvage what he could of the Alliance. In this mission, Mitre demonstrated the highest order of statesmanship and performed a tremendously valuable service for his country.

The Argentine-Brazilian clash also highlighted Bolivian claims to the Chaco Boreal. Too frequently historians have related Bolivia's Chaco claims to her losses in the War of the Pacific, but that war did not begin until 1879, long after Bolivia had pushed its claims to the Chaco. In all of the postwar negotiations, and before, Brazil had been solicitous of Bolivia's rights. Loss of the Pacific littoral may have intensified Bolivian desire for a port on the Paraguay River but certainly did not originate it. Argentina's refusal to take the Bolivian claim seriously was to be followed more than a half century later by her support of Paraguay in the Chaco War.

The Cotegipe-Loizaga Treaties, 1872

Cotegipe's threat to proceed to negotiate unilaterally was not supported by his instructions, although the baron knew well that Rio Branco would approve that course. After receiving reports of the Asunción conference, Rio Branco blamed Quintana and the opposition party in Paraguay for its failure and sought approval of the Council of State for separate negotiations.[1] In view of events in Asunción, Manuel Francisco Correia, Brazilian minister of foreign affairs, informed the council that agreement between Argentina and Paraguay seemed unlikely. He proposed two questions: Did the Treaty of May 1, 1865, obligate Brazil to support Argentina's claims? Should Brazil negotiate unilaterally with Paraguay? There was very little opposition in the council to continued interpretation of Article 16 as simply being the basis for negotiating boundaries, the Paraguayan government was competent to sign treaties, and if the Allies could not agree, each was free to negotiate separately.[2]

Correia, in authorizing Cotegipe to proceed, blamed Quintana for the failure of the Asunción conference. After all, Correia insisted, the

Buenos Aires protocols of 1870–1871 had established bases for peace, Quintana had no right to raise questions already settled, and Argentina could not insist that the Allies support its extreme Chaco claims. His Majesty's government realized the serious consequences that might result from separate negotiations and would do everything possible to prevent a rupture with Argentina. Brazil was bound to respect Bolivia's claim to the Chaco, and Argentina had never objected to that position. When General Emilio Mitre occupied Villa Occidental on November 23, 1869, Argentina had made no claim of permanent possession. These facts proved that Argentina recognized that no one of the three claimants had a perfect title to the Chaco, and it was absurd to expect Brazil to commit itself to supporting Argentina in the litigation. Correia concluded that Quintana's course left Brazil no choice but to negotiate definitive treaties with Paraguay, and Argentina would not go to war over the issue.[3]

Before leaving Asunción, Quintana tried feebly to prevent a Brazilian-Paraguayan negotiation by pretending that his absence would be temporary. Ortíz, the Paraguayan minister of foreign affairs, expressed his regrets that an agreement could not have been reached by the Allies, thus relieving Paraguay of the uncertainties that clouded its future. The Allies had made no proposals to Paraguay, something that Ortíz found very strange. In sending copies of these notes to Cotegipe, Ortíz wanted to know if the Brazilian, too, was going to delay negotiations or if he would proceed for the good of both nations. Pleased with this attitude, Cotegipe replied that he would begin as soon as President Jovellanos should appoint a plenipotentiary.[4] If Cotegipe himself had been writing the notes for Ortíz, as he probably was, Paraguay's position could not have been better for Brazilian purposes.

Perhaps confusion in the Paraguayan government explains why a negotiator was not named until January 5, 1872. At first Jovellanos appointed his new minister of foreign affairs, José Falcón, and Carlos Loizaga. Falcón, well acquainted with Paraguay's titles to the disputed territories, suggested that each country submit proofs; however, he was willing to give up the territories Brazil claimed in exchange for a waiver of prospective war indemnities. At this point Cotegipe decided to be rid of Falcón, since it would be easier to deal with Loizaga.[5] Jovellanos and Gill readily agreed to Cotegipe's demands. Falcón resigned and thereafter matters proceeded exactly as Cotegipe desired.

Throughout the brief discussions with Paraguayan officials, Cotegipe represented Brazil as the good friend of Paraguay who in former years had exerted pressure on other nations to recognize the country's independence, and now was asking only for territories to which she had legal title. After Cotegipe and Loizaga had done with exchanging notes, the Empire emerged with 3,324 square leagues of territory between the cordilleras Amambay and Maracayú and the Río Apa. Three treaties were signed: the first, a general treaty of peace and limits, on January 9; the second, a treaty of extradition, on January 16; and the third, a treaty of friendship, commerce, and navigation on January 18.[6]

Cotegipe could count on the Empire's good friends, Gill and Brizuela, to gain speedy approval of the treaties in Congress. To be certain that there would be no opposition, Gill assembled the legislators at his home, where he and Brizuela won their consent. Cotegipe had been concealed in another room and at the opportune moment appeared before the lawmakers, who must have been somewhat surprised, and promised that Brazil would oppose any territorial demand that Argentina might make. True to their word, Gill and Brizuela pushed the treaties through Congress with such ease that all were ratified by February 6 with almost no opposition.[7] A contemporary criticized Gill and Cotegipe severely for their actions in the whole affair:

> Baron Cotegipe always tried to bypass and actually did prescind the Executive Power in matters of his mission, arranging everything with Señor Gill, President of the Senate, who dominated the majority of the legislators with his influence, now using persuasion, now threats. One does not need much insight to understand that these threats were well known. . . . Gill had at his orders a battalion expressly organized by him, with special elements, and with which he dominated the town and kept it in constant apprehension. It was called "Batallón Guarará." This word means to fall suddenly on someone.[8]

Foreign diplomats were very critical of Brazil's treatment of Paraguay. The British minister in Buenos Aires considered ludicrous the article binding Paraguay to pay a war indemnity that could amount to more than $300,000,000 in gold.[9] Of course, no one expected that Paraguay would pay, and Gill later assured the American minister, John L. Stevens, that Brazil would not insist on payment as long as Paraguay refused to yield the Gran Chaco to Argentina. This was the understanding between Cotegipe and Loizaga when the treaties were negotiated. Paraguay would never consent to Argentine demands, and Brazil did not want to see Paraguay at the mercy of the Argentine Republic. Argentina, Stevens observed, was paying the penalty for having joined Brazil in destroying Paraguay and now "the security of the territorial existence of the Paraguay and Uruguay Republics is this strong jealousy between the Argentines and the Brazilians."[10] Despite the fact that Brazilian influence was dominant early in the Jovellanos regime, Stevens did not believe that Brazil would absorb Paraguay. No friend of the Empire, he predicted: "At no distant day the Argentines will see clearly what her [sic] true relations with Paraguay should be, and thereafter cherish it as a cardinal principle of her national policy to unite the Republics of the Río de la Plata in the bonds of friendship and peace, so that they may always maintain a compact front against the gross and bedizened civilization of the Empire."[11] The thought had also caused concern in Brazilian diplomatic circles.

Brinksmanship

Rio Branco predicted the great outcry that came from Buenos Aires as a result of the Cotegipe-Loizaga treaties and warned Cotegipe to take all necessary precautions, although he did not believe that war would result.[12] Bartolomé Mitre, in articles in *La Nación*, attempted to calm his countrymen, and Cotegipe assured Mitre that Argentine interests were not threatened.[13] But Mitre was not speaking for the government and did not have the treaties at hand. The official reaction was decisive. Argentine troops had occupied Villa Occidental since November, 1869; now President Sarmiento on January 31, 1872, ordered General Julio de Vedia to take formal possession as governor of Chaco Territory.[14] General Vedia was in favor of pushing the Argentine frontier to the Andes. To his mind, Paraguay had held the Chaco for sixty years by force and had done nothing with it. He would take possession of the Chaco in due time, and noted that various Paraguayans were asking for lots in Villa Occidental, the only place where life could be protected.[15]

Paraguay promptly protested the Argentine move. Appointment of a governor of Chaco Territory assumed that the area was incontestably Argentine and was an act of force against Paraguay, which had held uninterrupted possession of the Chaco. Loizaga reminded Tejedor that Argentine ambition to seize all of the Chaco was revealed for the first time by the Treaty of Alliance, which would extend Argentine territory to Bahía Negra. "The knowledge of that stipulation contributed much to making the war one of ferocity and extermination; moreover the Paraguayans who supported the Allies trusted the treaty which declared that the war was not against the Paraguayan people but against its tyrant dictator and the independence, sovereignty and integrity of Paraguay would be respected." The Allies had established a Provisional Government, and this government had protested Argentine occupation of Villa Occidental in 1869. At that time Argentina assured Paraguay that possession would be settled by legal title. The preliminary treaty of June 20, 1870, also promised negotiation, not unilateral action. Paraguay would never recognize any Argentine actions in Villa Occidental as legal. Tejedor replied sharply, blaming Brazil for the failure of the Asunción conference and reminding Paraguay that its claims to the Chaco were no more incontestable than its claims to Misiones. However, at the moment he was not going to enter into debate over the matter.[16]

The Argentine government and press protested vigorously against the Cotegipe-Loizaga treaties, Tejedor asked Brazil to evacuate Atajo Island, and Mitre urged Rio Branco not to forget the common sacrifices of the Allies. In his formal complaint, Tejedor charged that Brazil had created a protectorate in Paraguay and had broken the Alliance.[17] While the two foreign offices exchanged notes, Rio Branco summoned the Council of State to meet on March 1 to consider the treaties and the consequences of ratification. The Conde d'Eu gave voice to an old Brazilian concern: the annexation of Paraguay by Argentina must be prevented at all costs; while not as important as Uruguay, if the three republics were to become one, the new state would be a threat to Brazil's borders from Bahía Negra to the Atlantic. But the Visconde de Abaête objected; he was not convinced that a collective peace was impossible. São Vicente, who approved ratification, insisted that Argentina had no just cause for complaint and would not sever relations over the matter. In any event, Brazil should look after its own interests. Now was the chance, Bernardo de Sousa Franco argued, for Brazil to be rid of any obligation to support Argentina's Chaco claims and thus embarrass its relations with Bolivia. Brazil had been generous with Paraguay and the treaties should be ratified. The Council overwhelmingly approved Cotegipe's actions and recommended ratification.[18]

With the Council strongly supporting him, Correia replied firmly but reassuringly to Tejedor. Brazil was not assuming a unilateral protectorate over Paraguay, and he insisted that she had not demanded anything of Paraguay that the country could not grant to the other allies. Although futile discussions for two years had left the Empire no choice but to negotiate separately, on all other matters of the Alliance Brazil would remain faithful to its obligations. He closed with a thinly veiled warning:

> The Chaco question is the only difficulty appearing in definitive agreements of the Argentine Republic with Paraguay; and the Imperial Government is persuaded that the wisdom and prudence of the Buenos Aires cabinet will succeed in overcoming that difficulty without creating a painful situation for itself and its Allies, and without worsening the fate of

that unfortunate Paraguayan nation which owes much to the Alliance and merits the continuation of the same just and generous treatment.[19]

In the midst of this furor, Cotegipe left Asunción. He paid his respects to Jovellanos on February 15 and sailed for Buenos Aires two days later, leaving the consul-general, João Antônio Mendes Totta Filho, as chargé.[20] In Buenos Aires he visited President Sarmiento and Tejedor, encounters that were coldly formal. After defending his course in Asunción, Cotegipe continued to Rio de Janeiro, where he arrived on March 9, and on March 26 the Princess Imperial ratified the Cotegipe-Loizaga treaties. The British minister in Buenos Aires, a neutral observer, felt that this result was to have been expected. The Argentine policy had been one of deliberate delay in an attempt to gain all of the Chaco and now had only its own errors to blame. Argentina complained that the treaty of January 9 was a flagrant violation of the Alliance and reacted by seizing Villa Occidental, an act that revealed its own purpose and antagonized Bolivia. In short, the British minister found Argentine diplomacy peculiarly inept.[21]

Tejedor took his time in replying to Correia's defense of March 22, but when he did his "Ituzaingó note" was a masterpiece. Point by point he demolished Correia's arguments, leaving the Brazilian the solace of a strong squadron on the rivers, a powerful occupation force on land, and, he thought, firm control over the Paraguayan Congress. Writing bluntly, Tejedor asserted that Quintana had gone to Asunción in good faith, only to have Cotegipe raise issues impossible to resolve. How wonderful it was that Brazilians would impose their will upon a Paraguay decimated by the Allies! Brazil was neither loyal nor noble in seizing territories it claimed without supporting her ally in its demands, but this was to be expected, since Brazil had encroached on the territory of all its Spanish neighbors. Cotegipe, on passing through Buenos Aires on his way home, had been very conciliatory, then Brazil ratified the Cotegipe-Loizaga treaties with indecent haste. "The Argentine Government," Tejedor concluded, "does not wish to nor should conceal the gravity of the situation that all of these events create; trying to conceal the profound distress that these events have caused and to accept the proffered explanations would make it guilty of reprehensible hypocrisy." Although the Treaty of Alliance had been seriously compromised, Tejedor hoped that peace would prevail and the Allies would fulfill their obligations.[22]

Sarmiento and Tejedor were at a great disadvantage in dueling with Rio Branco and Cotegipe. Although Brazil had its own serious internal problems, the Empire was much more unified than Argentina, and its military strength was far greater than anything Argentina could muster. A noted Argentine scholar accurately assessed his country's weakness: "Imperial diplomacy expertly took advantage of the unfavorable conditions that complicated Argentina's political and military situation. The Paraguayan War had weakened and consumed our military elements. The formidable rebellions of López Jordán at the same time required extraordinary efforts; and the very bitter presidential struggle presaged a new civil war." [23] Despite the Brazilian military presence and Paraguayan resentment of Argentine occupation of Villa Occidental, there was a strong pro-Argentine party in Asunción that made life miserable for the Empire's man, Juan Bautista Gill.

Much of the war talk in Buenos Aires and Rio de Janeiro was political bombast intended to embarrass the government in power. Conservatives and Liberals sniped constantly at one another in Brazil, where uneasy relations with the Church, the abolition movement, and demands for electoral reform kept politics agitated. In Argentina, provincial caudillos continued their threats, highlighted by the murder of Justo José de Urquiza early in 1870 by followers of Ricardo López Jordán, a caudillo who kept Entre Ríos in turmoil. Epidemics of yellow fever, as in 1871, coupled with droughts and floods, imposed serious economic problems, and the emerging nation lacked everything to wage a successful war against an opponent like Brazil. In the presidential election year of 1874, Sarmiento wisely informed the Congress: "No question with Brazil can carry us into war." [24] His successor, Nicolás Avellaneda, was a frail young man of thirty-seven whose nickname "Taquito" (Little Heel) had no connection with his intellectual ability. Avellaneda was just as determined as Sarmiento to avoid war with Brazil, and the new foreign minister, Bernardo de Irigoyen, was much more conciliatory than Carlos Tejedor. Nevertheless, Argentine authorities would not neglect opportunities to embarrass the Brazilians in Paraguay by permitting revolutionary plots to mature on Argentine soil and providing sanctuary for defeated rebels. Eventually these plots would aid in wearing down Brazilian desire to continue a costly occupation.

The Fall of Juan Bautista Gill

Cotegipe's withdrawal from Asunción was catastrophic for Juan Bautista Gill. Representing Brazil after the baron's departure were Mendes Totta as chargé, General Guimarães in command of the army, and Admiral Francisco Pereira Pinto commanding the navy. All had instructions to support Jovellanos and all were inclined to favor

Benigno Ferreira, strong man in the cabinet.[25] Gill's power in Congress was impressive. Not only was he president of that body but also was named to succeed to the presidency.[26] The chief of police in Asunción, Col. Luís González, was Gill's man, and Gill frequently used his influence to free prisoners. Since Ferreira was minister of interior, González reported to him. Ferreira ordered an end to these irregularities.[27] This was but one incident in the Ferreira-Gill struggle for power: each was determined to become president, and each correctly accused the other of plotting to depose Jovellanos.

One may choose between two widely divergent versions of events that ended in Ferreira's victory in this struggle for supremacy. The anti-Gill account centers on a very minor incident. Ferreira was using some of the furniture that belonged to López and Madame Lynch. Gill sent a man to take the items to his own home, but Ferreira refused to let them go. Gill then demanded that Jovellanos dismiss Ferreira and threatened to depose the president! He sent a group of his *raidos* to seize Jovellanos, but one of the men betrayed the plan and Jovellanos escaped. Ferreira seized upon this abortive effort as justification for having Gill imprisoned on March 8.[28]

Gill's account of events leading to his arrest is more plausible. He had played a major role in placing Jovellanos in power, and perfect harmony appeared to exist within the government until Ferreira appointed his followers to key positions and plotted to overthrow Jovellanos. Gill knew of the conspiracy and, when he had absolute proof, urged Jovellanos to dismiss Ferreira, who would sell out to their enemies.[29] Unfortunately, Gill reported to Cotegipe, Jovellanos had come under Ferreira's influence and refused to dismiss him. Gill then told Jovellanos that he could no longer support the government and offered to leave the country, but Jovellanos said that this was not necessary. On March 8, Gill reported his conversation to Guimarães, who urged him not to leave Paraguay. While Guimarães and Gill were talking, Jovellanos alerted his troops. Guimarães hastened to confer with Mendes Totta while Gill went to the Cabildo to attend a session of Congress. Since a quorum was not present, Gill left the Cabildo. Fifty soldiers promptly surrounded him and escorted him to jail.[30]

The speed with which events then unfolded show clearly that Ferreira had plotted well to be rid of his rival. Gill was arrested at about 1:30 p.m., and the Senate convened two hours later with Juan José Brizuela presiding. Jovellanos informed the Senate that Gill had attempted a revolution, and the matter went to the committee on petitions, which recommended that Gill be stripped of his congressional immunities. Ferreira was present in the chamber and easily negated Brizuela's efforts to protect Gill.[31] On the next morning, March 9, General Guimarães and Admiral Pereira Pinto visited Gill in jail. Ferreira, who had been with Jovellanos during the conference with Guimarães and Mendes Totta, told the Brazilians that Gill had attempted to suborn the troops and overthrow Jovellanos. Hotly protesting his innocence, Gill warned Guimarães that his friends might start a revolt if he were left in jail, so the Brazilians obtained the government's consent to allow Gill to take refuge on the *Princesa* on March 11. Several of Gill's friends had warned Guimarães and Mendes Totta that the interests of Paraguay and the Empire would be seriously damaged by Ferreira's supremacy and pointed to the amnesty granted to Brazil's opponents as proof, but Mendes Totta followed his orders to uphold the government. [32]

Soon a rumor was circulating, as General Vedia reported: "All Paraguayans of the decent class at least, say that what happened is a triumph for the Argentine policy. There is something to this." [33] There was, indeed, but Vedia did not elaborate. He and Dr. Miguel Gallegos may have had a hand in the affair, but he may also have meant that Argentina was simply the beneficiary of Gill's reversal. Ferreira was determined to be rid of his rival, Jovellanos wanted to patch up the quarrel, and Gill decided it best to leave the country.[34] In the Senate, proceedings against Gill were suspended on March 14 because of his request for exile, but on March 15 the Senate voted to expel him on charges of conspiracy. Brizuela again tried valiantly to defend Gill, but Ferreira's partisans in the gallery raised so much of an uproar that he could not speak.[35] Ferreira now clearly dominated the Jovellanos government, and cabinet changes reflected his power.[36]

Gill had a poor opinion of Brazilian leadership in Asunción and warned Cotegipe that a capable minister should be sent. Guimarães and Pereira Pinto were competent military commanders, and Mendes Totta was good at attending to his own business. As for himself, Gill protested: "I have spared no effort to promote the prosperity of my Country and to increase constantly its friendship with Brazil. If I can do anything more in this regard I shall do it, but I am going to seek in private life more tranquillity than public life affords, above all in my country." [37]

Cotegipe did not lack for information. Brizuela, Gill, and Jovellanos all wrote to give their versions of events, while Guimarães sent long letters in which he reported in detail political moves from which he was unable to make much sense. Jovellanos maintained that his distinguished friend Gill was unjustified in his suspicion of Ferreira, who had always discharged his duties faithfully, and he did not know what caused Gill and Ferreira to be such bitter enemies. But Gill had appeared on the morning of March 8 at Jovellanos's home to demand Ferreira's dismissal. This was too much. To prevent turmoil, he had reluctantly ordered Gill to be imprisoned. "Gill's party is my own party," he wrote. "Gill left but the party remains." [38]

Better information came from other sources. A plausible interpretation of the events that led to Gill's expulsion reveals Jovellanos as anti-Brazilian if not pro-Argentine. The anti-Brazilian group was strong in Congress, and Jovellanos had been so discreet that Gill and Cotegipe had thought him to be a safe front man after getting rid of Rivarola. But Jovellanos was clever: in favoring Ferreira he had succeeded in greatly undermining Gill's position. Gill, therefore, demanded that Jovellanos expel Ferreira, and very likely did threaten the president. Gill overplayed his hand and Ferreira won the game. But there was another party to reckon with—the Lopiztas, or Bareiristas, to whom José Segundo Decoud had defected. To this party belonged Caballero, Escobar, Juan Silvano Godoy, the priests Fidel Maíz and Blas Ignacio Duarte, Juan Antonio Jara, and others of the Tacuaral rebels. At heart a liberal, Godoy cooperated with these Lopiztas because of his antagonism toward Brazil and the Gill family. Jovellanos seemed to be the best instrument of their policy, but neither Cotegipe nor Rio Branco trusted him. Guimarães made no effort to conceal his dislike for Ferreira, although he could see no reason for distrusting Jovellanos. Nevertheless, Jovellanos had been too severe with Gill and had acted unconstitutionally, which was not surprising in postwar Paraguay. [39]

Mitre's Mission to Rio de Janeiro

Diplomatic relations between Brazil and Argentina worsened steadily in 1872 after Brazil ratified the Cotegipe-Loizaga treaties. The press in each country assumed a belligerent tone, and for a time there appeared to be real danger of war. [40] Tejedor's "Ituzaingó note" of April 27 added to the tension, and Mitre, at first conciliatory, began to publish offensive articles in *La Nación*. For a time it appeared that Argentina was drifting blindly toward her own destruction, until Sarmiento decided to make overtures to both Paraguay and Brazil. To the latter he appointed Mitre as special envoy and indicated to President Jovellanos that a Paraguayan emissary would be welcome. [41]

Rumors of Argentine-Brazilian animosity caused concern in Washington, where Secretary of State Hamilton Fish reiterated fears that the Allies would absorb Paraguay, a country that could become an important "bulwark against encroachment from any of its neighbors."

Stevens replied that "there are strong reasons for the belief that the Emperor and the party in power secretly wish war if it can be made to appear to the world that the Argentines invoke it." With Brazil wishing to expand, Uruguay was much alarmed and hoped for moral assistance from the United States in maintaining neutrality.[42]

Desiring to see the situation first hand, Stevens left Montevideo on the *Wasp* for a leisurely trip to Asunción, where he arrived at the end of July. President Jovellanos greeted him cordially and, as Rivarola had done a year earlier, treated the minister and officers of the *Wasp* to a train ride. In his conferences with Jovellanos, Stevens learned that Cotegipe had given verbal assurances that the war claims would not be pressed if Paraguay held firm in its claim to the Chaco. This assurance failed to impress Stevens and he warned Jovellanos not to depend upon it. The treaty itself had been "carried through the Paraguayan Congress by the presence of Brazilian force and the clandestine use of Brazilian gold." Brazil, Stevens believed, "has adopted a kind of India rubber sliding-scale policy about as scrupulous as the diplomatic morality of the Europe of the 17th & 18th centuries." The Brazilians had accomplished all they could by maintaining armed forces in Paraguay and now it was time to withdraw them. Stevens fully believed that Brazil intended "to make the Rio de la Plata, the Parana & the Paraguay its southern boundary & its canal to the Sea,"[43] an opinion just the opposite of what he had believed earlier in the year.

While Argentina was negotiating with Brazil through the Mitre mission, Paraguay decided to respond positively to Sarmiento's overtures. Jovellanos named Carlos Loizaga to negotiate with Tejedor in Buenos Aires. If the new Brazilian minister to Paraguay, Joaquim Maria Nascentes de Azumbuja, did not aid in writing Loizaga's instructions, he was by no means uninformed. Loizaga was to demand Argentine evacuation of Villa Occidental and to claim all territory Paraguay had before the war. This would include Misiones and the Chaco. The boundaries of Paraguay's Chaco had never been determined but Loizaga was to claim north to Bahía Negra and west to 63°. Since the Allies had declared that the war was against López and not against the Paraguayan people, and an Argentine foreign minister had acknowledged that victory did not confer title to territory, Paraguay's demands were reasonable.[44]

Loizaga had a hard time in Buenos Aires. Dr. Rufino de Elizalde, who had been Mitre's minister of foreign affairs and was a frequent contributor to *La Nación*, had no faith in Loizaga's mission. The Paraguayan, he informed Mitre, could not have come without Brazilian instructions. Even if Loizaga did sign a treaty on terms acceptable to Argentina, Paraguay would not ratify. "To treat with Paraguay," he observed, "even with the assurance of coming to an agreement, is to follow in the waters of Cotegipe." [45] Nor did Azambuja trust Loizaga, and with good reason. In Buenos Aires, the hapless Loizaga showed his instructions to Tejedor and made his mission impossible by revealing his desire that Argentina annex Paraguay! Loizaga was authorized to offer Misiones in exchange for Argentine surrender of claims to the Chaco. Since Argentina had no good claim to anything except the Chaco Central, the area between the Bermejo and Pilcomayo rivers, Paraguay was offering a good trade, or what would have been a good trade under other circumstances. If Argentina refused to bargain, Loizaga was to offer a ten-year moratorium on the Chaco question provided that all Argentine troops were withdrawn from Paraguay, including Villa Occidental. Tejedor, naturally, said that they had nothing to discuss and the desperate Loizaga wrote for new instructions. Tejedor kept Mitre informed, since Loizaga's instructions obviously reflected Brazilian views.[46]

It is inconceivable that Paraguayan leaders had not discussed possible terms of settlement with Argentina, either among themselves or with the Brazilian envoys. An idea that was to appear again was Loizaga's suggestion to Jovellanos that Paraguay give up the Chaco in exchange for avoiding payment of war damages. Jovellanos refused to change Loizaga's instructions and ordered him to cease negotiations. This, of course, was a wise move, since there really was no need to haggle over war damages. Paraguay would never pay them regardless of treaty provisions, and no thinking person in Brazil or Argentina expected anything else. Jovellanos was by no means a free agent, and Tejedor knew that Brazil was dictating Paraguayan moves. The Brazilian foreign minister hoped that the territorial problems of Cerrito Island and the Chaco could be settled in Rio de Janeiro by negotiations among the Bolivian Mariano Reyes Cardona, Loizaga, and Tejedor, again proving that Brazil was fully cognizant of Bolivian claims to the Chaco and would not ignore them. But this assemblage could not meet. Tejedor was quite willing to treat with Bolivia and Paraguay on the Chaco, always reserving the rights of the other,[47] but not under Brazilian auspices. Elizalde, writing in *La Nación,* made the Argentine attitude quite clear. Argentina opposed the "protocols of Asunción," as Elizalde called the Cotegipe-Loizaga treaties. Paraguay had no right to territory on the right bank of the Río Paraguay, and the Treaty of May 1, 1865, merely confirmed Argentine title. Bolivia could, with some justice, claim part of the Chaco, and Urquiza's cession of the Chaco Central in 1852 was void since the Argentine Congress did not ratify it. Obviously, the Chaco belonged either to Argentina or to Bolivia, and if Brazil refused to recognize this, the Treaty of Alliance was nullified. However, Argentina would agree to an equal division of the Chaco north of Villa Occidental among the three claimants.[48] The other powers ignored this obvious feeler.

To Carlos Tejedor, the Paraguayans were incomprehensible. After Loizaga had taken his leave and just before Mitre came to an agreement with São Vicente, he observed:

> Paraguay continues to be undecipherable. Loizaga wants to overthrow Ferreira. Ferreira tries to disown Loizaga. Arambuya [Azambuja] is disgusted with Guimaraens and Pintos, and he, as well as the latter, wants to overthrow Ferreira after having praised him highly. In the spirit of Jovellanos, Arambuya also favors the resignation of Loizaga and propagandizes in favor of Gil. . . . I see in all of this a definite and frightening policy. The situation . . . is being prepared systematically for an indefinite occupation. Our policy, therefore, must be the opposite: To hasten negotiation, and if this does not bring results, to withdraw definitely from Paraguay. Paraguay left to its fate is better than Paraguay enslaved with our consent. To follow another course, that of the alliance, for example, or that of annexation, it would be necessary to be prepared for war, which we are not and do not want, and to count on a strong Paraguay in whose bruised or corrupted heart, at least for the present, there is little patriotic throbbing.[49]

Bartolomé Mitre met with a cool reception when he landed in Rio de Janeiro on July 5, but he conducted himself with admirable restraint and persevered until good relations once more were restored between the former allies. His instructions were conciliatory: "The Argentine Government, in the note of April 27, pronounced its final word, provoked by the attitude of the Brazilian Government, which in Asunción had joined the conquered and before foreign Governments charged its only ally with ambitious plans; but it has not delivered an ultimatum." Mitre should obtain explicit recognition of the Treaty of May 1 in all of its provisions, agreement to separate negotiation by Argentina, evacuation of Paraguay within three months, and Brazilian evacuation of Cerrito Island. Argentina would recognize the Cotegipe-Loizaga treaties to the extent that they did not violate these terms. In regard to war debts, there must be no privileged creditors.[50]

Ignored for the first few days, Mitre did receive a cordial reception when he called on Correia on July 9. After this meeting, he had several conferences with Rio Branco and Correia. His long dispatches to Tejedor reveal a leisurely, lengthy exchange in which both sides protested friendship but refused to yield on any significant points. After soothing Brazilian feelings hurt by the April 27 note, Mitre began to make progress.[51]

Brazil's military might did not impress Mitre. The Empire, according to his estimate, would have difficulty in mobilizing 15,000 men at a single point. There were fewer than 20,000 under arms, and they were scattered in Paraguay, Mato Grosso, and various places in the Empire. The army was poorly equipped, and considerable time must pass before Brazil could field a regular army of 25,000 men. Brazil wanted peace but was continuing to rearm.[52] Elizalde reinforced these conclusions, and Mitre may in part have been echoing Elizalde's opinion that Brazil, having achieved its territorial objectives, did not desire war. He was also correct in advising Mitre that Brazil did not wish the "Argentine Republic to recover its territories nor regularize its situation with Paraguay, and far from helping us and lending its guarantee as the treaty of alliance stipulates, it would oppose us and seek to inspire resistance on the part of Bolivia and Paraguay."[53] Confident that Mitre's mission would fail, Elizalde predicted that it would be easy to come to an agreement with Bolivia and Paraguay. There was no need to fear Brazil's army in Paraguay. Brazil could not risk increasing it, death and desertion would diminish the ranks. In the meantime, it was an expensive business for Brazil and benefited Paraguay. "The army in Paraguay is an absurdity," he concluded.[54]

One may surmise that Mitre was especially anxious to succeed in Rio de Janeiro and then go on to conclude peace with Paraguay. This would give him added strength in his attempt to be elected for a second term as president of Argentina. He rejected the good offices tendered by the United States, France, and Italy.[55] During the protracted discussions, Mitre dealt primarily with José Antônio Pimenta Bueno, Marquês de São Vicente, although both Rio Branco and Correia kept in close touch with the negotiations. There was also time for Dom Pedro II and Mitre to discuss literature, especially the work of Dante, whom both admired. In the intimacy of Dom Pedro's study, statesmen became philosophers and paved the way for renewal of good relations.[56]

Bolivia introduced a discordant note into the Mitre-São Vicente negotiations. Having made no headway in Buenos Aires, Reyes Cardona went to Rio de Janeiro, where he attempted to gain consideration of Bolivian claims to all of the Chaco north of the Pilcomayo and to promote the Madeira railway. Mitre refused to permit the Bolivian to complicate negotiations that were going smoothly.[57]

With justifiable satisfaction, Mitre was able to report the signing of an agreement on November 19. By its terms, Brazil reaffirmed its obligations under the Treaty of Alliance, and Argentina recognized the Cotegipe-Loizaga treaties, which would be effective only after the signing of a general treaty by the three allied powers. Uruguay and Argentina might negotiate separately or jointly with Paraguay, with Brazil lending its moral support, and if Paraguay should refuse to negotiate under the agreed terms, the Allies would cooperate to force an agreement. Argentine and Brazilian forces would evacuate Paraguay within three months after signing the definitive treaty of peace. Brazil would evacuate Cerrito Island. Paraguay would be compelled to pay war indemnities and would treat the Allies equally in payment of her debts; the war debt would bear no interest for ten years, then would reach 6 percent by a series of steps. The Allies would guarantee Paraguay's territorial integrity, all other terms of the alliance were in effect, and the Allies would agree on the solution of any difficulties that might arise in the future concerning Paraguay. Uruguay would be invited to adhere to the Mitre–São Vicente treaty.[58]

Mitre felt that his mission had been an unqualified success. The Treaty of the Triple Alliance had been reestablished and all questions between Brazil and Argentina had been settled.[59] Soon he would be going to Asunción to open negotiations with the Jovellanos government in company with the Brazilian minister to Argentina, Dr. Domingos José Gonçalves de Magalhaes, Barão de Araguáia. Unfortunately for their efforts, the volatile political condition in Asunción, combined with Brazilian support of Paraguay's claim to the Chaco, resulted in failure for Bartolomé Mitre.

8. Rails, Loans, and Immigrants

Brazil and Argentina were singularly unconcerned about problems basic to Paraguayan recovery from the war. Their rivalry for control of Paraguayan politics, their maneuvering for advantage, and their quarreling over the peace left the country with almost no economic guidance. The concept of postwar aid to a defeated enemy was entirely foreign to statesmen in Rio de Janeiro and Buenos Aires. The result was that politicians inexperienced in the intricacies of domestic and international finance, and motivated more by greed than by patriotism, involved Paraguay in projects so reprehensible as to cause one to wonder how the country survived at all.

The young Liberals knew that the transportation system must be developed, the railway must be repaired and extended, immigrants must be attracted if agriculture was to flourish, and financing must be sought abroad. Unfortunately, those who conceived the ideas were not the ones to carry them out. Leaders in the Congress and in the governments of Jovellanos and Rivarola generally were far more concerned with improving their own fortunes than with promoting the country's welfare. The Brazilians, refusing to risk war with Argentina by making Paraguay a protectorate, offered no guidance and almost no aid, and her ministers contented themselves with making cynical remarks about the venality of Paraguay's politicians.

The railway, loans, and immigrants were closely related. As a prime property of the government, the railway was both collateral for loans and the intended beneficiary. Proceeds from the loans would pay the cost of starting colonies, and colonists could expect an improved railway for transporting products to market.

Adventures of the Paraguay Central Railway

A principal architectural attraction in Asunción to this day is the Central, or San Francisco, Station. Located in the Plaza San Francisco,

129

now the Plaza Uruguaya, the building was designed by Alejandro Ravizza, the Italian architect who also began such ornaments as the Oratorio, a shrine now known as the Panteón Nacional. The station, newly finished before the War of the Triple Alliance, served as a music hall where bands entertained on Sunday mornings. Its spacious rooms became ballrooms for such occasions as the annual celebration of the birthday of Francisco Solano López on July 24, and during the war it became a military hospital.

The San Francisco Station was a fitting monument to the acumen and foresight of Carlos Antonio López, whose contributions to his country fully warrant his being dubbed "El Constructor." His finest material accomplishment was the building of the railway to Paraguarí, some seventy-two kilometers from Asunción, and only the beginning of hostilities prevented his successor from carrying the work forward as originally planned and built by English engineers.

Planning for construction of the railway had begun in the early 1850s, and one of the tasks ably discharged by Francisco Solano López when he went to Europe in 1853 was to further his father's plans to modernize Paraguay. The younger López contracted with John and Alfred Blyth of London to provide technical advice, technicians, and materials for many projects, primarily for the railway, shipyard, and foundry. The Blyths sent John William K. Whytehead to Asunción, where he studied the López projects and found them feasible. Carlos Antonio then moved rapidly. In 1856 he began to order materials for the first section of the line. A feeder spur of the railway connected the harbor with the Asunción San Francisco Station, while the main line ran eastward toward Paraguarí. Eventually the line was to continue to Villa Rica, then turn southeast to the Paraná River port of Encarnación. Principal engineer for the railway was George Paddison, who arrived in 1858. Other engineers were among the many technicians who signed contracts to serve in Paraguay. These men surveyed the route, directed construction of roadbed and bridges, and supervised the cutting and laying of sleepers. Rails and rolling stock arrived steadily fom England, all of which López paid for promptly. On June 14, 1861, a short train made the run from the harbor to the still incomplete San Francisco Station, and on the following September 21, formal ceremonies marked the opening of one of South America's first railways.[1] Work was still progressing when the war broke out in November, 1864. Prior to the conflict, the railway made no significant contribution to the Paraguayan economy, but completion of a spur to the military training camp at Cerro León facilitated the movement of troops and supplies.

A major casualty of war was this Ferro-Carril del Estado, or State Railway, which López attempted to destroy as he retreated before advancing Brazilian forces. When the Allies occupied Asunción, there was but one dilapidated locomotive in the city, and not until June 20, 1869, did an engine reach Pirayú.[2] By importing a few used locomotives, repairing what little rolling stock remained, patching the roadbed, and rebuilding destroyed bridges, the Allies restored a semblance of service. For a few months they operated four trains. The Ferro-Carril Empresa Brasileira (Brazilian Railway Enterprise) by October ran two trains between Asunción and Pirayú; the Argentine train went only to Areguá. Not to be outdone, the Uruguayans also had a train, which apparently went nowhere. Most of the rolling stock belonged to the Brazilian train. Its three locomotives, the "Gastão de Orleans," "Herval," and "Polidora," shared the task of pulling an assortment of forty-six wagons and coaches. The Argentines had one locomotive, "La Argentina," which had a stock of ten decrepit wagons, and the Uruguayans could boast of only the rickety "Constitución," which had a stable of two old cargo cars and one passenger coach.[3] Five locomotives and sixty wagons and coaches would have been respectable equipment had they been in good running order and placed under one manager, but riding the train was a hazardous venture:

> The train is miserable, shabby and uncomfortable; the high windows and hard benches suggest the notion that the first class carriages were originally intended for carrying horned cattle, but people need look for no creature comforts today in Paraguay, and it seems indeed unaccountable how a railway coach ever got into the country at all.[4]

Although the railway had improved very little within the next two years, the French traveler Forgues was inclined to see the more picturesque aspects of Paraguayan rail travel. He found the railway station "the most beautiful building in the country," swarming with people at departure time early in the morning. To this friendly observer, "Nothing was more bizarre than those savage looking people crowding on the cars and locomotives, those machines of a high civilization." Long North American cars had just arrived and were more commodious than those of the prewar period. Two flat cars, reserved entirely for the poor, were completely loaded. The train proceeded leisurely to Luque, where, after having taken an hour to traverse fourteen kilometers, the locomotive took on water and wood while travelers bought food and lace, especially *ñanduti*, from female vendors: "Women hang on the doors and offer us embroideries they have made with European net, or a special kind of net, or bottles of cold milk and chipa, a kind of mandioc bread in which eggs and starch are used, and for which Luque is famous as Dijon is with us for its spice bread," Forgues reported. The engineer was in no hurry and left his platform to talk at length with a friend until impatient passengers shouted at him. Resuming his post, the talkative driver managed to coax a speed of about fifteen miles per hour from his locomotive.[5] Considering the condition of roadbed and rails, the train was hurtling along the tracks.

Fifteen years later the scene had changed little when an Englishman from Buenos Aires traveled the route to Paraguarí:

> There is only one railway in Paraguay. It was built by Lopez the First. The excellence of earthworks, sleepers, rails, waggons and locomotives has been tested by wear and tear of the last 29 years. The cars and locomotives would form a valuable collection in a museum of railway antiquities: some of the locomotives did good work in the Crimean War before coming to Paraguay. In spite of their old age, these engines still hold together, and manage to pull a train daily to Paraguari and back—a distance of 45 miles.
>
> The daily departure of the train for Paraguari is one of the most interesting sights in Asunción. The general "getup" of the train, with its rickety engine, truck loads of dark and semi-nude women, and its shaky, antiquated first and second-class cars, is both amusing and interesting. The social standing of the sexes is immediately noticed—women only in the trucks and men in the cars, better still, shoes and stockings in the cars, bare feet and "typoys" in the trucks.[6]

All along the line of the railroad women were walking, baskets or pitchers on their heads, short black cigars in their mouths. Men lounged lazily about the stations, "with the despairing look of individuals in tight-fitting boots."[7] Poor as it was, this uncertain means of transportation and its run-down stations were a center of activity. The traveler able to ignore the imminent danger of derailment could enjoy the ride to Paraguarí:

> The railway from Asunción traverses a most delightful country for 40 miles, as far as Paraguari. On leaving the city the first object to attract notice is the house wherein the tyrant Francia lived and died. Close by is the quinta which belonged to the unfortunate Dr. Berjes [José Berges], minister of foreign affairs shot by López; here was a fine collection of exotic and rare plants, and at the foot of the cliff overlooking the river is the Chorro waterfall, a favourite bathing-place. . . . Soon we get sight of the Cordillera, clad to the summits in luxuriant vegetation, and now bursts upon the traveler's view the magnificent lake of Ypacaray (covering an area of 40 square miles), which begins at the village of Areguá. Now the line skirts the lake for some miles, passing the glorious peak of Ytaguá, at the foot of which was the summer-place of Mrs. Lynch during the López regime. The "cajón," or valley of Pirayu, offers a charming spectacle, wood-

ed hills rising up on either side, and appearing to close it in at the further end, where the Cerro Mbatovi lifts its head in the clear sky. There is a belief among the country people that St. Thomas the Apostle dwelt in a cave in this mountain, where a small chapel now exists. . . . Paraguari is a small village, only remarkable as one of the great Jesuit establishments in the seventeenth and eighteenth centuries; they had farms here with 30,000 head of cattle, and the old registers show the names of English or Irish fathers. . . . The route of the railway to Villa Rica would pass Cerro Acay, but the line will hardly be prolonged unless purchased from Government by an English company.[8]

The roadbed was in very bad condition, especially the stretch between Asunción and Luque, about fourteen kilometers, which was the oldest and poorest part of the line. One observer, whose spectacles must have been broken, enthused: "The line is the finest, best built, and most solid I have ever seen. . . . People wondered why Lopez when he fled the Lomas, did not destroy the railway, but it would take all Lopez' army when in the morning of the campaign to pull up a mile of it."[9] This exuberant evaluation was a wild exaggeration. Much more accurate was the report in August, 1869, that the railway was "in the worst possible condition" and could meet neither military nor civilian needs.[10]

The Brazilians had little or no use for the railway and were quite anxious to return it to Paraguayan operation. Apparently they made the effort in November, 1869, but the Provisional Government had no resources for operating the train. Brazilian operation continued until February 15, 1870, when service was suspended.[11] Theoretically, the transfer occurred early in April, 1870, and for a time the enterprise was referred to as the Ferro-Carril de la Asunción a la Villa Rica.[12]

Seeking a director of the railway, the Provisional Government turned to one of the foreigners who had miraculously survived the war, Col. Francisco Wisner von Morgenstern. As first director of the railway under the new regime, he proposed exploitation of public lands to finance needed expenditures.[13] The Brazilians claimed to have spent £20,000 on equipment and repairs, a sum obviously beyond Paraguayan resources to repay. The Brazilian minister agreed to sell the improvements for this amount, which was to be paid in three installments with interest at 6 percent on the unpaid balance. Each time the notes, given in July, 1870, became due, the Paraguayan minister of foreign affairs requested an extension, always for the same reason: there was no money to meet the payment that was due. And each request was granted, with interest added to the principal. By November, 1872, Paraguay owed $111,091.48 gold. By this time Paraguay had floated a second loan in London, and the Jovellanos government asked its agent there, Gregorio Benites, to send money to be applied on the notes. José Falcón promised to pay as soon as the money arrived.[14] This pattern of postponement and promise to pay was repeated frequently, although the government did pay $f50,000 on the debt in 1873 and asked for another postponement on the balance.[15]

The railway, in the meantime, experienced many changes of directors. James Horrocks, an Englishman, tried his hand briefly in 1870. He managed to assemble a group of notables for an excursion to Paraguarí on June 13. With wood piled high on its tender, the locomotive puffed out of the San Francisco Station at 9:00 a.m. and triumphantly completed the 45-mile run seven hours later. Laconically, a survivor reported that "the engine traversed its appointed course with more or less speed."[16] Freight and passenger traffic yielded little revenue. On August 6, 1870, for example, two cars of wood, fifty-two bales of yerba, ten bags of tobacco, one horse, one cow, and one car of railway ties came into Asunción. From August 6 to 8, there were 122 paying passengers and 356 officials who rode free. There was no money for repairs, and even the spare rails were being stolen. One boat left Asunción with purloined rails as ballast.[17] These conditions were enough to discourage Horrocks, who gave way to Lt. Col. Robert A. Chodasiewicz, a Polish officer who had served the Brazilians, as manager late in 1870. Despite some improvements made by the new manager, the general opinion was that the best thing for Paraguay would be to sell its railway.[18]

The Paraguay Central Railway, despite its deplorable condition, apparently was a valuable asset. When completed to Villa Rica, it would link the capital with the principal interior city and provide a means for moving agricultural and forest products to the port. There were huge areas of public lands that could be granted to entrepreneurs sufficiently daring to risk their capital in rejuvenating the enterprise. The Paraguayan government could neither finance reconstruction and extension of the line nor buy the new rolling stock that would be required.

The Provisional Government, always in financial distress, offered the railway and other properties as security for foreign loans. This collateral did not interest Argentine bankers when José Díaz de Bedoya sought a loan in Buenos Aires in December, 1869.[19] More luck attended the efforts of Máximo Terrero in London. The railway figured prominently among the properties pledged as security for the loans of 1871 and 1872, and a large proportion of those loans was supposed to have gone for extending the railway and for building other lines. The proceeds enriched a few foreigners and Paraguayans but not Paraguay.

Desperately seeking operating funds for the government, Congress early in 1871 provided for lease (*enagenación*) of "the railway from Asunción to Villa Rica." Pending consummation of the project, all receipts from the railway were to be used for maintenance. An act of May, 1871, set the lease period at a minimum of fifty years, and still another law sought to interest foreign and native merchants in the project.[20] Luís Patri, who had become wealthy supplying the Brazilian army, countered in 1872 with an unaccepted proposal to build a railroad southward to Paso de Patria, the government to guarantee a definite income per kilometer. Congress also rejected an offer to construct a railway or a corduroy road between the small river port of Rosario north of Asunción to San Estanislao to the east.[21] Nothing came of this project.

Seeking to sell the railway in England, Jovellanos and Ferreira early in 1872 sent Sinforiano Alcorta to London with powers that conflicted with those given to Máximo Terrero. Alcorta signed contracts with unidentified persons in May for the sale of the existing railway, its extension to Villa Rica, and the construction of various public works. Alcorta pledged proceeds from the 1872 loan to fulfill Paraguay's commitments; but Terrero had signed contracts with Waring Brothers for repair of the existing line and for its extension to Villa Rica, and had also pledged proceeds of the 1872 loan to pay for the work. When the Warings asked Terrero what was going on, he could only plead ignorance of Alcorta's powers while protesting to Jovellanos that his own mission had been seriously compromised. Just what kind of a game Alcorta was playing was a mystery to Terrero, but he assured the Warings that their contracts were valid. Waring Brothers sent an engineer to inspect the railway,[22] but his report discouraged them from proceeding.

Members of Congress were not easily discouraged and became more generous as they tried to dispose of the railway. A law in January, 1874, sought to sell the railway but with very attractive perquisites for the buyer, who would be given ten years to complete the line to Villa Rica "and would receive one league of land on each side of the railway or its equivalent from public lands" for each league of the entire line.[23] The government would guarantee the buyer a return of 7 percent on £8,000 per mile of new line. By this time, Paraguay had floated the two large loans in London that would be serviced by proceeds from the sale of the railway.[24]

Still no buyer appeared with the capital and the daring to take over the railroad. So Congress made the offer still more attractive by including a very generous banking concession that might lure cautious investors. This caution was fully justified by bickering among the Allies, the plots of 1872, and revolts of 1873–1874 that kept the country in turmoil. Conditions in Paraguay were reported with commendable accuracy by the highly respected *Standard* and the *Weekly Standard*, published in Buenos Aires by the Mulhalls, who were convinced that only English capital and management could save the railway.[25]

Cándido Bareiro, sent to London to negotiate a settlement with holders of the 1871 and 1872 bonds, came home in 1876 with a proposal that included transfer of the railway to a mammoth English enterprise; but the bondholders and the Paraguayans both rejected the plan. "That any enterprisers, individually or in company, wanted to try their hands at Paraguayan railroading is testimony enough to human daring and optimism. Fortunes could be made in Paraguay but almost invariably casual observers and even experienced travelers allowed the lush vegetation, the tropical exuberance and vast expanses of unexploited lands to blind them to almost insuperable difficulties in the way of establishing firm foundations for economic progress."[26] There were, among the Paraguayan leaders, men who urged agricultural colonization, expansion of cattle raising, creation of a lumber industry, and more intensive exploitation of the yerbales. For all of these projects, which would create traffic for the railway, Paraguay lacked people, capital, and political stability. Until the withdrawal of Allied troops in 1876, Paraguayan politicians were far from being free agents. After evacuation, political control passed into the hands of men who were strongly influenced by English capitalists, both directly from London and indirectly through their houses in Buenos Aires. These capitalists could be expected to regard the Paraguay Central Railway as an interesting property to add to the Argentine railways, which they controlled.

After more than five years of efforts to sell the railway, Congress finally succeeded in attracting a buyer in 1877. By now the country, deeply in debt, was floundering in a financial morass caused by widespread graft, incompetent administration, laws that stifled commerce, inconvertible paper money, and certificates of indebtedness. Some relief could be obtained by trading the railway for at least part of these internal obligations and enough additional money to pay the Brazilians the £16,000 they claimed to have spent on the railway. An act of December 30, 1876, offered the railway for sale at the absurdly low price of $f1,000,000 in internal obligations and the £16,000 owed to

Brazil. In addition to other privileges, the buyer would receive a generous land grant of about 12,800 acres.[27] Luis Patri, partner of Juan de Freitas Travassos in Travassos, Patri y Cia, accepted the gamble. He acquired the $f1,000,000 in government obligations for about $88,000 gold and gave his note for the balance of $f88,792.[28]

Trying to make a quick profit, Patri on July 12, 1878, sold the railway to Henrique Christiano Fernando Röhe for $f450,000, payable in seven months. At that time the company still owed Paraguay $f88,-792.75, the note given on October 24, 1877. Röhe had great plans to extend the railway to Villa Rica and petitioned the minister of the interior for a concession of two miles of land on each side of the railway and promised to bring in 1,500 colonists by February 1, 1884, for which he was to receive one square league for each 55 colonists.[29] Nothing came of Röhe's schemes, so Travassos, Patri y Cía retained possession of the railway.

Patri made very little from his investment, although he did enjoy the privilege of a special car and liked to stop the train at will. Expenses were high in comparison with receipts, and necessary repairs consumed what little was left.[30] Patri continued to operate the railway until 1886, when he sold it back to the government. Paraguay then entered into a complicated arrangement with British capitalists that resulted in completion of the railway to Encarnación in 1911, but it was never a profitable enterprise. So it was that at the beginning of the Colorado era, one of the country's major assets had passed to private ownership. The government had succeeded in divesting itself of a railway it could not operate; but the railway, the London loans, banking, and public lands had become inextricably entangled in a manner that was to influence Paraguayan politics and economic life for many decades.

Fantastic Financing: The London Loans of 1871 and 1872

The London money market in the nineteenth century was truly a thieves' paradise. Here came unscrupulous but needy borrowers to contract with equally unscrupulous brokers to sell stocks and bonds to a public sometimes greedy, usually naive, generally ignorant. These investors and the citizens of borrowing countries were victims of thievery so flagrant as to excite wonder that laws could be filled with loopholes so wide as to permit "respectable" houses to execute their plans with impunity. Their major concern was to sell bonds at handsome profits; the buyers could watch out for themselves. Ultimately so many investors had been deceived that they organized the Council of Foreign Bondholders in London, and through this powerful organization exercised a restraining influence on the financial pirates while also recovering a part of their investments.

Desperately seeking financing to maintain his shadowy government, President Rivarola grasped the dazzling opportunity offered for floating a loan of £1,000,000 in London.[31] Just how the business got started has not been discovered, although a contemporary gave credit to a syndicate "of a stockbroker, a banker's clerk, a newspaper writer, and an adventurous Spaniard or a Spanish adventurer."[32] This group sent a commissioner, Charles H. Ohlsen, to Asunción, where he persuaded Rivarola to authorize a loan of £1,000,000 and probably suggested the appointment of Dr. Máximo Terrero, an Argentine merchant residing in London, as Paraguay's financial agent.[33] Properly questioning his government's solvency, President Rivarola sent Carlos Loizaga to Rio de Janeiro to ask the Brazilian government to guarantee the loan. The statesmen at Itamaraty were too wary to be caught in such a scheme, especially since Paraguay owed both war indemnities and private claims in amounts far greater than could be paid for many years, if ever.[34] However, the impression got out that Brazil had offered some sort of guarantee that made the bond issue something more than "a reckless and unpardonable venture."[35]

Arrangements for the 1871 loan were completed quickly. Terrero and Waring Brothers signed the agreement on November 21, 1871. The Warings undertook to issue £1,000,000 in 6 percent bonds; while the issue price was 80, the Warings were to pay Paraguay 64, which would yield £160,000 for the bankers. The bondholder would pay £80 for a £100 bond, thus anticipating annual interest of 7.5 percent and a handsome capital gain of 25 percent. Waring Brothers formed a syndicate with Baron Albert Grant of Grant Brothers & Co. and Samuel Laing, a member of Parliament.[36] The syndicate floated the loan through Robinson, Fleming & Co., who also served as agents for carrying out projects contemplated by the Paraguayan government.

Although the underwriters and managers made superficial inquiries about Paraguay, the prospectus issued by Robinson, Fleming & Co. contained such wild exaggerations that persons acquainted with the country were appalled. Equally amazing were the guarantees offered by Paraguay, which pledged all of its revenues and properties to service the loan. The prospectus valued public lands at £35,000,000 and public buildings at £400,000, and asserted that the public debt was only £213,335. No figure was put on the seventy-two kilometers of railway. Proceeds from the loan would pay the public debt, extend the railway from Paraguarí to Villa Rica, restore roads, develop resources, construct public works, and promote education. One-fifth of the face amount, or £200,000, would be retained in London to meet interest and principal payments for two years. Thus the purchasers were assured of having one-fourth of the purchase price returned within two years; but of that £200,000 interest payments would require £160,000, and £40,000 would be principal payments.[37]

The syndicate pushed the price of the bonds through phony purchases, and speculators ran the price to 97.5 on April 15, 1872, a little more than four months after the initial offering. Of the £800,000 brought in by the 1871 loan, one-half was shipped to Paraguay, where the arrival of the gold sovereigns provided a temptation too great for government officials to withstand. The syndicate made £128,465 on the deal, including yields above the issue price. After paying Robinson, Fleming & Co. £14,000 in commissions, the syndicate had a considerable sum to divide.[38]

Congress had no difficulty in allocating the $2,000,000 in gold; in fact, they proposed to spend $3,000,000 to pay the public debt, repair the railway, promote agriculture and education, and capitalize a national bank.[39] Almost none of the money went for these purposes. The minister of hacienda admitted to having received £394,940, which went for state expenses. What President Jovellanos and his ministers did not steal outright, they squandered on graft-yielding contracts. Close to events and in a position to know, José Segundo Decoud condemned the Jovellanos clique: one minister bought 20,000 head of oxen in Corrientes at $7 a head and instead of sturdy oxen got scrawny young steers and calves; with the price of corn at 25¢ per arroba, a minister bought 80,000 arrobas for $160,000 at a personal profit of $140,000; to promote education, $50,000 was spent for three cases of primers and a batch of pamphlets on how to acquire virility, all of which cost $1,000.[40] The graft, of course, went to government leaders and other key figures, among whom were Jovellanos, Benigno Ferreira, Eduardo Aramburú, Pedro Recalde, Carlos Loizaga, Francisco Soteras, and Gregorio Benites. As president of the senate, Juan Bautista Gill was in a strategic position to benefit. His fellow senators were convinced of his guilt in stealing public funds and expelled him from the Senate. One writer charged that

. . . it was Gill who had most control over funds from the first loan; being president of the Senate, no law could be approved authorizing the executive to make payments that required legislative sanction unless a good part be given to him, as happened with the payments that were made to the sutler don Gumersindo Coll and many others; that if don Pedro Recalde had lived, being Minister of Hacienda, he could have counted on no payment being authorized without this man first handing him the sum or sums that Gill demanded of him; that on one occasion he [Gill] said these exact words to him: "E moí cheve co-ápe mil onzas, jhae ereicó-catúne." ("Put here for me"—pointing out a table—"a thousand ounces of gold, and you can do what you want.") And so it happened.[41]

The Brazilian minister, a very capable observer, had no illusions: "The ministers were spending without consulting their colleagues, appropriating whatever they could through fake contracts, or making gifts capriciously to their friends."[42] No one thought of using some of the money to prepare for the "agricultural" emigrants then being sent from London.

The loan of 1871 was a fantastic piece of financing; the second loan in 1872 was incredible. Having shown the government what could be done, the London crowd sent their emissary, Charles H. Ohlsen, to Asunción with a proposal that Paraguay borrow £2,000,000 and to explain the claims being pressed against Paraguay. Terrero assured Rivarola that Paraguay could easily meet the payments as its prosperity increased and warned against prodigality in granting lands to private persons. While Ohlsen was enroute to Asunción, Jovellanos approved Terrero's handling of the 1871 loan and on January 28 appointed him as Paraguayan chargé in London. Congress approved the second loan on March 8, 1872, with an act that earmarked the money for very laudable purposes: public works, immigration and colonization of public lands, government owned steamers, and banks. The law gave Jovellanos power to appoint a committee in London to sell public lands, the proceeds to be used for servicing the debt.[43]

Ohlsen returned to London in May with the documents necessary for getting the second loan under way. Terrero was much concerned about Sinforiano Alcorta, who had arrived early in 1872 with instructions to sell the railway. Since Alcorta, an Argentine citizen, appeared to be working against Terrero, the London financiers were worried. Terrero managed somehow to keep Alcorta quiet for a while, but Robinson, Fleming & Co. decided to hold up further shipments of gold to Paraguay pending clarification of the government's intentions.[44]

With Paraguayan bonds from the first loan selling at a premium, the syndicate had no trouble in starting the second issue at 85, an improvement over the first loan. Again the agreement mortgaged the "general revenue, property taxes, imposts, landed estates, quarries, mines, houses, buildings, railways and property and especially hypothecating the customs duties of the Republic (subject only to the hypothecation of the Public Works Loan of 1871)."[45] The prospectus, issued on June 1, was another hymn of praise, quoting the act of March 7 to show what Paraguay would do with the money. Rather smugly Terrero reported "it is a brilliant operation that has left the financial circles stunned," since the second loan came only six months after the first. Prospects were bright despite strenuous opposition from *The Brazil and River Plate Mail*, which warned the public of Paraguay's huge war debts; but Terrero rejoined that there was no debt, since mixed commissions had not determined Paraguay's liability, and Brazil had entered no objections to the loan.[46] Privately, the Brazilian minister of foreign affairs agreed with opponents of the loans who insisted that Paraguay could not meet its obligations, "the more so since it appears not to have had the necessary scruples in the use of the first loan."[47]

The market for Latin American bonds crashed at the end of June when Honduras, Costa Rica, and Bolivia defaulted. Bonds of the second Paraguayan loan had been available for only a few days before this catastrophe, and only about one-fourth of the issue could be sold. Bonds with a face value of £562,000 were sold at 85, yielding £477,870. Of this sum, £410,406 was due Paraguay, leaving a balance of £67,464 for the underwriters.[48] Terrero advised vigorous measures to meet the emergency. Paraguay should organize the proposed Banco Nacional at once, promote immigration, and allocate proceeds from the yerba trade to service the bonds. The bank would provide funds to develop industry and promote immigration. Paraguay's iron resources should be explored with a view to exporting the mineral to England. The faithful and much traveled Ohlsen was returning to Paraguay for conferences in which he would urge actions agreed upon by the financiers. But weeks passed with no word from Paraguay. Terrero lacked facts to counter the wild rumors current in London; Sinforiano Alcorta was once more causing trouble and refused to listen to reason. One John Torrens was returning to Asunción, charged with describing the situation to Jovellanos. In the meantime, Paraguayans must never forget that the whole future of their country was linked to its credit.[49]

Unhappy with results of the second loan, Jovellanos sent Gregorio Benites to investigate the whole affair, settle the claims against Paraguay, and attempt an arrangement of the religious question with the Vatican. Brazil, in accordance with its policy of noninterference in Paraguay's affairs that did not affect the Empire, had no objections to this mission.[50] When he reached London in September, 1872, Benites found Terrero, Robinson, Fleming & Co., and the Warings in a defiant mood. They had no intention of sending any more money to Paraguay.[51] Benites relieved Terrero of his post as chargé, demanded an accounting from the Flemings, then went off to Paris, where he drew a draft for £15,000 against Terrero. There were no funds to meet this draft, so Terrero refused to honor it; on his return to London in November, Benites engaged Dr. Leone Levi as his lawyer,[52] and instructed him to file suit in Chancery to compel an accounting from the underwriters. Soon there was a welter of suits and countersuits involving Paraguay, the López agent Alfred Blyth, the heirs of Solano López, Robinson, Fleming & Co., and the Warings.[53]

Terrero felt himself besieged in London. The actions of Benites had caused alarm in financial circles, opposition to the emigration scheme increased in Buenos Aires and London, and legal entanglements tied up all funds. Nevertheless, the London junta proceeded with plans to sell Paraguayan lands and sent William Warden Morice, brother of a faithful employee of Carlos Antonio López, to explain matters to Jovellanos and to locate the lands to be sold. Then Benites removed Terrero as consul general, and Paraguay's credit plummeted. Terrero, his pride wounded and his plans frustrated, advised Jovellanos that the charges against Robinson, Fleming & Co. were baseless, Paraguay's credit would be rescued only if laws were passed to designate income from the yerbales to service the bonds, and more of the 1872 issue could then be sold. However, both Benites and Alcorta were showing letters from Jovellanos and Ferreira that greatly undermined Terrero's position and cast doubts upon his integrity. Terrero continued to give sound counsel, which Jovellanos ignored because it would have required wise use of funds already stolen by Paraguayan politicians. Hampered by Alcorta's activities, completely thwarted by Benites, and distrusted by Jovellanos, who apparently knew little of the complicated transactions with the underwriters, Terrero gradually faded from the scene.[54]

Benites finally came to an agreement with the Flemings on March 12, 1873, which led to his persecution by the Gill regime when he returned to Paraguay. The accounting showed £416,000 due Paraguay, with a balance of £239,687 after meeting various expenses. On April 10, 1873, Benites accepted £242,899 in stocks and bonds to settle both loans. He realized £249,617 from their sale.[55] Benites said he sent £125,000 to Paraguay, although the minister of hacienda reported having received only £100,000 gold in June, 1873.[56]

The revolt of mid-1873 coincided with arrival of the £100,000 in gold sovereigns. The evaporation of this sum was so marvelously fast that President Jovellanos requested Congress to authorize the sale at public auction of all state-owned property to extinguish the internal debt. Congress gave its consent on August 20. Editorially the administration's mouthpiece warned that the budget had to be balanced and turned to classification and sale of public lands to meet the crisis.[57]

There was no question as to what happened to the gold—Paraguayan officials stole it. Forgotten were the good intentions legislated for use of the sovereigns surrendered so readily by gullible buyers of Paraguayan bonds.

The loans of 1871 and 1872 were major disasters for a country struggling to survive. Venal politicians and London financiers profited. Not only was Paraguay's credit ruined but also the country eventually surrendered a huge area of public lands, 2,177,344 acres, to the Council of Foreign Bondholders. While this settlement, which resulted in creation of the Anglo-Paraguay Land and Cattle Company, did bring a major enterprise into the country, the treasury lost revenue that could have been gained from sale of the land. Paraguay might well have repudiated the debt, but no statesman of stature ever considered the possibility. Paradoxically, politicians might be thieves but they were honorable men!

The Search for People

Paraguay desperately needed people after the war, people to resettle her abandoned lands, to revitalize the processing of raw materials, to provide for the nation's internal needs, and to produce surpluses for the Uruguayan and Argentine markets. A prime need was for healthy young men and women, principally agriculturalists, to exploit the fertile lands, huge forests, and extensive yerbales.

The attempt to promote immigration was an integral part of plans to increase agricultural production, which might provide needed exports to trade for tools, machinery, drugs, cloth, and innumerable products that Paraguay could not produce. Many Paraguayans were fully aware of this connection. From Buenos Aires, Carlos Saguier in letter after letter urged the promotion of agriculture, which would yield great wealth to Paraguay. Never did he consider the natural disasters of locusts, droughts, ants, and floods, or the lack of transportation and internal markets. Like so many of his fellow intellectuals, he exhorted and urged, but others were to do the work. The Saguiers and their kind were above working the soil; to themselves they relegated the roles of manager, political leader, and professional. They would be *estancieros, hacendados*, financiers, lawyers, doctors—but not farmers. They were no different than people in similar social strata in all countries and at all times.

A few hundred immigrants made their way to Paraguay in the postwar decade, but many of them gave up the struggle against overwhelming difficulties. Brazilian soldiers who deserted to go native, adventurers of many nationalities, camp followers of the armies, settled in the country; but so many Paraguayans, in the postwar decade and later, emigrated to the Argentine provinces of Formosa, Chaco, Corrientes, and Misiones that they and their descendants came to form a large proportion of their population.

The young Liberals urged the Triumvirate to promote immigration. They had seen Europeans arriving in ever larger numbers in Buenos Aires and were anxious to divert a part of the stream to Paraguay. An editor commented enthusiastically on a proposal in 1870 to settle 2,000 Swiss families in an agricultural colony: "This is what we want, that a hundred thousand immigrants should come. Immigration for Paraguay is the synonym of liberty, happiness, greatness, etc. Immigration is perhaps the most powerful weapon against tyrants."[58] But the Swiss did not come. Two years later it was rumored that Eduardo Aramburú, minister of war and marine, had signed a contract with the government to colonize many immigrants on the Río Apa.[59]

Europe offered excellent prospects for attracting immigrants, and the London loans of 1871 and 1872 provided funds. The Paraguayan Congress approved plans for an agricultural colony in April, 1871,[60] and the proposal to use a portion of the loan proceeds to finance an emigration scheme appealed strongly to the London financiers, who were easily misled by the effusive propaganda of Colonel Wisner, chief of the Paraguayan Immigration Office in 1871. In describing Paraguay's resources, Wisner was completely unfettered by a fine regard for accuracy as he mixed fact and fancy until the country appeared to be an unravished Eden waiting to lavish fantastic rewards upon those who ventured to exploit its riches.[61] Interested also in extending the railway, the financiers appreciated the need for generating traffic by promoting agricultural production along its route.

Although rumors of emigration schemes appeared before the war's end, the first serious effort was that which brought nearly 900 "Lincolnshire farmers" to Paraguay in 1872 and 1873. Terrero, prime mover in the plan, first attempted to lure immigrants from Alsace-Lorraine. When this effort failed, he signed an agreement with Robinson, Fleming & Co. to send 1,000 emigrants to Paraguay.[62] Colonel Wisner, in the name of the government, promised many concessions to agricultural immigrants: 80,000 sq. yds. (about 162 acres) of land close to Asunción for each head of family, provisions, implements, free passage, free use of the railway for one year, and adequate medical facilities. Robinson, Fleming & Co. then issued a glowing prospectus that grossly misrepresented conditions in Paraguay.[63] One John William Billiatt became the manager of the prospective colony and at once began to recruit "farmers" from the streets of London. Alarmed by adverse reports from Buenos Aires, the British Foreign Office warned the public not to be deceived. Captain Henry Cavendish Archibald Angelo, who had been sent to Paraguay to evaluate the country's mineral resources for Waring Brothers, reported accurately that Paraguay was in a shambles. But Billiatt went ahead and soon had 888 men, women, and children ready for the great adventure. Billiatt, who accompanied the first group of emigrants, which sailed on September 30, carried a letter in which Terrero recommended him in the most flattering terms. Prayerfully Terrero invoked the protection of Heaven "for this enterprise which has been arranged with so much zeal and care, since if the results are fortunate the future of Paraguay is secure," and Jovellanos would have the immortal honor of having started the country toward taking the high place that it deserved among the world's nations. Terrero urged upon Jovellanos how important it was for the enterprise to succeed and so attract other settlers. Both Brazil and Argentina were encouraging immigration, and Paraguay must do the same.[64]

The "Lincolnshire farmers" included almost no skilled agriculturists, a fact that would have assured the colony's failure under the most favorable circumstances. To prepare for their arrival, the contractors employed an unsuccessful rancher, Walter R. Seymour, as resident manager. Seymour had plenty of experience at failure in various Argentine ventures. Expecting to find preparations well under way in Asunción, Seymour was astonished to discover that government officials pretended to know nothing about the proposed colony! However, they told him he could settle the immigrants on any available public land; at the same time they instructed Gregorio Benites in London to deal severely with the agents who had proceeded so hastily to send out the colonists.[65]

Preparations for reception of the immigrants, for moving them to their land, and for care until they could produce crops were very incomplete when the first contingent arrived in November, 1872. Jovellanos and his ministers were fully informed about the immigration plan. Ohlsen had reported to them in June, and Terrero's letters were explicit.[66] The last of three groups reached the unpromising land in February, 1873, and brought to 794 the number who were destined to suffer severe hardship at the two sites, Itapé near Villa Rica and Itá, thirty-seven kilometers southwest of Asunción. Captain Angelo and others gave Seymour a hand in managing the undisciplined, disillusioned, hungry, and angry travelers, to whom nothing could have been more strange than the subtropical misery into which they had been plunged. Stories of the disaster appeared in Buenos Aires and London papers before the colonies broke up and the survivors began to dribble into Asunción. There they found assistance from the Italian consul and José Militão Segovia, a Brazilian merchant, who kept them alive until they could be sent to Buenos Aires. The British minister, F. R. St. John, and concerned citizens in the port city raised money for their passage, and by November, 1873, most of the "Lincolnshire farmers" were in Buenos Aires.[67]

The failure of this first important attempt to establish an agricultural colony was assured by a complete lack of cooperation between Paraguayan officials and their London agents. Terrero had obligated the government to provide the colony with land and assistance when, in fact, it could offer nothing but land and had only the most hazy notion as to what land was available. The London agents had recruited hundreds of people entirely innocent of agriculture and generally unfit to face the hardships of pioneering in a country torn by revolution, occupied by foreign troops, and misgoverned, with magnificent disregard for the people's welfare, by a regime whose authority was nonexistent beyond the environs of Asunción. Since promotion of immigration was one of the principal activities to be supported by the loans of 1871 and 1872, Robinson, Fleming & Co. were fully justified in proceeding; they could not be excused for failure to exercise better control over the project, for not having prepared the way carefully in Paraguay, and, finally, for abandoning the colonists when the enterprise failed so miserably. Segovia in 1873 agreed to provide supplies worth $f59,198, bearing 2 percent monthly interest. His efforts to collect from the Paraguayan government were futile for many years. Benites agreed to recognize the claim when he was in London, and Juan Bautista Gill approved the agreement "because Segovia gave Gill several thousand pesos."[68]

The Lincolnshire fiasco did not discourage efforts to give Paraguay a people transfusion. The British minister to Argentina estimated that there were, in 1875, about 200,000 Paraguayans, two-thirds of them women who made themselves available with such reckless abandon that the birth rate was high. The postwar generation would not be economically productive until the 1880s, and in the meantime Paraguay must attract European immigrants, who would not come until good government, or at least stable government, put an end to turmoil. The failure of the French colony at Nuevo Burdeos (Villa Occidental) in 1854 and of the "Lincolnshire farmers" did not mean that Paraguay was no place for agricultural colonies. Intelligent farmers could succeed if peace prevailed and government assistance was real.[69]

Not more than twenty British subjects were in Paraguay in 1875, but one of them, Dr. William Stewart, was very active. As agent for one

John Alston, Stewart obtained a concession north of Concepción to grow coffee and sugar cane. Any private owners were to be compensated for their claims. Since future concessions, especially in the 1880s, were to follow the Alston grant closely, its terms are significant. The grant had a width of about seven leagues (2.69 miles per league) and a depth varying from two to five leagues in the department of Salvador. The Villa de Salvador had been abandoned because of Indian raids. The company agreed to plant 200,000 coffee trees and to put 200 hectares (494.2 acres) into sugar cane within five years, under penalty of losing the grant. For each 100 immigrants, the company would receive another square league. Goods needed in the enterprise would be free of import duties for three years; exports were exempt from duties for ten years, and no taxes could be levied on the property for twenty years. Alston himself came to Paraguay late in September, 1876, "to give impulse to an industrial enterprise" in Villa de Salvador, a ghost town of no importance.[70]

Another concession in the postwar decade went to George R. Usher, American vice-consul at Villa Rica, who received a princely grant of 36 square leagues in the delta of the Tebicuarí-mi and Tebicuaríguazú for planting sugar cane. Unlike the Alston grant, Usher's concession required a performance bond.[71] The Alston, Usher, and smaller grants caused a shortlived wave of optimism that private enterprise would rescue Paraguay. The government was bankrupt, unable to provide aid, and the London loans "had caused more damage than the long military occupation of five years!"[72] Still the time was not right for immigration; extensive colonization efforts were to be delayed a few more years and became a principal contribution of the first Colorado era.

The most important immigrant during the 1870s was the French botanist Benjamín Balanza (or Balansa), who arrived in Paraguay for a three-year scientific survey in 1874, left in 1877, and returned in 1878 for a nine-year stay. Apparently Balanza was a member of the Scientific Commission made up of several men sent by Waring Brothers at various times. Captain Angelo was one of the group. Balanza made surveys for the government, and his bill of $f7,400 was paid with national land, which he was to select. During the year of this arrangement, 1876, Balanza started the petit-grain oil industry at Yaguarón to use the massive crops of wild oranges. By August, 1883, he had three other factories, which soon produced the majority of the world supply.[73]

A few other immigrants who came during the postwar decade made lasting contributions to the nation. The Spaniard Victorino Abente y Lago gave impulse to the rebirth of poetry, and when he died in 1935 he left a literary legacy that guaranteed his permanent place in Paraguayan letters. Abente began his literary career with poems in *El Pueblo*, as did other foreigners who were editors, poets, and essayists. Teodoro Chacón, a Bolivian, also contributed to *El Pueblo* and in 1884 published an elementary text on agriculture.[74] Francisco Martínez, a Spaniard killed in the Molas revolt of 1877, edited *La Patria*. The sutlers Luís Patri and Juan de Freitas Travassos came with the Brazilian army and remained to become prominent entrepreneurs. There were many more, some of whom became progenitors of Paraguayan families and others who drifted away into oblivion.

9. Paraguayan Society
in the Postwar Decade

War is a great social catalyst from which neither victor nor vanquished can escape. In conflicts that result in catastrophic loss of life, the very foundations of society are seriously weakened. But, so long as a viable remnant of the old order remains, historical continuities are not completely destroyed and the opportunity exists for starting anew. These generalizations are especially applicable to Paraguay. Old families, some whose ancestors had come with founders of Asunción in 1537, were decimated and some disappeared entirely. Others, more fortunate, survived in the persons of those who had miraculously escaped death or who had been out of the country during the terrible conflict. They would become the rulers of Paraguay, not of a new Paraguay but of one in which profound changes were inevitable.

A new order of things was the vision of the young Liberals who, safe from the war, exhorted their fellow citizens with the cry of *Manos a la obra!* (Hands to the task!). There was much work to be done. New political institutions must be established, and they needed time to build a body of precedents, to gain respect and acceptance. Even while these new institutions were being created, as in the Constitution of 1870, old attitudes persisted. Tolerance of dissent, freedom of the press, and protection of political liberties enjoyed no more than feeble support during the post-López years. Very few men of any age with political experience survived the war, and among these few the moderates were almost non-existent. A new generation would have to be trained, hopefully imbued with ideas and convictions harmonious with the Paraguayan psyche.

A shattered economy must be restored. Immigrants must be sought to replace thousands of people destroyed by war. Paraguay had never been a haven for immigrants, and the disastrous result of the French

149

colony of Nuevo Burdeos (now Villa Hayes) under the elder López made European governments hesitant about endorsing new ventures. The fiasco of the "Lincolnshire farmers" was the only venture of its kind during the postwar decade, but in the 1880s agricultural colonies brought industrious immigrants who were to exert an exceptional influence on Paraguayan society.

The dictatorships of Francia and the López had held crime to a very low level, but after the war law enforcement disappeared in much of the country. Argentine troops maintained order in Villa Occidental and its immediate neighborhood, but Brazilians left a much poorer record in Asunción and its satellite villages. The postwar decade witnessed the worst outbreak of individual crime and revolts in more than four centuries of Paraguayan history.

Despite their poverty and uncertain tenure, postwar governments were ever mindful of the need to create an educational system. A few foreigners were attracted to the country, but most of the teachers were native Paraguayans, many of whom had been educated abroad. The best elementary and secondary schools developed in Asunción and Villa Rica, while village schools varied in quality from very poor to almost worthless.

Paraguay desperately needed a free and responsible press, a need still unmet at the end of a decade. However, the many newspapers that appeared provided outlets for literary efforts, and copies that have been preserved are invaluable sources of information. They reveal clearly that a decade was altogether too short a time for the solution of the many social problems that all but overwhelmed Paraguay.

The Church, a powerful institution in colonial Paraguay, was reduced to impotence by Francia and failed to regain much of its power under the López. Dominated by foreigners during the occupation, the Church also met opposition from the Liberals. The native clergy and Congress struggled to regain control and finally recovered the right to nominate their own bishop.

Health, Morality, and Crime

Aside from the physical condition of the country and the destruction of its economy, the most obvious effects of the war involved health and personal relationships. The population as a whole was unable to withstand diseases that had previously been kept under control. Undernourished and even starving people offered little resistance to gastrointestinal, pulmonary, venereal, and other infections. To prevent a smallpox epidemic, the Brazilians offered free vaccination,[1] but there was little they could do about other dread diseases. A group of Paraguayan prisoners of war, repatriated in 1870, started an epidemic of yellow fever that physicians diagnosed as "bilious icteroid." The death toll was heavy, several died on ships quarantined in the harbor, and fear of the disease drove many out of Asunción to seek safety in the country. To a survivor it seemed that "the hand of God is against poor Paraguay."[2] In this emergency early in 1871, the Junta de Higiene (Health Commission) ceased to function when its members resigned. President Rivarola fled to the country; Vice-President Cayo Miltos died.[3] The Buenos Aires *Standard* insisted that the disease was not yellow fever but a gastric epidemic and considered as trifling the daily death toll of twenty-five. Two years later, President Jovellanos made Humaitá a quarantine station to prevent yellow fever from being brought again to Asunción.[4]

Sanitary conditions were terrible. The city government lacked resources to organize essential services. "The town of Asunción," wrote one correspondent, "is still in a horribly filthy state, and is likely to remain so, until the energetic commander-in-chief pays it another visit."[5] People threw trash, garbage, and filthy water into the streets, undeterred by stern threats of heavy fines. Brazilian troops were notorious offenders, as they allowed huge garbage dumps to accumulate by their quarters. All of the filth from the Argentine hospital was carried to the street by a sewer that emptied into the Río Paraguay. In contrast, the Brazilian naval hospital was praised for its cleanliness.[6]

Disposal of the dead presented an annoying problem. Refugees not only died on roads leading to Asunción but also fell in the streets, victims of hunger and disease. With packs of hungry dogs roaming at will, removal of corpses was of paramount importance, yet the dead often lay for hours where they fell. Government carts did make daily rounds to pick up the bodies, but this was slow business. The streets were "immense foci of infection."[7]

Attempting to do something about health and sanitation, the Provisional Government appointed a Council of Medicine and Public Hygiene. If this council tried to do anything, it made little or no impact on the horrible conditions in Asunción. There were so few doctors in Asunción in 1871 that Brazil permitted three of its army doctors to serve on the council. Later governments continued to make gestures. President Gill in 1876 appointed another Commission of Public Hygiene with Dr. William Stewart as president. Such commissions made little progress, and years were to pass before sanitary conditions could be deemed acceptable.[8]

There were few professional people to serve Asunción immediately after the war, and interior towns and villages rarely saw a doctor or dentist. Most of the foreign physicians who had been with López were not available, for various reasons. Dr. William Stewart was more interested in mending his personal fortunes, although he did establish a thriving practice after 1880; Dr. Frederick Skinner died in an accident in 1872. Only a few other physicians can be identified with certainty.[9] One dentist, Dr. Rosa de Florencia, advertised in early issues of *La Regeneración* under the slogan: "Sacar no es curar; es destruir"—Pulling is not curing; it is destroying. Several doctors advertised their specialization in venereal and urinary diseases. A Portuguese doctor had "a remedy prepared by a practitioner [himself?] for infallible cure in a few days and without pain. Venereal and other cankers, as well as gonorrhea."[10] He could have had a land-office business if the people had been able to afford his services. Doctors did enjoy one privilege: together with soldiers on active duty, they were permitted to gallop their horses through the streets of Asunción, a concession denied to all others.[11] Many lawyers, a few engineers, several aspiring poets and others who sought fame through literature, foreign scientists, and the clergy rounded out the professional sector of the population. Among the lawyers one may note Dr. Facundo Machaín, the Uruguayan Dr. José Sienra Carranza, and Dr. Benjamín Aceval. Two who advertised as lawyers had names altogether too good to be true: Ynocencia Avaricia and Pedro Sietepartidas.[12] Humor was not dead in postwar Paraguay.

Shocking social conditions could be expected after the war. There was no police force of any consequence for several years, and Allied troops were a rowdy lot. Travelers in the suburbs of Asunción and in rural areas encountered "gangs of deserters and hungry Paraguayans.[13] Vagabonds and criminals roamed the streets, serious crimes occurred daily in Asunción, and rape was so common that no woman was safe without a strong male escort.[14] Child-stealing occurred frequently as kidnappers attempted to obtain ransom from distraught parents; but the result generally was to turn the children into "the streets and roads to starve and die."[15] Vandalism was common while there was anything left to smash or steal. Even street lamps were stolen. Indignantly an editor asked: "How long must we endure this condition, and how long will the perversion and vice of these creatures continue?"[16]

If one can believe the journalists, sexual morality had disappeared in postwar Paraguay. In rural areas there were supposedly "50 women for each man," while in Asunción the ratio was three to one. A horrified Juan José Decoud wrote that "the corruption of the masses is difficult to comprehend without seeing it." He urged easy marriage and the civil ceremony, a proposal that brought a protest from a group "of old women who have nothing to do except to finger their rosaries and kiss the feet of saints in the Church."[17] Marriage was not very popular, for personal dignity seems to have all but disappeared. Prostitution flourished among the large number of nearly naked people, most of them females, who roamed the streets. The Paraguayan male, once so industrious, became a loafer and bandit. Free love prevailed "in the plazas, streets, and meeting places."[18] This was no exaggeration:

> We call the attention of the Municipality to the scandal that occurs not only in the Market but in every place where there is a gathering of women, a scandal that consists in the immorality of men without modesty, who believe they have license to enjoy love in public places. There are even those who take a woman and scandalize everyone who sees them, without respect for the public or for morality.[19]

The situation must indeed have been one of unrestrained bestiality: "Men without modesty who are more like beasts than rational beings may be found, even in the corridors of the Church and of the cemetery, atrociously scandalizing even during the day to satiate their brutal passions."[20] More than 400 women were reported as living in squalor in the unfinished theater, which had become an immense brothel. Riotous orgies occurred nightly in more than a score of brothels, and an anti-Brazilian paper in Buenos Aires charged that Asunción had become "a brothel for the Brazilian army."[21] To blame this immorality on the Brazilians is to ignore Argentine culpability. Although there were relatively few Argentine troops stationed in Paraguay, they had their share of Paraguayan women. When the National Guard embarked for Buenos Aires, they took some 300 of their *paraguayitas* along.[22]

Truly, the Provisional Government had an immense task as it strove to curtail banditry, prostitution, and gambling. *La Regeneración* never tired of urging greater efforts, of providing remedies in the form of work, resettlement of families, public relief, and better policing. Although these deplorable conditions improved with the passing of time, there were still so many women without gainful occupation in 1873 that the chief of police ordered them to be collected and sent to rural areas. Another order required every citizen to have an identification card, which would show up vagrants, and unemployed persons were to be put to work on public projects.[23]

Moral laxity could be expected during the postwar period when Allied troops occupied the country. However, one should understand that nothing like a Puritan morality ever had prevailed in Paraguay.

The numbers of "natural" children were always high, and little if any stigma attached to such origins. The extraordinary surplus of women was in itself sufficient explanation for looseness in family ties. Perhaps a French writer was correct: "But the women saved Paraguay, since they bore nameless children, and that liberty of morals that they instinctively practiced in place of marriage . . . assured the continuance of the race."[24] When Benjamín Balanza, the French botanist, visited Asunción in 1877, he observed that there was one man for each twenty-eight women. The imbalance between males and females continued for many years, although by 1900 at least the numbers of each sex should have been about the same. A factor sometimes overlooked was the tendency in postwar years for males to seek employment in Argentina and Brazil. These emigrant workers, although they might return to Paraguay, generally were unmarried.

Paraguayans, like any other people, had their share of immoral men and women: but common law marriage, or pairing off in more or less permanent alliances, was never generally considered immoral. Priests from time to time inveighed against the practice, but these men of God frequently indulged in the same custom. The Paraguayan woman had an excellent reputation for her attachment to her man, "to whom she is rarely united by the sacred ties of marriage, and for her great sobriety of speech, her fastidious neatness, her industry and her intelligence."[25]

Security of life and property was precarious in postwar Paraguay. No reliable police force existed in the country; indeed, a civilian policeman was a rare sight. The police force in Asunción, a paramilitary organization, confronted a task of mammoth proportions with meager resources. No matter how often the press might deplore lawlessness, crimes of violence continued. Brazilian troops kept a degree of order by maintaining a guard under arms. Late in December, 1871, a riot developed in the port when police arrested a Portuguese sailor for attacking a Paraguayan woman. Such sexual attacks in full daylight and in plain view were so common that the arrest infuriated a gang of fifty sailors, among whom Italians and Portuguese (or Brazilians) were prominent. The mob marched on the office of Benigno Ferreira, captain of the port, and threatened to shoot him unless the sailor were released. The mob cut down the flagstaff, threw the flag into the street, and probably would have lynched Ferreira had not a Brazilian patrol charged the hoodlums. Loaded with irons, the ringleaders spent some time in jail.[26] Unable to depend on police protection, citizens who could afford the expense carried firearms; others were never without a knife. The chief of police tried to stop the practice by levying fines and confiscating the weapons,[27] an effort doomed to failure.

One would think that in Asunción, at least, a sound basis for order would have been established by the Brazilians if not the Paraguayans. But shortly after the last Brazilian troops had embarked for Mato Grosso in 1876, near anarchy prevailed in the capital. "Paraguay is in a state of complete social dissolution," the Brazilian chargé complained. "Not a day passes without serious crimes of every sort, which are committed with impunity because of complete lack of action by police."[28] Courts were inept and corrupt, arrested criminals generally went free, and nearly all murderers were found innocent. "Thefts, disorders, and murders occur with alarming continuity," *Los Debates* asserted.[29] While the press called for more severe measures to protect life and property, the Brazilian chargé wearied of reporting "the innumerable crimes that are daily perpetrated with impunity in this miserable country."[30]

That these conditions prevailed should have surprised no one. The court "system" existed merely in outline, and few judges had formal training in the law. Appointments to the highest court in the land, the Superior Tribunal of Justice, were dictated by political expediency, and the press frequently took it to task for neglecting its work.[31] Paraguay had developed no law codes of its own and took over the various Argentine codes with little variation. When an effort was made to prepare a civil code, the Congress ended by adopting the Argentine Civil Code, written by Dalmacio Vélez Sársfield in 1875. The Rural Code, promulgated on August 8, 1877, was more Paraguayan in origin,[32] but the Argentine Penal Code was adopted in 1880. This failure to develop its own codes continued to plague Paraguay into the next century and was one of the *infortunios* for which a legal expert severely condemned successive administrations.

Society and Diversion

Profound changes in Paraguayan society occurred as a result of the war. A very large percentage of troops were mestizos of various mixtures, and it is unlikely that there were many "pure-blooded" Indians in the armies of López. By 1864, when the war began, Guaraní blood had been thinned by *mestizaje*, or miscegenation. Military occupation may have intensified the negroid strain somewhat, since there were many Brazilian Negro troops. This was not a new strain in the Paraguayan people, for there had been Negroes in Paraguay throughout the colonial period and there were still a few hundred slaves in the country when the war began. Slavery was not abolished until the Provisional

Government issued the necessary decree in 1869, despite the law of 1842 which decreed "freedom of the womb" effective on January 1, 1843. A more ironical situation would be hard to find, in view of Paraguayan propaganda against the Brazilians because of slavery in the Empire. Although accustomed to racial mixture, Paraguayan women probably had few children as the result of liaisons with black Brazilian soldiers.[33]

Upper-class Paraguayans boasted of their *limpieza de sangre* (purity of blood), and the presence of some racial prejudice is indicated by the charge that Carlos Antonio López had Guaycurú blood. Many who were "pure" European, whatever that might mean, had fled from Paraguay before the war. Many Paraguayan women of the upper class were not so fortunate. Dr. William Stewart's wife, Venancia Triay Yegros, was one among many who were forced to leave Asunción and suffered great privation in the interior.[34] There was only a sprinkling of such fine women, but they played an important role in postwar Paraguayan society.

The lower-class Paraguayan women, especially when young, elicited admiring comments from foreign visitors. The common women of Villa Occidental may have had more Indian blood than those across the river. A traveler admired the jaunty walk of these barefoot women as they went for water, empty jars on their heads, enormous black cigars in their mouths, white rebozos contrasting sharply with bronze skin. Their principal garment was a white cotton chemise, "embroidered around the neck and at the top of the sleeves with black wool." Caught at the waist with a narrow belt or cord, the top of this garment served as a carryall for cigars, money, food, and various other articles. Some of the women had attractive figures, nearly all had beautiful teeth. Their high cheekbones, square chins, "big black eyes shaded by thick eyebrows, with hair as black as the wings of the raven," hardly met a Frenchman's standards of beauty, but he could appreciate a trim ankle and a well rounded bosom. Unencumbered by corsets or other articles of torture, young women quickly lost their lithe figures, a fate common to women everywhere. Consumption of tobacco was universal among the Paraguayans: "Not even nursing infants abstain from tobacco," Laurentian Forgues remarked, "and I even recall having seen a Guaraní woman, her small infant riding on her hip, attempting to appease the cries of the little fellow by putting between its lips, not the maternal breast, but the half chewed end of her vile cigar."[35]

An almost new set of social relationships had to be established in postwar Paraguay. Many of the old and honored families had been wiped out by the war; others had lost their wealth and with it their prestige and position; a few had survived, some in exile and some by various miracles in Paraguay itself. Until 1876, Brazilian troops occupied Asunción, and, for a time, Argentine forces shared occupation tasks with Brazilians in villages near the capital. These men would find entertainment somewhere, and what was left of the Paraguayan population could not avoid close relationships with the conquerors. That immorality was rife cannot be denied; but there is considerable evidence that Brazilian and Argentine soldiers were strongly attached to their half-Paraguayan offspring, and when they left the country many Paraguayan women went with them. Liaisons were not confined to the lower classes. Doña Rafaela, sister of Francisco Solano López, who had been widowed by her brother's command, married the Judge Advocate General, Dr. Milciades Augusto de Azevedo Pedra.[36]

The majority of Paraguayans chafed under the presence of Brazilian troops. Officially, relations were cordial, but this surface congeniality deceived no one. Brazilian ministers never really trusted their Paraguayan puppets, and none but officials participated in Brazilian festivities. To ask Paraguayans to observe Brazil's independence day, September 7, was expecting too much. Nevertheless, this was an annual occasion in Asunción. At the 1872 celebration of the Grito de Ypiranga, gaudy decorations smothered the Cathedral for the Te Deum observed in honor of the occasion. Paraguayan officials, foreign representatives, and Brazilian officers made up the crowd that welcomed Joaquim Maria Nascentes de Azambuja, who arrived late. Resplendent in white cashmere trousers and elaborately embroidered coat, and with white plumes waving from his tricorn, the Brazilian minister dismounted from his carriage, which had gotten stuck in the deep sand. The guard presented arms while the army and navy bands each struck up a different air. Undaunted by this frightful cacophony punctuated by fireworks and military commands, Azambuja strode majestically into the Cathedral, passed through the lines of welcoming dignitaries, and took his seat close to the choir. After the service, the Brazilian Rio Grande cavalry unit added smartness to the military review; and in the evening officers presented a theatrical performance, which was followed by the inevitable dance. In similar fashion the occupation forces celebrated Pedro II's birthday on December 2: Te Deum, parades, banquet, music, fireworks, and dance.[37]

Inevitably there were clashes between Brazilian soldiers and Paraguayans, some of which were violent. Murders occurred with alarming frequency, both in Asunción and the interior towns, with the score of dead Brazilians and Paraguayans appearing to be about even. These incidents, unimportant individually, in the broad picture had a cumulative effect that increased Paraguayan animosity. Argentine troops, most of whom were held at Villa Occidental, not only avoided these conflicts but also provided protection for refugees from across the river.

An almost constant stream of complaints poured in from Brazilians in the interior. So many crimes occurred that a Brazilian living in Villa Rica complained: "The rights and guarantees that the Constitution of the Republic bestows upon all of its inhabitants are a chimera for the Brazilians." Criminals escaped punishment because officials ignored their crimes, pleading lack of resources to punish them. More than 300 Brazilians living in Villa Rica, Caazapá, and Yuty feared that they would lose their investments.[38] The number of Brazilians seeking financial gain in the interior in 1872 is surprising, and Paraguayan resentment was to be expected. Elections were farcical, with government candidates always winning. Calling such officials barbarians, Azambuja described arbitrary confiscation of Brazilian property in Humaitá and Piribebuy, and complained that the freely roving Chaco Indians indiscriminately seized Paraguayans, Argentines, and Brazilians.[39]

Brazilian complaints were well founded. Paraguayan officials, needing horses, simply took them from Brazilian civilians. Despite orders from Asunción to let the horses alone, Paraguayans continued to provide themselves with mounts at the expense of the hated foreigner.[40] Brazilians were by no means innocent of transgressions. Paraguayans complained about Brazilian recruiting of their nationals, or accepting them for the army. Brazilians in turn complained that Paraguayans harbored numerous deserters who were living with native women.

Several prominent Brazilians had significant claims, which Paraguay generally ignored. Ricardo Antônio Mendes Gonçalves, who supposedly received £10,000 from Gregorio Benites for munitions, met constant frustration in his efforts to recover $f767,655.87 for supplies. José M. Segovia, who had helped the "Lincolnshire farmers" escape from Paraguay, vainly claimed $f49,680 for horses taken by the government or stolen by rebels.[41]

Despite the poverty, crime, disease, and resentment, that weighed so heavily on Paraguayan society, people did find a measure of entertainment. Asunción, much better off than interior towns, was far from being surfeited with opportunities for interesting diversion. Cockfights continued to be popular, Brazilian and Argentine officers occasionally staged amateur theatricals for their own amusement, and a few groups of players made the long trip from Buenos Aires and Montevideo; but Asunción was a drab place during the first years of occupation. The Sociedad Paraguaya, whose members have not been identified, staged a dance for foreigners late in September, 1869. Every woman, the reporter wrote gallantly, was queen of the ball. Dances celebrated the end of the war, the birthday of Pedro II, the founding of Asunción. Dances sometimes ended in brawls, as did one on Saturday, April 26, 1873, when a group of rowdy Paraguayans chased twenty Argentines through the streets to the Brazilian barracks, where the pursued found refuge.[42]

Argentine troops at Patiño-cué, a few kilometers to the east, organized the Teatro Nacional Argentino, which offered its second production in November, 1869. An orchestra entertained between acts. A company called El Alcázar Lírico played in Asunción in November and December, but its popularity suffered somewhat when Mme. Gooz Y Gattier added spice with a cancan performance that showed her legs freely and shocked the drama critic of La Regeneración. A charity performance on December 17 ended the stay of "La Gooz" and company. Nevertheless, the cancan was not forgotten. Less than a year later, a Madame Blanche appeared as a singer on a program that included an operetta and concluded with a bit of cancan. "Bravichimo!" was La Regeneración's reaction, apparently written by someone less prudish than the critic of "La Gooz." This performance was followed by a father-and-son team that presented various songs and acts, including "The head that speaks without a body," and ending with "The Fountain of Fire."[43]

Entertainment improved little over the next two years. The French traveler Laurentian Forgues watched a cockfight in a cleared spot in the woods, along with some fifty spectators who were "very excited by that horrible spectacle." Attending a Brazilian dance in Asunción, he met Paraguayan high society "composed exclusively of the families of higher officials." With less than Gallic gallantry he observed that "most of the women I am going to see tonight [September 12, 1872] in full dress had no more than a simple loin cloth to wear three years ago." The party was at one of Madame Lynch's old houses, probably the one that at present is part of the National University. Forgues was much impressed by Madame Lynch's taste in decoration, and even more so by the young women, whom he described as pretty, "astonishingly graceful and alluring," although their dresses were not cut low enough. He was also impressed by the mothers, who sat in their chairs,

> leaning against the walls, gaunt faces, long gray hair carelessly gathered on the top of the head by a comb. Wrapped rather than enveloped in their shawls of various somber colors, neither speaking nor moving, and appearing asleep; it is difficult to imagine anything more repulsive; these are the mothers. Now turn and look at these groups of brown-skinned young women with large black eyes and ebony hair and smiling lips who dance our European dances: these are the daughters.[44]

Still, living in Asunción was monotonous, "a long succession of matés, interrupted by meals, the siesta and cigars." Men simply vegetated: "The few Paraguayan men whom I know," Forgues observed, "raise idleness to the height of an institution; the women, on the contrary, are active."[45] This monotony, relieved by constant revolutionary plots, occasionally was broken by theater performances. To benefit victims of yellow fever in Montevideo, an ambitious performance graced the Teatro Nacional on May 16, 1873. Juan Risso directed the drama La cosecha del vicio (The wages of sin), with Señora Zacconide Musella and Señora Risso singing principal roles. Arthur Loreau, a piano teacher, played between acts.[46]

Rural areas were even less impressive than Asunción. People lived isolated from one another, doing little to increase opportunities for social intercourse. This isolation, because of a lack of roads or other means of transportation, was to continue for many decades. Where people escaped the war's desolation, they made their own entertainment. Vicente Fleytas, whose estancia near Villa Rica was so isolated by unbridged rivers that it escaped unscathed, was rich and apparently lacked for few of the rude comforts. When Forgues visited the place, Fleytas held a dance in his honor. Together they rode through huge virgin forests to deliver the invitations, which attracted seventy women and only four men! The guests brought their own chairs, and again Forgues observed that party dresses were cut higher than in France.[47]

The Press

Independent journalism began in Paraguay in October 1, 1869, with the first issue of La Regeneración. All newspapers published under the López had been official organs of the government. El Paraguayo Independiente (1845–1852) bore the slogan "Independencia o Muerte!" Then came El Semanario, published continuously until 1869, except for 1855–1857, when El Eco del Paraguay took its place. Two other papers, La Época and La Aurora, were student papers of slight importance. Several other journals appeared during the war as propaganda vehicles: Cabichuí, Cacique Lambaré, El Centinela, and La Estrella. Illustrated with interesting cartoons, written in Spanish and Guaraní, Cabichuí was the best of the four and an outstanding propaganda organ. Cacique Lambaré, written in almost uncorrupted Guaraní, was printed on caraguatá (wild pineapple) paper produced by Richard Friedrich Eberhard von Fischer Treuenfeld, one of the foreign technicians brought to Paraguay by Carlos Antonio López.[48]

More than a score of papers appeared in the postwar decade. There are no complete files, and only scattered copies of most have been preserved. All but one, the weekly *El Comercio* (1877–1880), were political, ephemeral, and polemical. Several ran out of funds or into official displeasure after a few numbers. Starting a paper was difficult and hazardous, even for those with the means; keeping it going was much more difficult. Freedom of the press was an ideal never realized under postwar governments, which forcibly closed opposition papers. Unwillingness to permit journalistic criticism is an attitude that has prevailed through most of Paraguay's history, with some notable exceptions in the late nineteenth century. Journalists, too, lacked a sense of responsibility to the public, a weakness by no means peculiar to Paraguay. The law did provide safeguards: there could be no anonymous newspapers, and each must have a responsible editor known to the public. Silva Paranhos and his successors must share some of the blame for failure to start a healthy press, since no paper could survive without Brazilian approval, and several presses suffered violent attacks by Brazilians or their thugs.[49] In a society as small and closely knit as was Asunción, anonymity was almost impossible, and although many columnists assumed pen names, these could not have concealed them from their contemporaries. Some of the papers attracted very capable writers, most of them young men. Political essays, editorials, and gleanings from the foreign press were standard fare, with frequent poems to brighten the pages.

Most interesting of all postwar papers was *La Regeneración*, begun by the Decouds on October 1, 1869. Col. Juan Francisco Decoud financed the paper, and the Provisional Government paid a monthly subsidy for printing official announcements. Silva Paranhos agreed to the enterprise provided it would support the Alliance, and Rivarola was anxious to have an official forum.[50] The war had not ended, and it would have been unthinkable for the Allies to have permitted complete freedom of the press.

Most of the young contributors to *La Regeneración* had spent their formative years in Argentina. Some of them as boys had seen the fall of Juan Manuel Rosas at Caseros in 1852 and had observed the schism between Buenos Aires and the provinces and between Bartolomé Mitre and Justo José de Urquiza, giants both, and the decisive battle of Pavón in 1861. They had read Mitre, Sarmiento, and Alberdi. Voltaire, Rousseau, Diderot, and other French and English writers had helped to shape their political ideology. They were unusually literate: some were poets, others essayists who wrote in polished Spanish, and all were skilled polemicists. For the most part, they were political virgins, unravished by experience in government, glowing with idealism, inspired by a missionary fervor. The five sons of Juan Francisco Decoud and

Doña Concepción Domecq de Decoud dominated, with Juan José and José Segundo as editors. Their brothers, Héctor Francisco, Diógenes, and Adolfo, were contributors, as were several other well educated young men.[51]

These writers analyzed Paraguay's needs accurately. Successive issues of *La Regeneración* explored forms of government, favored civil marriage, advocated separation of church and state, championed honesty in government, opposed standing armies, urged full political rights for women, and turned to immigration as a means of peopling the country with sober industrial and agricultural workers. To the new Paraguay, Adolfo Decoud sought to give a slogan: *"Manos a la obra, y el porvenir es nuestro!"* (Hands to the task, and the future is ours!).[52] Time after time in years to come, statesmen and publicists would invoke this slogan.

In his first editorial, Juan José Decoud declared war against López and all his works: "We shall fight Francisco S. López as the most monstrous incarnation of all despotism, crimes, and vices—we shall fight him on all possible fields until he disappears from the face of the earth, whose very bosom has been stained by the immense slime in which he has lived."[53] On the positive side, the paper would respect individual opinions, fight any tyrants, support the Alliance, and strive for democratic republican government: "Our lodestar is the happiness of Paraguay; our norm is the law, our party is the people, our flag is liberty and progress, our social science the education of the people, and the means we shall use is reasonable discussion in the serene world of principles." Returning to the anti-Lopizta theme, Decoud made certain of antagonizing a considerable number of Paraguayans: "Our continuous desire will be that all Paraguayans without exception fight López by all possible means, that each one be an intransigent enemy of that despot, that each free citizen be the terror of tyrants, and that the memory of that evil one be evoked only to condemn and to execrate him." In this vein, through verse and prose, *La Regeneración* boldly challenged the Lopiztas while stridently urging democracy for a country that had never known anything other than authoritarianism: "The tradition of blood that the tyrants and despots have left, the innocent immolated victims, are the living testament of the truth that presents itself now, as an example for the future and for raising the pedestal of the Fatherland and the temple of Democracy that unfortunately has never existed."[54] The columns of *La Regeneración* contained gossip and tidbits that would have been lost forever. "Casi-miro" turned frequently to satire, "Otelo" was more urbane, "Hassan" surpassed his fellows as a polemicist. To attract reader interest, advertisements often had such tricky heads as "Revolución en Buenos Aires!" "MADAMA LINCH," and "Resurrección de López."

A subsidiary of *La Regeneración* was the short-lived *La Luz*, a weekly that appeared on April 12, 1870. The combined circulation of the two was claimed as 800 with 4,000 readers. Another companion, *El Paraguay*, edited by Juan José Brizuela, began on May 21, 1870, and appeared three times a week before it folded on June 16. As spokesman for El Gran Club del Pueblo, it proposed to support truth, justice, responsible journalism, good government, individual rights, immigration, and good candidates, and to oppose evil.[55] Although it is easy to assume that Cándido Bareiro, unable to withstand *La Regeneración*'s attacks, directed Lopiztas in destroying the paper on September 23, 1870, one close to events and by no means friendly to Bareiro denied government responsibility.[56]

Bareiro and his followers in El Club del Pueblo wanted to start a rival paper. First it was necessary to obtain permission from Silva Paranhos and Rivarola, who agreed to the venture when assured that the journal would eschew the country's militant politics. Dr. Miguel Gallegos, head of the Argentine hospital and angel of the new venture, "a coarse and dull writer," was not cut out for journalism. Two colleagues were a fellow Argentine, Miguel Macías, who was a hot-tempered enthusiast, and Victorino Abente y Lago, a Spaniard who had a bright and witty style.[57] The first issue of *La Voz del Pueblo* appeared on March 31, 1870, with the best wishes of *La Regeneración*. Soon the two papers were engaged in a contest of vituperation as "Otelo," "Hassan," and "Casi-miro" crossed pens with "Saccam." The Lopizta priest, Fidel Maíz, and the young and brilliant Cayo Miltos were the best Paraguayan writers for *La Voz del Pueblo*. Juan Silvano Godoy was right when he charged that the paper was "directed for the most part by men foreign to the misfortunes of our country, perhaps paid by some exagent of the tyrant."[58] Brazilian thugs are accused of destroying the press of *La Voz del Pueblo*,[59] probably because of anti-Brazilian views expressed by its writers.

The Decouds, tireless in their journalistic efforts, also started *La Situación* and *La Ley* in October and November, 1870. These they followed with *La Opinión Pública*, ostensibly directed by Pedro N. Vera, on November 6; but this paper's attacks on President Rivarola caused a warning that no anonymous paper would be permitted.[60] Extremely embittered by the overthrow of the Liberals in the Convention of 1870 and feeling betrayed by the Brazilians, José Segundo Decoud and his friends used *La Opinión Pública* to attack the government without restraint. Tired of insults, such as the charge that he had stolen Madame

Lynch's furniture, President Rivarola closed the paper on November 20, 1870.[61] Seven issues had appeared.

The Rivarola and Jovellanos administrations had their own papers that would benefit from government printing. Rivarola could take comfort from reading *El Pueblo*, a triweekly begun on October 14, 1870, and edited by Miguel Macías. Among its contributors was the poet Victorino Abente y Lago, whose graceful work had embellished *La Voz del Pueblo*. After Macías had left for Buenos Aires, José de María and Francisco Martínez, both Spaniards, edited the paper, which changed drastically.[62] The Jovellanos government had the support of Paraguay's first daily, *Nación Paraguaya*, which began on December 18, 1872, and survived into 1874. Well printed and large, *Nación Paraguaya* carried many official announcements, proceedings of the Congress, and decrees and orders of courts, and provided readers with editorials defining the official position on current issues. After having crushed the second phase of the Bareiro-Caballero revolt in July, 1873, the government's mouthpiece reprimanded Argentine papers that charged that Paraguay continued to be the focus of tyranny in which personal liberty and individual guarantees were so many words. Modesty did not characterize its columns:

> The paternal government of Jovellanos which, almost from its inception, opened the ports of the fatherland to those exiled by former administrations, confided the direction of affairs to the energetic as well as intelligent hands of the young ministers Ferreira, Miranda, and Soteras, who had been making so much progress when the ill-omened rebellion broke out, bringing with it so many disasters, causing so many calamities, so many other crimes that they can be compared only with those that afflicted humanity in times of Tiberius, Caligula, and Nero.[63]

Whether describing the Te Deum celebrated to honor the victory over Caballero, or exuberantly welcoming the victors, restraint was never apparent in the paper's editorials. The only significant paper published outside of Asunción in the postwar decade was *El Guaireño* of Villa Rica, whose appearance in October, 1873, brought effusive praise from *Nación Paraguaya*.[64]

Several newspapers openly served the Empire. Probably the first was *Saudade*, an army organ published in 1869. Rio Branco had authorized payment of a subsidy to establish *El Derecho*, which suspended publication on October 21, 1872.[65] *El Progreso*, edited by Cándido Piquiló, appeared in April, 1873, and managed to get out twenty-five issues before President Jovellanos closed it on May 4. Another *El Derecho*, unique with its three wide columns, began publication in January,

1874,[66] and probably lasted less than a year. Piquiló reappeared as the editor of *A Gazeta Brazileira* in 1875, but his career was cut short when President Gill took exception to the paper's anti-administration policy.[67]

Attempts by opposition elements to keep a newspaper functioning were in general notably unsuccessful. *La República*, edited by Francisco Fernández, began publication on August 22, 1872, and stayed alive until June 7, 1873, when its last issue was a single sheet announcing its demise by government order. Ostensibly to serve the interests of foreigners, *El Fénix* began its uncertain career on May 9, 1873, probably edited by Cándido Piquiló, whose *El Progreso* had been closed on May 4. *El Fénix* ceased publication about the middle of June, to be followed on July 2, 1873, by *El Imparcial*, also edited by Piquiló, which survived into 1880.[68]

Journalists had a difficult time in the postwar decade and could survive only with some sort of subsidy. Official organs had the advantage of being paid to publish various government documents not only in their columns but also as pamphlets. Piquiló analyzed the situation correctly when he editorialized that public spirit was being extinguished, a frightful apathy had fallen over the people, "public opinion has died, and it would appear that this glacial indifferentism may be the precursor of greater evils." A true press did not exist: "There is not a periodical that dares to discuss the most vital interests related to actuality; and if anyone takes the initiative in any question it is to eulogize the acts of the government but never to condemn them with the severity of this writer, of the *Imparcial*." [69] Another Piquiló could have written the same thing with equal truth a hundred years later.

A paper with excellent promise was *La Reforma*, first edited by José Segundo Decoud, which appeared on July 1, 1875, and survived for a decade with various editors. Benjamín Aceval and Decoud published penetrating analyses of governmental actions in its columns. Less fortunate was *Los Debates*, begun by Adolfo Decoud on July 3, 1876, but which died in 1877.[70] As he had in *La Regeneración*, Decoud bemoaned the state of things in Paraguay, condemned the people's indolence, noted the theft of the London loans, and charged the government with responsibility for attracting foreign enterprise and immigrants.[71] The weekly *El Comercio*, begun in 1877 by Carlos Pisaca and edited by the Colombian Próspero Pereira Gamba, appears to have been the only paper concerned primarily with economic matters. By August, 1877, the Asunción press counted only three papers—*El Imparcial*, *La Reforma*, and *El Comercio*. José Segundo Decoud, editor of *La Reforma*, was a "virulent and traditional enemy of Brazil." [72]

Experience in the postwar decade was an accurate forecast of what lay in store for Paraguayan journalists. That papers should be partisan organs was to be expected, but their lack of restraint invited retaliation by the government. Only by refraining from criticism could an opposition organ expect to survive, and then it would fail to attract readers and the needed advertising. Although records are not available, it is apparent that newspapers could not pay their way. Many years were to elapse before Paraguayan journalism matured, but the threats of censorship and violent action against an opposition paper have never ceased.

Education

When the Allies occupied Asunción, the city was a cultural wasteland. There was no school, no academy of science, no libraries or bookstores, no museum. Public gardens, fountains, or even attractive plazas were nonexistent.[73] Paraguayans, well aware of this deficiency, moved with admirable determination toward a rebirth of a cultural life that Carlos Antonio López had done so much to invigorate.

Education in the postwar period presented an encouraging picture, highlighting the few efforts to keep alive an activity never very prominent. In view of the country's economic prostration, educational endeavors were surprisingly numerous. Men who led postwar governments, most of them in their twenties, were much concerned with promoting education. Numerous editorials appeared in the first newspapers championing schools and praising those who served as teachers. Both public and private schools appeared, but it is impossible to determine how much financial aid come from the perennially strapped national government. Financing was primarily a function of municipalities and patrons.

The first schools opened in Asunción early in November, 1869, under municipal auspices. The Escuela Central de Niñas (Central School for Girls), after a few false starts, opened on November 7 under the direction of Doña Asunción Escalada, niece of the Argentine teacher Juan Pedro Escalada, who had settled in Paraguay. Beautiful and brilliant, Doña Asunción wrote an article, which appeared in the first issue of *La Regeneración*, championing education for women. Silva Paranhos, the triumvirs, generals of the Allied armies, and Sinforiano Alcorta, president (mayor) of the Municipal Corporation of Asunción, graced the opening ceremonies with their presence.[74] The Escuela Municipal de Niños (Municipal School for Boys), under the direction of Francisco Valteti and his wife, Doña Cristina S. de Valteti, opened at the same time.[75] The curriculum in each school offered basic work in Spanish, arithmetic, geography, natural history, ethics, and domestic arts. Attendance initially was encouraging, considering "the poverty and misery in which the greater part of the Paraguayan population finds itself." [76] There were other elementary schools in San Lorenzo and Carapeguá; attendance at the four schools was 582 by the end of November, and the editor of *La Regeneración* observed: "A school is worth a hundred times more than a convent or chapel, where the parasites give themselves to eating and drinking, fanaticizing the public and making it stupid." [77]

This promising start caused the Triumvirate on March 7, 1870, to order *jefes políticos* (political leaders) in every department and the *comandantes* (commanders with military, police, and civilian powers) of the towns to establish one or more elementary schools. Education was compulsory. Preceptors, or teachers, were to be selected by the *jefe* in consultation with the parents and were to be paid monthly by them; fees for orphans were a charge against the national government. Apparently the only requirement that teachers must possess was the ability to read and write correctly. The decree required parents not to let their children be absent without good cause, and teachers had to report delinquents. Teachers must, as a rule, treat all students with consideration. No Guaraní could be spoken in the schools. Teachers must require children to be neat, "having hands, face, and the entire body clean, accustoming them to maintain moderation and honesty in all their acts, without allowing obscene gestures nor the use of obscene expressions and any kind of grossness." Teachers must inculcate religious principles. *Jefes políticos* must assiduously promote the schools, visit them monthly, hear examinations every three months, and report on all matters to the Ministry of Public Instruction.[78]

The order against using Guaraní reveals a social aberration among the young men in Asunción who were putting their hands to the task by attempting to erase as much as possible of the past. Although relatively few Guaraní Indians survived in eastern Paraguay, their language, much changed by Spanish influence, continued to be the language of the people. All Paraguayans spoke it, even the legionnaires who had been educated in Argentina. Such war journals as *Cabichuí* published many poems and other material in Guaraní; captions of cartoons in the Indian language, which missionaries had reduced to writing very early in the colonial period, made use of colloquialisms understood by all. Guaraní, despite efforts to repress its use, continued to flourish as an integral part of Paraguayan culture.[79]

Asunción set the example for establishing city schools by opening a Colegio Municipal (Municipal High School) on April 1, 1870, under the direction of Prof. Alejandro Vietinghoff. As in the elementary schools, the curriculum stressed mathematics, grammar, geography, history, religion, moral philosophy, and Spanish. English, German, Italian, Greek, and Latin were in the curriculum, although it is doubtful that all were taught. The typical school day began at 7:00 a.m. An hour each was given to writing and French, reading, and arithmetic. Pupils were released at 10:00 a.m. and returned at 2:00 p.m. for Spanish, English, and geography.[80] Although the school day was long, the midday break allowed plenty of time for a siesta.

Interior towns at least made an effort to provide elementary schools. Nearly every town, from Villa Rica to the small hamlets, had a school of sorts that operated sporadically. At Capilla Borjas, south of Villa Rica, there were 365 children in 1872, of whom 310 were orphans. The school enrolled 125 pupils. To meet the general shortage of teachers, Congress authorized the employment of foreigners "of recognized morality and intelligence." [81] Whatever their motives may have been, teachers were not lured by financial considerations. The 1873 national budget listed teachers' salaries at a range of $f21.50 to $f68 per month. Paid in depreciated paper, these salaries could not encourage qualified persons, native or foreign, to answer the call of "Manos a la obra!" Late in 1870, President Rivarola had appointed Jaime Sosa Escalada to reorganize the school system, and two years later President Jovellanos appointed a Council of Public Instruction, made up of Dr. Facundo Machaín, José Segundo Decoud, Jaime Sosa, and José C. Mano—young men all.[82] There were 350 schools in 1876, all admittedly deficient in materials and teachers, but schools nevertheless. Of these, 320 were for boys, 30 for girls. Of the 12,000 pupils, only 2,000 were girls.[83] "So long as we lack means for a radical reform," President Higinio Uriarte informed the Congress in 1878, "those establishments will always be of very little use because of the total lack of knowledge by the majority of the men who are in charge of them." [84]

There has been much confusion about the Colegio Nacional (National High School). The first school to bear that name opened on December 1, 1870, with an enrollment of 180.[85] The second secondary school was the Colegio Nacional de Segunda Enseñanza (National School of Secondary Education), which began in 1872 under Padre Luis Blaschère. This school continued until October 29, 1877, when its director, Dr. Facundo Machaín, was murdered in jail.[86]

Before the demise of the Colegio Nacional de Segunda Enseñanza, Congress on December 20, 1876, authorized creation of the Colegio Nacional de Enseñanza Superior (National School of Higher Education). Another law increased customs duties by 4 percent to provide funds,[87] and soon a commission was appointed to receive funds and carry out the project. There were unexpected delays. A member of the commission, Dr. Benjamín Aceval, was sent to the United States to represent Paraguay in the Chaco arbitration, and money collected for the Colegio was used to pay his expenses. Successful in pleading Paraguay's case, Aceval returned to a hero's welcome on March 25, 1879, but he had not forgotten the Colegio Nacional, which finally got underway when Aceval became its fourth director on April 30. The Colegio apparently had a good enrollment, since Congress approved the purchase of additional property to enlarge it in 1879.[88]

The last educational institution to be started in the postwar decade was the Seminario Conciliar (Conciliar Seminary) to train clergymen. The government appropriated $f2,000 to begin the project, which finally opened on April 4, 1880. A French Lazarist, Padre Julio C. Montagne, became director and served until 1921.[89] This institution exercised a salutary influence on the Church.

One of the amazing enterprises in 1869 was the effort to establish a public library. Jaime Sosa Escalada, Francisco Guanes, and the Decouds were all prime movers in the enterprise.[90] Through private donations the first public library in Paraguay came into being late in 1869 or early in 1870, and by October, 1871, there were 526 volumes in the collection, "the majority of which came from Sosa Escalada himself."[91] This small start was the beginning of the Biblioteca Nacional (National Library), an institution that has never had more than token support from the national government. Two Italian doctors poking around Asunción discovered the bones of a megatherium, which they donated to the nation. To house the fossils, President Gill in 1875 ordered a national museum to be added to the library and placed the combined institution under the direction of the Junta Económica Administrativa (Economic Administration Committee) of Asunción. More or less haphazard support was provided in 1881, when Congress authorized the president to make a monthly payment to the institution.[92]

The Church and the Religious Question

Religion and religious institutions were by no means thriving in the postwar decade. Anti-Jesuit feeling persisted from the colonial period, and the controversial role played by several clerics during the dictatorships of Francia and the two López could not be forgotten. The three dictators had forced priests to violate the secrecy of the confessional, until no one but a fool would confess to any but the most innocuous of faults. After having suffered cruel torture himself, Padre Fidel Maíz served Francisco Solano López as one of the judges of the infamous *tri-*

bunales de sangre (literally, "tribunals of blood"). Padre Gerónimo Becchis had been editor of the war journals *Cabichuí* and *La Estrella*, neither of which was noted for its Christian charity. Church buildings had suffered deterioration but not demolition during the war, and practically all vessels and ornaments had been stolen or removed for safe keeping.

Although organized religious observances were sporadic, the Christian tradition persisted despite the long subordination of church to state, systematic betrayal of the confessional, and worldly priests. The very observant Forgues noted, "There is not a single house that does not have its household deities, coarse images in wood of some saints who, enclosed in a glass case, are the object of incessant worship."[93] Churches in the country districts were reopened as soon as priests could be found to serve them. Priests assigned to Asunción's three churches— the Cathedral, San Roque, and Encarnación—celebrated mass regularly as a crushed but hopeful people sought solace in their holy religion. Even the Liberal intellectuals thought it proper to celebrate special occasions with a Te Deum in the Cathedral. When the Day of Assumption, August 15, came in 1873, the editor of *Nación Paraguaya* exulted in Paraguay's choice of the Mother of God as her patroness. Linking church and state, he called the observance "an act of national sovereignty." Whether that or merely a religious expression, it was good to mark the day by resting from daily labors and consecrating it with genuine rejoicing. Concluding with "Eternal glory to Mary full of grace! Eternal glory to sovereign and Christian Paraguay!" this official paper served notice that Paraguay would be independent in politics and religion. Here was the heart of the "religious question"—Paraguayans demanded religious independence and resented Brazilian control of the Church.

Priests were extremely unpopular with the young Liberals. While singling out Presbíteros Blas Ignacio Duarte and Gerónimo Becchis for special condemnation, *La Regeneración* charged that the Paraguayan clergy were corrupt supporters of despotism. Becchis denounced his tormentors from the pulpit, but the combined rhetoric of Bernardo Recalde, Juan Silvano Godoy, and Jaime Sosa Escalada painted him as a spy, traitor, jester and valet to Madame Lynch, and craven glorifier of López.[94]

Attempts by Jesuits and Capuchins to re-establish themselves in Paraguay were met by strong opposition from the noisy Liberals. *El Paraguay*, closely associated with *La Regeneración*, expressed its sorrow: "Poor Fatherland! Poor Paraguay!" Jesuits had caused Paraguay's colonial troubles, wrote the editor, and now were returning as missionaries and were living in Madame Lynch's house. Irrelevantly asking, "How many Indians do we have to convert?" the writer betrayed his ignorance by replying "None," and reminded his readers that the United States had converted more than a million Indians without a single Jesuit.[95] Jesuits and Capuchins were trying to start schools, an activity that infuriated one of the young firebrands:

> . . . these *black crows* are unworthy of anyone's protection, as much because their doctrines are those of regression and tyranny as because that evil race of men has been the cause of all our misfortunes.
>
> Why not protect and dignify the Paraguayan clergy in place of calling in obscure mercenaries whose only religion is worship of gold?
>
> The Paraguayan priests of our holy religion find themselves relegated to oblivion, while others now appear to educate the youth in the fatal doctrines of oppression and servilism.
>
> Out with them! [96]

This was a new tack for *La Regeneración* and revealed that the Liberals were not against religion, not opposed to all priests. The Brazilians had provided clergy to serve the Cathedral, and the few surviving native clergy found ready champions in the press. Five priests were elected as members of the Constitutional Convention in 1870, but Becchis and Duarte were not among them.

One of the main victims of the López fury was Bishop Manuel Antonio Palacios, who fell before a firing squad on December 21, 1868. Pius IX, understandably disturbed by this disrespect for his bishop, declared the Paraguayan diocese suffragan to Buenos Aires, and not until 1930 did the country regain its ecclesiastical independence. For ten years the "religious question" was a minor but persistent irritant in Paraguayan affairs. The question was not one of doctrine but of politics, and provisions of the Constitution of 1870 could not have pleased His Holiness. This charter, while recognizing Roman Catholicism as the country's official religion, decreed religious freedom for all inhabitants. Complete liberty in marriage, whether among Christians or non-Christians, followed in 1872, and justices of the peace were permitted to perform marriages.[97]

The focus of this tempest in a maté bowl was Padre Fidel Maíz, without whom there would have been much less to agitate souls over religious matters. The Paraguayan clergy, divided in their attitude toward Maíz, either supported him strongly or condemned him bitterly. Maíz had several counts against him. He had been excommunicated by Bishop Palacios, had contributed to the López war journals, had "refuted" the bull of Pius IX that made the Paraguayan diocese suffragan to Buenos Aires, had served as a judge on the *tribunales de sangre* that had condemned hundreds of Paraguayans and foreigners to death, and had functioned as a priest after having been forbidden to do so.

Fidel Maíz, priest, judge, author, teacher, and journalist, was a belligerent polemicist who loved to display his knowledge of Latin, the Bible, and the classics. No occasion found him lacking a relevant quotation from the classics or scripture. Born in 1833 at Arroyos y Esteros, Maíz died eighty-seven years later in the same community. An uncle, Padre Marco Antonio Maíz, had taught Fidel and Francisco Solano López in the same class. The elder López in 1859 had appointed Fidel· Maíz as the first head of the Seminario Conciliar, where he taught moral theology, religious oratory, and liturgy. Somehow, perhaps because of his brilliance, Maíz incurred the enmity of Bishop Palacios. This prelate, Maíz complained, had spies in the Seminario. Maíz had refused to baptize one of Madame Lynch's children at home, although he would have performed the sacrament in the Cathedral,[98] and so had probably infuriated the dictator's influential mistress.

The *via crucis* began for Maíz in 1863 when he was imprisoned and tried on the charge of heresy. Convicted and excommunicated, the unfortunate priest remained in prison, loaded with heavy fetters, until 1866. The dictator then intervened and gradually restored Maíz to favor. After having written a cringing confession of his sins, Maíz was favored with a López pardon and became a judge who heard the "confessions" of supposed conspirators. Bishop Palacios was one of the victims. Padre Maíz refused to repent his role in the torture and execution of hundreds of victims who could not possibly have conspired to overthrow the dictator. He disclaimed responsibility for the cruelty of the laws and did not admit his role in condemning Palacios. At the battle of Itá-Ybaté he commanded a battalion, and when the papal internuncio in Rio de Janeiro later charged that he had exterminated a regiment, Maíz replied that he was only doing his duty. Captured at Cerro Corá, he was taken to Rio de Janeiro, where he asked to be restored to his priestly functions. The apostolic delegate, Domingo Sanguini, had come to no opinion when Maíz accepted the chance to be repatriated.[99]

The confused political situation in Asunción was one from which Maíz could hardly have gained advantage. A chaplain of the Brazilian army, Padre Fidelis Maria de Avola, an Italian Capuchin, was acting vicar with the title of Vicario Foráneo Apostólico, with Padre Fortunato José de Sousa, another Brazilian chaplain, as secretary. Padre Fidelis informed Maíz that Sanguini had confirmed his suspension. Then Padre Blas Ignacio Duarte, priest of San Roque church, invited Maíz to preach on February 13, 1871, day of San Blas, patron saint of Paraguay.

Despite his suspension, Maíz delivered a fighting sermon in which he accused his enemies of being tyrants. Padre Fidelis had ordered a novena to Saint Cecilia "and a Pater Noster and Ave María for the lost soul of Father Maíz."[100] Sacrilege! Maíz cried, an inquisitorial auto-da-fé! President Rivarola attempted to cancel the exequatur of Padre Fidelis, but the resourceful Capuchin refused to be displaced until a successor was appointed by the Vatican. Then the administration paper, El Pueblo, entered the religious battle with an editorial scathingly denouncing the Capuchins:

> So far we do not know what mission these *good people* are performing in this capital; however, we see that they inhabit an excellent and comfortable government house, greatly needed for the Superior Tribunal of Justice; that they stretch out at their ease on luxurious benches; that they eat sumptuously and regularly; that they sleep in soft and voluptuous beds, and that in the morning hours and in the evening when the fresh breeze cools their bearded faces full of patriarchal gravity, they say mass, intone four responsories, pray a novena to San Roque that he free them from pestilence and sickness; but all this after previous pecuniary compensation by the faithful. . . . the Capuchins in Paraguay are doing nothing except usurping the rights of the national clergy and making the people more fanatical.[101]

El Pueblo, Rivarola's paper, steadily attacked Padre Fidelis, the Apostolic Vicar, who was an obvious target. The Brazilian military commander, General Guimarães, badly misinformed his superiors by saying there was no problem until El Pueblo began its anti-Capuchin campaign. Apparently he had not been reading La Regeneración and El Paraguay. Rio Branco indignantly called the attack on Padre Fidelis a major mistake by the Paraguayan government; neither the virtuous Capuchin nor Brazil deserved such treatment, and he warned Rivarola to mend his ways. The difficulty lay in the requirement of the constitution that the head of the church be a Paraguayan.[102] To obtain the appointment of Padre Manuel Vicente Moreno, a native of Limpio, was the principal purpose of the Benites mission to Rome in 1873. Brazilians opposed the Benites mission because its object was to get rid of Fidelis, but Pius IX approved the nomination of Padre Moreno to be administrator of the diocese of Paraguay.[103] The fortunes of Maíz improved at once. Moreno restored him to his duties and made him his secretary and successor as ad interim administrator before he died on May 31, 1874. This illegal appointment met with papal disapproval. Moreno had no power to appoint a successor and Maíz was out of favor until cleared of charges against him.[104]

The religious question now became more intense. The "very sadly notorious Padre Maíz" was a bad choice, the Brazilian minister observed, and warned Juan Bautista Gill, the president-designate, to be wary.[105] Gill promised to be on his guard, but he misled the Brazilian. Following Gill's orders, Higinio Uriarte, the Paraguayan envoy to St. James's and other courts, promised to do everything possible to put Maíz in the place the government wanted him to occupy, that is, the bishopric. To gain favorable action from the Pope, Uriarte must have "the pecuniary resources to overcome the difficulties that may be in the way."[106] President Jovellanos convened the Paraguayan clergy and asked for a list of three candidates for the bishopric. This group put Maíz at the head of the list, but Gill hoped that the Senate would disapprove and so extricate him from an uncomfortable position. Papal and Brazilian officials did not trust the domineering, rancorous, haughty priest; but Maíz had worked hard to secure Gill's election. Noting the executive's failure to take a positive stand, the Senate, succumbing to lobbying by Maíz and his partisans, approved the list and sent it to the president. After Gill's election had been verified, Jovellanos wisely left the problem to his successor. Maíz pressed for action, but Gill told him that, in view of the internuncio's opposition, his name could not be presented. Maíz then threatened to resign his ad interim position and withdraw to the country, a move that would leave the Paraguayan church headless and have serious consequences for the clergy. The cabinet finally decided that Maíz should continue in office until the government, "after a previous and confidential agreement with the Holy See," could persuade the clergy to put the Brazilian candidate at the head of the list. Becchis, who opposed Maíz, gave up the fight and went to Buenos Aires.[107]

Efforts to rehabilitate Maíz ended for the moment, and Jaime Sosa tried to solve the religious question by negotiation in Rio de Janeiro with the internuncio. Two matters had to be resolved—the rehabilitation of Fidel Maíz and appointment of a Paraguayan as bishop of Paraguay. Sosa failed in his attempt, but others continued the struggle. After many efforts, including a trip by Maíz to Rome, the errant priest was absolved of all charges against him but barred from any connection with administration of the diocese. The settlement with Rome provided that the Paraguayan church would be completely organized, a Paraguayan bishop would be appointed, and a seminary would be established.[108]

Peace had come to the Paraguayan church. The new administrator, Padre Dionisio Riveros, was growing old, and it was time that a Paraguayan bishop be named. The clergy met on April 30, 1879, and presented a list of three candidates to Congress. Heading the list was Padre Pedro Juan Aponte of Villa Rica. His name was sent to His Holiness as the Paraguayan nominee, and the Pope gave his approval. Before the president, the cabinet, the diplomatic corps, and other officials, Padre Aponte took the oath of loyalty to Paraguay on Saturday, October 13, and was consecrated the following day. Maíz, properly chastised, served briefly as priest of Encarnación parish in Asunción, then retired to Arroyos y Esteros, where he founded a primary school that he conducted for thirty years without pay. Bishop Aponte died in 1891, and eight years later his successor, Juan Sinforiano Bogarín, supported the plea of Maíz that the prohibition against his participating in diocesan affairs be lifted. Leo XIII approved on June 9, thus completing the rehabilitation of Padre Fidel Maíz.[109]

10. Jovellanos and the Plots of 1872–1873

Few periods in the history of postwar Paraguay were more critical than the years when Salvador Jovellanos was president. Argentina and Brazil continued their bitter rivalry, and only the good sense of a few men prevented an open rupture. There was an intense struggle for power among rival Paraguayan leaders. At this stage what were to become the principal parties had not emerged with unmistakable clarity. Lopiztas, legionnaires, Liberals—the terms were bandied about carelessly. Lopiztas became Liberals, Liberals became Colorados, and legionnaires joined Lopiztas to organize the Colorado Party. Convenience, not conviction, and selfish interest, not patriotism, determined political affiliation. While many still spoke scornfully of the legionnaires, twenty-three of them were charter members of the Colorado Party when it organized formally in 1887; indeed, two former legionnaires served as Colorado presidents before 1904. Lopizmo was a cult not formalized until 1904, when Juan Emiliano O'Leary and his young friends deliberately created it to promote Paraguayan patriotism. To call a political enemy a Lopizta in the 1870s was no more damaging than the counter-retort of *legionario*. What did matter was loyalty to Paraguay and resistance to demands for territorial cessions. Herein lies the key to the Brazilian attitude toward the revolts of 1872–1874. Ferreira, despite his admiration for Argentina, was adamant in his refusal to yield one inch of the Chaco north of the Río Bermejo. But the rebel leaders, Caballero and Bareiro, were willing to accept the Brazilian proposal that Argentina be given the Chaco Central between the Bermejo and the Pilcomayo, and in 1871 Bareiro was accused of being willing to give up all of the Chaco.

Each year of the postwar decade was crowded with events significant for Paraguay's future, but 1872 brought far more than the remnant of a country could encompass. The Cotegipe-Loizaga treaties, Gill's break with Jovellanos, floating the second London loan, the threat of war between Argentina and Brazil, and the struggle of the pro-Argentine party to control the Jovellanos government would have been enough to try the most skillful of statesmen. Further complications were added by the numerous plots that eventually led to the successful Bareiro-Caballero-Decoud coalition. A flurry of plots in 1872 preceded the first phase of the Bareiro-Caballero revolt in October. These plots multiplied after the departure of Cotegipe from Asunción in February. Individually insignificant, collectively they revealed the strength of the pro-Argentine party and the necessity for the Empire to send a skillful diplomat to follow Cotegipe, a diplomat who could exercise some control over events.

Rivals for Power

The central military figure in all of the 1872–1874 revolts was General Bernardino Caballero, a name with "eight golden syllables that ring with glory."[1] Born in the village of Ybicuí on March 20, 1839, his early years were unexceptional. He was a handsome youth, blond with clear blue eyes and endowed with a remarkable physique and a very unremarkable mind. His photograph as an adult in civilian clothes shows a full head of wavy hair, receding at the temples, that topped a high forehead. The tip of his aquiline nose was all but lost in a long curving mustache whose ends drooped into a medium beard that concealed the bow of his string tie. Drafted into military services at Cerro León in March, 1864, Caballero's rise to high command was meteoric in 1867. He is said to have come to the attention of López by means of his attractive sister, who became one of the dictator's mistresses.[2] He fought in many bloody battles during the war, including Itá-Ybaté, after which he protected the fleeing López by rearguard actions. When López was killed at Cerro Corá, Caballero was off on a foraging expedition. Had he been in camp, his fearlessness and devotion to López might have caused him to fight to the death. Instead, he became a prisoner of war.

Caballero's luck was simply phenomenal. He emerged unscathed from battles in which casualties were heavy, perhaps because he was careful not to expose himself, as an enemy has insisted. He participated in revolutionary movements and became the front man, if not the embodiment, of the dictatorial regime known as Caballerismo that held sway in Paraguay, often precariously, from 1880 to 1904. His political acumen has been vastly overrated, since it was Cándido Bareiro who laid the foundations for the Colorado Party and it was José Segundo Decoud, onetime legionnaire and dedicated Liberal, who became the philosopher and architect of the Colorado Party when it was formally organized. Caballero was a simple, barely literate man whose mental processes could easily encompass a tactical situation on the battlefield; but in the whirlpools and crosscurrents of Paraguayan politics he would have drowned quickly, as did Rivarola, had he not clung to Decoud as a lifesaver. These two men made a formidable combination. One's credulity is severely tried by the wild assertion that Caballero was a man of destiny whom López himself had marked for future greatness: "His destiny was to live, to be saved, to survive because he was the worker necessary for future reconstruction. Marshal López preserved him in the final hour because he had assigned this civil role to him, as cyclopean and heroic as that of the battles in which he had participated." [3] Another writer, a contemporary, pictures him as a bloody executioner. As a leader, "what he always did was to sacrifice his soldiers, leading them not to victory, because he never won a battle, but to a certain death." [4] But today, with the glorification of Francisco Solano López accomplished, Bernardino Caballero is honored as one of the great heroes of Paraguay, his remains resting in the Panteón Nacional.[5]

Salvador Jovellanos, who had succeeded Rivarola with the title of Vice-President in Exercise of the Executive Power, was a very weak, good natured man who was also probably very corrupt, "a man with nothing but a good address and pleasant manners to recommend him." [6] Because he was no threat to such ambitious politicians as Gill, Bareiro, and Ferreira, the vice-presidency under Rivarola had appeared to be a safe spot for him. He was by no means a cipher but was unable to inspire trust and confidence among his colleagues.

Far different was Benigno Ferreira. Born in Limpió near Asunción on February 13, 1846, he studied first in Paraguay and at the age of thirteen was sent to the prestigious Colegio Nacional in Concepción, Uruguay. Completing the course there, he went to Buenos Aires to study law. A charter member of the Asociación Paraguaya, Ferreira joined and left the Paraguayan Legion but served with General Wenceslao Paunero in the Argentine army, emerging with the rank of captain. Like many young exiles, he returned to Paraguay in 1869 and enjoyed political preferment. Unlike Juan Bautista Gill, Gregorio Benites, and Zacarías Jara, he was not among the 377 who signed a petition on January 30, 1869, asking that the Allies organize a corps of volunteers, a second legion, to fight López to the death. Sporting the usual mustache and beard, Ferreira's confident bearing and vigorous rhetoric made him a leader of the Liberals despite his youth. A principal editor of *La Regeneración*, he recognized the need to cooperate with the Allies while he fought their territorial demands with a vigor unmatched by his contemporaries. Captain of the port and commander of the 529 men who

formed the National Guard in Asunción, he had gone far for a young-
ster of twenty-three. Minister of war and marine in 1871 and of interior in 1873, it fell to Ferreira to suppress the Bareiro-Caballero revolts
of 1873. A grateful Jovellanos promoted him to the rank of colonel
major. One who knew Ferreira well, and disliked him equally well,
characterized him as a cold, practical, astute politician with well defined
objectives. Eliminated with Brazilian aid in March, 1874, Ferreira went
to Buenos Aires and won a law degree. He returned to Paraguay late
in 1894, became president of the Liberal Party in 1895, and later became president of the Superior Court. He led the revolt of 1904 that
overthrew Caballerismo and served as president from November 25,
1906, until he was overthrown by Albino Jara on July 2, 1908. He
spent the rest of his life in exile until his death in 1920. Ferreira was
brilliant and ruthless, a young man in a hurry, convinced that Paraguay needed him to save her territory from the Allies. He completely
overshadowed Jovellanos.[7]

The other two ministers during the Bareiro-Caballero revolts were
both Ferreira's creatures. Francisco Soteras, handling Hacienda and
other portfolios from time to time, was known as "a notorious robber."
José del Rosario Miranda, minister of foreign affairs and of war and
marine, was "a quiet gentlemanly man with fair capacity and nothing
particularly remarkable about him."[8] Although Ferreira dominated
the government, his tenure would last only so long as he was useful to
Brazil. The Empire was not ready to jettison Ferreira in mid-1873 despite his anti-Brazilian stance, since it was widely believed that his
chief rival, Bareiro, would surrender the Chaco to Argentina had he
the opportunity. Ferreira would never betray Paraguay's best interests,
despite his having been called "the traitor of 65, the despot of 73."[9]

Cándido Bareiro, faithful lieutenant of López, had been a diplomat
and propagandist in England and France.[10] When he returned to Asunción in February, 1869, Bareiro at once became leader of the Lopiztas
with full cooperation from Cayo Miltos, Antonio Jara, and the priests
Fidel Maíz, Gerónimo Becchis, and Blas Ignacio Duarte. Capable and
ruthless, he attracted such military men as Caballero, Patricio Escobar,
and Germán Serrano, all of whom were far inferior to him in intellect,
education, and political sophistication. Higinio Uriarte and Gregorio
Benites, prominent civilians, were his followers when it suited them.
An English resident observed: "He is a man of some capacity, but very
ambitious and extremely proud and reserved; I should consider him
the most capable man in Paraguay to take a leading position, but as
President he would be most despotic, and his character for temperance
and sobriety does not stand too high."[11] Bareiro had few friends, and

Juan Bautista Gill, eventually to profit most from the Bareiro-Caballero revolts, was not one of them. For the Brazilians to impose Gill on the country as president following Jovellanos was a hard blow to Bareiro; but, when Gill was assassinated in 1877, Bareiro was clearly the man to succeed to the presidency.

José Segundo Decoud, urbane, sophisticated, and brilliant, was born in Asunción in 1848. As a youth he had the advantage of being tutored by the Spaniard Ildefonso Antonio Bermejo, who was one of the "civilizers" brought to Paraguay by Carlos Antonio López. At the age of twelve he attended the Colegio Nacional in Concepción, Uruguay, and then moved on to the Seminario Anglo-Argentino of Buenos Aires, where he studied philosophy. In the port city he quickly moved into the circle of the Asociación Paraguaya and then served for a time in the Argentine army. When he learned the terms of the "secret" Treaty of the Triple Alliance, he withdrew from military service and resumed his studies in Buenos Aires. He returned to Asunción in 1869, served the Triumvirate and the Constitutional Convention, and championed liberal causes. His swing to conservatism in the late 1870s may have been caused by disenchantment wtih the bickering Liberals; more sympathetic toward Argentina than toward Brazil, he would sacrifice his country's interests to no foreign power.

Decoud was an excellent student, a linguist at home in Spanish, French, English, and Latin. Editor or director of *La Regeneración, La Opinión Pública*, and *La Reforma*, he also contributed many essays to other papers. Although not a good writer, he was author of several books and reports to Congress. Translator, student of government and economics, he was the brains of the Colorado Party even before its formal organization. No matter how scathingly *El Látigo* and other papers of the late nineteenth century might lampoon him in editorials and cartoons, Decoud continued his service to Paraguay until his last illness, which caused his death in 1909.[12]

This Liberal turned conservative presents a fine study in contrasts. Here was a man who enlisted in the Legion to fight the tyrant, who raised his voice fearlessly for liberal principles, who joined in the struggle for a genuinely democratic constitution—and who readily went over to the reactionaries, encouraged Caballero in violating the Constitution of 1870, and became the stalwart defender of principles he abhorred as a youth. Decoud was a turncoat, an opportunist, who changed sides so frequently in the 1870s that one wonders how any one of the principal politicians could have trusted him. Decoud served Rivarola, Jovellanos, Gill, Uriarte, and Bareiro. He was with Caballero in the revolt of 1873; when it failed, Decoud fled to Corrientes and attacked the rebel leaders in a manifesto. Through General Guimarães he obtained a pardon and accepted an appointment to the Superior Tribunal. Here the successful revolt of 1874 caught him. No one had been more critical of Juan Bautista Gill; but, when Gill returned from exile, Decoud hastened to praise him. Gill assigned to Decoud the role of defending him in the press. His anonymous critics pronounced a harsh judgment:

> José S. Decoud as a man is perfidious; as a friend, disloyal; as a partisan, he is a turncoat, and as a public man he is venal and fickle and his ambition is fathomless. To him all means are good and he is capable of every villainy. . . . He defended Rivarola only to fight him later. He fought Jovellanos, Bareiro, Gill and the lackeys of López, . . . only to make obeisance to them later, praising and exalting them.[13]

The motives of the revolutionary leaders were complex. Each protested his patriotism, his conviction that Paraguay needed his peculiar skills and talents; each proclaimed the faithlessness of the *situacionistas* (office holders). No leader, from Rivarola to Bareiro, had any doubts about his own ability to guide Paraguay toward a better future. These convictions command wonder if not credence, for those who protested them were willing to risk their lives in an effort to seize power. The cynical view that political control opened the way to personal wealth through peculiar opportunities may be accepted without serious challenge. Presidential access to the public treasury had ever been the norm in Paraguay's short history as an independent nation, although Francia probably had been scrupulously honest. No matter how much the revolutionists accused the incumbent party of looting the treasury, they had no intention of foregoing that prize of successful rebellion. But to say that this was the major motive for revolution is to deny the validity, the credibility, of aims stated in calls for support in various manifestoes. The preferments of high office included access to opportunities for personal gain, and however limited such opportunities were in the postwar decade, they were relatively important. Nevertheless, who can say that Bareiro, Gill, and Caballero were not sincere? That their own contemporaries challenged this sincerity is not a valid counter-argument: such challenges were and continue to be part of the political game as played in Paraguay. The seeker after high office wanted the totality of political power, and attracted supporters to the degree that he could persuade others of his probability of success. Many of those supporters viewed themselves as eventual heirs to a power that would be easier to seize provided they subordinated their own ambitions for a time. In doing so they were deceiving no one, for the revolutionary leader, however visionary he may have been, was wise in the ways of politics. And, despite the condemnation of all parties, revolution definitely was accepted as a valid political process.

Prelude to Rebellion—the Plots of 1872

Trouble was brewing for Jovellanos in Corrientes, where the Tacuaral refugees had gathered, assured of Argentine benevolence. Rumors that Caballero and other leaders had a force of 400 men preparing an invasion were circulating in Asunción a few days after Cotegipe left on February 17, 1872. A vessel, the *Pampa*, was supposedly leaving Buenos Aires with arms for the rebels. Cotegipe suggested that a boat stationed above Corrientes would suffice to discourage an invasion. Although Argentina would not use force, the Correntinos probably would provide aid for such men as Serrano and Caballero. The Paraguayan government should be careful, very careful.[14] Brizuela was certain that a coup of some sort was in the making as Serrano, Godoy, José Segundo Decoud, and several others returned unmolested to Asunción late in February and early in March, and were said to be waiting for Caballero and Padre Duarte. Their presence gave added strength to the opposition. Jovellanos assured Brizuela that none of them, except perhaps the more moderate, would be given positions. If Jovellanos held fast, the country would be safe; if not, the pro-Argentine opposition would take over. Gill was needed in the country to prevent their triumph. Argentina was preparing to send a minister to Asunción, and if Gill was not sent back soon, Brizuela foresaw a serious reversal for the Brazilian party.[15]

The anti-Brazilian plots of April and May, 1872, focused on attempts to assassinate Jovellanos, Ferreira, Brizuela, and others. Siesta time was hardly over on April 18 when the agitated chief executive called on General Guimarães. A very trustworthy person had exposed a plan attributed to Bareiro and Rivarola to murder Jovellanos and Ferreira that very day and to imprison others on April 19. Taking no chances, Guimarães kept armed patrols in the streets; Colonels Serrano and Fernández went to jail on April 22, while Jovellanos sent men to arrest Rivarola, who joined his fellow conspirators on April 25. Irritated by this aborted plot, Cotegipe urged Jovellanos to deal sternly with the opposition. Paraguayans apparently "failed to appreciate the precarious condition of their country, which could make no progress without external peace and internal tranquillity."[16]

Ferreira was using every means at his command to dominate the Congress, as Brizuela discovered when he returned from Montevideo on May 13. Cirilo Solalinde and José Mateo Collar, who had opposed the Cotegipe-Loizaga treaties, controlled the Senate. A week later,

Senator Guillermo Federico Báez introduced a resolution to expel Brizuela, charging him with a trumped-up criminal act. Brizuela complained to Guimarães, who told Jovellanos to stop the intrigue. Then Brizuela counterattacked. Báez was an Argentine citizen never naturalized in Paraguay, so the Senate expelled him. Solalinde, infuriated by this turn, offered his resignation, which was accepted unanimously. "So this comedy ended," Brizuela reported, "resulting in the defeat of Brazil's enemies and the complete triumph of her friends, leaving Palacios and me master of the Senate and with a majority that we shall take care to maintain firmly." He still believed Jovellanos to be "an excellent person but weak and tolerant of everyone."[17]

A major reason for the frenetic political activity in Asunción in 1872 was the desire of politicians to get their hands on some of the gold that had arrived from the first London loan and was expected from the second loan. The first shipment of £100,000 had reached Asunción in mid-February, 1872. Gill was imprisoned on March 8, so he had no chance to participate in disposing of the rest of the loan, some £300,-000, that came in July. The corrupting influence was apparent to Brizuela: "The loan has been an evil for the country, corruption and immorality is [sic] at its height, and the loan, without a third of it having arrived yet at Buenos Aires, has already disappeared with no one knowing what happened to it."[18]

Brizuela's control over the Senate was very uncertain, and he feared that Argentine partisans would triumph. Pedro Recalde as minister of hacienda was a key figure in handling the vanished loan money, and now was a candidate for the Senate seat vacated by Báez. He could, Brizuela knew, buy enough votes to win the election. Recalde would strengthen Ferreira and the Argentine party. To counteract the growing power of Ferreira, Brizuela called his friends to meet in his home on June 6 to form a political club. While persuading Jovellanos that this was a plot against the government, the Ferreira circle also formed a club. Since Miguel Gallegos and Guillermo Federico Báez, both Argentines, joined with José Segundo Decoud, Facundo Machaín, Juan Silvano Godoy, and other friends of Argentina, this was definitely an anti-Brazilian move.[19]

The Rivarolas were the most likely suspects in a loosely contrived plot to get rid of Brazil's partisans and to dispose of Jovellanos. Two poncho-clad ruffians attacked Brizuela on the night of June 10. Despite his shouts, a policeman stationed nearby made no move to help the victim, who was rescued by his neighbors. Other known friends of Brazil were also mauled by thugs. Believing that Jovellanos was responsible, Brizuela enlisted the support of Guimarães and Mendes

Totta for a visit to the vice-president. Jovellanos, protesting no knowledge of the assault, ordered the policeman to be arrested and started a search for the attackers. Brizuela and his friends then accused Ferreira with having ordered the beatings, but Ferreira replied scornfully that "if he had any complaints about Brizuela, he would confront him man to man and never resort to treachery." Brizuela and Palacios warned the Brazilian commanders that the government was under Argentine influence; Jovellanos and Ferreira protested mightily that Brizuela's suspicions were unfounded, that they were the ones most in accord with Brazil's policy. Guimarães had to agree that this did appear to be the case, but he could not vouch for the Paraguayans, who would not be friendly with anyone unless it suited their own interest.[20]

Political confusion in Paraguay and apparently increasing Argentine influence required the presence of a skilled diplomat. Guimarães was a good soldier but could not cope with the complicated situation that had developed after Cotegipe's departure. To fill the important Paraguayan post, the Brazilian Foreign Office appointed Joaquim Maria Nascentes de Azambuja in June, 1872. Enroute to his post, Azambuja laid over in Buenos Aires for a few days, where Juan Bautista Gill, anxious to end his galling exile, asked the minister to take him along so that he might see his family and look after personal interests. He promised to take no part in public affairs. Since the Brazilian minister in Buenos Aires had no objection, Azambuja was willing but warned Gill he would be on his own. However, he would try to persuade Jovellanos not to be harsh with Gill, upon whose aid the Empire could depend in an emergency. Correia advised caution in dealing with Gill and instructed Azambuja to determine Paraguayan reaction before doing anything.[21] This reaction was easy to obtain, since Gregorio Benites, on his way to London to investigate the shady loan transaction of 1871, opposed Gill's return. At the same time, La Prensa of Buenos Aires charged that a plot against Jovellanos was under way. Regretfully Azambuja told Gill to stay in Buenos Aires, where he would be useful in breaking up anti-Brazilian plots.[22]

If Azambuja found the Paraguayan weather pleasant when he arrived in Asunción on August 3, the political climate was far less to his liking. He assured his superiors that he would proceed "with moderation, but with firmness and solicitude." In his first conference with Jovellanos, he urged conciliation with Bolivia and arbitration with Argentina. He found Brazil's position anything but secure, the Paraguayans not to be trusted, and politicians out to steal all they could for themselves regardless of their country's fate. President Jovellanos, married to an Argentine, he regarded as a necessary evil; Rivarola, out of office but very ambitious, was an enemy of Brazil; Congress, disliking the boundary commission, was hostile. The best friends of the Empire were Miguel Palacios, president of the Senate, Brizuela, and the exiled Gill. Higinio Uriarte, president of the Chamber of Deputies, pretended to favor Brazil but could not be trusted. "One cannot count on Paraguayan loyalty," Azambuja observed, and recommended that the armed forces be alert.[23]

The principal task facing the Brazilian minister during the 1872–1874 plotting was that of deciding which of the Paraguayan politicians should have the support of the Empire, since he could not avoid being involved in the machinations of rebels and *situacionistas*. Azambuja, after all, was the most powerful man in Paraguay, with land and naval forces at his command to enforce his will but restrained by the Empire's policy of avoiding an open break with Argentina. Azambuja was not opposed to revolutions provided the victors remained pro-Brazilian in sentiment. As events unfolded, he became increasingly cool toward the Jovellanos regime.

After two weeks in Asunción, the Brazilian envoy was completely cynical. He identified Brizuela, Palacios, Uriarte, and Gill as leaders of the Brazilian faction, but each was working for his own interest. Everything was in a profound mess among a people who, Azambuja asserted, lacked the intelligence necessary to organize their national life. The men most favorable to Brazil during Cotegipe's mission were out of favor. Relatives of Jovellanos ran the courts, and the Macháin clan, Azambuja discovered, could not be counted as friendly. Ferreira dominated the government and had support from the Macháins, Francisco Guanes, and the Decouds. Ferreira and Aramburú stoutly resisted efforts to get Brizuela and Palacios into the cabinet. The expected arrival of funds from the second London loan would have some effect on the men now out of power! As a result of the first loan, Recalde, Brizuela, Gill and Palacios had all become wealthy:

> Pedro Recalde, who had nothing before being Minister of Hacienda, today ostentatiously displays his wealth. Brizuela maintains a fine house in Montevideo; Gill ordered 70 crates of furniture that entered here recently without paying duty, and now is trying to buy a house for some thousand ounces [about $16,000 gold]; Palacios, as President of the Senate, also carried out a good deal with the sum that was ordered paid, with the consent of Congress, to a Señor [Gumercindo] Coll, in the amount of 240,000 patacones.[24]

From this deal, Palacios was said to be collecting 3 percent interest, compounded quarterly. But Ferreira, "who was unable to get from Gill a large sum from the theft made under pretext of buying some 20,000 cattle and 400,000 arrobas of meal to distribute to the people . . . wants to assure himself of a share in the deals being prepared for next October . . . And it is known that Señor Loizaga is very amenable to short *transactions*." There was really little choice among these men, Azambuja continued, "all of whom want to be rich even though they sacrifice the credit, the future, and the very fate of the country." However, probably more could be gained by backing Brizuela, Gill, and Palacios against Ferreira and his followers. In the meantime, Jovellanos consulted Azambuja about everything. As to Gill, Azambuja had no doubt that he was Brazil's man and could be very useful in Asunción, but he could not return without the consent of Jovellanos.[25]

His first impressions having been confirmed, Azambuja had no difficulty in analyzing the political situation. Ferreira, who was subsidizing *El Diario*, an anti-Brazilian paper, was definitely hostile. Azambuja warned Jovellanos that he should be taking measures to avoid deplorable events, but Ferreira was too strong for the president.[26] The Brazilian was obviously referring to a possible revolution.

Gill's friends vainly sought to persuade Azambuja to bring their leader back to Asunción. While refusing to grant their request, Azambuja was careful not to offend Gill, and the latter, resigned to being in exile for a time, sent for his family. In response to a letter taken by Brizuela to Montevideo, Gill had expressed his appreciation for the Brazilian's efforts. Azambuja remarked that Gill's letter was "proof that we can always depend on his favorable attitude toward the policy of the Empire."[27]

Azambuja's description of Paraguay's public men distressed Correia, who advised circumspection in dealing with Jovellanos. As to Brizuela and Gill, they merited Brazilian benevolence "but within certain limits. We cannot trust blindly," he warned Azambuja, "in the sincerity and constancy of their friendship toward Brazil." In any aid given to the Paraguayan government, whether in domestic or foreign affairs, care must be taken not to make it appear that Brazil desired to control the government, "neither do we take moral responsibility for its acts." Correia advised his envoy to urge upon Paraguay the highest regard for fiscal responsibility, especially that it meet the obligations incurred in the London loans.[28]

Azambuja, very circumspect in his relations with Jovellanos, found his suspicions of Ferreira deepening. He despaired of other members of the cabinet and so was indifferent to the recurring ministerial changes. Aramburú was something of a cipher; Falcón, an old Lopizta, would bend with political winds. Although Ferreira was pro-Argentine, he would never agree to cede any of the Chaco. On this point Brazil had nothing to fear so long as the Empire provided its moral and material aid. Azambuja's language is significant for understanding subsequent revolts against the Jovellanos government: "In the other political questions, our adversaries are more impertinent and clever, more condescending and circumspect. And this is why Gill was not permitted to return to the Republic, why Brizuela was compelled to flee in order not to become a victim of some ambush, why Palacios and others are excluded from office and at the same time their enemies acquire more influence every day." Nevertheless, it might be necessary to make use of Gill, Brizuela, and Palacios in order to keep the gains won by Cotegipe; if not, Brazil should be prepared to abstain entirely from involvement in the Chaco question. There was a growing demand for Brazilian evacuation of Paraguayan territory, but this demand should be resisted until the boundary had been run and Brazil's claims had been satisfied. "It will not be a protectorate that we wish to exercise nor shall we exercise it, faithful as we are to the limits imposed by the Treaty of Alliance, but an effective protection of Brazilian interests, which we must not allow to be compromised after so much sacrifice of blood and money." Azambuja was convinced that withdrawal of Brazilian forces would result in Argentine absorption of Paraguay; therefore, in the forthcoming negotiations with Mitre, the independence of Paraguay must be guaranteed.[29]

The Climate of Revolt

Mutual suspicions among Paraguayan politicians, quarreling between Brazil's civil and military representatives, and surreptitious Argentine aid to possible rebel leaders created an excellent climate for revolution. These factors kept the pot boiling after October, 1872. The revolts that ended with the triumph of Juan Bautista Gill in 1874 began with various plots in the last quarter of 1872. Rivarola, smarting from the coup that drove him from power in 1871, tried to organize a countercoup and suffered imprisonment as a result. Released, he resumed plotting, was again imprisoned in April, 1872, and released with no injury except to his ego. In a bitter, almost hysterical manifesto, he complained about the perfidy of his fellow men and referred to the grafting of the ministers, especially Gill, when proceeds of the London loan of 1871 had arrived. The Brazilian minister correctly estimated that Rivarola, now a confirmed enemy of the Empire, had very little support; but there was no lack of power-hungry men, among whom Caballero and Juan Silvano Godoy would bear watching.[30]

The most serious plot in 1872 was one said to be promoted by the

Argentine government through its consul, Dr. Miguel Gallegos, who was working with Germán Serrano, Cándido Bareiro, Juan Francisco and Adolfo Decoud, Godoy, Caballero, and Padre Fidel Maíz. The presence of the Decouds and Godoy in this group can be explained by their jealousy of Ferreira. Approached by one of the plotters in Montevideo, Gill promptly reported to Azambuja and Cotegipe that the plan was to overthrow the government, denounce the Brazilian treaties, and form a defensive and offensive alliance with Argentina. Once the Brazilians were defeated, a plebiscite would be held to annul the Cotegipe-Loizaga treaties, "an easy thing to do, considering the moral qualities of the mass of our people," Gill observed smugly. Either Gill or Bareiro would replace Jovellanos if the latter refused to go along. Cotegipe replied that the conspiracy was a piece of madness that Brazil had no reason to fear. If Paraguay annulled the treaties, war would result and that would be the end of Paraguay. But Cotegipe must have been worried, since he promised an effort to get Gill back to Asunción.[31] Azambuja had already expressed his fear that Brazil might have to provide a subsidy in order to maintain Paraguay's independence, since new loans were impossible and, even as things were, the Paraguayan government could not survive without the presence of Brazilian troops.

Azambuja was ready to move in the troops. To counter the threat of the Argentine plot, he asked the president of Mato Grosso to have 500 men ready to send to Paraguay. The Brazilians had 1,200 men in Asunción, about 4,800 close by, and enough reserves in Mato Grosso to permit the concentration within a fortnight of 15,000 men wherever needed. Although the military commanders, General Guimarães and Admiral Pereira Pinto, advised immediate reinforcements from Mato Grosso, Azambuja cautioned restraint unless matters threatened to get out of hand.[32] The Brazilian minister of foreign affairs, suspicious of Gill, advised his minister in Asunción not "to receive his confidences without reservation and caution" and to be wary about what their supposed friends had to say, since they wanted political office and would try to get Brazil committed to their cause. Brazil must not intervene in the country's affairs except to give advice in special cases and to keep the government out of difficulties. As to any secret moves by the Paraguayan government, Azambuja should get the facts and be governed accordingly.[33]

Jovellanos obviously had no control over his cabinet. Aramburú and Falcón attacked Ferreira in the columns of *Nación Paraguaya*; Ferreira struck back through *El Orden*. Azambuja advised Jovellanos to reorganize the cabinet, but the vice-president would rather resign than fight constant intrigues. Azambuja then attempted to reconcile the quarreling ministers, without any noticeable success, and complained to his superiors that the Empire's efforts to help Paraguay were shattered "by the obstacles of a tortuous and stormy politics that repels good sense and the spirit of conciliation that should be the basis of the administration."[34] To promote Brazilian interests, Azambuja had continued to pay 250 patacones monthly to the editor of *El Derecho*, who filled his columns with material written by enemies of the Empire! Prudently the minister suspended publication of *El Derecho* on October 21. It was just as well, since everyone knew that Brazil had been supporting the paper.[35]

Additional evidence of a plot appeared in the distribution of insulting pasquinades, handbills attacking Brazil, which came from a "secret, criminal hand" and were printed on a hidden press. Taking note of this propaganda, Jovellanos ordered the chief of police to investigate and close the press, and authorized any citizen to arrest the offender.[36] After a month or more of rumors and of quarreling in Jovellanos's cabinet, Aramburú and Ferreira appeared to be reconciled, and talk of an Argentine plot died down. According to Gill, the revolt would come in December; but Azambuja saw no signs of it, so he asked the president of Mato Grosso to suspend preparations to send troops to Asunción. Ferreira strengthened his position by persuading Jovellanos to make Francisco Soteras minister of hacienda, leaving Aramburú with war and marine.[37]

The Argentines were playing a sharp game in Asunción, taking advantage of Ferreira's unpopularity, the innate Paraguayan distrust of Brazil, a favorable press, and disagreement between Azambuja and Guimarães. Ferreira, by no means a charismatic leader, attracted adherents who saw a chance to further their own interests, nor was Jovellanos a strong leader, and the Argentines found ready access to him through his Argentine wife. Despite a steady stream of reports from Guimarães to Cotegipe in which Jovellanos and Ferreira were presented as cordial to Brazil, the faceless "man in the street" still regarded Brazilians as black monkeys, and the Lopiztas could never forgive the Empire for having led the Allies to a victory that nearly annihilated Paraguay. Caballero and his circle had no difficulty in finding support in the country, since they represented what the people had been accustomed to and not the strange egalitarian doctrines of the still-new democratic institutions. Except for the papers they subsidized, the Brazilians generally found little support in the press: even *Nación Paraguaya*, owned by officials kept in power by Brazilian support, published caustic anti-Brazilian editorials. Azambuja had faith in none of the Paraguayan leaders and resented the refusal of Jovellanos and Ferreira to take his advice. Guimarães, who certainly had been privy to the plot that ousted Rivarola and elevated Jovellanos, refused to believe that Azambuja was the right man to represent the Empire. While Rio Branco and Cotegipe were in Asunción, Guimarães had no trouble, but he quarreled with their successors. This was a civilian-military conflict in part, one in which Guimarães would support no Brazilian minister who refused to accept his own evaluations of the Paraguayan scene and his interpretation of the Rio Branco-Cotegipe policies.

Since political quarrels in Asunción had apparently subsided for the time being, Brizuela returned to the capital on December 13, only to discover that the government was hostile to anyone who was friendly with Gill. Elections were to be held on January 25, 1873, and all candidates were hand picked by Jovellanos and Ferreira. Many of them were relatives of Jovellanos, and many spoke nothing but Guaraní. With money from the second London loan expected soon, the government must have a supine Congress.[38] While Brizuela was taking soundings in Asunción, Gill went to Rio de Janeiro to ask Cotegipe for aid, but his mentor had gone to Bahia. Gill complained that he had received no help from Brazil and became importunate: "I must again bother you, asking that you agree to do something for one who is always disposed to showing you his greatest gratitude." If he returned to Paraguay, he would stay out of politics as long as Cotegipe thought it wise.[39] The time obviously had not come for Gill to return, and he could not avoid becoming more amenable to revolutionary proposals from the Bareiro-Caballero clique. Gill was the Empire's man in reserve, and if the Paraguayans wanted a revolution, Brazil would see to it that Gill became its head.

The elections went off smoothly on January 25, but the Jovellanos regime was not happy. Although still loyal to Brazil, the government did not like the Mitre–São Vicente agreement, which might mean a Brazilian withdrawal from Paraguay, as that would leave the country in chaos. Guimarães, who made this report to Rio de Janeiro, assured Cotegipe that Jovellanos had no confidence in Azambuja. Jovellanos himself accused Azambuja of plotting against him, trying to enlist Aramburú and Falcón in a revolution to overthrow the regime. Azambuja obviously was *persona non grata*.[40]

Continuing the practice of moving from crisis to crisis, the Jovellanos cabinet endured another shakeup on February 8, 1873. Falcón, Loizaga, and Aramburú all resigned, thus ending the stormy experiment with a coalition cabinet. Loizaga, minister of justice, was angry because a justice of the peace in the interior had been imprisoned for openly opposing Ferreira. Aramburú simply refused to associate with Ferreira any longer, and Falcón had drawn a sharp rebuke from Ferreira for having published an attack on the Allies in *Nación Paraguaya*. Jovellanos had no choice but to disavow Falcón. This multiple resignation left the cabinet composed of Ferreira, Soteras, and José del Rosario Miranda, who was appointed minister of war and marine and acting minister of foreign relations.[41]

Jovellanos and Ferreira had no illusions as to their strength. If they lost the support of Brazil, their tenuous tenure would end abruptly, and the key to this support was their attitude toward Argentina's territorial demands. Brazil's policy was clear: Paraguay should acknowledge Argentine title to the Chaco Central between the Bermejo and the Pilcomayo; the area north to the Arroyo Verde, which lay just north of Villa Occidental, should be submitted to arbitration. No Paraguayan who opposed this policy would have Brazilian support. Bartolomé Mitre had been to Rio de Janeiro to restore the appearances of friendship between the Allies, whose relations had cooled to the freezing point; now, early in 1873, the great Porteño was preparing for a mission to Paraguay, where he would attempt to gain Argentina's territorial demands. This was an awkward time for Brazil to change ministers, but Azambuja took his leave on February 11, 1873, and left Alfredo Sergio Teixeira de Macedo as chargé.[42] Azambuja left when plans for the Bareiro-Caballero revolt were rapidly maturing. Teixeira de Macedo was certain that the Argentines were planning to replace the Jovellanos government with one more amenable to their territorial ambitions, an interpretation strengthened by revolutionary movements just before the arrival of Mitre.

As a preliminary to the revolt of March 22, Cirilo Antonio Rivarola caused a little flurry on March 6 with a harebrained attempt to overthrow Jovellanos. The plan was to detain the chief of police, place Jovellanos under house arrest, and then have Congress assembled to consider the situation. A committee of twenty-one was to inform Jovellanos, a committee of five was to ask the Allied representative to remain neutral, and a group of forty was to be at the cavalry barracks at 12:30 p. m. Rivarola left his house at 12:15 for the barracks, where he arrived at the appointed time—only to learn that his companions had understood the designated time to be 2:30! With five men following at a discreet distance, Rivarola then went to the police headquarters. Two men were to guard the chief of police, Col. Luis González, and keep him from leaving; followed by the other three, Rivarola went on to the guardroom, where a sergeant was asleep. Rudely awakened from his siesta, the sergeant listened to Rivarola's chit-chat for a time, boldly refused to join the coup, and quickly locked the door when the would-be rebels departed. Rivarola insisted that the government had no knowledge of his plans.[43]

After the failure of his muddled plot, Rivarola sought refuge in the Brazilian barracks. Guimarães reported to Jovellanos, and soon Paraguayan soldiers surrounded the place to prevent Rivarola's escape. Jovellanos suggested that Rivarola write a letter confessing the plot and requesting permission for permanent exile. But Rivarola was too canny to fall for this trick, or refused to abandon his accomplices, and preferred to trust his fate to the courts while remaining safely with the Brazilians. Guimarães again conferred with Jovellanos; Rivarola changed his mind and decided to surrender, then his sanity returned and he accepted a Brazilian escort, which took him aboard the *Princesa* on March 14. Enroute to Buenos Aires, he dropped off at Corrientes, the favorite spot for rebels to gather before invading Paraguay.[44]

While on board the *Princesa*, Rivarola fired off an impassioned manifesto against the regime. His accusations, couched in highly charged rhetoric, were essentially true. There was no freedom of speech, since no one could express a political opinion without being imprisoned or attacked by government thugs. Arbitrary imprisonment, torture, and fines occurred without any respect for the rights of the accused. The government had sacked the treasury, sold public properties secretly, abandoned education, shackled commerce, thrown the monetary system into chaos, and made a mockery of justice.[45]

All of these accusations were true, but knowing the truth made no one free and proclaiming it was an invitation to persecution. Rivarola had failed miserably as a revolutionist, but more capable leaders were preparing a revolt that would enlist the aid of all enemies of the Jovellanos-Ferreira coalition.

11. The Triumph of Juan Bautista Gill

After his expulsion from Paraguay early in 1872, Juan Bautista Gill made every possible effort to return and resume the struggle against Ferreira. In this critical year, when plots were as thick and intertwined as vines in a tropical forest, there were plenty of opportunities for Gill. He was too clever to become identified with a losing cause, too astute to antagonize key Brazilian officials and leaders of successful revolution in Paraguay. Gill's power had its source in the favors of Cotegipe and Rio Branco, a fact that Cándido Bareiro and Bernardino Caballero, principal movers in the only serious plots that disturbed the Jovellanos regime, soon came to realize. This combination of powerful and unrepentant Lopiztas proved to be too much for Ferreira to combat successfully. There is no doubt that Argentine influence and aid were present in the plots of 1872, but the Argentines were cautious. Having restored a semblance of good relations with Brazil, they were not going to risk an open break with the Empire.

While Brazilian statesmen had no illusions about the loyalty of Jovellanos, Gill, and Brizuela, they could see no choice other than to support them against the obviously unreliable Argentine party. Paraguayans generally were adamant in their refusal to cede any part of the Chaco Boreal to Argentina, but there was always the possibility that some group might do so in exchange for trade concessions or cancellation of war debts and indemnities.

One of the ironical results of the revolutions of 1873–1874 was the restoration of Gill to a powerful position. Ferreira had won the first confrontation in the Jovellanos cabinet. In the second confrontation, Gill enjoyed continued Brazilian support as well as reluctant backing from Bareiro and Caballero, neither of whom liked or trusted him. These two Lopiztas provided the brains and the military leadership for the revolts, while Gill stepped in to be the principal immediate beneficiary. Even so, if the Brazilians had been satisfied with Jovellanos and

Ferreira, they would not have permitted the Bareiro-Caballero revolt to succeed. When the Brazilian ministers became certain that the revolution did have popular support, they moved in as more or less honest brokers to negotiate a settlement that eliminated Ferreira and placed Gill in a position to become the next president. Bareiro, who had lost the prize temporarily, knew how to wait until events should place him in a position to win the presidency.

Bartolomé Mitre arrived in Asunción immediately after the first phase of the Bareiro-Caballero revolt had failed. Although he was conciliatory, his negotiations with the Jovellanos government failed to produce an agreement. However, the mission did provide Mitre with a close view of Paraguayan politics and very likely lessened any desire he might have had for Argentina to become more deeply involved in Paraguayan affairs.

The Bareiro-Caballero Revolt—Phase One, March, 1873

Jovellanos feared that the Brazilians would withdraw their troops from Asunción and leave him with no support against his enemies. He had no more than 350 men under arms and was totally dependent upon the Brazilians for military supplies. There was widespread sympathy for the Lopizta, or Bareiro-Caballero, party, and Jovellanos had reason to believe that the Brazilian Foreign Office resented Ferreira's success in getting rid of Gill. Why had Brazil not kept a minister in Asunción? Teixeira de Macedo certainly lacked prestige, and Jovellanos would not last a day if Guimarães should decide to allow a revolt to succeed.[1]

Caballero, Bareiro, and their associates apparently believed they could bring off a successful revolt with the minimum of resources and without having determined what actions the Brazilians might take. They may have had some surreptitious Argentine aid, but Argentina was in no position to challenge Brazil openly, and Mitre was soon to arrive for negotiations with the government. The time was so unpropitious for a revolt that one finds it difficult to believe the charges of either Brazilian or Argentine complicity.

At seven o'clock on the morning of Saturday, March 22, 1873, the rickety train to Paraguarí began its customary tortured journey. The cars were full of men who intended to fight with Caballero, and although government officials knew of the plot they made no effort to stop the train nor to place police aboard. To do so, they feared, would be a confession of weakness. The rebels took possession of the train at Pirayú, but the conductor escaped, obtained a horse, and galloped back to Asunción with the news. Rumors then ran wild: the rebels had 900 men supplied by Argentina with arms and money, several towns had adhered to Caballero, and the rebels would attack Asunción with 1,500 men. To reconnoiter, Ferreira rode out at the head of his cavalry, 50 strong; but when he reached Pirayú he turned back to gather a stronger force.[2]

Jovellanos learned of the revolt before the conductor escaped from his captured train. One of the rebels had invited a member of Congress to join them; instead, the legislator reported to Guimarães, who advised him to warn Jovellanos. The vice-president asked for arms and ammunition to suppress the revolt and got them only after promising Guimarães that he was following Azambuja's instructions and would continue to support Brazil's policy. The chargé reported that, although somewhat in the dark, Guimarães and he had no choice but to support Jovellanos, but they would do so "in the least direct way possible." Brazilian troops would be used to protect the capital if necessary, since the government had only 100 cavalry, 200 infantry, and 50 urbanos (city and rural police) under arms. Guimarães advised Jovellanos to call the citizens to arms to augment his small force but did not offer to provide weapons for them. The Brazilians were careful not to arouse Argentine suspicions that they were arbitrarily protecting a weak government. Upon Guimarães's advice, Jovellanos summoned the Argentine commander, Major José María Ferreira, and told him of the rumors that Argentina was supporting the revolt. Major Ferreira denied involvement and promised aid in supporting Jovellanos.[3] With this backing, Jovellanos immediately declared a state of siege, and Benigno Ferreira prepared to attack the rebels.

The classic Latin American revolt must have a pronunciamiento, a declaration to condemn the existing government and to justify the armed effort of the rebels. Caballero and Bareiro did not neglect this honored formula. Bareiro informed Macedo and Guimarães that patriotic Paraguayans could not continue to tolerate ruin, discredit, and perdition carried out by a group of avaricious men who would sacrifice everything for a little gold. They must, therefore, attempt to overthrow the corrupt government and willingly faced expatriation should they fail. The rebels were not attacking legitimate interests of the Allies, they would agree to any reasonable settlement, but they insisted that Ferreira must leave. Bareiro sent along a copy of Caballero's proclamation of March 22, a proclamation that showed no signs of Lopizmo: "The hecatomb of the Paraguayan people carried to the sacrifice by the fierce will of a dictator who himself suffered the same fate, is a lesson so cruel that the people might forget that it is preferable to rise and to fight to guarantee liberty than to bow cowardly to the will of tyrants." Now, Caballero continued, the time has come to reap the rewards of that long struggle; but the people had permitted a small group of self-ish men to seize control with the aid of the Allies. These men were ene-mies of the people, concerned only with making their own fortunes, stealing from the people, and especially stealing the loans raised in for-eign markets. Paraguayans must overthrow this system, must restore constitutional government, must oppose forced military service, must restore free elections. The pronunciamiento then became more specific: Paraguayans deserved to be imprisoned, whipped, or shot if they did not protest against the theft of the London loan, or if they allowed the government to maintain a force of 150 terrorists to intimidate the peo-ple and the Congress, or if they consented to continued deception and exploitation of the immigrants. Paraguayans must protest arbitrary po-lice acts, resist the imprisonment and exile of the best citizens, prevent summary executions, property seizure, and illegal deportations. All men in the Gran Partido Nacional were supporting him, Caballero—or whoever wrote the proclamation—concluded. The party's program was summarized in five points: reestablish the Constitution, end looting of the public treasury, respect international promises, make peace with the Allies, and religiously meet debt payments and convert paper money.[4]

This pronunciamiento is especially important because it contains the first statement of principles of what was to become the Colorado Party. The use of "Gran Partido Nacional" was not infrequent to designate the Bareiro-Caballero group. The Colorados, of course, would not fol-low the principles they so loudly proclaimed in 1873, nor have they ever followed them.

The proclamation issued over Caballero's name found sympathetic reading in the Brazilian legation. Teixeira de Macedo observed that the rebel's points were well taken and accurate; but would the rebels, if victorious, be any better than the regime then in power, and would they protect Brazilian interests? As to getting rid of Ferreira, a waiting policy would be best, since Jovellanos was ready to sacrifice his chief minister to avoid bloodshed, despite his refusal to desert Ferreira and the latter's offer to resign during a conference at the Brazilian legation.[5]

Acting vigorously to suppress the revolt, Jovellanos on Sunday, March 23, called the people to arms and sent a force of 350 men along the railway toward Pirayú. Ferreira followed with more men on Mon-day, reached the outskirts of Paraguarí, and halted to reconnoiter. Con-vinced that the rebels had little strength, he swept into the small town on Tuesday, encountered about thirty poorly armed men, and captured several supposed leaders. Among them were Col. Juan Francisco De-coud and his son Adolfo, who protested that they were in Paraguarí on

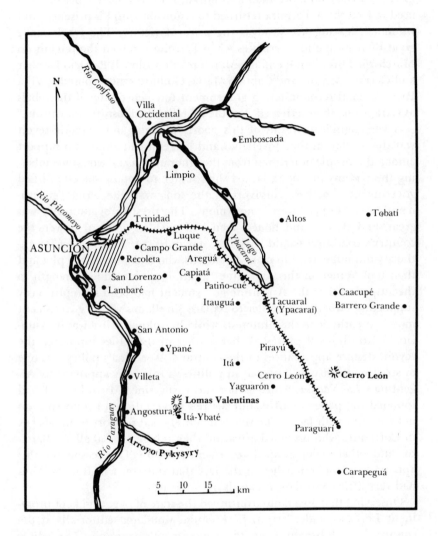

Map 5. Asunción Area

business. The principal leaders had fled with the larger part of their force, probably no more than a hundred, since two beeves per day sufficed to feed them. Ferreira returned to Asunción with his prisoners and wounded, leaving five dead as the price of victory. The rebels made good their escape to Corrientes when Ferreira resumed the pursuit on March 26. This did not end the March revolt. Colonels Patricio Escobar and Germán Serrano and Captain Matías Goiburú rendezvoused at Villa Rica. A small reconnoitering government force encountered the rebels at Carapeguá, then retreated; but the rebellion had lost its momentum.[6]

A very significant result of this poorly planned and quixotic revolt was the revelation that Jovellanos and Ferreira had almost no support among the people other than from the ignorant masses, who, remembering the tyranny of López, lacked the courage to oppose the established government. To these survivors of the long war, the terms "government" and "López" were synonymous. The prestige of authority was great, and if wise and honest men had wielded political power, the country's condition would have been far different. This respect for authority did not extend to many Spaniards who had entered the plot and then took refuge in the Argentine Legation, giving added strength to the suspicion that the Argentine government had been surreptitiously supporting Caballero in order to replace Jovellanos with a government more sympathetic to their interests while Bartolomé Mitre was in Asunción. Mitre himself protested that neither of the Allies supported the revolt, despite appearances to the contrary. Argentina's policy was one of strict neutrality in Paraguayan politics, a role fully approved by Argentina's *La Nación*, which is not surprising since Mitre himself had founded the paper in 1870. But Mitre's protestations of innocence do not conform with facts. The rebels definitely had support from officials in Corrientes who provided arms and then refuge for Caballero, Bareiro, and others who escaped to Argentine soil.[7] The reason for this apparent contradiction lies in the fact that statesmen in Buenos Aires had very little control over officials in Corrientes.

Observing that Jovellanos continued the state of siege and kept prominent Lopiztas under arrest, *El Progreso* wondered editorially if the country would benefit from the government's triumph. The editor agreed that Guimarães had conducted himself loyally and generously by providing guns and sabers, but not one Brazilian soldier had stepped out of the city during the revolt. Gradually *El Progreso* stepped up its criticism of the Jovellanos regime, reminding the vice-president that he had imprisoned his political mentors, Rivarola and Gill, and had complacently permitted the first loan to be stolen. Police responded by closing the paper on May 3, an event announced in a single sheet published the next day. The editor protested that once more the constitution was being violated and that the revolution, contrary to official claims, was growing in strength.[8] Guimarães, too, feared that Caballero would return, with a better prepared force and aided by Argentina, to overthrow the government, which refused to cede a single palm of the Chaco territory because it was subservient to Brazil. The leaders, notorious Lopiztas, wanted to throw out the Negroes, as they called Brazilians.[9]

The Mitre Mission to Asunción

Bartolomé Mitre's negotiations in Rio de Janeiro apparently had succeeded in closing the rift between Argentina and Brazil. Since the Cotegipe-Loizaga treaties had precluded a general settlement, it remained for Argentina and Uruguay to negotiate separately with Paraguay. This task President Sarmiento entrusted to Mitre, whose reputation as a statesman was unexcelled by any of his countrymen. Sarmiento was confident that difficulties with Brazil and Paraguay could be solved readily, but Mitre was dubious.[10] Clearly, this was no time for the Empire to be represented by a chargé in Asunción. To fill the post left by Azambuja, Itamaraty sent on special mission Dr. Domingos José Gonçalves de Magalhães, Barão de Araguáia, an experienced diplomat who was also a famous poet, dramatist, and historian.[11] The baron may not have been very diplomatic in Buenos Aires, where in one private conversation he "spoke as if the time had come for playing out that grand farce, known as the Republic of Paraguay." [12]

The two envoys, on their first visit to Asunción, sailed a few days apart. Experienced, sophisticated, prominent men of letters, and at the height of their intellectual powers, they must have had some interesting conversations in Asunción. The Argentine colony, government officials, and Brazilian troops greeted General Mitre when he arrived on April 2, and ten days later gave a similar welcome to Araguáia. Government officials, convinced of Argentine complicity in the revolt, were cool but proper when they greeted the distinguished Porteño who had been commander-in-chief of the Allies during the first part of the war.[13]

Mitre was pleased to have Araguáia's moderating influence on Jovellanos and Ferreira. This was well, for Carlos Tejedor had left him very little room to maneuver in his conferences with Paraguay's acting foreign minister, youthful José del Rosario Miranda. Mitre was ordered to obtain Misiones and Cerrito island, incontestable title to the Chaco Central, and submission of all of the Chaco north of the Pilcomayo to arbitration.[14] The Paraguayans balked at submitting the northern portion to arbitration; at best, they would agree to arbitration of the Villa

Occidental area. However, Ferreira continued to oppose cession of the Chaco Central, an attitude that made him unacceptable to Argentina, frustrated the Brazilian policy of compromise, and eventually brought his downfall.

Sparring between Brazil and Argentina made itself felt in Paraguayan politics. Argentine policy was to find and support Paraguayans who would be willing to surrender the Chaco at least as far north as Villa Occidental. Brazilian policy had to be one of supporting politicians who would hold fast to the Pilcomayo line, with possible arbitration north to the Arroyo Verde. In this game, Brazil had much the better position, not only because of military superiority in Paraguay but also because there were few Paraguayans who would do anything more than pretend to support Argentina's demands.

Mitre's negotiations with Miranda got off to a good start with the agreement that Misiones and the islands of Cerrito and Apipé should go to Argentina, while Paraguay retained Yacyretá. After the May-June phase of the Bareiro-Caballero revolt had ended, Miranda made a dangerous move in presenting Bolivia's claim to the Chaco in order to complicate matters,[15] but Jovellanos quickly corrected his minister and rejected any Bolivian claim north of the Pilcomayo. Mitre then adopted the Brazilian position on arbitration and tried to persuade Tejedor that Villa Occidental would be only a liability to Argentina. By stopping at the Pilcomayo, a boundary dispute with Bolivia could be avoided, there would be no more bickering with Brazil, and a flourishing colony could be established in the Chaco Central. But there was a presidential election in Argentina, and Mitre was a candidate. If he succeeded in this mission to Paraguay, Sarmiento's candidate probably would lose. Tejedor therefore changed Mitre's original instructions by adding the provision that if arbitration were required, then Mitre could agree on the Pilcomayo, keeping Villa Occidental with its natural boundaries. Mitre, Miranda, Araguáia, and Jovellanos had a crucial conference on July 6. Jovellanos insisted that either all of the Chaco north of the Bermejo be arbitrated or, if Paraguay abandoned the Chaco Central, Argentina must accept the Pilcomayo. This stand, which ran counter to the Brazilian position, ended the exchange.[16]

Araguáia took credit for persuading Jovellanos to agree to cession of the Chaco Central and attempted to convince Argentina not to insist on claiming more of the Chaco.[17] In the Mitre-Miranda negotiation, he had played the honest broker, and he left Asunción early in September knowing that the situation was essentially unchanged.[18] Argentine-Brazilian rivalry in Paraguay was to continue for more than two years, and the British ministers in Buenos Aires and Rio de Janeiro both thought that the two countries were on a collision course and that Argentina was backing the revolt against Jovellanos. Argentina increased her armaments at home, and Brazil strengthened its units in Mato Grosso. President Sarmiento pointedly remarked that Argentina would have preferred that Brazil spend its money on a dockyard to build river steamers. Almost unnoticed in the turmoil was the successful negotiation of treaties of peace, friendship, commerce, and navigation with Uruguay. Dr. José Sienra Carranza signed these agreements on December 13, 1873.[19]

The Bareiro-Caballero Revolt, Phase Two (May–June, 1873)

The revolutionary movement was by no means over, and plotting continued while Mitre and Miranda carried on their less than satisfactory discussions. An old Paraguayan hand and veteran of the War of the Triple Alliance, Col. George Thompson, despaired for the future of the country he had served so well. He came to the conclusion

> that nothing can offer a prospect of improvement in that country, despite its marvelous fertility of soil and the richness of its products, save annexation to the Empire of Brazil; an eventuality which he [Thompson] seems to think by no means improbable. That the members of the present Government, though the best ever known in that unhappy country, are guided in their actions by the sole desin [sic] of amassing wealth, till replaced by others, still more corrupt and rapacious than themselves.[20]

Among those who had escaped from the March fiasco was José Segundo Decoud, now leaning more and more toward the nebulous Gran Partido Nacional. Not directly involved in the revolt and strongly opposed to the means employed by its leaders, he claimed that he was compromised with no "militant party in Paraguayan politics" and held himself ready to serve where he could best help the country.[21] Decoud refused to return to Asunción even though Guimarães did promise protection.

Jovellanos had reason to be worried. *El Fénix* boldly criticized the government for ignoring journalistic strictures as though it would be debased by acknowledging their truth; indifferentism or apathy of the masses, accustomed to tyranny, must be overcome. The country from Pirayú to Villa Rica was deserted, the farmers having fled to the hills. There were no draft animals; a food crisis could be expected, and the monetary crisis continued unabated. Congress was paralyzed, artisans feared to work, journalists were muzzled. Well might Jovellanos's ability to rule be questioned. In an effort to counter these gloomy conditions, Jovellanos issued a proclamation urging greater effort by all, war against those traitorous Paraguayans, and strong support for Ferreira, victor over the rebels.[22]

The next serious phase of the revolt was to come in June after the rebels had made more careful preparations in Corrientes and in Paraguayan villages favorable to them. Caballero's activities steadily increased during the last of May and the first two weeks of June. The appetites of both rebels and government officials were whetted by news that £100,000 had arrived in Buenos Aires from the London loans and that another £200,000 could be expected soon. The first shipment was to come on the *Taraguí* as soon as possible, and politicians were drooling as they waited. True or not, the belief was widespread that this hoard encouraged the rebels and made the *situacionistas* determined to stay in power.[23] They used some of the money to buy war matériel in Buenos Aires, but the Argentine minister of war held up the export license despite the posting of a suitable bond, on the excuse that the munitions might reach Argentine rebels in Entre Ríos. This business confirmed Brazilian suspicion that Argentina favored Caballero and brought Rio Branco and Caravellas to repeat their instructions to Araguáia to protect the Jovellanos government.[24]

Caballero and Bareiro struck again before the gold arrived in Asunción. The country had not been pacified after the March revolt, and revolution seethed so widely in the countryside that an exact date for the resumption of hostilities is difficult to fix. Certainly by June 4, Caballero and Bareiro were on the move, actively aided by Serrano and Escobar. While rumors credited Gill and Rivarola with financing the revolt, some believed that Brazil was encouraging the rebels, others that Argentina was their patron. Although Brazilians had lost faith in Jovellanos and especially in Ferreira, they were not supporting Caballero and Bareiro at this stage.

Caballero's forces apparently gathered near Carapeguá, a village about fifteen kilometers south of Paraguarí. Some came up from Corrientes to Pilar by boat and then took the road to Carapeguá, others came in from the hills, while some left their refuge at Villa Occidental to join Caballero. Benigno Ferreira, commanding some 1,500 troops, occupied Paraguarí to protect the capital. Caballero led a force to threaten Asunción while Col. Germán Serrano with 800 men drove on June 7 to cut the railway between Cerro León and Pirayú. They succeeded in derailing two locomotives and tore up some track before a detachment sent by Ferreira drove them off. Caballero then moved swiftly toward Asunción, and by June 8 rebel troops were in Villeta, San Antonio, and San Lorenzo, the latter on the southern outskirts of Asunción. Another rebel group reached the railway at Patiño-cué and turned toward Asunción.[25]

With Caballero's forces poised for an attack on the capital, Mitre and Araguáia had to decide the Allied course. Mitre's negotiations with Miranda did not appear to affect their decision materially. Caballero had troops on the very edge of the city at Recoleta on June 17 and could easily have advanced to the Plaza Constitución with little opposition. Bareiro and Caballero sent a note to the Allied ministers asking that they be treated as belligerents, with the right to overthrow Jovellanos. They would disarm the government's partisans, protect foreigners, and hold a free election. Mitre and Araguáia replied that the fighting must end and that Asunción was under Allied protection. When the rebels precipitated a crisis by sending 600 troops into the city, Mitre, Araguáia, Guimarães, and Admiral Pinto rode out to the San Roque church close to the railway station to warn the rebel leaders that they would be met by the bayonets of Allied troops. Bareiro argued convincingly as he proposed a four-point plan: retain Jovellanos but change the cabinet, declare an armistice pending settlement of the conflict, disband all armed forces other than police, and hold new elections. The objective, of course, was to get rid of Ferreira and his two close colleagues, Miranda and Soteras. Warning the rebels not to advance until the morning, the Allied leaders conveyed Bareiro's proposals to Jovellanos, who indignantly rejected them and requested protection. Mitre and Araguáia rather bitingly asked why they should protect the government when Jovellanos had done nothing. By way of reply, at 11:00 p.m. on June 17 Jovellanos ordered hasty fortifications to be thrown up in the Plaza Constitución: "Bales of hay, barrels of sand, stakes, and 4 guns formed the defense of the Plaza, in which Jovellanos, his two ministers, and all available forces were concentrated."[26] Jovellanos had received a message from Ferreira, who was pushing rapidly toward Asunción, but the rebels could attack the Plaza at will while Allied troops formed in the Plaza San Francisco opposite the railway station. Practically all of these troops were Brazilians, since General Vedia had been recalled to fight Argentine rebels in Entre Ríos.

The rebels attacked with 700 cavalry and 300 infantry on the morning of June 18 but were unable to win the advantage. Finally, the approach of Ferreira's forces caused them to flee in confusion, and the victorious government leader entered the Plaza Constitución at 4:00 p.m. After only a brief pause, the victor turned quickly to pursue the enemy and engage him wherever encountered.[27]

Jovellanos sought to end the revolt by offering a pardon to all rebels who would come in by June 29,[28] but they wanted another chance, not a pardon. They hid out in Paraguay or fled to Argentine territory. General Caballero and his men made for Encarnación and crossed the Paraná to Posadas on the Argentine *Cadete*. They remained there under arms, a circumstance that led to Paraguayan demands for Argentine neutrality.[29] Villa Occidental received scores of refugees, some of whom might find work in the large sawmill imported and then sold by Edward Augustus Hopkins. The influx of Paraguayans, who would be protected by the Argentine flag, temporarily swelled the population until enthusiasts expected a model town to develop.[30] After chasing and catching a few rebels, the victorious government troops returned to Asunción for a triumphant entrance on July 27. Estimated at about 1,200 troops, Ferreira's force was made up mostly of teenagers: "Every man-jack of them had something green stuck in the mouth of his rifle or musket, and a great many had their necks adorned with martial wreaths of flowers." [31] Ferreira hailed the government's victory as definitive. Caballero, a correspondent exulted, would never return to Paraguay because he would have to answer for crimes committed during the rebellion.[32] He was an extremely poor prophet.

Paraguay needed more than words. *El Imparcial* advised Jovellanos to reform his administration and appoint an advisory council for economic affairs made up of Col. George Thompson, director of the railway, Col. Francisco Wisner von Morgenstern, head of the immigration office, and Robert Chodasiewicz, director of public works. These men would advise on such matters as roads, canals, ports, railways, telegraphs, public and private buildings, streets, plazas, fortifications, agriculture, mining, and other matters.[33] Jovellanos ignored the advice.

Bareiro-Caballero Revolt: Phase Three
(December, 1873–February, 1874)

Paraguayan historians have long maintained that the impetus for the revolution that succeeded in deposing Ferreira early in 1874 was Brazilian in origin.[34] Actually, the rebellion was Paraguayan in origin, supported from the beginning by Argentina and eventually accepted reluctantly by Brazil. The rebels needed the support of Gill and his friends, and they knew that Gill was their only bridge to the Brazilians. Caballero, Rivarola, Escobar, and Bareiro did not trust Gill but they knew how to bide their time. If the only way they could gain Brazilian support was to accept Gill, then this they would do and trust to the future and to José Segundo Decoud to extricate them from an unwanted alliance.

Attempting to take advantage of the June 29 amnesty, Gill arrived in

Asunción about September 10 and sought permission to land in order to look after his business affairs. When Jovellanos refused to let his former friend go ashore and even arrested some who visited him, Guimarães had Gill transferred to the Brazilian gunboat, *Barroso*, which soon returned him to Montevideo. This incident caused an Argentine correspondent in Asunción to accuse Brazil of having promoted a revolutionary plot to put Gill in office, an accusation hotly denied in Asunción.[35]

The rebels kept Gill well informed about their plans, and Gill faithfully reported to Rio Branco and Cotegipe. A well armed invasion force was ready at Corrientes, and the rebels offered its leadership to Gill, who was inclined to accept; but first he must obtain the advice of his Brazilian mentors. While protesting again his loyalty to Brazil, he asked only that Brazilian troops remain neutral. Cotegipe reminded Gill that he disapproved of all revolutions in Paraguay, which was so badly in need of peace to restore its strength. Definitely not needed was "a call for liberty that its people are not able to understand and that revolutionary leaders would not bring, no matter what their promises. As soon as they triumphed, they would put in practice the same measures of repression and oppression so common in Paraguay and accepted by everyone as the norm of government." Paraguay's misery as a result of the war, the bad state of finances made worse by the theft of the London loans, and its other problems could be remedied only by peace. Brazilian forces would not permit Asunción to become a battlefield. Once Paraguay's foreign problems were settled, Brazil would evacuate its forces, hoping that annihilation—that is, absorption by Argentina—would not follow. Now certainly was not the time for Gill to join the rebels; he should wait for a better occasion. But Gill was restless. He conferred with Araguáia and Antônio José Duarte de Araújo Gondim, Brazilian minister to Paraguay, and endeavored to get Rio Branco's approval for his return to Asunción, promising to be useful to Brazil in the future. Rio Branco assured him that Brazil appreciated his past services and would use its good offices to persuade the government to permit his return to Paraguay.[36]

Argentine involvement in the Bareiro-Caballero plotting was obvious and, Rio Branco observed impatiently, was designed to force Brazil's hand. The Empire would have to take costly precautions. What else could be done? "The Argentines, at least, declare they will not modify their proposals to Paraguay and invite us to support them or agree to withdraw our forces. As you know," he reminded Cotegipe, "their proposals are: the Pilcomayo with Villa Occidental separated [from the rest of the Chaco] by a certain line to be drawn; or definitive agreement on the Pilcomayo, arbitration of the rest, and status quo meanwhile." He hoped that there would be no war.[37]

Instructions to the Empire's chargé in Asunción were very explicit. The Vizconde Caravellas[38] ordered Amaral Valente to protect Jovellanos and prevent rebel success if Argentina were aiding the uprising. In the event of a strictly Paraguayan revolution, Brazil would remain neutral, but no outside interference would be tolerated. However, it would not be to the Allied advantage to have former López chieftains, such as Caballero and Bareiro, overthrow a friendly regime, and Araguáia had been instructed to inform Tejedor of the imperial position. When Gill wrote to Rio Branco from Montevideo on June 1, 1873, advising him that he was going to join the rebels in Corrientes, Rio Branco warned him that Brazil would protect Jovellanos. Under these conditions, Caravellas reminded his chargé in Asunción, Jovellanos should weigh well his actions and do nothing to antagonize Brazil. In acknowledging these instructions, the chargé reported Jovellanos as being very effusive in his protestations of friendship for Brazil and his appreciation of Brazilian efforts on his behalf. That rebels were preparing in Buenos Aires and Corrientes was well known. The chargé observed significantly: "We are prepared for any and every emergency; and with God's favor I hope to overcome the difficulties that may arise during the absence of my illustrious chief, the Councillor Gondim." At about the same time, the rebel leaders informed Gill that everything was ready.[39]

There was no doubt whatever that rebels were using Argentine territory, especially Corrientes, as a base of operations, although the official Argentine policy was properly that of neutrality. While waiting in Buenos Aires, Gill had an active part in the revolution. General Caballero and Colonel Escobar kept in touch with him from Corrientes, and late in 1873 confidently predicted victory for their cause. Anyone, apparently, was welcome in the rebel camp. For Caballero, Escobar, and Bareiro to work together was no miracle; but add Germán Serrano, Francisco Soteras, Gill, and Rivarola, and one is entitled to wonder at the alchemy that held them together.[40] At one stage, after the revolution had begun, Rivarola offered to sell out to Brazil and to make important revelations about the aims of the rebels and of their agreements with the Argentine government. All of this he would do for payment by Brazil of the $24,000 he claimed to have provided to the rebels. This could be done, but the Brazilian minister seemed dubious about accepting the offer. On another occasion, Rivarola asserted that Gill and he were financing the revolt, not Argentina.[41] This immediately raises the question as to how two politicians, penniless in 1870, obtained the money to finance a revolution!

Brazilian support of Jovellanos and Ferreira began to waver late in 1873. The Brazilian press was very critical of the way in which the loans had been squandered, and Caravellas instructed Gondim to urge Jovellanos to correct the irregularities that undoubtedly had occurred. The rebels grew stronger as Gill, Bareiro, Rivarola, Caballero, and Serrano cooperated, at least temporarily. The key influence in this shift in Brazilian attitude was the new minister to Paraguay, the Councillor Gondim, who arrived at his post on December 1, 1873.[42] Gondim was Gill's champion, a fact that could not have been lost on the rebel leaders, none of whom trusted Gill. Impatiently Gill pressed Rio Branco for a favorable stance but there was delay, until by mid December authorities in Rio de Janeiro felt that perhaps a change in the Paraguayan ministry might be a good thing, although Gondim should be careful not to upset Jovellanos. Some attention should be paid to complaints against the government, sacrificing personal interest to the good of the country, but Jovellanos could count on Brazil's good will.[43] Caravellas instructed Gondim to promote Gill's return to Paraguay, and the diplomat assured Jovellanos that Gill had repeatedly refused to accept leadership of the revolution, but Jovellanos and Miranda were skeptical. They knew that Gill had provided a launch for the rebels and so informed Gondim that they could never permit Gill to return to Paraguay, at least not until new elections were held. Gill's complicity in the planning is undeniable and he had indeed provided a boat. The rebels had expected him to accompany them, but Gill held back despite assurance that everything would succeed.[44] Jovellanos and Ferreira might well have wondered just what sort of game Gondim was playing, but there was no doubt about Gill's attitude: he would show up in Asunción when he was guaranteed a welcome and not before.

In an attempt to justify the renewal of efforts to overthrow Jovellanos, the rebel proclamation charged the government with arbitrary arrests and executions, pilfering of public funds, and maintaining conditions that prevented economic recovery. Sympathizers with the March revolt had been forced to flee the country; but this time, General Caballero proclaimed on December 31, 1873, the whole country would rise and join the revolution.[45]

Rumors of this new invasion, which had been launched on the last day of 1873, spread swiftly and brought first a weak denial and then bitter denunciation as *Nación Paraguaya* called it an attempt to oust Ferreira. The minister of war, Francisco L. Cabriza, immediately made a foray from Asunción but found no rebel troops—he went in the wrong direction. A few days later he pursued a party of cavalry near Pilar but failed to engage them. Congress approved a state of siege and voted $f200,000 to crush the revolt. Gondim asked Guimarães to move a battalion of artillery from Corumbá to Asunción and assured Miranda that Jovellanos could depend upon Brazilian protection. At this stage the Brazilians had not fully decided whether to support the government, and the reenforcements would make it easier to move against the rebels. Although they refused to sell a gunboat to Paraguay, which obviously could not pay for it, the Brazilians forced Caballero to dismantle a battery he had placed at the mouth of the Tebicuary.[46]

The prospect of renewed civil war distressed Gondim, who knew Paraguay's limited resources could not stand more domestic turmoil. Many of Paraguay's most capable men despaired of their country's future as an independent nation once Brazil's occupation ended. The government's annual income was about $500,000, yet almost $600,000 was required just to service the London loans! Suppression of the last insurrection had absorbed almost a year's income, and the current invasion would cost at least as much, in addition to the loss of work oxen, which would be disastrous for agriculture. News of the revolt also disturbed Caravellas. His instructions of October 21, 1873, still held, and Brazil must lend its moral support to the government. However, the attitude of the people, the strength of the rebels, and the resources of the government must be considered. The Paraguayan government must not believe that it could avoid responsibilities and depend on Brazil to support it at any cost. Although the revolution had been nurtured on foreign soil, still, if the Paraguayan people supported it, Brazilian intervention should be confined to defense of life and property in the capital, not permitting hostilities there. If, however, as Caravellas believed, the revolt did not have support by a majority, or if Argentina intervened on behalf of the opposition, then the Brazilian forces must be placed in full support of Jovellanos. Brazilian involvement must be limited as much as possible, and must not prevent the triumph of a popular and legal cause. The revolution was not to be considered a civil war; there must be no interference with river navigation, and Brazilian naval forces must destroy any batteries that Caballero might establish on the river banks. So far as Caravellas could see, the revolt promised nothing better than what Paraguay already had: Rivarola had himself been deposed by his present associates; Gill also fought against his present associates when he was in the Jovellanos government. Caravellas was no admirer of Bareiro, who, he wrote, had "no prestige at all . . . he was a López representative, and a relative of the ex-dictator's family," and during the war he served as a subordinate employee of an Argentine sutler! Caballero, Serrano, and others were tools, some with ominous antecedents, and nothing more. "Nevertheless," Caravellas concluded, "direct Brazilian aid would be frowned upon abroad." Should events permit, Gondim should consult with the Brazilian envoy in Buenos Aires; however, he "should be guided by developments and the best interests of Paraguay and the Empire." Caravellas was deeply concerned about Argentine support of the rebellion. As he assured the British minister, Brazil wanted peace but would not consent to Argentine domination of Paraguay or to Paraguayan cession of the Chaco.[47]

In order to avoid bloodshed, Gondim persuaded Jovellanos to declare a general amnesty on February 3; but Ferreira, who controlled the Chamber of Deputies, opposed the move and prevented publication of the decree. Jovellanos issued a full pardon to Gill, thus enabling Gondim's man to return. This was very important for Gondim, who wanted to settle matters without a show of brute strength. Argentina, not Brazil, provided most of the rebel support. Gill, by assuring the Brazilians of his cooperation, and by contributing financial aid to the rebels, was able to move into a commanding position. Gondim surely was playing Gill's game, but it would be a serious error to believe that Brazilians began the revolt in order to make Gill president.[48]

The critical period in the revolt came between February 2 and 12. Jovellanos and his government were completely unable to defend themselves. When some 2,000 rebel troops moved against the capital on February 12, Ferreira and Cabriza met them at Campo Grande near Luque. The battle began at 10:00 a.m.; four hours later the government troops were routed. Gondim and Guimarães warned Caballero not to attack Asunción. Argentina reinforced its Villa Occidental garrison with a national guard battalion, and 300 of her troops were reported to be fighting with Caballero. This did not worry Guimarães, who had about 1,000 men in Asunción. Still, the Argentine attitude was threatening.[49]

Caballero entered into negotiations with the Brazilians when he realized that they would defend Asunción. Bareiro, representing Caballero, demanded that Jovellanos resign; Gondim, planning to put Gill into the presidency, refused. Bareiro threatened to establish another capital at Villeta, but Gondim persuaded him not to be so foolish. Bareiro then threatened to lay siege to Asunción, but again the Brazilian called his bluff. Finally, Gondim assembled the principal rebel leaders to meet with Jovellanos in the Brazilian legation on February 15 to solve the impasse. The agreement provided for a new cabinet without the hated Ferreira. Gill drew Hacienda, Caballero went to Interior, Bareiro took over Foreign Affairs, Germán Serrano became minister of War and Marine, while the weakest of them all, Francisco Soteras, would preside over Justice, Worship, and Public Instruction. This was a pro-Brazilian cabinet, Gondim observed with satisfaction but with amazing self-deception. Bareiro and Caballero had even sworn on their word of honor that they had no commitments to Argentina and would not hesitate to support Brazil in event of a conflict between the Allies.[50]

Caravellas hoped that Gondim was right in saying that peace and constitutional order had returned to Paraguay. Brazil would be most pleased to see the republic emerge from the depths into which it had been plunged by its last dictator's tyranny and blindness. But Gondim's actions might prove to be very disadvantageous, and he did not like the minister's delay in supporting Jovellanos; he disapproved of using the legation as a meeting place between the rebels and Jovellanos, since this gave Bareiro and Caballero a status they did not deserve, and leaving Rivarola out of the cabinet might prove to be a blunder. Caravellas assessed the situation accurately: Jovellanos was critically weakened; Caballero, "who can scarcely sign his name, will be nothing but a weak instrument of Sr. Bareiro." Moreover, to what extent had Gondim compromised Brazil? Was it only a moral commitment or something deeper? And how could Paraguay pay for the revolution? Recognizing that the deed was done, Caravellas accepted the situation reluctantly. But, he warned Gondim, Brazil did not want Paraguay to cede the Chaco: "What Brazil would be unable to see with indifference in any case would be the abdication of the sovereignty and independence of Paraguay." Since a ministerial shakeup was certain to occur, Gondim should consider such men as Miguel Palacios, Gregorio Benites, Carlos Loizaga, and Juan B. Egusquiza—all patriotic Paraguayans.[51]

A detailed account of the revolt published in Buenos Aires denied Argentine complicity, asserted Paraguayan leadership, and confirmed Brazil's turning to Gill in an attempt to salvage what was left of its moral authority. The author, probably Dr. Miguel Gallegos, condemned Brazil's vacillating policy and inability to control Paraguay. The criticism was justified. Brazil's policy was primarily a negative one of preventing Argentine aggrandizement and not promotion of Paraguayan recovery.[52]

The February agreement certainly did not end bickering among the victors. Juan Bautista Gill was in an orbit that put Cándido Bareiro into a long eclipse. Benigno Ferreira was gone, but Bareiro discovered quickly that Gondim was determined to make Gill president of Paraguay. This adventurer, whose personal fortune had improved so dramatically with the arrival of gold from the London loans, reached Asunción on the night of March 2, shortly after a Brazilian battalion arrived from Corumbá. Gill called at once on Gondim, then the two visited Jovellanos. Gill not only reasserted his adherence to Brazil but also maintained that neither Bareiro nor Caballero had an agreement with Argentina. Gill was profuse in his thanks to Cotegipe for having helped him return to Paraguay, but, he asserted, he could have stopped the bloodshed at Luque had he returned earlier. Now Jovellaños, Serrano, and he were following Gondim's advice; despite efforts of their opponents, who followed the advice of Miguel Gallegos, they would establish a firm government and hoped to merit Brazil's continued protection.[53]

Political confusion continued for another three months as rivals for the presidency jockeyed for advantage. Gallegos, supported discreetly by General Julio de Vedia, threw Argentine support to General Caballero, who was Bareiro's candidate. Gondim continued to support Gill, and Serrano lined up with Gill and Jovellanos. In preparation for the coming presidential campaign, Gill and his brother Emilio worked assiduously to repair old fences, especially in Congress. Gondim pretended neutrality in these political struggles, but all knew where his sympathies lay. At the end of March, Bareiro and Caballero attempted a coup by imprisoning their enemies and reconstituting the cabinet. There was a flurry of activity, conferences, and innumerable rumors; but Jovellanos, Serrano and Gill had Gondim's support, and Vedia's suggestion that Jovellanos resign met with a less than sympathetic response. The result was a new cabinet that left Bareiro still dissatisfied. Bareiro was minister of foreign affairs briefly and then resigned on April 6, giving way to Higinio Uriarte, a strong Gill supporter. Dr. Gallegos, who had been involved in the March 29–30 turmoil, became *persona non grata* with Jovellanos, who revoked his exequatur. Gondim saw in this action proof that Caballero and Serrano had no commitments to Argentina. These events clearly showed that the Argentine party had lost the game, although José Dolores Molas and Rivarola led a final forlorn revolt in April that might well have succeeded had not the Brazilians fielded 2,500 men to oppose them. The Molas counterrevolution began on April 17, 1874, and enjoyed brief success when Serrano was defeated in a short engagement a week later, but Brazilian troops took the field on April 27. The revolutionists fled, pursued relentlessly by Serrano. Molas and the notorious bandit, Matías Goiburú, fled to Argentine territory; Rivarola was captured and imprisoned.[54]

President Sarmiento ordered General Vedia to withdraw to Villa Occidental with all of his troops, thus eliminating any further prospect of a clash with the Brazilians.[55] Assessing the situation from Buenos Aires, one editor detailed five blunders in Argentine policy and concluded:

> The final result is, the submission of Paraguay to Brazil. Are we to undertake a second war to liberate her against her will? If Paraguay has succumbed not ten armies could restore her. If we beat the Brazilians we should only take their place, for it is absurd to suppose for a moment that Paraguay can subsist without a foreign Protectorate. Hence the position of Brazil is correct. The Cotegipe treaties have been recognized by our Government. Councillor Gondim has simply carried these out, as in duty bound. We cannot grumble in the matter, unless we pretend to be more Paraguayan than the Paraguayans themselves, and undertake over again the war of 1865 without any allies on our side.[56]

Revolutions out of the way temporarily, Gill proceeded with plans to win the presidency. He was assured of widespread support as "the only one who can rescue the country from the almost bottomless mire in which it finds itself."[57] Gondim could see no obstacles to fulfillment of Brazil's plan to make Gill president. His candidate "almost daily" protested his gratitude for Brazil's aid. Caravellas had made Brazil's preference clear. The Empire must have a friendly president. Gill was the first choice; Gregorio Benites would be acceptable if it were impossible to get Gill. There was some argument about the vice-presidential candidate, but Asunción papers solidly supported Higinio Uriarte, Gill's cousin. The election for presidential electors occurred on June 21 as scheduled, and, also as scheduled, candidates favorable to Gill and Uriarte were elected unanimously. No violence marked the election, manifest proof to the Brazilians that Gill and Uriarte were truly popular candidates, but the Argentines had by no means given up the game. There were rumors of a plot by Caballero and Serrano to oppose Gill; if this was indeed true, Gill countered the threat by having Congress approve a plan to send Uriarte and Caballero to England to investigate the loans situation. The two men, who might check on each other, left Asunción in July. Uriarte, therefore, was absent when formalities of the election ended in September and missed the inauguration on November 25. Apparently old wounds were healed, the press hailed Brazil and Gondim as saviors of Paraguay, and even Padre Fidel Maíz and Dr. Facundo Machaín, chief justice of the Superior Tribunal, expressed their gratitude for Brazil's friendly intervention.[58] Juan Bautista Gill had set his feet on the path that was to leave him dead on an Asunción street, victim of poncho-clad assassins.

12. In the Toils of the Past

Juan Bautista Gill became president of a country that was just beginning to show faint signs of recovery from the terrible war. The revolt against Jovellanos had won considerable popular support, interest in promoting immigration persisted in spite of the "Lincolnshire farmers" fiasco, there was concern over relations with the Church, and a few people still sought to promote education. Although trade and commerce were primarily in Italian and Portuguese-Brazilian hands, English and German enterprisers were showing increased interest.

Paraguay had no intention of repudiating the scandalous London loans and sought to make the best settlement possible with the bond-holders. Proposals to sell the railway and public lands were heard with increasing frequency, and both were aimed at attracting capital and energetic immigrants. Although President Gill sought earnestly to solve the many problems that weighed so heavily on the shattered country, government resources were unequal to the very severe tasks that would have taxed the most enlightened of regimes. Whatever popularity Gill may have enjoyed with the Brazilian military leaders had been completely eroded by his previous political activities, and his reputation had been badly tarnished by the old charges of embezzlement, which would not die.

Brazilian military and civilian representatives fought among themselves, giving Gill an opportunity to be far more independent than one might expect. When Brazil replaced its minister, the situation became even more intolerable for Gill, whose complaints helped to bring about a change. Jovellanos had sent Gregorio Benites to investigate the loans in London, and when this envoy returned he suffered persecution by the Gill administration. Gill's treatment of Benites and his rejection of Madame Lynch cost him support among the Lopiztas. Elisa Lynch, proving again her fearlessness and confidence, returned to Asunción, where she challenged the government boldly. Gill, after having posed

215

as her friend, found it convenient to order her deportation before her presence further complicated the maze of domestic and foreign problems through which he was stumbling bravely.

Gill in the Political Vortex

President Gill's term began auspiciously with a conciliatory inaugural that extended political amnesty to all Paraguayans. "This is a solemn day," he declared, "the first day which the history of Paraguay will record as having effected the legal transmission of power after a free election, not as a family heritage nor as a coup in the shadows of the night." Gill came to office without a program, since Paraguay's condition, "after so many disasters and calamitous mistakes, does not permit it." He promised to keep the peace, called for reconciliation of all factions, and urged all citizens to forget the past and raise the country from the slough of tyranny. He echoed, probably unconsciously, Thomas Jefferson's plea for nonpartisanship: "As for me, I assure you that from this day forward I recognize no parties in Paraguay, because there is no reason for them under the folds of our beautiful flag; all people have the perfect right to live peacefully in the land in which they were born, in which they saw the first and clearest light of our beautiful sky, in which the perfumed aura from our forests animates our souls." He concluded his short address with a plea for unity, for hard work from which the country could not fail to progress. General public rejoicing and a big celebration launched Gill's term under the best auspices, or at least so thought Gondim.[1]

Gill's administration did appear to have begun under enviable conditions. A civilian caudillo, imposed leader of the revolutionary coalition, he was supported by Brazilian forces and had no rivals, no imitators—or so it seemed. Cabinet positions he parceled out for blatantly political reasons, not because of the demonstrated ability of the appointees. The very important post of Minister of Interior went to General Germán Serrano. Another general, Patricio Escobar, drew War and Marine, while General Bernardino Caballero, strongest military man in the revolt, had to be content with Justice, Worship, and Public Instruction. To his brother, General Emilio Gill, the President assigned Hacienda, while Dr. Facundo Machaín directed Foreign Affairs.[2] As consul-general and then as minister to Argentina, Gill named his old friend Carlos Saguier. This was a good choice. Saguier held one of Paraguay's two sensitive posts, and his dealings with President Nicolás Avellaneda and Foreign Minister Bernardo de Irigoyen were marked by wise restraint. Vigilant in all things, Saguier cultivated good relations with the press, kept Argentine authorities informed about rebel activities in Corrientes, and reported faithfully to his president, whom he lectured from time to time on the need for promoting immigration, free trade, and agriculture, maintaining political peace, winning popular support, and conducting an economical government.[3]

No matter how necessary it was for the president to be master in his own house, Gill could not ignore the Brazilian presence. His every move was observed closely by the Brazilians, with open hostility by the military and, after the departure of Gondim, with suspicion by the legation. To gain control over the government, he removed nearly all foreigners from office, leaving only a few Italians. Others, such as Dr. William Stewart, were so closely identified with the country that their services could be used advantageously on various commissions. Italians, Spaniards, Frenchmen, Uruguayans, and Brazilians were all involved, although a small group of the latter attempted to promote the "false and absurd" idea that the measure was directed exclusively against them.[4]

Very much concerned about internal conditions, which, according to all observers, bordered on anarchy, President Gill early in December, 1874, sent Generals Serrano and Escobar on a tour of the interior charged with strengthening the police, recruiting an armed escort for the president, and reporting on general conditions. They carried commissions for justices of the peace and jefes políticos, both important local and departmental positions. The jefe, more than a political leader, was an administrator with a wide variety of duties. To find qualified persons without making use of foreigners was extremely difficult, and the result was so unsatisfactory that justices of the peace were abolished in 1876 and their functions absorbed by the jefes políticos. Dictated also by a shortage of funds, this change resulted in no harmful effect, according to the acting president, Higinio Uriarte.[5]

The president was very energetic, fully cognizant of his country's needs, and impressed the American minister, General John C. Caldwell, as "a man of limited education, but of much natural sagacity, and [he] appears to possess great firmness and decision." [6] Caldwell was impressed by the professed friendship for the United States: "It is impossible to exaggerate the veneration which this people entertains for the United States. Their model and exemplar in theory at least is always the Grand Republic of the North." After this exuberant nonsense, the minister returned to earth with the usual platitude about a possible great future, which he followed with a masterpiece of understatement: "Both rulers and people are yet to be educated to a sense of their duties and responsibilities." [7]

Brazilians in Asunción continued to be divided in their attitudes toward Gill. Gondim was a strong supporter of the man he had placed in the presidency, but the military commander, General João Auto da Silva Guimarães, Barão Jaguarão, entertained a violent dislike for Gill. The disagreement between these two men may have been precipitated by the attack of Lt. Col. José Thomas Gonçalves, commander of the 8th Infantry Battalion, on the legation's secretary, Dr. Gurgal do Amaral Valente. Antipathy between the diplomats and the military was of long standing, and Gondim recommended that Jaguarão be relieved of his command.[8] The military fought back with two newspapers that had been established to counter Argentine influence. Manoel Antônio Guimarães directed *El Cabrión* for a short time. The military founded *A Gazeta Brazileira*, directed and edited by Cándido Piquiló, which constantly insulted the president, his cabinet, and Gondim.[9] The Argentines, of course, gleefully repeated the *Gazeta*'s strictures in their *Amigo del Pueblo*, founded in 1875 to counter Brazilian propaganda. "Sad it is," Gondim lamented, "that there should be Brazilians who thus oppose the policy of the Imperial Government, but the fact is that they have begun an open campaign against the Government of Snr Gill, and our own land forces are lending support to this."[10] Jaguarão and Gondim sent conflicting reports to Rio de Janeiro. Early in 1875, the military commander complained against "the system of terror inaugurated by the new President . . . by means of arbitrary imprisonment and tortures to which the victims of those violent acts were subjected and whose screams horrify those who live near the police station." Gill denied the tortures, assured Gondim that Gregorio Benites, imprisoned because of alleged corruption during his London mission, was in as good health as one subjected to solitary confinement could be, and asserted that rumors about Eduardo Aramburú having gone crazy as a result of torture were also false.[11]

The complaints against Gill had begun with his inauguration and concerned a series of attacks, some of them violent, against Brazilian soldiers and civilians. *A Gazeta Brazileira* on January 14, 1875, had complained of such attacks, but Jaguarão had made no official complaint to Gondim, so the latter had ignored them. *A Gazeta*, Gondim asserted, was the instrument for a circle of complaining persons "so blind that they do not see that by such action they only work in favor of the Argentine influence, which seeks to increase under the protection of such senseless propaganda." The issue of March 11 reprinted from Buenos Aires papers the calumnies of the Italian priest Gerónimo Becchis, although the latter's hatred of Brazil was well known. *A Gazeta*, Gondim complained bitterly, invented the wildest stories, such as the yarn that he had permitted the Asunción chief of police to drag Becchis from his refuge in the Brazilian legation. Gondim could see no solution except to remove Jaguarão. The Brazilian cabinet solved the problem by recalling both of the quarreling chiefs.[12]

While awaiting their replacements, Jaguarão and Gondim went on with their feuding. *Cabrión* and *A Gazeta Brazileira* continued to delight the Argentines with attacks against Gill. Finally, tired of the libelous articles in *Cabrión*, President Gill had the editor summoned before the Criminal Judge. Manoel Antônio Guimarães, accompanied by more than a dozen Brazilian officers who invaded the court to intimidate the judge, denied that he had written the offensive articles: he had merely published unsigned articles as he received them. The court gave him twenty-four hours to recall the name of the guilty party. To avoid conflict, Gondim and Emilio Gill urged Jaguarão to take proper measures against the offending officers. Their visit was in vain. On his second trip to court, Guimarães had the company of two Brazilian officers, with a more distant escort of at least twenty Brazilian, Portuguese, and Italian supporters, "all of bad fame." This escort prevented the Paraguayan judge from sending the young editor to jail. Upon leaving the police station, the editor hurried to Jaguarão's headquarters and then under escort to the Brazilian consulate. President Gill ordered both *Cabrión* and *A Gazeta Brazileira* closed forthwith.[13] Gill, obviously, was very sure of himself or he would not have dared to take such strong action. On April 1, 1875, Cándido Piquiló also appeared before the Criminal Judge with a Brazilian escort and, of course, escaped punishment.[14] Gondim, in response to a complaint from Facundo Machaín, demanded an investigation by Jaguarão into this censurable conduct of his officers, "conduct that is in flagrant contradiction to the enlightened policy of the Imperial Government toward this unfortunate country." A commission of three Brazilian officers who investigated the conduct of their fellows surprised no one by exonerating them. Nevertheless, Gill won the argument. Piquiló left Paraguay secretly on the *Cuyabá* on April 10, along with Jaguarão's secretary. Less than three weeks later, Gondim presented his letter of recall and Felippe José Pereira Leal, Barão de Maracajú, became Brazil's minister on April 28. Jaguarão, too, soon ended his tour. General Federico Augusto de Mesquita assumed command of Brazil's occupation forces on May 9.[15] If President Gill expected to benefit greatly from these changes, he was disappointed.

Pereira Leal, who had been expelled from Paraguay by Carlos Antonio López in 1858, was no friend of Paraguay or of President Gill. Nevertheless, Gill convinced him that Paraguay considered Brazilian friendship indispensable, and his private conference with the new minister on

April 24 went off well. Gill had no other choice at the time, especially with the prospect of an invasion from Argentina, where Rivarola, Soteras, Molas, Ferreira, and others were reported to be planning an invasion for June or July. They had obtained artillery in Montevideo, guns and ammunition in Buenos Aires. Carlos Saguier kept up a stream of protests and was assured that the rebels would get no aid from Argentina. Pereira Leal promised Gill Brazil's support and asked the Brazilian naval commander, Delfim Carlos de Carvalho, Barão do Passagem, to prevent any river expedition from landing men and arms in Paraguay. General Mesquita kept a force ready for any eventuality. This threat from abroad soon faded, but Pereira Leal became disillusioned with President Gill and allied himself with the Brazilian officers, who began to encourage General Serrano in his plans to overthrow the government.[16]

Pereira Leal's opinion of Paraguay and Paraguayans was colored by his constant ill health. He suffered from colds and bronchitis, and often was so weak that he had Dr. Daltro go with him to see the president. His personal letters to Cotegipe frequently began with a health report; safely back in Bahia, he referred to "that infernal Paraguay." Health problems aside, he had good reason to be suspicious of Gill and his ministers. Long before the Serrano revolt, he condemned Gill's economic policies, excoriated the President for closing the Asociación General del Comercio Paraguayo (General Association of Paraguayan Commerce), and reported that Gill and his brother Pedro were making money by stealing from funds yielded by the tobacco monopoly and that Gill and Serrano bought state properties with payment orders that sold in the market for not more than 6 percent of their face value. Gill acquired a large property in the suburbs for his wife using payment orders worth 300 patacones; Serrano bought the Solano López quinta for about 600 patacones. Gill sent 150 Paraguayan soldiers every day to improve and cultivate his wife's property. By refusing to pay large sums owed to Ricardo Mendes Gonçalves, João de Freitas Travassos, and José Miltiades Segovia, Gill had ruined these Brazilians, all of whom had aided in starting the Caja de Conversión (Exchange Office),[17] which tried to introduce some order into the confused monetary situation.

Plots of his enemies abroad and at home, furor over the Sosa-Tejedor Treaty, and failure of his economic program weighed heavily on President Gill in 1875. Add to these troubles the efforts of his emissaries to settle the London loans and the visit of Madame Lynch to Asunción, and one begins to sympathize with the beleaguered president.

The Economic Legacy

For more than fifty years after becoming independent, Paraguay enjoyed a favorable balance of trade that enabled the dictators to pay for imports and accumulate a small reserve of gold and silver. The principal items of export were maté, hides, and such forest products as logs, for the Buenos Aires market. Francia and the López had monopolized foreign trade to such an extent that the commercial community was very small. The war destroyed this export trade. Maté exports were first to recover, but many years were to pass before a flourishing trade once more provided an important source of income.

During the years of occupation, Brazilian and Argentine troops consumed most of the imported goods, and nearly all of their supplies had to be imported since only small quantities could be provided by Paraguay. This trade was in the hands of such sutlers as Travassos, Patri, and Segovia. They paid no import duties on goods destined for Allied troops, and used this cover to avoid payment of duties on goods that trickled into the general market. A few vessels plied the river, gradually increasing in number during the postwar decade, but even by 1880 the river trade was much less than it had been in 1864.

Trade was confined almost entirely to the capital. A few small houses survived in the northern departments, Villa Rica, and Encarnación; animal husbandry and agriculture had scarcely begun to revive in the interior by 1874. Seeking to invite capital, Congress on July 11, 1874, enacted a law to guarantee 7 percent return on capital investments of $f200,000 in railways, telegraphs, steamers, roads, or industrial establishments, to a maximum of $f15,000,000.[18] The proposal, given the condition of finances, was hardly realistic.

Export items continued to be tobacco, maté, timber, quebracho bark, and oranges. Hides, so prominent in the prewar trade, were not available, for nearly all of Paraguay's cattle had perished in the war and animals had to be imported from Corrientes. Imports, excluding supplies for the occupation forces, included textiles, hardware, liquor, clothing, shoes, and a wide variety of miscellaneous manufactures. Gill became president during a period of economic stagnation within a generally stagnant decade. The total value of imports and exports was $f1,685,886 in 1873; the figure plunged to $f490,138 in 1874, and to $f267,509 in 1875. From this trade customs duties yielded $f322,485, $f319,129, and $f137,112 in the respective years. Paraguay depended primarily on Argentine and Uruguayan markets for its exports, but these outlets suffered from severe economic difficulties in mid-1875. Gill's financial program of 1875, undertaken with excellent advice and in the best of faith, made matters worse, and the accumulated effects of a series of bad harvests caused by droughts and locust plagues contributed to the economic disorder.[19]

Government finances obviously would be strongly affected by the economy. Paraguay lacked population to exploit its natural resources. The languishing trade severely limited income from customs duties, personal taxation in the poverty-stricken nation was impossible, capital levies would have been ludicrous, and such excises as license fees and stamped paper for legal documents would yield but a pittance. There remained three possible sources of income: subsidies by the Allies, loans, and sale of government property.

Neither Brazil nor Argentina offered Paraguay substantial financial aid. Brazil did finance restoration of railway service after a fashion but then kept dunning the bankrupt country to pay the bill. The small military force, primarily a guard, created during the first months of occupation was equipped and maintained by Brazil. How much Brazilians paid to various politicians is not known, but we are justified in assuming that Rivarola, Jovellanos, Brizuela, and Gill were among those who received subsidies.

Paraguayan success in obtaining loans in London was incredible, although Argentine bankers were on far safer ground in having refused to make any loans until Saguier obtained a small advance of $50,000 in 1876.[20] Because the London loans had been squandered, it was absurd to believe that Paraguay could obtain significant foreign financing until provision had been made for satisfying the bondholders.

The sale of government property was especially tempting. This consisted of the railway, 16,239 square leagues of public lands, and 500 buildings, of which 148 were in Asunción. From time to time these assets were pledged as security for paper money or foreign loans and were offered for sale. Efforts to sell the railway were unsuccessful until 1877 and then yielded little advantage to the government. Land sales, which began as early as 1873, did not really get under way until after 1880, when Bernardino Caballero seized the presidency. Government buildings available for sale attracted few buyers.[21]

Government revenues constantly failed to meet budgeted expenditures. For the years 1870–1873 inclusive, revenue from all sources other than the London loans was estimated at £186,000 or about $930,000. There appears to be no reasonably accurate record of expenditures, but they greatly exceeded income. Records for 1873 are fairly reliable. Congress voted a budget of $f444,085 for that year, a sum which the Brazilian minister found very unrealistic. The Paraguayans, he grumbled, should stop depending upon foreigners and create a system that would impose taxes on those best able to pay and establish a customs schedule that would not discourage nascent industry. This was exactly what Congress, in a bumbling way, was trying to accomplish when it imposed duties varying from 25 to 40 percent on imports, the highest rates being assessed against such competing products as yerba, wood, and liquor. Export duties were very light: 6 reales (60¢) per hide, 3 reales per arroba (25 lbs.) of maté, and 6 percent ad valorem on other goods.[22] Congress could not anticipate the heavy expenses incurred in crushing the first phases of the Bareiro-Caballero revolt. Despite application of some of the London gold, expenses far exceeded revenues.[23] Most of the receipts in 1873, exclusive of the gold from London, came from customs duties, which averaged about $f36,000 monthly.[24]

Government finances obviously were in desperate straits when the Bareiro-Caballero revolt succeeded in 1874. Congress had voted a modest budget of about $f440,000 for the year, whereas expenses would exceed $f1,000,000. No wonder the Gill administration sought desperately to uncover large sums supposedly concealed by Gregorio Benites when he came to a settlement with the London bankers in 1873![25]

Paraguay's postwar banking history began with efforts to raise money in England to start a bank of issue. After failing to use the London loans for this purpose, Congress on July 11, 1874, authorized a bank capitalized at £1,000,000. Agents sent to England to raise this sum understandably encountered difficulty, but Congress persisted and on September 19, 1874, authorized formation of the Asociación General del Comercio Paraguayo.[26] This enterprise had a nominal capital of $f500,000 consisting of 5,000 shares of $f100 each, only 10 percent of which had to be paid in, the rest being used as a reserve to be called when needed. Its banking functions included issuing paper, receiving deposits, issuing drafts, and discounting commercial paper. The bank could issue bonos de caja, or bank notes, in an amount equal to discounted paper or anticipated funds; the bonos were to be redeemed in gold when due. A unique provision enabled a merchant to deposit goods in the Asociación warehouse and receive a loan in bonos de caja, but the merchant signed a short-term note that bore weekly interest of 7 percent! The Asociación operated the Caja de Conversión, which greatly facilitated commerce. Partners with the government in this enterprise were Travassos, Segovia, and Ricardo Antônio Mendes Gonçalves, all Allied sutlers.[27] Unfortunately, this banking venture was not permitted to realize its full potential.

Gill's Financial Program of 1875

Paraguay lacked experts who might point the way out of an extremely dismal economic swamp. There was no one in the Gill Administration to play the role of an Alexander Hamilton, although one was desperately needed. No one, apparently, knew how to compile a budget. A schedule of salaries totaling $f43,525 monthly for 1875 was called the national budget,[28] and this was far beyond possible income. A comprehensive budget was required, one that would present a fairly accurate estimate of revenues and allot them realistically.

The Brazilian mission in Asunción advised calling in Baron Mauá's financial secretary, an expert who proposed several measures that Congress dutifully enacted. First came an ambitious program to be financed by issuing $f2,500,000 in bonds called *consolidados paraguayos*. This issue was to pay the floating debt, establish trade missions abroad, create a Junta de Crédito Público (Public Credit Committee), pay expenses of the scientific mission then in Paraguay, reorganize public instruction, help establish a bank, rebuild the telegraph line to the Paraná, develop a merchant marine, and provide backing for paper money. Bearing 9 percent interest, the bonds were to be serviced by a registry tax and a capital levy.[29]

Corollary acts rounded out these "laws of Dorión." Most important were taxes to service the consolidateds. The Public Credit Committee of three members was to administer the loan, receive taxes and customs, transmit funds to banking houses for payment of interest and redemptions, and supervise the Office of Public Lands, the Department of Topography, the General Statistical Office, and the mortgage registry. Major governmental functions, therefore, were assigned to this agency.[30] A commission of three members was to prepare an economic report and a general plan for public administration and to propose general tariff and financial reform. The Office of Public Lands was to bring order out of the title chaos. All land claimants were to present their titles or other proof of ownership within ninety days, and all land to which private title could not be proved reverted to the nation. During the ninety-day period there could be no land transactions, and no public lands could be alienated to pay debts.[31] One should remember that Paraguay had pledged its public lands as collateral for the London loans of 1871 and 1872, a detail easily overlooked by Congress.

Gondim, while praising the proposed measures, was dubious about their success. It was an admirable program that might work and relieve the government of "the permanent pressure exerted on it by the bearers of letters, payment orders, and other bills of a floating debt in excess of one million patacones; causing it constant embarrassment, besides the complaints and resentment of dissatisfied parties."[32] The executive expected new taxes to yield 240,000 patacones, an estimate altogether too sanguine, since most of the government's income derived from customs duties. Withdrawal of Brazilian forces would greatly decrease the amount of metallic money in circulation. Since gold brought in to pay troops supported most of the country's trade, its sudden end would be catastrophic. Public order would suffer because Gill, notwithstanding his energy and firmness, lacked forces to defeat revolutionary plots.[33]

The "laws of Dorión" failed miserably. Their success was predicated upon receipt of considerable sums from the various tax levies, but that income failed to materialize. By March, 1875, the country's economic picture, greatly worsened by four years of locust plagues and droughts, was so gloomy that even Carlos Saguier in Buenos Aires was advising President Gill to issue $f3,000,000 in paper while desperately trying to get an agricultural surplus to exchange for gold. As economic depression deepened, many merchants went out of business, imports of needed foodstuffs fell off drastically, and the government's principal income came from the sale of stamped paper.[34]

President Gill's next measure compounded Paraguay's economic trouble. Laws of April 22, 1875, provided for an issue of $f1,000,000 in paper and a tobacco monopoly. Retroactive to January 1, the monopoly permitted seizure of the existing supply of cigars and unprocessed tobacco. Owners were paid in paper at absurdly low prices, and speculators bought the paper at discounts up to 90 percent. To obtain maximum advantage from the monopoly, a Comisión de Crédito Nacional (National Credit Commission) was created with power to carry out tobacco transactions, supervise issue of paper money, administer funds, and control conversion. This ended the operations of the Asociación General del Comercio Paraguayo and its affiliated Caja de Conversión, which were nationalized.[35]

Results of the new measures were catastrophic. The house in Buenos Aires that handled the tobacco failed, and, since Pedro Gill claimed that Paraguay owed him 40,000 patacones, cynics again charged the Gill brothers with grafting. Tobacco planting fell off drastically. Trade was at a standstill as many merchants who had loaded goods for Asunción returned the cargoes to warehouses, and commercial houses in Asunción were being liquidated. The tobacco monopoly and expropriation of the Asociación General, combined with the new issue of paper, destroyed what little confidence remained among merchants.[36]

President Gill attempted to inject a bit of gaiety into Asunción's somber social scene by ordering his birthday to be celebrated on June 24, one month earlier than former celebrations held in honor of Francisco Solano's natal day. The "martyr of Cerro Corá" had been dead for only five years, too short a time for the apotheosis so avidly promoted four decades later. So it was that the diplomatic corps, government employees, and a few stragglers attended the Te Deum at the Cathedral and completed the celebration with a great dance in the evening. Merchants celebrated with less joy, for more than a score of them closed their doors in the week following. Paper money was worthless, but those who refused to accept it were reported by spies and suffered fines and imprisonment. To register their protest, thirty-three merchants still at large met to consider the economic situation but could find no solution. As if to see how much worse he could make things, Gill obtained a law on August 17 to establish a government monopoly on salt and soap for three years, but this was soon modified to permit any merchant to import and sell the commodities on payment of $f2 per arroba of soap and $f1 per arroba of salt.[37]

Perhaps the stream of advice from Saguier in Buenos Aires was to have a beneficial effect on Gill. His faithful agent repeatedly urged development of commerce, promotion of immigration, abolition of monopolies, and extreme caution with paper money. He referred to the commercial crisis in Argentina, Uruguayan turmoil, and Brazilian unrest as results of bad economic policies. Attempts to increase the army should be dropped, since Paraguayan exiles feared to return lest they be drafted. The army was an expensive luxury and should be reduced to 500 men.[38]

Confronted with the obvious failure of his elaborate program of 1875, President Gill on October 5 decreed an end to the monopolies and summoned Congress to revise the constitution. Although Congress had no such power, important measures could be expected. A conflict was also developing between the president and his ministers and was resolved in mid October by appointing Cándido Bareiro as minister of hacienda to replace Emilio Gill. That Bareiro should have been left out of the reconstituted cabinet in the first place is surprising, and was probably the result of pressure from Juan Bautista Gill to obtain an office for his brother Emilio. Bareiro was in London in October, 1875, so Adolfo Saguier, younger brother of the envoy in Buenos Aires, served in his place until June 16, 1876. As minister of interior, José Urdapilleta replaced Serrano, who was never one of Gill's favorites.[39] Serrano resented his dismissal and immediately began plotting a rebellion, encouraged by dissident Brazilian officers. While observers in Buenos Aires were applauding repeal of the monopolies, Congress quickly passed legislation to ratify the president's decree. Following this came repeal of the "laws of Dorión," which had precipitated the crisis, and another act provided for resumption of land sales to the amount of $f6,000,000 to service the London debt and amortize the *consolidados paraguayos.* Tobacco on hand was earmarked for creditors of the Comisión de Crédito Nacional. Issues of paper money stopped after $f351,486 of the authorized million had been placed in circulation; the rest was burned. The Caja de Conversión, revived on October 21, received compensation for its losses from the confiscation of a few months earlier.[40]

The new financial program and cabinet changes marked a decided turning-point in the postwar decade. Large mercantile interests in Montevideo and Buenos Aires rushed to buy land. By the end of October, some £22,168 had been received from sales that varied in price from $2.00 to $1.50 per cuadra of 100 square varas, or 94.71 sq. yds. (the Paraguayan vara equals 34.09 inches), depending on the distance from Asunción. Since payment was in gold and silver, the government was rescued for the moment. José Segundo Decoud turned his considerable talents to writing a series for *La Reforma* in which he urged an end of the occupation and a quick treaty with Argentina. It was time for Brazil and Argentina to stop using Paraguay as a pawn in their game of power politics. Whether this October reversal of policy was indeed the cause of successful negotiation with Argentina, there is no doubt that continued occupation of the country could serve no good purpose. A meeting called for December 8, right after the pilgrimage to the shrine of the Virgin of Caacupé, was to have registered popular protest against the occupation but was canceled at Brazilian request.[41] Decoud's articles were timely and may be taken as an indication of President Gill's disillusionment with Brazil and his determination to be his own man. Once more Brazil had shown no inclination whatever to aid its former enemy toward economic recovery. It was time for the Empire's troops to go home.

Benites under Fire

The Gill crowd was critical of the Benites mission from its beginning in 1872. Gregorio Benites, in middle age an elder statesman, was an unreformed Lopizta who may have had the confidence of President Jovellanos, but neither Gill nor Ferreira, who hated each other cordially, placed any trust in him. In Congress, Brizuela, Palacios, Higinio Uriarte, and Emilio Gill asked embarrassing questions that continued until Azambuja played the peacemaker and advised the Ferreira circle to avoid a conflict with Congress and urged the Gill clique, which he called "our old friends," to be moderate.[42] Gill's antagonism had not lessened by the time he became president in 1874.

The political situation in Asunción was vastly different when Benites went home in 1874 from what it had been when he left in 1872. The Bareiro-Caballero revolt had sent Ferreira into exile and left Jovellanos with only a shadow of his former power. In Rio de Janeiro on his way home, Benites conferred with Caravellas, who found him to be a very cultured, ambitious man with a deep dislike for Gill, whom he accused of having "stolen a large sum from the first loan." Caravellas was careful not to give Benites the idea that he was their "candidate for any political position in the Republic." The Brazilian foreign minister continued: "We desire that Paraguay be governed with probity, patriotism, and intelligence. In this context let us advise Sr. Jovellanos that he freely exhort his ministers and not fear offending the Imperial Government." [43]

Benites either badly misjudged the reception he might receive in Asunción or trusted too much to Brazilian protection. He dawdled for a while in Montevideo. Then, encouraged by letters from Asunción and the immunity previously enjoyed by defrauders of the public treasury, he returned to Asunción in April to participate in the elections, or to seek a cabinet post or foreign appointment. Congress, under control of the Gill circle, flatly rejected the accounts Benites presented. Everyone knew that £125,000 had been received in Asunción and had promptly disappeared but that was not the fault of Benites. He was especially criticized for having paid debts of the López regime: $30,500 in subsidies to European newspapers, $14,000 to United States newspapers, $125,000 to Alfred Blyth, $3,000 to Abate Paris for expenses of students, $5,000 to a French contractor in Havre, $10,000 to Percy Burrell and Henry Valpy, and $5,000 to Dr. Simon du Graty. President Jovellanos appointed a committee to examine Benites's accounts.[44]

Despite suspicion that Benites had embezzled large amounts, he was not molested for a few days. For rest and possibly fancied security, he went to the estate of his brother-in-law, Eduardo Aramburú, on San Francisco Island off Villa Occidental, close to the Argentine garrison. The committee concluded that Benites was indeed an embezzler, that he had joined Robinson, Fleming & Co. in speculating on the exchange in order to cause Paraguayan bonds to fall in price. Ordered to appear at the Ministry of Hacienda, presided over by Juan Bautista Gill, Benites refused. The government then sent an armed force to seize him on May 8. Benites took refuge in the Brazilian barracks, but Gondim ordered Jaguarão to surrender the fugitive, who was immediately clapped in prison for a confinement that was to last well over a year.[45]

Benites refused to break under the pressure of real or fancied torture. Then, so the story goes, police intercepted a letter from the prisoner to a correspondent in Montevideo that not only referred to a credit of $35,000 but also to sums he had in his London account. Threatened with severe torture, Benites "confessed" his crimes on May 18. Receipts that he denied having were later found between the mattresses of his wife's bed. Thus encouraged, emissaries were sent to Montevideo in an attempt to find the $35,000. Benites also confessed that he had given £15,000 to his brother-in-law; Aramburú in turn said that his sister had it; but Señora Benites denied any knowledge of the money. If there was any truth in the confession of May 18, Benites was one of Paraguay's most accomplished embezzlers. He accounted for £361,000 in deposits and payments:

In banks		£129,000
Union Bank, London	£98,000	
Pedro Gil, Paris	27,000	
Bank of London and Río de la Plata, Montevideo	4,000	
Entrusted to individuals		18,000
Eduardo Aramburú	15,000	
Augusto Lascages, Montevideo	3,000	
Payments		214,000
To lawyers in London	14,000	
Dr. Leone Levi, London	28,000	
Felix Aucaigne, Washington	5,000	
Robinson, Fleming & Co.	167,000	
Total		361,000[46]

In addition to these funds, Benites had £3,000 of what he claimed to be his own savings on deposit in the Banking Association of London. His tormentors forced him to give a power of attorney that enabled Higinio Uriarte to get the money.

Benites probably was lying, both in his original accounting and his confession of May 18. However, the emissary to Montevideo recovered more than $30,000 in patacones and a box of important papers. The Brazilian minister was convinced that these papers proved that Benites, "besides enriching himself with the product of the second loan, even intentionally contributed to the depreciation of the bonds" that ruined the country's credit.[47] It is very unlikely that the whole truth of this affair will ever be known. Neither Robinson, Fleming & Co. nor Alfred Blyth would make their books available to the emissaries sent to investigate the Benites caper, and the various statements made by Benites cannot be reconciled.

Among critics of the entire proceedings was the Argentine commander, General Julio de Vedia, who had a very low opinion of President Jovellanos, "a refined Tartuffe—a vulgar ambitious man who uses the post he occupies for no purpose other than to steal—nothing else matters to him." As to Benites, that unfortunate victim of the Jovellanos-Gill torture had been forced to confess to having some $1,500,000 in his possession; but, Vedia vowed, Paraguayans were the greatest liars and under torture would confess to anything. Vedia thought better of Gill: "But Jovellanos? . . . Puf!!!"[48] Reports of torture applied to Benites and widespread police brutality reached Rio de Janeiro and disturbed Caravellas, who asked Gondim to investigate. Gondim assured his superiors that the reports were greatly exaggerated, but torture, an accepted part of the Paraguayan judicial process, definitely had been used on Benites. After the new minister, Pereira Leal, remonstrated with President Gill, Benites was released on July 29, 1875, and immediately left for Montevideo, where he published his impassioned defenses.[49] Gill, floundering in the aftermath of the Sosa-Tejedor Treaty and overwhelmed by economic troubles, must have been glad to see him go; but the book Benites published, *Las imposturas de Juan Bautista Gill*, has cast heavy shadows on Gill's reputation ever since.

The Uriarte-Caballero Mission to London, 1874–1875

The large sums that Benites confessed to having deposited abroad would have aroused the cupidity of almost any Paraguayan politician. Gill certainly could use the money and, while he was preparing for his election to the presidency, General Caballero's presence might prove embarrassing. Clearly the duty of the administration was to recover whatever money might remain abroad; still, there was no good reason for sending the general, a man completely unencumbered with knowledge of finance or diplomacy, on a foreign mission—except to get him out of the way and possibly to strike a bargain with Madame Elisa Alicia Lynch. If Francisco Solano López had indeed buried treasure along the route of his final retreat, his mistress might well know the hiding places. If she would reveal the secret, Gill would help her to recover property she claimed in Paraguay. Although no documentary proof has been found to support this supposition, later developments do give the idea a tantalizing credence. At least someone should hasten to London and Paris to seize Benites's deposits. Efforts should be made to persuade the financiers to establish a bank and to extend the railway to Villa Rica. Relations with the Papacy should be normalized, a bishop should be appointed for Paraguay to put an end to the bickering among rival clerics, and the Lopiztas wanted to rehabilitate Padre Fidel Maíz. To accomplish these objectives, President Jovellanos, acting for Gill, named Higinio Uriarte and Bernardino Caballero, with Cayetano Uriburú as secretary.[50]

In London the Paraguayan envoys met the whole crew who were involved in the loans of 1871 and 1872. In addition to Máximo Terrero, there were Charles Ohlsen, Albert Grant, Samuel Laing, Alfred Blyth,

George Fleming, Henry Luke Robinson, Leone Levi, and others with whom Benites had dealt. A key figure in the whole complicated mess was in Asunción—Dr. William Stewart, who had been appointed to the commission that audited the Benites accounts and who undoubtedly kept Robinson, Fleming & Co. well informed about affairs in Asunción. This information filtered through to Máximo Terrero, who attempted some much-needed fence repairs. Expressing a hope that Gill would be victorious in the presidential elections, Terrero advised him to consider seriously Paraguay's need to meet its obligations. If Paraguay could service the loans, the unsold securities from the second loan, totaling £1,438,000, could be placed and then Paraguay's obligations in London and Buenos Aires could be met. To service the £1,562,000 outstanding, a quarterly payment of £29,000 should be sent to London. To expect Paraguay to send $145,000 in gold to London each quarter was ludicrous in view of the government's financial position, and no one knew that better than Terrero. His Asunción correspondent kept him well posted on the troubles of Benites, and he observed that an investigation of Benites's disastrous mission to Europe was highly proper. Some of the charges against Benites were baseless, others exaggerated, but the truth should be heard.[51] One can imagine Gill's reaction to this advice.

Uriarte and Caballero spent more than a year in frustration. The vast sums they expected to recover simply were not to be found. From the Union Bank they drew £1,168 and hoped to get £3,000 from Benites's account in the Banking Association. They also discovered that Benites had withdrawn £12,000 from the Bank of London and Brazil before he left and advised that Gill find out what he did with the money. Robinson, Fleming & Co. would discuss nothing until Paraguay had accepted the Benites settlement. Exasperated, the envoys turned their papers over to a lawyer who advised Uriarte to annul everything done by Benites, an obviously impossible course.[52] Terrero, discredited by Benites, continued to pose as Paraguay's friend. Gill's brother Pedro had married Terrero's sister, and Terrero attempted to use this family connection. Uriarte countered by warning Gill to place no trust in Terrero "because he is very close to the house of Fleming, and is their accomplice in the scandalous affairs of the loans."[53]

General Caballero, who did not really have much to do in London, took time to renew an old friendship. Madame Lynch in Paris invited Uriarte and the general to her birthday party on November 19.[54] Caballero accepted and apparently enjoyed some interesting conversation, which he reported to Uriarte. As soon as the weather and his health permitted, Uriarte hastened to Paris. In the course of his conferences with her, Madame Lynch promised, in return for aid in recovering property in Paraguay, "to make various revelations about money that belongs to the State, and about which no one knows anything now." Uriarte was cautious and simply promised to write to the president in her behalf if she would reveal her secrets, but Madame Lynch said she would go to London in a fortnight and there talk things over calmly before she left for Asunción. Uriarte advised Gill to come to an agreement with the lady, because he believed "that she must know about some burials [of treasure] made by López."[55] The newly elected vice-president clearly believed the stories of buried treasure. But one must remember that Madame Lynch wanted above all to return to Paraguay to recover her property, and the "revelations" probably were no more than a trick to gain aid from President Gill. If she knew about buried treasure, why did she not reveal the hiding places to her children? One son, Enrique Solano López, to whom she gave her shadowy land claims, lived in Asunción for many years in genteel poverty. Anyway, Madame Lynch did give the emissaries a document "to collect some armaments that López ordered made in Scotland, whose value is 5 to 8,000 pounds."[56]

Frustration, aggravated by bad colds, continued to plague the Paraguayan envoys. Their lawyers advised suing Robinson, Fleming & Co., claiming that Benites had been deceived and the March 12, 1873, agreement should be nullified. But the underwriters were not frightened, and Uriarte claimed that they were trying to intimidate the Paraguayans. Convinced that Dr. William Stewart was advising their enemies from Asunción, Uriarte repeatedly warned President Gill not to trust him. Gill, in turn, warned his envoys to be wary of Charles Ohlsen, who was advising them. By February, 1875, they were thoroughly disillusioned. The Benites agreement tied their hands; their instructions, written by Sinforiano Alcorta, were impossible to follow, and they saw no prospect whatever of raising more money. For a while Uriarte believed that Fleming might advance enough money to pay the arrears in interest and to establish a bank, but news from Paraguay ended that hope. President and Congress, the underwriters complained, showed no concern about the foreign debt, for all decrees and laws related only to internal obligations. In the meantime, the mission was desperate for money, a condition that did not improve until June, when the Banking Association, after a court order and another power of attorney had been received, finally paid over £3,000 belonging to Benites. Since Benites had confessed to having £27,000 deposited with the banking firm of Pedro Gil in Paris, Uriarte went over in March to present his credentials, visit Madame Lynch, and see if he could get the money. Not having the proper documents, Uriarte was unable to determine if there was such a deposit.[57] Again hopes rose when Alfred Blyth and his two sons visited him. Uriarte guessed that the underwriters were afraid of what the parliamentary inquiry into foreign loans might reveal. Their fears were unfounded. The inquiry merely showed the public how gullible buyers had been deceived by unscrupulous underwriters.[58] President Gill wrote that a revolutionary threat was disturbing the country, causing more concern and bringing a plea from General Caballero that he be allowed to return to fight for the government.[59]

Although Gill was not ready to end the mission, his agents had given up. They despaired of gaining anything in the courts and wanted only to get home. Three or four years would be needed to fight the legal battle, and the Benites agreement of 1873 made it practically impossible to win a suit against Robinson, Fleming & Co. Paraguay, they advised, should drop the suit and do everything possible to start a bank and extend the railway. So the envoys were willing to accept the stipulations made by Robinson, Fleming & Co. before they would negotiate about a bank and the railway: they must accept the Benites agreement. Again progress slowed to a halt. Another six weeks passed. Robinson, Fleming & Co. insisted that Paraguay must improve its credit so that the unsold bonds could be placed at 70, and the government must be able to pay £15,000 monthly to service the loans.[60] In the meantime, Gill informed his emissaries that Cándido Bareiro would replace them. This was good news, since Robinson, Fleming & Co. had an agent in Asunción who was dealing with Gill.[61] Caballero and Uriburú, the mission's secretary, had nothing to do while Uriarte was in Rome trying vainly to persuade the Pope to appoint the notorious Fidel Maíz as vicar. The envoys left London in November and early in December were back in Buenos Aires,[62] happy to have Bareiro try his hand at the game in London. Disappointed though he surely was with the Caballero-Uriarte mission, President Gill had a brief diversion when Madame Lynch returned for a visit in Asunción.

The Rejection of Madame Lynch

Elisa Alicia Lynch, beautiful Irish mistress of Francisco Solano López, had refused to abandon her lover in the final weeks of the war. However much moralists may condemn her and enemies heap calumnies upon her, Madame Lynch lived her finest hours while the sun was setting on the Paraguay of the great dictators. At Cerro Corá she saw her eldest son, Francisco, lanced when the boy resisted a Brazilian soldier, and she buried him with the fallen dictator in a shallow grave that, according to a tradition that has never been proven, she herself scraped out of the ground. During the next few years, Madame Lynch fought tenaciously to recover from Dr. William Stewart the large sums entrusted to him and to secure restitution of her Paraguayan lands and houses. Lopiztas sympathized with her, and in Juan Bautista Gill, Germán Serrano, Higinio Uriarte, and Bernardino Caballero she thought she had redoubtable friends; but the postwar decade brought mainly disappointments.

Soon after her capture at Cerro Corá, Madame Lynch was included in a decree of the Provisional Government that embargoed all possessions of the López family: Referred to as "the woman Elisa Linch, concubine and accomplice of the criminal traitor Solano López,"[63] she was then on board the Brazilian *Princesa* in the harbor, having just arrived from the north after a trip on foot and by oxcart from Cerro Corá to Concepción. Madame Lynch had with her a quantity of jewels, which caused ninety Paraguayan women to present a petition to Silva Paranhos for their return on the charge that the jewels had been stolen; but Silva Paranhos, more chivalrous than the women and certainly more practical, in rejecting the petition asserted that the inventory showed only modest possessions, which Madame Lynch could keep. Elisa protested from the *Princesa* that she had been grossly slandered: the property embargoed by the government was legally hers, and she challenged the women to prove that she had ever taken anything or had ever been seen with jewels not her own.[64]

Attacking Madame Lynch was a safe amusement for journalists and officials. Even *La Voz del Pueblo*, mouthpiece of the Lopiztas, used its venomous ink generously in its first number:

> All of Paraguayan society knows how that bad woman stole their jewels, seized their goods, and even took the fine clothes they wore, sometimes violently, sometimes with serious injury. Every family has a claim against her and every citizen has full knowledge of the violence she committed in the epoch of her reign. . . . That woman now leaves for Europe, where she will enjoy the wealth and the fortunes of many unfortunates who today lack a piece of bread for their children and a mouthful of meat to appease their hunger.[65]

A decree of the Triumvirate on May 4, 1870, confiscated all property belonging to López, provisionally distrained all of Madame Lynch's possessions subject to civil or criminal actions, and ordered her to be tried as a war criminal. Informed of this decree, the persecuted woman refused to sign an acknowledgment of the notice and pointed to several provisions of the Constitution of 1870 that, she claimed, nullified the decrees of March 19 and May 4. She was on uncertain legal ground, since the Constitution of 1870 was not adopted until several months after the decrees had been issued. By this time she was in Buenos Aires, where she sought protection from the British minister. Rebuffed, she continued to Montevideo, where her agent tried to recover the seized property, and on to Rio de Janeiro, where she talked freely to reporters. The Emperor refused to see her. Dom Pedro II could have learned some interesting things from Madame Lynch, who was talking freely, but his Braganza pride would not permit an encounter with this notorious courtesan. In London and Scotland, Madame Lynch became entangled in a series of legal actions in an effort to recover very large sums from Dr. William Stewart and his brother Robert and from the firm of J. and A. Blyth, long-time agents of the López. Only partly successful after many months, she crossed over to Paris, where she was living when Uriarte and Caballero were in London.[66]

While Madame Lynch was in London in 1870–1871, the Paraguayan Congress enacted three laws to ratify the various punitive decrees against the López family. The law of June 14, 1871, held that the family, including Elisa Lynch, were accomplices and inheritors of property stolen from the nation since Carlos Antonio López took office in 1841. This property was to be sold to indemnify claimants, who had until the end of 1872 to present their claims. President Rivarola, who had signed the punitive decrees as a member of the Provisional Government, vetoed the law as being unconstitutional. The courts were open and claimants should make use of established legal remedies. This veto message was an eloquent defense of individual rights and of due process, couched in language far beyond the limited vocabulary of President Rivarola, and probably was written by José Segundo Decoud. Congress overrode the veto but Rivarola, as noted previously, dissolved the Congress.[67]

Madame Lynch's lawyer in Asunción, Edmond Berchon des Essarts, had many documents that the Paraguayan government desperately wanted. Berchon, whose wife may have been Elisa Lynch's aunt, had managed to deliver the most critical documents to his client on board the *Princesa* in 1870. The rest of them were concealed in his home when Jovellanos sent ruffians to break in and steal them. Berchon surprised the thieves, who stabbed him to death. The French consul, Vicomte Paul d'Abzac, hurried to Berchon's home, found the papers, and put them aboard the Italian gunboat *Confianza*. Fearing for his life, d'Abzac himself fled to the *Confianza* on December 23, 1872, and went to Buenos Aires. Understandably, Jovellanos cancelled his exequatur. Gregorio Benites made efforts to see the papers, which, after various adventures, were delivered to the French minister in London, and eventually Madame Lynch recovered them.[68]

Armed with her recently retrieved documents, Madame Lynch resolved to return to Asunción to face the criminal charges ordered by the government in 1870, "confronting," she wrote, "all of my enemies in the very theater of their power and when I counted on no help other than that of my confidence and of my deeds."[69] She could, however, count on much more substantial aid, or so she believed. Juan Bautista Gill, in exile in Montevideo in 1872, assured Madame Lynch that he would gladly help her after his plans had succeeded. After he had become minister of hacienda in 1874, Gill advised her to come to Asunción as soon as possible; he renewed the offer of his services, assuring her that he would do whatever was possible. Unless unexpected misfortune should occur, the time was ripe for presenting her claims.[70] And when Uriarte and Caballero went to England, Gill repeated his offer: "I shall do whatever is possible IN ORDER TO REPAY THE FAVORS WHICH YOU BESTOWED UPON MY FAMILY ON ANOTHER OCCASION." Uriarte would report on conditions in Paraguay.[71]

So it was that Madame Lynch resolved to make the daring effort in 1875 to obtain action in her favor. The attempt testifies more to her courage than to her wisdom, but she was counting on President Gill's friendship, and Caballero and Uriarte must have reassured her. In Buenos Aires in July, she asked the British minister, L. S. Sackville West, for protection. West, who was about to leave for a short visit to Asunción, was forearmed: his predecessor in 1870 had asked the Foreign Office what responsibility the British had toward Madame Lynch and had been instructed to provide "all the protection" that her position might require, but was told that she had no claim as a British subject unless she could prove that she had not been legally married to a French subject.[72] Obviously, having been legally married to Jean Louis Armand de Quatrefages, she was not going to compound her problems by denying the union.

Madame Lynch had business with the Argentine government. She resented the use of her furniture in the Casa Rosada, but all efforts to recover her property had been in vain. Pending the outcome of this claim, she had written again to President Gill and sent a sash and band, which he promised to wear on his birthday. Again Gill assured Madame Lynch that she would find in him "a good and loyal servant."[73] This was more than just a polite nothing, a meaningless bit of courtesy so often used by writers of Spanish. But Madame Lynch was concerned. The Buenos Aires press published scandalous attacks, and enemies in Asunción joined in baiting the supposedly friendless woman. These attacks distressed President Gill, who again protested his friendship and promised her full protection of the laws.[74] Some of Madame Lynch's few friends in Buenos Aires feared that Gill was trying to lure her to Asunción and then to force her to reveal where López had buried jewels and treasure. They would have been even more convinced had they known that Carlos Saguier thought it probable that La Lynch was going to Paraguay "to take out some great amount of money buried by López during the war."[75] In view of her hints to Higinio Uriarte in Paris, which are not mentioned in the *Esposición y protesta*, there might have been a slight basis for thinking that President Gill, like many Paraguayans a century later, put some stock in the stories of buried treasure; if he did, the friends were on solid ground. But Madame Lynch trusted President Gill, at least as much as she could trust any Paraguayan in public life at that time. After some especially vicious letters in *La Tribuna* of Buenos Aires, she was determined to accept the challenge.

With her son Enrique, Elisa Lynch boarded the *Cisne* on October 16 for her last trip to Paraguay. At Rosario she met West returning from Asunción, and the British minister gallantly gave her his card with a note commending her to Commander Henry Fawkes, HMS *Cracker*, then stationed in Paraguayan waters. The imminent return of Madame Lynch sent waves of excitement through Asunción as both friends and enemies prepared to greet her. At Pilar below the capital, many people welcomed her affectionately, and on the next day, Saturday, October 24, a large crowd waited on the wharf at Asunción when the *Cisne* dropped anchor. Before going ashore, Madame Lynch very prudently sent West's card to Commander Fawkes, who despatched an officer to determine her wishes. Prepared to defend herself in court against the decrees of 1869 and 1870, Elisa had a packet of documents. These she sent to Fawkes for safety until she could claim the protection President Gill had so positively promised.[76] Unfortunately, Germán Serrano, a faithful Lopizta whom she had counted as a strong supporter, was no longer in the cabinet.

Expecting important friends to come aboard, Madame Lynch waited until all other passengers had landed. The friends did not come, but if this was an ominous sign she could ignore it as cries of "Viva!" came from the crowd when she went ashore with Enrique. Far from being stoned, as her enemies reported,[77] Elisa protested that she was nearly suffocated by the embraces of women who greeted her with unrestrained joy. Surrounded by a large throng, she went through customs and then to the tramway, whose director, James Horrocks, had a special car waiting.[78] She approached the car slowly, pressed from all sides, she wrote, "by people who embraced me, kissed me, and pressed my hands; all, men and women alike, wanted to touch me and speak to me, and everyone had a friendly greeting for me." [79] People who recognized her waved from their doorways as the car moved slowly to the San Francisco station, where many had gathered. Vendors from the Plaza San Francisco crowded around Madame Lynch and went with her to the San Roque church, where she "offered a fervent prayer to the Almighty." Well-wishers and curious idlers escorted her to the house of Señorita Isidora Díaz, where she had arranged to stay. "All day there was a real procession of people," she wrote in her diary, "bringing me messages from the most distinguished families, who wanted to visit me, and of poor people who brought me little gifts to show me that they had not forgotten me and that they held grateful memories." [80]

Elsewhere in the city there was feverish activity to have Elisa expelled promptly. Fifty or more women gathered at the home of Señora Machaín de Haedo, where they signed a petition urging the president to expel La Lynch at once. All of the accumulated hatred against López surfaced in this outpouring of indignation that Elisa should dare to show herself in Asunción.[81] President Gill sent two emissaries to inform the astonished and mortified woman that she must leave at once. Infuriated, Elisa replied that, having come to face the charges against her, she was at the government's command and invited the officers to arrest her; but this was not in President Gill's plans. Madame Lynch then sent Enrique and a woman friend to see the president, who was taking his siesta. Gill promised to see Elisa, but she must not expose herself publicly. The two then called on the Brazilian minister to deliver letters of recommendation from the Duke of Caxias and Rio Branco. Pereira Leal promised to receive Madame Lynch on Monday, probably knowing full well that she would be out of the country by then. Gill had no intention of risking a face-to-face encounter and sent Colonel Ignacio Genes to order Madame Lynch to leave. Again the frustrated Elisa demanded to be arrested. Genes refused the request but did say that the president would see her at midnight if she had to have an interview. Then another officer came and told Madame Lynch that she had two hours in which to embark. Fearing for her life, Elisa sent a messenger to ask Commander Fawkes for an escort, which arrived promptly. Armed with a pistol, Elisa hurried through the streets with the English officers and boarded the gunboat before midnight. October 24 had been a busy day! Curious people visited the harbor on Sunday to catch a glimpse of Madame Lynch on the British vessel, which sailed the next day.[82]

British protection probably saved Madame Lynch from imprisonment or assassination, of which measures the government of President Gill was fully capable. Reviewing the humiliating events that ended her visit on October 24, Madame Lynch could hardly find words to express her indignation. Gill, she charged, had spent four years in weaving the web to entrap her, she had been denied her constitutional rights, and Gill had no power to expel her. Why had not the government, under the decrees of 1869 and 1870, brought her to trial? She had part of the answer: men of the government dared not risk loss of the properties seized from Lynch and López. She charged that Gill had instigated the petition to have her expelled, thus denying her the right to defend herself in court.[83] Madame Lynch probably was close to the truth. It is easy to believe that President Gill had lured Elisa to Asunción in order to destroy her, and had changed his plans when he discovered that she had the protection of Commander Fawkes. West might have mentioned the matter when he was in Asunción. But all of this is speculation. Too, it would be difficult to trace the fate of her properties, her houses and estancias and leagues of unexploited lands, which surely fell into the hands of her enemies at little or no cost to them. Madame Lynch struck back by publishing Gill's letters in her *Esposición y protesta* before the end of 1875. Carlos Saguier may have been reflecting what he believed to be President Gill's real sentiments when he reported on Madame Lynch's return from Asunción:

> La Linch has arrived in this city [Buenos Aires] and I hope that this evil woman will profit from the lesson she has received in that capital, not to attempt in the future to harbor pretensions about imaginary claims. The English government has rejected her, as well as the French; thus, she has the help of no one; without doubt in just punishment of her crimes.[84]

The tragic career of Madame Lynch had more than a decade to run. Although her movements after 1875 have not been documented satisfactorily, apparently she visited Ireland and England, lived for a while in Paris, and spent some three years in Constantinople and the Holy Land. These trips could have been made on limited resources, but obviously she had more money than has been accounted for, since she also educated her surviving sons and a daughter of López by another woman. She returned to Buenos Aires in 1885, transferred her claims to 3,105 square leagues of Paraguayan lands to her son Enrique, and returned alone to Paris, where she died in very modest quarters on July 25, 1886. Buried in a pauper's cemetery, her remains eventually were brought back to Asunción to rest in an urn in the Museo Histórico Militar. Lopiztas, stubbornly opposing leaders of the Church and pious Catholics, still strive to have them placed in the Panteón Nacional.

13. Diplomacy and Revolution, 1875–1876

President Gill faced so many problems during his administration that selection of one as having been paramount is hardly possible. To remain in power he had to prevent or disrupt revolutionary plots and retain Brazilian support. The Empire's statesmen, confronted by many domestic problems, including the increasing agitation over slavery, sincerely wanted to end the costly occupation and regularize relations with Argentina. The failure of Mitre's mission to Asunción in 1873 was disheartening, although a possible break in the stalemate was indicated by Mitre's willingness to arbitrate claims north of the Pilcomayo. This moderate stand was rejected by his superiors, and in the negotiations with Jaime Sosa in Rio de Janeiro, Carlos Tejedor appeared to have won. But Brazil's violent reaction caused a quick reassessment.

Sosa's mission to Rio de Janeiro is one of the most controversial episodes in Paraguayan diplomacy. The controversy swirls around the instructions given to him by Juan Bautista Gill and Salvador Jovellanos. There is no argument about the written instructions, but did President Jovellanos actually give his envoy oral instructions to negotiate a treaty favorable to Argentina? Probably this question will never be answered satisfactorily. Available evidence clearly shows that Sosa was carrying out the orders of Jovellanos and not those of Gill. At this stage in the occupation of Paraguay, Gill had not broken with Brazil, and he was definitely dependent upon Brazilian troops to keep him in power when he assumed the presidency on November 25, 1874. Jovellanos had no reason to be grateful to the Brazilians for their part in bringing to a successful conclusion the revolts of 1873–1874.

Crises precipitated by the Sosa-Tejedor treaty had scarcely receded when Germán Serrano launched a revolution with encouragement from aggrieved Brazilian citizens. President Gill was convinced that he could never be safe as long as such enemies were in Paraguay. At the same time his genuine desire to sign a treaty with Argentina led him to send

241

Facundo Macháin to deal with an Argentine foreign minister who was more conciliatory than the irascible Tejedor. Macháin's success was one of the most notable events of the postwar decade. The treaty quickly led to the evacuation of Paraguayan territory by Allied troops, and the resulting arbitration eliminated Argentine claims to the Chaco north of the Pilcomayo. President Gill saw the last Brazilian troops leave the capital, but he was not to enjoy the great satisfaction of seeing Paraguay's claim to the Chaco validated by the arbitral decision of President Rutherford B. Hayes in 1878.

Brazilian intrigue and intervention in Paraguayan politics contributed to political confusion, retarded recovery, and sharpened animosities; but the Brazilians did make two positive contributions in the seven years of occupation: they prevented anarchy and nullified Argentina's extreme territorial demands. One could at least have expected an occupation army to maintain order, provide relief for the destitute, and aid in establishing political institutions. Brazil's record in these areas was less than imposing. There was no organized policing of the entire country, not even of Asunción and its surrounding communities; the destitute were allowed to shift for themselves; and, except for establishing the Provisional Government, the Allies did not guide the creation of political institutions to replace the dictatorship. Since Brazil dominated the Alliance, the failures of the occupation were overwhelmingly the result of the Empire's policies. While Argentina might conspire with Paraguayan rebels to overthrow Brazilian puppet regimes, those rebels themselves did not fail to reassure Brazilian representatives of their loyalty to Brazil. The game was one of constant frustration for Argentina until the Macháin-Irigoyen treaty promised an end to the long struggle with Brazil for the domination of Paraguay.

The Sosa-Tejedor Treaty

Sparring between Brazil and Argentina over the Chaco question continued throughout 1874. Brazil had no intention whatever of abandoning Paraguay or of allowing Argentina to gain its territorial objectives in the Chaco. The Empire's troops would protect the country, and their presence alone would deter bellicose moves by Argentina. Failure of the Molas revolt deprived the Argentines of any lingering hopes they may have had of displacing the new pro-Brazilian government. Argentina still maintained that the Treaty of Alliance, signed hurriedly in 1865, set definite boundaries; but Argentine claims had been eroded steadily by Paraguay, the Argentine foreign minister complained, although that country never had any legal basis for its supposed rights to the Chaco and now was claiming the whole area, while Argentina's allies had betrayed her and even Bolivia was asserting ownership of much of the Chaco. Sustaining disputes with Chile, Bolivia, and Paraguay, Tejedor insisted that Argentina had offered excellent terms through Mitre; rejection of those terms would not result in war and negotiations would continue. Earlier in the year, Araguáia had been willing for Argentina to have Villa Occidental, giving up all claims to the area north of Arroyo Verde, but Caravellas refused to make this concession. As to keeping troops in Paraguay, he instructed Gondim to determine Paraguayan wishes, but Brazil would retain whatever force was necessary to support the government.[1]

Sosa's mission to Rio de Janeiro originated in the desire of Gondim and of the Paraguayans not to break off negotiations with Argentina. Despite definite advantages obtained from Brazilian occupation, many Paraguayans were restive and resented Brazilian dictation. In Brazil, too, there was rising criticism of Brazilian policy that had brought the Empire to the brink of war with Argentina. A kind of "bring-the-boys-home" movement had considerable support. To still this criticism, Rio Branco urged Tejedor to come to Rio de Janeiro for negotiations with Paraguay, and at the same time Gondim pressed for the appointment of a special envoy from Paraguay.[2]

Paraguay had an agent in Rio de Janeiro who had been instructed to report on conditions in the Brazilian capital and to feel out Rio Branco This envoy, Higinio Uriarte, arrived on July 29 en route to London. He conferred with Caravellas, was received by Pedro II on July 31, and then visited Rio Branco, who discussed the question of Paraguay's boundaries with Argentina. If Tejedor would accept the Pilcomayo, leaving Villa Occidental to Paraguay, Brazil was willing to surrender Cerrito (Atajo) Island to Argentina, and, Uriarte reported, Brazilian troops would remain in Asunción as long as Brazil thought it necessary.[3] This proposal concerning Cerrito was no sacrifice, for Brazil's occupation had no legal foundation, and the island had little economic and limited strategic value. The time was propitious for a settlement, since President Sarmiento wanted to end the diplomatic quarrel as soon as possible.

Before naming the special Paraguayan envoy, Jovellanos, Gill, and Serrano discussed boundaries with Gondim. The latter's principal proposal was that Paraguay accept the Pilcomayo line as offered by Mitre, with the understanding that Brazil and Argentina would withdraw their forces simultaneously. An alternative was for Brazil to continue occupying Cerrito Island. Although Paraguayans were still reluctant to give up the Chaco Central, since they had already agreed to cede Misiones and Apipé Island to Argentina, Gondim urged them to accept the

Pilcomayo line and let Argentina have Cerrito. Jovellanos was willing to accept this advice but wanted Brazilian troops to remain until the government could establish itself firmly. He exaggerated grossly in assuring Gondim that both natives and foreigners agreed on the need for continued occupation, although the material contribution of the military payroll was appreciated. The Paraguayans were willing to accept the Pilcomayo line if Argentina would withdraw from Villa Occidental and renounce indemnification; Paraguay in turn would recognize individual land titles acquired during Argentine occupation.[4]

Having brought the Paraguayans around to his views, Gondim proceeded to select an envoy to treat with Tejedor in Rio de Janeiro. Upon his recommendation, Gill proposed the appointment of Jaime Sosa Escalada, "formerly Minister of Finance and a young man of considerable talent combined with great modesty." Sosa had behaved very commendably since his removal from office in February. Serrano was opposed to Sosa's appointment but agreed when Gondim asked for his support. Jovellanos sent Sosa's name to the Senate, which gave its approval for his nomination as Envoy Extraordinary and Minister Plenipotentiary on Special Mission, with authority to sign a treaty of limits with Tejedor or some other envoy on terms already agreed upon.[5]

Before Sosa left for Rio de Janeiro, the Argentines wanted to know just where he stood. Tejedor sent Sinforiano Alcorta, a relative of Jovellanos well acquainted with Asunción, to be consul-general in the Paraguayan capital. Alcorta was pleased to discover that Sosa was friendly toward Argentina. On the day that he left for Buenos Aires, Sosa asked Alcorta to tell Tejedor that he was not going as a "blind instrument of Brazilian diplomats." [6] The Brazilian ship that took Sosa to Buenos Aires also bore a letter from Gondim to the Brazilian chargé in Buenos Aires informing him that Paraguay wanted Argentina to send an envoy to Rio de Janeiro to sign a treaty. Tejedor was quite willing to sign a treaty with Sosa on Argentine terms; but, since he wanted immediate and complete evacuation by Brazil, these terms would not be harsh. When Tejedor replied to an inquiry from Gill in the same terms, Gondim reported that Sarmiento was being deceitful. Jovellanos, Gill, and Gondim decided not to reply to the Argentine note. Throughout these preliminaries Jovellanos and Gill obviously followed Gondim's recommendations closely.[7] In the meantime, Sosa had joined Uriarte in Rio de Janeiro. There was little for him to do until Tejedor arrived from Buenos Aires, other than to enjoy himself and hear occasional lectures from Brazilian officials as to Paraguay's best interests. Someone in Asunción, undoubtedly Gill, had instructed Sosa and Uriarte to request that Brazil remove the unpopular Jaguarão. Rio Branco was not very receptive to the idea at first and refused to believe the accusations that reached him through diplomatic channels.[8]

Jaime Sosa definitely was pro-Argentine in sentiment, feared the absorption of his country by Brazil, and could see no reason for toadying to the Empire. He knew that officially Jovellanos and Gill wanted Brazilian troops to remain in Paraguay. His instructions were practically identical with those sent to Uriarte: insist on the Pilcomayo as the northern limit of Argentine territory, obtain the withdrawal of both Argentine and Brazilian forces, cede Misiones to Argentina, make every effort to have Villa Occidental returned without indemnification. If possible, Sosa was to secure Argentine withdrawal from Villa Occidental and Brazilian withdrawal from Cerrito Island.[9] Sosa's *Negociaciones*, revised and corrected by Tejedor, contains a letter from Jovellanos to Sosa admitting that Brazilian troops provided political stability and that their expenditures were vital to the Paraguayan economy, even though the smuggling of the sutlers was brazen; but Brazil was impatient to be out of Paraguay, Jovellanos correctly stated, and continued the occupation only to prevent Argentina from gaining territory north of the Pilcomayo. Nevertheless, Jovellanos made it clear that all patriotic Paraguayans wanted to end the ignominious Brazilian occupation and that Brazil was the principal obstacle to peace and had forced treaties on Paraguay that stripped her of immense territories. "I authorize you," Jovellanos is supposed to have written, "to enter into treaties with the Argentine Republic on the basis of immediate Brazilian evacuation, no matter how much the official instructions may be to the contrary, [since they] as you know were drafted in the Brazilian Legation."[10]

When Sosa arrived in Rio de Janeiro, he learned quickly that Rio Branco, Caravellas, and other officials expected to dictate his negotiations with Tejedor. The Brazilians would not evacuate Cerrito Island before a treaty was signed, and they constantly warned Sosa not to cede Villa Occidental to Argentina. The young Paraguayan argued strongly. He reminded the Brazilian minister of foreign affairs that Brazil had gotten everything stipulated by the Treaty of Alliance of 1865, and it was time that the Paraguayan-Argentine territorial dispute ended. Cession of Villa Occidental, Sosa sincerely believed, in exchange for Argentine surrender of reparations and any other territory north of the Pilcomayo, was a good bargain for Paraguay. Caravellas argued that Argentina wanted Villa Occidental in order to carry on intrigues against Paraguay, to promote smuggling, and eventually to absorb all of Paraguay, and that Brazil was Paraguay's best friend, the guardian of its independence and integrity. These arguments failed to impress Sosa.

He could see no more danger from an Argentine-held Villa Occidental than from any other part of the frontier. Moreover, Villa Occidental would be an easy refuge for Paraguayans escaping from possible tyranny, and he had no fear that Argentina would absorb his country. Anyway, he would sign a treaty *ad referendum* that would require the executive's approval. Caravellas warned Sosa that if he persisted in signing away Villa Occidental, reactions in Paraguay would be violently against him. He should at least submit the Villa Occidental area to arbitration.[11]

Rio Branco, Caravellas, Tejedor, and Sosa held a critical conference on May 11. At this third meeting, Tejedor presented two proposals as his last word: Argentina would accept the Pilcomayo as its boundary, but with cession of Villa Occidental and an area around it, and cancel any claims for damages, and the Allies would evacuate Paraguay immediately. If this proposal were refused, Argentina would accept arbitration of the Villa Occidental area, immediate indemnity for expenses in improving the village, recognition of existing property rights, evacuation by Brazil of Cerrito Island and its delivery to Argentina, and reduction of Brazilian forces in Paraguay to equal the Argentine force at Villa Occidental until the arbitral award. Although Sosa admitted that he had no authority to agree to the cession of Villa Occidental, he was very much in favor of the first proposal. Rio Branco called this attitude disastrous if not treasonable.[12]

Even while Rio Branco and Caravellas were warning him not to do so, Sosa met with Tejedor at the Hotel dos Estrangeiros and signed the treaty of May 20 by which Paraguay ceded Misiones, the Chaco north to the Pilcomayo, and Villa Occidental to Argentina.[13] Rio Branco, outraged by the territorial provisions and Argentina's cancellation of war debts, immediately advised the Emperor that Brazil should take a strong stand against the treaty. In agreeing with his minister, Dom Pedro exclaimed that the Brazilians were better Paraguayans than Sosa.[14]

Sosa argued strongly for acceptance of the treaty and urged against hasty action that might result in its rejection. Paraguay's economic future, he insisted, depended upon Argentina, and it was time to settle all outstanding difficulties with Argentina and to stop accepting Brazilian dictation.[15] Sosa, acting solely from patriotic motives, thought he had served Paraguay well. Villa Occidental was not essential for Chaco development, he believed, and in Argentine hands it would be a guarantee against would-be Paraguayan dictators, "a refuge where exiles could find means to counterattack and destroy the power of tyranny."[16] This was a peculiar argument! Villa Occidental should be ceded so that future rebels might have a convenient base for operations against Paraguay!

Tejedor refused to remain in Rio de Janeiro for protracted discussions. He and his wife were anxious to return to Buenos Aires and would not postpone their departure, which had been set for June 2. They had tried to have a farewell audience with the Emperor and Empress but one could not be arranged at a satisfactory time. The Brazilians were insulted. During his last days in Rio de Janeiro, Tejedor refused to modify his stand, so Rio Branco moved quickly to prevent approval of the treaty in Asunción.[17] While the Council of State was assembling, Rio Branco made sure that Argentina would be unable to gain any advantage from the treaty. The secretary of war ordered reinforcements to Asunción and Cerrito Island; Caravellas wired Pereira Leal, via Montevideo, to inform President Gill of Sosa's actions against Brazil's advice but to bring no pressure and to wait for further instructions. Rio Branco had to wait for the Council of State to act, and when that body met on June 11, it decided by a close vote to protest against the treaty.[18]

News of the Sosa-Tejedor treaty struck Asunción with thunderbolt force and shocked Gill and Pereira Leal into intense activity. Informed by telegram on June 14 of the details, Pereira Leal went at once to see Dr. Facundo Macháin, who cried that Sosa's act was treason. Together they hurried to the president's home. When Gill heard the news, he vowed indignantly that he "would never accept the agreement that Sosa had made with Tejedor in violation of his instructions and contrary to the advice of the Imperial Government." At Gill's request, Pereira Leal repeated the news in a cabinet meeting on June 15. Gill unequivocally disavowed Sosa's treaty. To prove that he was not double-dealing, Gill showed the Brazilian a copy of Sosa's instructions and promised to send a special envoy to Rio de Janeiro to undo the damage caused by Sosa's "treachery" and to assure the court that Paraguay would insist on the Bermejo as a boundary, with the island of Cerrito going to Paraguay, if Brazil would back the demand. When Sosa's despatch, urging approval of his agreement, arrived on June 17, Pereira Leal again attended a cabinet conference. Now Gill asked Pereira Leal's opinion about the Bermejo line and Cerrito. Avoiding an answer to this critical question, the Brazilian minister vowed that he exerted no pressure but advised Gill to have Saguier in Buenos Aires formally inform Argentina that Paraguay disavowed the Sosa-Tejedor agreement. As to the special envoy, he should be one who enjoyed Paraguay's complete confidence. To this Gill replied he would send Dr. Facundo Macháin, and Pereira Leal agreed to have a Brazilian gunboat take him down river. Gill issued decrees on June 17 that disavowed the treaty and discharged Sosa, and on June 18 he issued the decree appointing Machaín as minister to Brazil.[19] In this emergency, Pereira Leal reported, President Gill and his cabinet had acted "with the loyalty of a Government and of a people who see in Brazil the guarantee of their political existence in the integrity of their territory."[20] He might have added that the Paraguayan government rarely moved so promptly and decisively.

Pereira Leal and the Brazilian commander feared that Argentina might react violently to Gill's rejection of the treaty by seizing Cerrito Island and possibly the disputed territory. In Asunción the Brazilians had the 8th and 17th Infantry Battalions, seriously understrength by 400 men. Argentina had landed 300 reinforcements at Villa Occidental and Corrientes. General Federico Augusto de Mesquita advised that his brigade of about 1,400 men could keep Gill in power against a Paraguayan revolt, but if Argentina were to support the rebels, it would be prudent to have the 2nd Battalion of Foot Artillery and the 19th and 21st Infantry Battalions alerted for possible service in Asunción.[21]

Well aware of Brazilian and Paraguayan reactions, Argentina nevertheless pressed for approval of the Sosa-Tejedor treaty. For this unenviable task President Avellaneda selected Senator Dardo Rocha, who arrived in Asunción on June 19 in the midst of a fiesta celebrating rejection of the treaty. Rocha conferred with Machaín, who expressed Paraguay's determination never to cede Villa Occidental, and reported that Pereira Leal had a spy who peered at them through the blinds. On two occasions the Argentine had appointments with Gill, and each time Pereira Leal appeared and broke up the conference. Rocha suspected that Gill was toying with him, but the president invited him to his home on a Sunday and this time told Rocha that he was sending Machaín to Buenos Aires to renew negotiations after the envoy completed the Rio de Janeiro mission. Rocha promised territorial concessions in exchange for Villa Occidental, plus free entry of Paraguay's principal exports for many years. Gill, apparently, was quite cordial; but when Rocha called to complete arrangements for a treaty, Gill refused to see him. This, according to a widely accepted version, was the result of Pereira Leal's warnings. Gill was surrounded by spies and dared not be cordial with Rocha, who left for Buenos Aires on July 10.[22]

The appearance of Argentine reinforcements at Villa Occidental with Dr. Dardo Rocha gave rise to rumors that Argentina would support a revolution to overthrow Gill if the Sosa-Tejedor agreement were not ratified within fifteen days, and that Rocha would not present his letter of credence if Sosa were disavowed. Rocha, according to rumor, was authorized to accept Villa Occidental with less territory and surrender

Argentina's war debt claims, provide Paraguay with arms and warships, and station 2,000 men in Corrientes and 2,000 in Villa Occidental to protect Paraguay from Brazil. Villa Occidental was a point of honor with Argentina, hence the generous offer. But this overture, supposedly made to an aide of President Gill, was received coldly. Gill considered Villa Occidental vital to Paraguay's future, and his offer to cede Villa Occidental and two leagues of the Chaco to the Arroyo Verde was made with the knowledge that Argentina would reject it—according to Pereira Leal's reports. Argentina was aiding rebels who were gathering in Corrientes, but Gill was completely dependent upon Brazil, thanks to his disastrous financial policy. The Brazilian legation, Pereira Leal assured his superiors, "has given and is giving every moral support and will provide the material support of the Imperial Forces if it should be necessary to defend the government in this capital." In the meantime, reinforcements would be kept on the alert.[23] Actually, Dr. Rocha had found President Gill ready to throw off his Brazilian shackles. Pereira Leal had gone too far in forcing renunciation of the Sosa-Tejedor treaty, although Paraguay gained as a result. Gill promised that Paraguay would negotiate behind Brazil's back, and with this understanding Rocha returned to Buenos Aires. By this time Pereira Leal had fallen under the influence of the anti-Gill faction of Brazilian army officers and had no faith in the president.[24]

Much to Gill's displeasure, Machaín spent more than three months in Rio de Janeiro. The city, Machaín explained, was not like Asunción, which could be covered in two or three days. In Rio de Janeiro one needed appointments to see officials and often they were not available. He found that Brizuela, Aramburú, Benites, and many more had done little good for Paraguay. Machaín earnestly attempted to reassure Brazilians of Paraguay's faithfulness to the Empire, but he received too little news from Paraguay to enable him to counteract unfavorable reports. Sosa had failed to leave official papers in the Paraguayan legation, and Machaín, fearing that confidential letters might compromise Paraguay, was relieved when Gill assured him that Sosa's journalistic activity in Buenos Aires could hurt no one. He would be pleased to negotiate with Argentina and hoped that Brazil, having made its position clear, would stay out of it; but, being blamed for Paraguay's bad government and being criticized for a costly occupation that gained nothing, the Empire would gladly see the Argentine-Paraguayan question settled. Argentina, too, would be pleased to bring the dispute to an end without war that could result only in its ruin.[25] Having reassured the Brazilians, Machaín returned to Asunción, where he found the government in serious difficulty.

There is little reason to doubt that President Gill continued to negotiate with Argentina through its messenger Adeodato Gondra, who conferred with Bernardo de Irigoyen, Tejedor's successor in the Argentine Foreign Office. Gill was willing to accept the Pilcomayo line with arbitration of a strip of territory on the Paraguay extending north of Villa Occidental. For this, Argentina would renounce reparations if Paraguay so requested in five years, and offered trade concessions. Gondra returned to Asunción with these proposals, which Gill and Urdapilleta accepted.[26] President Avellaneda on November 2 named Dr. Manuel Derqui of Corrientes as chargé d'affaires to negotiate with Paraguay. Derqui, he of the small body and large head, spoke "Spanish like an academician and Guaraní like an Indian." It was at this stage, according to one version, that Pereira Leal promoted the Serrano revolt, but that event is difficult to connect with the Derqui-Gill negotiations except in time.[27]

Derqui attempted to conduct his mission in great secrecy so as not to arouse Brazilian hostility. Gill, expressing growing impatience with military occupation, demanded that the Allies evacuate all of their troops simultaneously. Derqui, who kept in touch with Irigoyen by frequent trips of his secretaries, was able to keep negotiations going to the point that Gill was willing to send Machaín to Buenos Aires to sign a treaty. At this stage, Argentina officially invited Paraguay and Brazil to send envoys to Buenos Aires. Machaín left Asunción for the port city on December 8, the day when Serrano started his revolt. And, if we are to believe Freire Esteves, Pereira Leal knew nothing about the preliminary negotiations that Derqui had carried on. This is too much to accept. Adolfo Saguier and Germán Serrano had kept Pereira Leal informed about what was going on, and the Brazilian knew early in November that Derqui was coming to Asunción as Argentina's representative. Saguier assured Pereira Leal that Paraguay would not cede the Chaco to Argentina unless forced to do so by war or arbitration. He believed that loss of the Chaco to Argentina would mean the death of Paraguay, since the small country would be completely surrounded by Argentina and Brazil and future growth would be severely restricted. Urdapilleta, too, was unfaithful to Gill, for he joined Machaín in reporting to Pereira Leal.[28] All of the elaborate precautions for secrecy may have appealed to a romantic streak in Derqui and Gondra, but they were entirely useless.

The Sosa-Tejedor treaty shook up chancelleries and brought an end to the prolonged diplomatic stalemate.[29] Rio Branco's policies had again resulted in a humiliating defeat for the Empire, and on June 25, 1875, Pedro II entrusted the Council of State to the Duke of Caxias, conqueror of Paraguay, and called upon Juan Maurice de Wanderley, Barão de Cotegipe, to organize the cabinet. Cotegipe replaced Caravellas as minister of foreign affairs.[30]

Another casualty of the Sosa-Tejedor crisis was Dr. Miguel Gallegos, who had meddled in Paraguayan politics for several years and was notoriously anti-Gill. Gallegos represented the old Argentine policy of opposing Brazil by every possible means, and his accusations against both Gill and Brazil could not go unchallenged. Toward the end of June, Gill ordered Gallegos imprisoned because of his outspoken opposition, but the Argentine consul, Sinforiano Alcorta, secured his release. Gill then canceled Gallegos's exequatur and the Argentine government appointed Alcorta to succeed him as consul-general.[31]

The Serrano Revolt, December, 1875

Juan Bautista Gill, in the view of some of his colleagues in the revolt of 1873–1874, had no real claim to the presidency. They knew that Gondim had imposed him on the country in the belief that Gill would be Brazil's puppet. Gill was well aware of these feelings, and so at no time really trusted his cabinet, especially General Germán Serrano. Rumors of continued plotting by émigrés inevitably were linked with cabinet members, and by the end of July, 1875, Gill was convinced that a real threat was developing.[32] Nevertheless, in these critical winter months, President Gill was preparing to escape from Brazilian tutelage. He needed to go slowly in view of a possible need for Brazilian troops to repel an invasion of émigrés, and he had to convince Argentina that he was not, in fact, Brazil's puppet. Both in Paraguay and in Argentina resentment was rising against Brazil's continued occupation, and everyone knew that Gill had rejected the Sosa-Tejedor treaty at Brazil's command. Lionel S. Sackville West, the British minister to Argentina, concluded after a visit to Asunción that Brazil was in complete control of Paraguay and had no concern for its future. Argentina, West observed, was at a disadvantage because of its own internal dissension; nevertheless, so long as Brazil occupied Cerrito Island, Argentina would keep its troops at Villa Occidental. He could see no use in Gill's attempting to oppose Brazil at that time. The situation of Paraguay appeared to be very critical:

> Thus the country is languishing under a foreign occupation which is gradually extinguishing its already feeble resources and which must . . . end in its annexation to either one of the occupying powers. Such a solution is anticipated, but at the same time, a hope emerges from this situation that the question of annexation may produce a war between the parties contending for it, which may result in forcing them to recognize its independence,

and I am inclined to think that it is the policy of the present President secretly to foment the discord existing between the Brazilian and Argentine Governments in view of such a possible contingency[.] The shrewdness of Brazilian diplomacy may thus overreach itself, and eventually bring about exactly what it is now directed against.[33]

President Gill had a good and faithful servant in Buenos Aires. Carlos Saguier cultivated good relations with editors and government officials and carried on a voluminous correspondence with Gill. When Tejedor reached Rio de Janeiro, Saguier reported that the time was ripe for a peaceful settlement of the Argentine-Brazilian impasse over the treaty. About a month later he reported that Tejedor had signed the treaty with Sosa and anticipated Argentine anger over rejection of the treaty. When Gill disavowed the treaty, Saguier asked for a letter stating that Sosa had violated his instructions. Argentina must not be antagonized. There was a considerable amount of resentment in Buenos Aires, but Saguier believed it would not last, and his good relations with most of the editors had a restraining effect. The only solution would be arbitration, and the change of ministry in Rio de Janeiro should further this happy solution. Whether he really did have so much influence is a moot question, but, by mid-July, Saguier believed he had mollified the Argentine government, which showed its friendliness by giving peremptory orders against any gathering of armed men in Corrientes to support Rivarola's planned revolt. Whatever Gill was planning, he needed assurance that rebels would receive no aid from Argentina. After a long talk with Bernardo de Irigoyen, Saguier could assure President Gill that officials in Corrientes had strict orders to prevent an invasion.[34]

President Gill's cabinet changes in mid-October, 1875, marked a fairly obvious break with Pereira Leal if not with Brazil. Urdapilleta, Saguier, and Bareiro were notoriously friendly to Argentina, but at least they would not be blind followers of Gill.[35] Serrano, angry because of his dismissal, spread rumors that the new cabinet was hostile to Brazil and that the Brazilian minister and armed forces were opposed to Gill. Brazilian leaders reassured the president, but Adolfo Saguier called on Pereira Leal to complain that Brazilian doctors and others were speaking disparagingly of Gill's government and that Dr. Antônio da Silva Daltro had tried to bribe a police officer to cooperate in a revolution against Gill. Daltro denied the story and felt that this was poor compensation for his medical services to President Gill. Urdapilleta also visited Pereira Leal to assure him that there was no substance to rumors that Paraguay would cede Villa Occidental to Argentina.[36]

Convinced that Gill was involved in an intrigue with Argentina in order to lessen Brazilian influence, Pereira Leal resolved to be neutral in the Gill-Serrano quarrel. Profoundly cynical, he trusted none of the politicians and considered Gill "in character and perfidy a worthy successor of the two López" who was consumed by pecuniary ambition. The game obviously was to promote a quarrel between Brazil and Argentina, and if the Paraguayans hoped to use Brazilian fingers to pull their chestnuts from the fire, he hoped that theirs would be the ones to be burned.[37] Adolfo Saguier reassured Pereira Leal that the cabinet would resign rather than agree to ceding Villa Occidental, a cession that "would be the death of Paraguay's nationality." But the Brazilian believed that Gill was capable at any given moment of changing his ministers and, depending on a servile Congress, ceding Villa Occidental to Argentina.[38]

Rumors of invasion from Argentine territory continued as a choice group of émigrés plotted means of returning to Paraguay. Even while Carlos Saguier was once more complaining to Irigoyen, the Paraguayan Congress issued a decree on October 27 to extend amnesty for political crimes to all exiles except José Dolores Molas and Matías Goiburú. Rivarola, Jovellanos, Ferreira, Soteras, and many others could now return —where Gill could keep his eye on them. Very few were expected to take advantage of the offer.[39]

The most pitiful among deposed leaders was Cirilo Antonio Rivarola. Frequently linked with revolutionary plots, he was never able to gain much of a following. A Montevideo paper surmised that Sosa and Tejedor had an agreement with him to head the rebels at Corrientes who would have Argentine aid. Rivarola complained that Gill's partisans had planted the story in order to discredit him. Indignantly, the former president protested his loyalty to Paraguay and his independence from Argentine and Brazilian influence. As to his involvement in a revolt, he boasted that he needed no foreign aid to overthrow a government as corrupt as that headed by Gill, since "the entire Republic was opposed to that infamous thief." As to Argentine aid, Rivarola referred to orders that no one provide him with assistance. The Argentine government believed that Gill would approve the Sosa-Tejedor treaty but that Rivarola, if victorious in a revolt, would oppose it. He would, indeed; and if Gill should approve the treaty, Rivarola boasted that he would launch his own revolution at once, with or without arms, since the people would rise in his support.[40] Rivarola was living in a dream world. He had no support among the exiles in Corrientes and his hope for a general uprising in his favor was pure fantasy. He was at Corrientes in October when the general amnesty decree was published and soon decided to return to Paraguay, counting on Brazilian protection.

Before retiring to his home in Barrero Grande, he visited Pereira Leal and warned him that Gill was about to cede Villa Occidental to Argentina. Although Pereira Leal doubted this intelligence, he could not forget the Sosa-Tejedor treaty, which would have done the same thing.[41]

There were so many would-be leaders among the exiles that each was a political faction unto himself. Among those who had taken refuge in Buenos Aires were Adolfo Decoud, Jovellanos, and Ferreira. Decoud had a bitter pen that used gall instead of ink. *La Tribuna* published a Decoud article that sent Jovellanos and Ferreira into a rage. Together they went to Decoud's house to seek vengeance at the very inconsiderate hour of nine in the morning. While Jovellanos remained discreetly at the gate, Ferreira confronted Decoud with a heavy whip. Decoud met the attack with a revolver. Among the curious who came to witness the battle were the landlady and the police. Ferreira went to the hospital, where he recovered from two bullet wounds; Decoud, not seriously hurt, went to jail, whence Carlos Saguier eventually rescued him.[42]

This sort of bickering annoyed Saguier, who had far more important matters at hand. He watched anxiously while Machaín was sparring with the Argentine minister of foreign affairs. Pereira Leal reported on Saguier's efforts to persuade foreigners, mainly English and Argentines, to start a bank in Asunción and on the presence of Benjamín Aceval and Juan Silvano Godoy in the port city, supposedly seeking to recover $f100,000 from the estate of José Díaz de Bedoya, the absconding triumvir who had sold Paraguayan church silver in Buenos Aires for his own account. Aceval actually was carrying on highly secret conferences with Irigoyen and even denied that he was on any mission whatever. Saguier was very hopeful that a new era was about to dawn for Paraguay. Argentina wanted to settle the territorial problem and would allow no armed invasion of Paraguay, and he advised Gill to broaden Paraguay's diplomatic representation by sending Eusebio Machaín to Paris as minister and José Machaín to the United States to participate in the Centennial celebration. While Saguier was reporting nice things about Argentina, *La Nación* in Buenos Aires commented favorably on Gill's cabinet changes and the political amnesty.[43]

The Serrano revolt of December, 1875, appears to have been aided by Brazilian sutlers who had been injured financially, in cooperation with a small group of officers who persisted in their animosity toward President Gill. Pereira Leal, despite his protestations of innocence, was at least aware of the plans. Although absolute proof of these assertions is lacking, available evidence strongly supports them. The October cabinet changes were in part designed to weaken Brazilian influence. General Germán Serrano, the principal victim of the shakeup, was so active that Gill ordered him to leave the country early in November. Significantly, he sought asylum in the Brazilian legation, but Pereira Leal refused to let him stay more than twenty-four hours. General Serrano went to Corrientes, where he obtained some support, including that of Colonel Molas. On December 8, during the annual pilgrimage to the shrine of the Virgin of Caacupé, Serrano and Molas started their revolt in Caacupé. A few rebels joined the movement in Itauguá and Pirayú, but the total could not have been more than 100 men. President Gill immediately declared a state of siege, authorized the commandeering of all horses and cattle needed for military activities, called the newly uniformed national guard to assemble on December 10, declared Serrano a rebel, and sent General Escobar at the head of 350 men to combat his former comrade. Gill found unexpected support in Asunción, where *La Reforma*, so often critical, attacked Molas in violent language. Merchants met to raise money for the government, and the Argentines moved a few soldiers and a military band from Villa Occidental to Asunción, a gesture of support that has been greatly exaggerated. The Brazilian, Argentine, and Italian ministers all offered Gill their support. General Escobar needed no help and reported from Paraguarí on December 11 that the rebels were in full retreat. A relentless pursuit resulted in the capture of the leaders and the dispersal of their followers. Then came a typical *ley fuga* incident in which General Serrano was killed while trying to escape, an event that President Gill could lament during the Te Deum held in the Cathedral to celebrate the return of peace on January 11, 1876.[44]

Failure of the Serrano revolt was met with unrestrained glee by the Buenos Aires press, which did everything possible to encourage the belief that Brazil had backed Serrano, and they reported that Derqui had been received cordially in Asunción. Higinio Uriarte, in Buenos Aires returning from his mission to London, urged the Argentines to strengthen their forces in Paraguay, since Serrano's revolt could not possibly have occurred without Brazilian aid. *El Nacional*, never friendly to Brazil, editorialized on January 8, 1876, that Brazil had lost control of Paraguay, that Paraguay's true interest lay on the side of Argentina because her only commerce with Brazil had to go through Argentine rivers. In Asunción, too, the belief was widespread that Brazilians had supported Serrano. President Gill was careful to reassure Pereira Leal, who had no faith whatever in the president, that he would never depart from Brazilian policy and the minister's advice.[45]

Recovery of Sovereignty: The Machain-Irigoyen Treaties

By mid-1875, Argentine, Brazilian, and Paraguayan officials were thoroughly tired of the protracted occupation. Failure of the Sosa-Tejedor agreement, financial difficulties in Asunción, and domestic troubles in Brazil and Argentina combined to bring about evacuation. The three governments were approaching an understanding made possible primarily by Argentine retreat from Tejedor's refusal to arbitrate any part of the Chaco. Saguier in Buenos Aires was a personal friend of Bernardo de Irigoyen, so there was no barrier to a free exchange of views. His advice to President Gill was to be firm with Argentina and Brazil, recognize Argentine possession of the Chaco Central provided Argentina would renounce claim to territory north of Villa Occidental, and submit to arbitration the area south of Villa Occidental to the Pilcomayo. Confident of Paraguay's victory in such an arbitration, Saguier strongly urged these terms, which were practically identical with the Brazilian position.[46]

Shrewdly reading through Pereira Leal's official denials of antagonism toward Gill, Cotegipe decided to change ministers in Asunción. He ordered Gondim, then minister to Argentina, to relieve Pereira Leal; since Derqui was in Asunción, it was possible for negotiations to be carried on there. Brazil did not really care about what Paraguay finally accepted as a boundary, however much the Foreign Office favored arbitration of the Villa Occidental zone. After ascertaining Argentine intentions, Gondim should proceed at once to Asunción, settle matters there, and then return to his post in Buenos Aires.[47]

Cotegipe's exasperation with his bungling representatives in Asunción shows clearly in his analysis of the situation. Had Pereira Leal and the military commanders followed instructions, there would have been no misunderstanding with Paraguay. If Gill's new policy of coming to an agreement with Argentina "does not violate the treaty of alliance or our essential rights and interests," he commented, "there will be no reason for concealing it from us. . . . It is possible that Paraguay, publicly or secretly, has obliged itself to demand evacuation of our forces, which is the objective of the Argentine Republic." In that case, Gondim was to impress upon Gill the fatal consequences of such an act. Brazil's occupation was by right of conquest, did not rest on the consent of Paraguay, and would not end as long as Argentina occupied any Paraguayan territory. A responsible government, like that of Brazil, would not aid or promote revolutions against legal authority, but it could not consent to actions contrary to good government and the public welfare. The Imperial Government would limit itself to giving friendly counsel and would not interfere in internal affairs, and private Brazilian citizens must also be on their good behavior.[48] Cotegipe believed that Gill was still loyal to Brazil because that was in Paraguay's interest; he must be reassured, and suspicions of Pereira Leal must be allayed; the Brazilian military must have no relations with the Paraguayan government.[49]

In view of Brazil's military position, the Empire conducted itself with great restraint. Not only were its troops completely in control of Paraguay but also of the upper Paraguay River area. The British minister in Buenos Aires decided to go up the river to inspect Brazilian installations at Corumbá. HMS *Cracker* took him to Asunción, where he transferred to the small steamer *Venezia* on September 26, 1875, and two days later had reached Concepción, which he described as a collection of about one thousand people "miserably housed in mud huts." Concepción sent a few products to Buenos Aires, mainly yerba, and cordage and cloth from the caraguatay plant. No other settlements were encountered before reaching Bahía Negra, northern limit of Argentina's claims, "and where the Bolivian Government has a guard." West reached Corumbá on October 2 to be greeted by two military bands and a guard of honor. He found the works, under construction since 1873, to be "of considerable extent, and when completed will form the only important naval station in these waters." This station, with Brazilians in possession of Cerrito Island, gave Brazil complete control of the Paraguay River. If Brazil were to absorb Paraguay, the question of free navigation of the river would be important. When West returned from this trip, Dr. Bernardo de Irigoyen called and the Englishman advised him that the time had come to end the occupation of Paraguay. Irigoyen agreed and noted that he would know more about Brazilian intentions when his special envoy, Dr. Manuel Derqui, returned from Asunción.[50]

When Gondim arrived in Paraguay at the end of 1875 for his second tour of duty, he found the situation vastly changed from what it had been in April. President Gill, greatly pleased by the change in ministers, was convinced that Pereira Leal had plotted with Serrano and Molas to remove him from the presidency and made the accusation in a cabinet meeting attended by Gondim. However, the president assured his old mentor that his policy toward Brazil had not changed. In evaluating the situation, Gondim believed that Gill's success in dealing with Serrano and Machaín's favorable reception in Buenos Aires on December 21 greatly strengthened the government. The machinations of Pereira Leal and the Brazilian army clique had intensified Paraguayan desire for evacuation. Although it might be possible to restore cordial relations with Gill, recent events would make the task extremely difficult. The Argentines were encouraging Gill to show his strength, and those who were ambitious to overthrow him would be at complete liberty to do so once Brazil withdrew. Revolutions, as Gondim knew well, were easily organized in Paraguay, and he did not believe that Gill

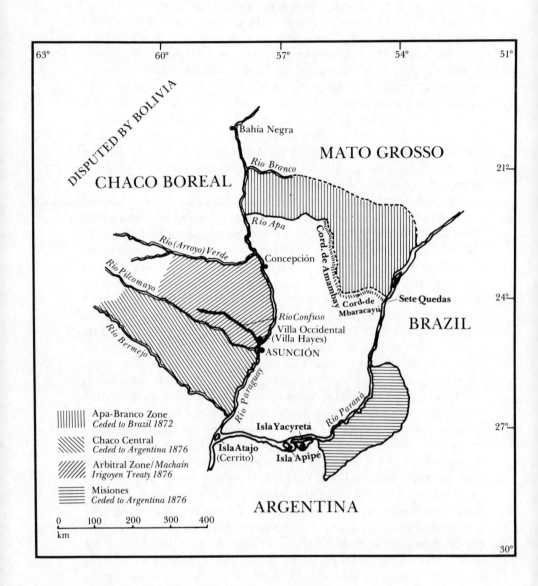

Map 6. Territorial Arrangements after the Paraguayan War

could last long after Brazil withdrew, but this was a risk that should be taken. Now the best service that he could give would be to promote a treaty that would provide for arbitration of the Villa Occidental zone and the evacuation of Allied troops.[51]

Gondim apparently succeeded in mollifying the aggrieved Paraguayans, and within two weeks he was able to report that Gill, Saguier, and Urdapilleta were friendly and there was less talk about Brazilian complicity in Serrano's revolt. Gondim's recommendations for the treaty with Argentina went to Machaín as instructions: Paraguay would cede the Chaco Central and Misiones and agree to arbitrate the Villa Occidental zone. If Argentina would accept these terms, then Gill wanted simultaneous withdrawal of Argentine and Brazilian forces; if Argentina wanted to stay on in Villa Occidental until the arbitral decision, Gill desired Brazilian forces to remain. To end further embarrassment, Gill promised to suppress any evidence that Pereira Leal had been involved in the Serrano revolt and to stop the nasty articles that José Segundo Decoud was publishing in La Reforma. Gondim urged General Mesquita to get rid of his recalcitrant officers.[52]

There are various versions of how the Machaín-Irigoyen treaty came about, so many versions that the details are still in doubt. According to leading Paraguayan historians, President Gill carried on a conspiracy behind Brazilian backs after he had been forced to renounce the Sosa-Tejedor treaty. Gill had turned to Dr. Benjamín Aceval, José Urdapilleta, and José Segundo Decoud for advice after his financial and other measures had made a mess of Paraguay's affairs. Gill decided to open negotiations secretly with Argentina after Machaín's mission to Rio de Janeiro had resulted in no financial aid or other gain for Paraguay. Gill's messenger to Argentina was Adeodato Gondra, brother-in-law to Urdapilleta.[53]

Argentina was generous in helping Paraguay to pay for suppressing the Serrano revolt. Carlos Saguier persuaded the government to loan Paraguay $50,000 and was happy to announce that the entire sum would be sent before the end of January.[54] The Argentine consul-general observed later that "in those days the National bank of this capital made a generous loan to the Government of Paraguay, and which ended up entirely in the strongbox of Don Juan Bautista Gill." [55] Perhaps this helps to explain why, when negotiations were nearly completed in Buenos Aires, Gill suddenly on January 28, 1876, sent Benjamín Aceval and José Falcón to offer all of the Chaco to Bahía Negra in exchange for free trade for five to ten years! Fortunately, Machaín and Irigoyen already had signed the treaty of February 3, 1876, which ended the long controversy.[56]

In the first of two treaties signed in Buenos Aires, Paraguay recognized the Chaco Central as Argentine territory; on the south and east, the Paraná was the boundary, which was recognition of Argentine title to Misiones. The Chaco was divided into two parts: Argentina renounced any claim north of the Arroyo Verde at 23°10′ S; from that line south to the Pilcomayo was to be submitted to arbitration by the President of the United States. All Allied military forces were to be withdrawn no later than July 3, 1876, but Argentina was to administer Villa Occidental until the arbitral decision. Paraguay agreed to pay all expenses of the war "and indemnization for damage done to public and private property." [57] This provision, of course, was meaningless.

General rejoicing followed the announcement that peace at last was assured. As José Segundo Decoud had predicted two months earlier, Paraguay had no fear of being absorbed by Brazil and the prolonged stalemate must end.[58] In his annual message to the Argentine Congress, President Avellaneda hailed the treaty as finally ending the worst of all South American wars and wished for Paraguay a felicitous future.[59] Aceval wrote in La Reforma that Paraguay would continue to be "the most loyal and consistent friend of Brazil and the Argentine Republic" after their troops had left. In Buenos Aires, El Nacional saluted the treaty as ending the danger of another war.[60] General Caldwell found that leading Argentine officials were all friendly toward Paraguay and "disposed to do everything possible to rehabilitate that unfortunate country. They now see plainly that the alliance with Brazil was a suicidal policy, and are striving to repair that great error." [61]

Graciously the Argentine government provided its gunboat Paraná to carry the impoverished Paraguayan delegates to Asunción with the treaties, which a joint session of Congress approved on February 21.[62] There was rejoicing in Asunción, except among the Argentines who resented the possible loss of Villa Occidental. President Gill sent a band of musicians to serenade Gondim, who then called on Gill and reported with satisfaction that President Gill "received me with signs of great pleasure, embracing me affectionately, and showing me the sentiments of Paraguay's deep gratitude for the generous and effective aid of the Imperial Government, without which they would never have recovered Villa Occidental [which is] so necessary for its independence." [63]

In presenting the treaty to the Argentine Congress, Irigoyen once more reiterated the oft-stated Argentine position: Paraguay had never had permanent establishments in the Chaco, its limits never crossed the river, the dictators had made temporary incursions to punish Indian marauders, Argentina had never given up its claims, which had been recognized clearly in the Treaty of Alliance, and this was not an attempt to injure Paraguay but simply a reassertion of Argentine sovereignty. Animated by fraternal feelings for a people so crushed by adversity, Argentina had allowed Paraguay to propose modifications to the limits defined in the Treaty of Alliance; this concession inspired Paraguay to claim the Chaco to the Bermejo, and then only to the Pilcomayo. Generously Argentina gave up the territory north of the Arroyo Verde, agreeing to submit the Villa Occidental zone to arbitration. Brazil hailed the treaties of February 3 as a great triumph of international justice and ordered evacuation of Paraguay and Cerrito Island; Argentina had reduced its forces at Villa Occidental, and this mutual withdrawal ended the long uncertainty over Paraguay's future. The question of free trade between Argentina and Paraguay should not be linked with the treaties; however, Congress should consider the impetus that free trade might give to Paraguayan industry.[64]

The signing and ratification of the Machaín-Irigoyen treaties removed a major block in the way of liquidating the War of the Triple Alliance. Almost unnoticed was the protocol signed on July 30, 1877, by which the three Allies jointly guaranteed Paraguayan sovereignty, independence, and territorial integrity for five years.[65] Ahead lay two immediate goals, evacuation of Allied troops and winning the arbitration.

Brazilian insistence on the Pilcomayo line had been the crucial issue until Argentina finally surrendered, with a face-saving provision for arbitration. If there was any serious thought of war by Argentine statesmen in order to force Brazil to accept their claim to all of the Chaco, realism forced them to retreat. Argentina was still becoming a nation, and leaders in Buenos Aires could not depend upon the loyalty of other provinces in a confrontation with the Empire. There was left to Argentina no more than diplomatic maneuvers, all of which Brazilians could abort through domination of Paraguay.

Absorption of Paraguay was never a part of Pedro II's Platine policy. The Empire would insist on having the territory it claimed and on preventing Argentine aggrandizement at Paraguayan expense. Only reluctantly did Brazil agree to Argentina's retention of Misiones and the Chaco Central. Rio Branco and Cotegipe probably did not care whether Bolivia or Paraguay had the Chaco north of the Pilcomayo, but they did not want that vast area to be Argentine. Astute and extraordinarily well informed statesmen, they had no fear that Argentina would emerge victor in the Chaco arbitration.

14. End of an Era

Eighteen seventy-six was a banner year for Paraguay. The end of occupation was in sight, and with the evacuation of its troops Brazil would have a decreasing influence in Paraguayan affairs. Retention of a strong force in Mato Grosso, however, would be a deterrent to Paraguayan waywardness and Argentine ambition. President Gill could look forward hopefully to finishing his term with honor. The plague of sutlers would disappear when Allied troops left, customs receipts would flow into the treasury, and finances could be put in order.

Paraguay desperately needed a sound financial institution, a settlement with holders of bonds issued in London, rehabilitation and extension of the railway, and an influx of agricultural immigrants. The key to prosperity lay in restoring agriculture, animal husbandry, and exploitation of the vast yerbales and forests, combined with political stability. Bareiro's agreement with the Council of Foreign Bondholders held great promise that these objectives would be realized and that Paraguay's credit would be restored.

The Bareiro agreement might have been an excellent arrangement for Paraguay had it functioned as intended. To be sure, the exercise of certain attributes of sovereignty would have been delegated to the powerful bank that was the central part of the arrangement. The proposal aroused intense criticism, much of it politically motivated, from persons who refused to recognize Paraguay's complete dependence upon foreign investors. Brazilian opposition killed the Bareiro agreement, although approval by the bondholders in London was by no means certain.

The evacuation of foreign troops, so long desired by Paraguayan politicians, occurred with reasonable dispatch after the approval of the Machaín-Irigoyen treaties. There were some who realized the shock that Paraguay's staggering economy would suffer when the Brazilians left, but evacuation appeared to be so important that all other considerations were overshadowed by the prospect of complete restoration of the country's sovereignty. Argentine statesmen fully expected that Paraguay would become an economic if not a political satellite of their country.

Paraguay's economic difficulties of 1876 were compounded by Brazil's entirely unrealistic effort to obtain payment of war damages. This insistence caused a violent reaction in Asunción, where such influential writers as José Segundo Decoud excoriated the Empire without restraint. President Gill earnestly attempted to solve Paraguay's economic problems, but fate was soon to remove him from the scene of a very stormy career.

Paraguayan leaders, no longer restrained by the Brazilian presence, crushed the revolt of 1877 with exceptional severity and followed that success with a series of brutal murders that still cloud the presidencies of Higinio Uriarte and Cándido Bareiro. After having been bypassed by Brazil, Bareiro waited patiently for the proper time to assume the presidency. His success in 1878 caused another ambitious caudillo, Bernardino Caballero, to bide his time. Paraguayan success in the Chaco arbitration was the highlight of Bareiro's administration, which marked the end of the postwar decade.

Bareiro's Mission to London, 1875–1876

The winter of 1875 brought no relief for Paraguay's economic problems. The failure of the "laws of Dorión" and the inability of the Uriarte mission to make any headway in London left Paraguay's finances in a dismal condition. Responding to pleas from his envoys, President Gill decided to replace them with Cándido Bareiro. This prominent Lopizta, whose appointment won the quick approval of Carlos Saguier, had lived in London for several years and was "a practical man" who might come to a definite agreement with the London financiers. At the same time, President Gill ended the imprisonment of Gregorio Benites and Eduardo Aramburú, admitting failure to recover the huge sums Benites was supposed to have embezzled, although the amounts seized in Montevideo and London were not insignificant. Bareiro proceeded promptly to London via Bordeaux and reached his post in September.[1]

Bareiro found that Robinson, Fleming & Co. had turned over to the Council of Foreign Bondholders all matters relating to the loans of 1871 and 1872, and that Paraguay could obtain no credit until payments on the loans were resumed. His principal dealings were with Joseph Rodney Croskey, who represented the council, and Samuel Leith Tomkins of Willis, Perceval & Co., London bankers. He solicited the aid of Alfred Blyth and his son, Henry David Blyth. Bareiro and his helpers put together a closely knit scheme of many parts for the purpose of rescuing Paraguay's prostrate economy. The council, with many misgivings, tentatively approved this imaginative plan, which was put into final form on March 23, 1876.[2]

Paraguay's lack of a real bank had long been recognized as a major handicap to economic recovery. Bareiro's arrangement proposed to fill this need by creating a Banco Nacional del Paraguay with such great powers that Paraguay's sovereignty would be imperiled. To be capitalized at £300,000, the bank would begin operations as soon as £50,000 had been subscribed and sent to Paraguay and not less than four months after the agreement had been ratified by Paraguay. This would be a powerful institution, operating under a thirty-year concession dating from July 1, 1876, and renewable until the external debt had been paid. The bank could issue paper money that was legal tender redeemable in gold or silver on demand, coin money, set its own interest rates to a maximum of 15 percent, exploit the yerbales for twenty years, be exempt from taxation or contributions, and have preference in every public works concession. It could extend the railway through a separate company and serve as fiscal agent for the government, and would pay £90,000 annually to the treasury in monthly quotas, using the balance of its revenues to service the internal and external debts. Bank employees were to be exempt from military service, forced loans, and personal contributions. Of the five to seven directors, who would reside in London, Paraguay would name three.[3]

Paraguay would own one-half of the £300,000 capital, but this would be in shares to be received from the bank in exchange for the railway. The bank would obtain the railway to Paraguarí, with one mile of public lands on each side, and could extend the road to Villa Rica or other points with the same land grant. The bank, of course, could sell the land. There were to be 2,500 Class A 6-percent preferred, and 12,500 Class B, or common shares. Actually, Paraguay stood an excellent chance of obtaining only its 2,500 Class A shares, with a par value of £25,000, since the Class B shares must be paid for in gold or silver by July 1, 1876. After that date, the council could sell them and use the proceeds to buy bonds on the exchange and to pay dividends on the bonds,[4] thus increasing the value of the 1871 and 1872 issues.

Support for the Bareiro agreement was by no means unanimous in London. In view of what had happened to the gold sovereigns that had gone to Paraguay a few years earlier, investor reluctance to throw more into the pit is easy to understand. Alexander Francis Baillie, secretary of the council, charged that the Blyths had deceived Bareiro and had not subscribed for any of the bank's stock. Only £20,000 had been subscribed by February, and more would not be subscribed until Paraguay ratified the agreement. News that the Machaín-Irigoyen treaty had been signed should have been encouraging to investors, but this event appeared to have little influence in the markets. José Segundo Decoud, long a bitter enemy of Bareiro, opposed the agreement, charging that the bank would be a monster that would retard progress. Nevertheless, President Gill submitted the plan to Congress shortly after Bareiro returned. Saguier hoped that this action would be favorable, since something had to be done to restore Paraguayan credit. During the negotiation of the Machaín-Irigoyen treaty, Argentina had implied that Paraguayan products would be allowed entry free of duties; but when Machaín appeared in May to start informal negotiations, he met with no encouragement. Argentina, in a severe economic depression, could not be counted on for extensive aid, and the best that Paraguay could expect from Buenos Aires would be a reciprocal trade treaty.[5]

Evacuation of Allied Troops

Juan Bautista Gill had been an extremely busy president since his inauguration in 1874. Desperate measures to bring in revenue, efforts to discover funds supposedly stolen by Benites, two missions to London, successful negotiations with Argentina, crushing the Serrano revolt, and sparring with Brazilian diplomats had left him with little leisure time. The completion of the Machaín-Irigoyen treaty gave Gill an opportunity to make a long-delayed tour of the interior. Leaving his cousin, Vice-President Uriarte, in charge, Gill left Asunción on March 1, 1876, taking with him his brother Emilio and General Bernardino Caballero. Gill visited the principal towns, observed the abandoned fields and homes, and made some political changes. The country was calm, the people cordial, and Gill returned to Asunción on April 17 to relieve Uriarte, who had had his fill of "watching the Cabildo." The financial situation had been eased somewhat by the arrival of the final installment of the $50,000 loan from the Banco Nacional in Buenos Aires, and Uriarte had not stolen a penny of it! An Argentine envoy had arrived to discuss a reciprocal trade agreement, and some obstreperous deputies had prevented Congress from opening as scheduled on April 1. After having waited for two hours, the chagrined Uriarte and the small diplomatic corps, more amused than provoked, gave up and went home. Little else of moment had occurred in the capital during Gill's absence.[6]

Brazil prepared to evacuate Paraguay with almost indecent speed after having approved the Machaín-Irigoyen treaty in April. Brizuela's letters from Paraguay reflected the second thoughts of beneficiaries of the occupation. Trade would be brought to an end, whole families were emigrating to Corrientes and Corumbá, and every day Gill's government became more unpopular. Argentine agents continued efforts to picture evacuation as a great bonanza, but people continued to flee the country.[7] Gill, rested from his trip through the interior, watched Brazilian preparations with undisguised pleasure. He did not share Brizuela's fear that withdrawal of the last Brazilian soldier would mark the beginning of further economic decline and inaugurate a period of revolutions, daily assassinations, and the most frightful anarchy. "You will recall," Brizuela reminded Cotegipe, "that some time ago in my first letters I told Your Excellency that Gill would take Paraguay to the precipice, and now he is on the verge of doing so; two more months and events will prove me correct."[8] He was an excellent prophet, although his timing was inaccurate.

Gondim presented his letter of recall on May 6 and left Eduardo Callado as chargé. At the port on May 11 to bid the minister *buen viaje* as he boarded the *Jaurú* were President Gill, Vice-President Uriarte, the cabinet, high Brazilian officers, the Italian chargé, four bands, and a battalion of Paraguayan gendarmes.[9] Two days later, the Brazilian 17th Battalion left for Rio de Janeiro and President Gill hailed a new era for Paraguay. During the six years of occupation, Gill proclaimed, Paraguay had "reconstructed its nationality and reestablished the authority required for the free exercise of our rights, as a sovereign and independent nation." Now that international agreements had been concluded, there was no pretext or reason that might excuse Paraguay in the eyes of history if she consented to further occupation. Gill thanked the Allies for the sacrifices they had made in order to maintain the occupation and claimed full credit for bringing it to an end through the treaty of February 3. Paraguay could maintain law and order. The president concluded with a passage reeking with sarcasm:

> . . . and now that we witness the embarkation of the foreign forces . . . we comply with the duty of offering a cordial farewell to those disciplined troops who have been our guests for six years; in all sincerity we wish them a prosperous and pleasant voyage; and we would ask that of their stay among us they preserve a memory as pleasant as the one they leave with us.[10]

When Gondim left Asunción, Gill assured Cotegipe of Paraguay's complete satisfaction and advised him that in a few days he would issue a manifesto in which he would again express his gratitude for the successful solution under the Empire's auspices of Paraguay's problems with Argentina.[11] Gill's heavy sarcasm was not lost on Cotegipe, who replied that the President's calculated phrases seemed to imply that a new golden age was about to begin for Paraguay. He reminded Gill that

the services provided by the Brazilian occupation are so obvious that only ingratitude or bad faith can belittle them. If any agent or employee of ours involved himself in internal intrigues, it was never with the consent, order, or approval of the Brazilian Government. We always left to Paraguay the free exercise of its rights, even when this or that matter might contradict our desires or damage our interests.[12]

Cotegipe considered the manifesto "inaccurate, unjust, and impolitic." He could understand Gill's bombast but not his failure to express gratitude for Brazil's services. He defended Brazil's occupation as a treaty right; contrary to the manifesto, Allied evacuation was not the result of negotiations in which Paraguay had to use force. Gill's implication that Paraguay had brought about evacuation through brilliant diplomacy was ridiculous.[13]

The river port was unusually busy during the next five weeks. The 2nd Cavalry Regiment embarked for Rio Grande do Sul on May 22 and the 2nd Artillery Battalion went upstream to Mato Grosso on the same day, taking about 1,500 Paraguayan women along. On June 22, the last of the 8,000 troops, the 8th Infantry Battalion, boarded the transport *Visconde de Inhaúma* enroute to Corumbá. General Mesquita took leave of the government and people of Paraguay but waited for the *Inhaúma*'s return to sail for Rio de Janeiro with his staff. Congress decreed June 22 a national holiday, and Benjamín Aceval noted in *La Reforma* the general happiness with which Paraguayans watched the last of the troops embark. The sudden lack of 8,000 consumers who had left between May 13 and 22 produced predictable results. A great many merchants hastened to liquidate their businesses and to leave the country.[14]

Porteño leaders, expecting to establish their influence over Paraguay, regarded the evacuation with satisfaction. Carlos Saguier again advised President Gill to put finances in order, maintain peace, guarantee the safety of life and property, protect the immigrant, and with liberal laws promote agriculture and industry. For once, no hostile force was gathering on Argentine soil, and Argentina had issued orders to recall its troops, leaving only a token force to hold Villa Occidental until its fate should be decided by arbitration. The treaties of February 3 were approved by the Argentine Congress on July 1, and Saguier correctly predicted a very special place in history for Juan Bautista Gill.[15]

The Allied evacuation and the Bareiro agreement with the Council of Foreign Bondholders undoubtedly gave the president great satisfaction. Continued plotting by Rivarola and José Dolores Molas came to a head in May but was little more than a nuisance. Gill put Rivarola under house arrest on his estancia at Barrero Grande. André Decoud, one of the conspirators, sought asylum on the Brazilian gunboat *Barroso*, and Molas remained in jail, where he had been since the Serrano revolt.[16] The major problems facing Paraguay were financial, and these, President Gill hoped, would be solved by the arrival of fresh capital from London to put the Bareiro agreement into effect.

Crisis of 1876–1877: Rejection of the Bareiro Agreement

To represent the Council of Foreign Bondholders in matters concerning the Bareiro agreement, Joseph Rodney Croskey arrived in Asunción on June 11, 1876, hoping to start the Banco Nacional del Paraguay. Congress approved the agreement on June 23 and Croskey returned to London, where his report aroused much opposition to going through with the plan. Unaware of this opposition in London, Congress designated the Club Nacional on Calle Palma as headquarters for the bank, authorized the president to deliver the railway upon receipt of the 15,000 shares of stock, and created the yerba monopoly.[17]

At this point the Brazilian government entered a vigorous protest. The last of its troops had left for Corumbá on June 22, but no one doubted for a moment that they could return quickly if needed. Cotegipe argued that the Bareiro agreement impaired Paraguayan sovereignty and imperiled its ability to meet obligations arising from the war. Brazil had prevented Argentina from indemnifying itself by seizing Paraguayan territory; now Paraguay was surrendering its public lands to private speculators! After having recognized its debt to Brazil in the Cotegipe-Loizaga treaty, Paraguay by this agreement would deliver its assets to the bondholders. And, asked Cotegipe, where would Paraguay get the money to amortize the war debt? "There will be no revenue for this purpose for many years," he concluded.[18] Brazil had invited Argentina to join in the protest, but Bernardo de Irigoyen declined. Instead, it was believed, Argentina planned to abolish all import duties on Paraguayan products. Paraguay might yet gain some benefit from the affair if Argentina could take advantage of Brazil's opposition; but Argentina, enduring a severe economic crisis, had no intention of granting economic favors to Paraguay.[19] For Brazil to interpose at this juncture was not very reasonable, since Paraguay by the Bareiro agreement was doing no more than was promised when the contracts were signed for floating the loans of 1871 and 1872, except for the proposal to create a powerful bank. All of the government's assets had been pledged as security for the loans, and Brazil would have been far wiser to have killed those contracts in 1871 and 1872 than to prevent a settlement several years later.

Paraguay rejected the Brazilian protest in language that no foreign minister would have used while occupation troops were present. Facundo Machaín reiterated his government's intention of meeting its obligations, but first the Allies must agree among themselves in order that all might be treated fairly. He commented sharply and not without a bit of sarcasm: "If Paraguay's independence had not been solemnly acknowledged by secret treaties, she would be justified in interpreting the protest as a threat to her sovereignty; but, since it is unthinkable to mistrust a Government with which she is linked by bonds of close friendship, she must attribute the act to other motives." Obviously, Cotegipe had failed to analyze the agreement with the council. Paraguay, as co-owner of the bank, would receive half of the profits, and the Bareiro agreement thus was much less onerous than the loans of 1871 and 1872, for which Paraguay had pledged all of its revenues and public property. Why had not Brazil entered a protest then? Now, if Brazil wanted to stop the settlement, Paraguay's subsequent troubles would be the fault of the Empire.[20]

Cotegipe replied indignantly in a patronizing but less dictatorial tone. He reminded Machaín that Paraguay owed two war debts, one for general costs of the war and the other for damages to be paid in bonds, and Paraguay's resources were tacitly mortgaged to paying off the war debts. Brazil would respect Paraguay's independence but must protect her own interests. In Asunción, Callado maintained social contacts with Gill, Machaín, and Bareiro, attempting to follow Cotegipe's instructions to maintain good relations. However cordial some officials might appear to be, the Paraguayan press continued harsh attacks against the protest.[21]

Brazil's objection may well have been a decisive factor in the decision of the Council of Foreign Bondholders not to carry out the Bareiro agreement. "Are the English coming or not?" was the question asked widely in Asunción while Argentine enterprisers, ready to invest in Paraguay, held back for fear of Brazilian intervention.[22] President Gill, convinced that Cotegipe's note had killed the project, was obviously cool toward Callado. The Spanish-born journalist Ricardo Brugada voiced Gill's resentment and called Brazil's attitude outrageous. Newspapers in Buenos Aires and Montevideo echoed Brugada's criticism and saw in the Bareiro agreement Paraguay's only chance to redeem the $f250,000 paper in circulation and to increase its revenue. Anticipating the failure of the Bareiro agreement, Saguier tried unsuccessfully to persuade the Banco de Italia y Río de la Plata to establish a branch in Asunción.[23]

Disregarding Paraguay's obvious bankruptcy, the Brazilians continued to press for payment of the *polizas,* or certificates issued by the government to meet awards approved by the Mixed Claims Commission that had been at work since 1872. The commission had awarded $767,000 to settle 52 claims by the end of October, 1876, but 741 claims remained to be adjudicated. Callado concluded that Paraguay would never be able to meet these obligations.[24]

The Paraguayan papers *La Reforma* and *Los Debates* were both very critical of Brazil. *Los Debates* lost no opportunity to condemn practically everything the Brazilians had done, and *La Reforma* was almost as vitriolic. José Segundo Decoud, later to be a chief architect of the Colorado Party, unleashed a savage anti-Brazilian attack in *La Reforma*: Brazilian guidance had perpetuated despotism, ruined commerce, promoted smuggling, and corrupted the people; Brazilian money had corrupted administrators who should have been in jail. "Feigned sympathies, shameful humiliations, hypocritical manifestations of friendship and sincerity, fabulous offers to corrupt the hearts of patriots, tricks and traps, perpetual conspiracies against the legal order, bloody threats of death, all capably carried out as if the prophetic genius and shadow of Philip II inspired those infernal souls, nurtured in the dark caverns of iniquity."[25] This journalistic attack was a clear expression of Paraguayan resentment of Brazil's role in killing the Bareiro agreement. *Los Debates* was more moderate and supported Gill's efforts to get back into the Empire's good graces. Facundo Machaín, who had left Gill's cabinet at the end of November, 1876, felt that his dismissal was the result of having defended Paraguayan interests. Henceforth he was an irreconcilable enemy of the Gill circle.[26]

Realizing that the Bareiro agreement was dead, President Gill reluctantly called Congress into session to consider the best course of action. Congress repealed all of the June laws, which were enacted to put the agreement into effect, and passed new revenue measures that included a substantial increase in import duties. Other laws made provisions to start paying the internal debt, amortize paper money, and create a Colegio Nacional. Once more public lands, by act of December 16, 1876, were put on sale. To Carlos Saguier, the view from Buenos Aires was hopeful. The new economic measures would attract financiers, who could not fail to note Paraguay's astonishing recovery under Gill; with peace assured, foreign capitalists would invest in the country and Paraguay would merit the confidence of civilized people. Even during the general economic depression in the Plata area, Paraguay could depend on increased custom revenues as a result of the Brazilian evacuation, since goods formerly smuggled in by sutlers and sold in the open market could now be taxed.[27] But the measures of December, 1876, failed to produce favorable results during the next few months, and Saguier's hope that the Banco Nacional in Buenos Aires would establish an Asunción branch was not realized. Nor was an effort to revive the Bareiro agreement in 1877 successful.[28]

Death in the Morning

President Gill may have believed that he was strong enough to control Paraguay without the support of Brazilian troops or that he was favored with supernal protection. Peace with Argentina removed the major threat of aid to rebels at Corrientes, and there was very little chance for a revolutionary plot to develop successfully within Paraguay. Gill made the fatal mistake of overestimating his strength. His political career, whether in Congress, the cabinet, or the presidency, had produced a large number of enemies even within the group that would become the Colorado Party. Among his most uncompromising enemies after the Serrano revolt were Juan Silvano and Nicanor Godoy, José Dolores Molas, Matías Goiburú, and Cirilo Antonio Rivarola.

Although Molas and Goiburú are given credit for leading the revolt of April, 1877, its principal architect was Juan Silvano Godoy. This fiery revolutionist was born in Asunción in 1850, received a legal education in Argentina, and returned to Paraguay with scores of other exiles in 1869, and was probably the youngest member of the Constitutional Convention of 1870. A handsome youth with dark brown hair parted on the left, a strong and slightly dimpled chin, well set brown eyes and a high forehead, the young Godoy was a natural leader who wasted his talents in futile jousting with Paraguayan political windmills. He participated in the revolts of 1871 and 1873 and held important judicial positions, including membership on the Tribunal Superior de Justicia, or Supreme Court. He was deeply involved in planning the revolt of 1877 but left for Corrientes on April 5, one week before his plot succeeded in its first objective, to prepare for the planned invasion that was not to materialize. Unable to return to Paraguay, he lived in Argentina until 1902, then went back to Asunción as director of the National Library, Archives, and Museum, a post he held until his death in 1926. Author of many books, editor, and connoisseur of the arts, Godoy was one of the country's prominent intellectuals.[29]

Having crushed all revolts and plots to overthrow him, President Gill was too complacent about his ability to survive. He was assured that Argentina would permit no gathering of rebels on its soil for possible cooperation with Rivarola, who was still eluding capture near Barrero Grande. Perhaps this explains his apparent indifference in the face of numerous warnings on that fatal April 12, 1877. Twice the plotters had failed to carry out Godoy's plan; but on that morning there were six armed men, ponchos concealing their weapons, well positioned for the third attempt. Nicanor Godoy, Molas, José Dolores Franco, and Mariano Galeano had moved into a doorway the president must pass, while two blocks away were their colleagues Juan Regúnega and Matías Goiburú.

President Gill with two aides left his home at 10:00 a.m. to walk to his office on the lower floor of the Cabildo. His wife, Doña Concepción de Bedoya, urged him not to go. Along the route several others, having observed the suspicious movements of the poncho-clad figures, warned the president. Apparently depending on his aides, Gill continued along his customary route. Nicanor Godoy stepped out of the doorway and fired twice at him from a distance of about four yards. The president fell dead. Then Molas, Galeano, and Franco shot at the aides, one of whom managed an ineffective return shot. Both of the aides were wounded. Goiburú came riding up, shouted "The tyrant dies!" and fired into the inert body. Police then attacked the assassins but were driven off after Molas had suffered a saber cut. The dead president was taken to the Policía, where Dr. William Stewart examined the body. The assassins managed to keep their rendezvous at the railway station and then galloped off toward Luque. The group of fleeing horsemen met General Emilio Gill, whom Goiburú murdered without warning.[30]

These vicious murders were intended to be the opening move in a revolution. There must, of course, be a manifesto, and Godoy had written one, which was released at Corrientes on the day of the crime. In florid periods, this manifesto proclaimed freedom from the tyrant. Then came a bill of particulars that called Gill a murderer, thief, traitor, and torturer. He had made a farce of elections. So great were his crimes and so numerous his relatives that the only way to prevent another family tyranny was to kill him.[31] But the murder was primarily one of personal vengeance, not the beginning of a successful revolt, since none of the principals could attract a strong following.

President Gill certainly had not solved Paraguay's many problems, but there is little reason to believe that any of his contemporaries could have done much better. The Machaín-Irigoyen treaty and the evacuation of foreign troops were the most notable achievements of his regime. His efforts to come to terms with the Council of Foreign Bondholders were commendable, but the Bareiro agreement would have ended Brazil's position as a preferred creditor. To condemn Gill for the emigration of hundreds of families to Corrientes, the failure of monopolies to produce revenue, the decline in value of both internal and external obligations, the increase in paper money, Brazilian intervention in Paraguayan politics, and the sale of the railway to Luis Patri is to ignore the country's desperate economic plight. That he persecuted such political enemies as Rivarola, Ferreira, and Urdapilleta was true but also to be expected. Like his predecessors, Rivarola and Jovellanos, he dealt harshly with journalistic opponents. The death of Germán Serrano in a *ley fuga* incident may or may not have been ordered by Gill; in any case, the rebellious general fully deserved his fate. To Juan Bautista Gill belongs the dubious honor of having been the only Paraguayan president to be assassinated in office, a record that was to endure for at least a century.

Uriarte and the Colorado Terror

Higinio Uriarte promptly assumed the presidency and prepared to deal with the revolt. He declared a state of siege, announced his cabinet, and sent troops under General Patricio Escobar and Colonel Ignacio Genes to thwart the rebels, who had little time to gather their forces. Regúnega succeeded in reaching Rivarola at Barrero Grande, where Goiburú joined them a day later with his men, bringing the total to about 300. This small band marched to Pirayú, where General Escobar waited with a superior force. The battle, joined on the afternoon of April 17, was an easy victory for Escobar. Completely routed, the rebels fled as best they could. Rivarola and Nicanor Godoy made good their escape, Mariano Galeano was captured on the river bank while waiting for a canoe to take him to Villa Occidental, and Molas, badly wounded, surrendered on April 18. During the relentless pursuit, government troops killed Goiburú and captured Franco when he was trying to cross the Paraná.[32] Events were to prove that all of the prisoners would have been better off had they been killed outright.

Uriarte proclaimed peace restored, but several months of turmoil lay ahead, months in which Cándido Bareiro left no doubt about his political ambitions. He had been the brains behind the 1873–1874 revolt, and one can but admire his restraint in not thrusting Uriarte aside and seizing the presidency; before giving him too much credit, one should remember that General Caballero had to be taken into consideration. Unable to trust his cabinet, Uriarte assigned to Ricardo Brugada the tasks of editing documents and writing diplomatic notes. Vasconcellos, the Brazilian chargé, said that "he is the oracle consulted in all matters, and nothing, absolutely nothing, is done without his advice and approval." Brugada was on intimate terms with Gill's widow and served as her lawyer in the bizarre case in which she claimed that Vasconcellos had stolen many of her husband's documents.[33]

President Gill's financial measures had left the treasury in a deplorable condition. The $50,000 Argentine loan had to be repaid; the Council of Foreign Bondholders would demand further negotiations; an astronomical war debt hung over the country, and damages in the millions were being assessed against Paraguay by the Mixed Claims Commissions. The Uriarte government had no income other than insignificant customs revenues and no credit in foreign capital markets, and public administration was notoriously corrupt. The Brazilian chargé despaired of the future:

> I find this Government in the most critical circumstances, deprived of the indispensable means to meet its most urgent needs. There have been heavy rains for nearly five months in all the Republic, almost without ceasing, causing not only the total loss of plantings and making it impossible to transport the few products of the country to this market, but also destroying the houses which for the most part are built of earth. More than a hundred have fallen in the city and almost all of the rest are threatened with ruin. It has been a real calamity, and the consequences of such rain are terrible: misery and hunger.[34]

After the failure of the Bareiro agreement and its modified version of 1877, the Council of Foreign Bondholders urged renewed efforts by Paraguay to meet its obligations. Saguier in Buenos Aires replied that the time was not propitious. He, too, referred to the rains that had destroyed some 200 houses and had devastated many plantations; government income was sufficient to meet about one-third of the necessary expenses and the bondholders would have to be patient.[35]

Succession to the presidency was the principal political question in 1877. The strongest candidates were Bareiro, Urdapilleta, and Adolfo Saguier. Brother of the Paraguayan chargé in Buenos Aires, Adolfo Saguier was one of the students sent to Europe for education by Carlos Antonio López. Upon his return to Paraguay, he entered the army and served with distinction as commander of artillery at Curupaity. Saguier later became a founder of the Liberal Party. Caballero supported Bareiro, Decoud backed Saguier, and Escobar was thought to be for Urdapilleta. This alignment early in 1877 changed rapidly. Urdapilleta lost support when he left the cabinet, and neither he nor Saguier had Brazil's endorsement. Some observers feared a revolution, but the chances were remote with Godoy in Argentina, Rivarola a fugitive, and neither able to attract a following. Dr. Facundo Machaín was Paraguay's leading Liberal, a young man of brilliant promise whose stature had increased immeasurably because of his successful negotiations with Irigoyen. His principal rival was José Segundo Decoud, whose thirst for power was steadily cementing his adherence to the Bareiro-Caballero circle. To bring about greater cooperation among rivals for power and preferment, Machaín inspired the organization of the Sociabilidad Paraguaya on May 20, 1877, a group formed to promote culture and the common welfare.[36]

Facundo Machaín had held himself aloof from the many revolutionary plots that kept Paraguayan politics in a turmoil. His reputation for personal integrity was spotless, his fame as a jurist and advocate well deserved. When the captives Molas, Regúnega, Franco, and Galeano asked that he represent them, Machaín ignored the pleas and advice of his friends and accepted the case. There was reason for concern. Shortly after their capture in April, fear for the lives of the prisoners was shown by anonymous letters received by cabinet members and some senators. These letters threatened retaliation against officials and their families should harm come to the prisoners. Indignantly, El Comercio asked if a band of carbonarios existed in the city.[37] These threats may have been the result of rumors that the prisoners would never be brought to trial, or they could have come from someone with a good knowledge of how the Uriarte cabinet would operate. Whatever their origin, they were all too prophetic of what awaited the prisoners.

Doing his best for his clients, Machaín protested their maltreatment and aroused much public sympathy for them. This infuriated Uriarte's circle, which was, of course, dominated by Bareiro, who inspired rumors that Machaín himself was plotting revolution! Although he had no plans at all for resorting to revolution to overthrow the Bareiro-Caballero-Escobar coalition, Machaín was caught up in a net of intrigue. Major Marcelino Gamarra, a great admirer, urged Rivarola to renew the April revolt. Rivarola, widely held to be insane and at most no more than a nuisance, had few followers and would have been easy to find any time the government wanted to take him. But his presence offered a plausible excuse for repressive measures, so he was permitted to serve as a lure for such rash enthusiasts as Gamarra. The plot had scarcely begun to take shape when Gamarra was seized and imprisoned. Benjamín Aceval, a moderate influence in the cabinet, left for the United States on August 3 to present Paraguay's case in the Chaco arbitration. Urdapilleta, who had never been happy in the Gill cabinet, again resigned, leaving Bareiro, Caballero, Juan Antonio Jara, Adolfo

Saguier, and Patricio Escobar in the cabinet.[38] Gill's death caused no sorrow to any of this group, but leaders of the April revolt were a constant threat to them, and this fact is sufficient to explain the tragic events that soon occurred.

Jailbreaks were so easily organized that official complicity must be suspected. One on August 4 gave Comandante Molas, the principal prisoner from the April revolt, an opportunity to escape; but, with the end of his trial approaching, the popular hero of Paraguay's famed attack on Brazilian ironclads during the war refused to flee. He was confident that Machaín could win acquittal in the appellate court, the Tribunal de Jurados, which was to receive the case on September 5. Very conveniently on that day a police informer reported that Machaín was plotting with Rivarola. Pretending to believe this utterly absurd fiction, General Caballero ordered Machaín imprisoned on September 6, then released him on bond a week later. Machaín had great support in Congress, and public opinion ran strongly in his favor. The triumvirate of Bareiro, Caballero, and Escobar concocted a brazen plot to discredit Machaín: they sent agents among the Liberals who sought an alliance with Rivarola in an effort to overthrow the government. Caballero let the plotting continue until October 15, when he ordered Machaín, Dr. Francisco Galeano, and several others sent to jail. Theoretically, the plot was to proclaim either Machaín or Rivarola as president.[39]

Political events continued on their tragic course. There were widespread rumors of an impending mass murder of prisoners, but Machaín refused to believe them. Molas was less naïve and laid plans to escape during a jailbreak scheduled for the night of October 28–29. The police, of course, knew about the plan and were ready to carry out the slaughter approved by Caballero, Bareiro, and Escobar. Major Gamarra, Regúnega, and a few others were allowed to escape, then a strong force of officers rushed to the jail where they brutally murdered several manacled prisoners, including Molas, Machaín, Mariano Galeano, and Franco.[40]

These atrocious murders set off a wave of revulsion that is still felt by all Paraguayans who know their country's history, however much they may argue the question of guilt. Machaín was "without doubt the most illustrious Paraguayan, whose faults were simply political."[41] That eventually the Bareiro circle would turn to murder to be rid of its opposition surprised no one who knew Paraguayan politics. The country's major political weakness was the lack of capable and honest men to staff the various branches of government, a situation that would hinder progress for many decades. Reflecting contemporary opinion, the Brazilian chargé blamed the fanaticism of the Jesuits and of the dictators for Paraguay's complete ignorance of ways to promote civilization and to guarantee public freedoms. With no plan of government, no source of funds to meet pressing needs, this observer concluded, selfish men would go to any length to promote their personal interests. Men like Gill, Rivarola, Jovellanos, Bareiro, and most of their associates regarded public office not as a trust but as an opportunity for aggrandizement.[42]

The brutal murders of October 28 served notice that the Bareiro-Caballero-Escobar combine would brook no opposition in the 1878 election. José Segundo Decoud, whatever his role had been, was satisfied with a Bareiro-Saguier slate. The ruling clique formed the Club Libertad on February 17, 1878, with its only object that of securing the election of Bareiro and Saguier.[43] Caballero, who was very popular in the country, was the only one who could have beaten Bareiro in a fair election had such an event been possible. Vasconcellos, however, as had Rio Branco earlier, asserted that Caballero was illiterate.[44]

Notably pro-Argentine in former years, Bareiro now posed as a friend of Brazil; but, Vasconcellos asserted, like all Paraguayans he could not be trusted. As a defeated and almost annihilated people, Paraguayans hated Brazil, the chargé continued, and their state of civilization could be compared only with Central Africa, their government and administration were beneath ridicule, and poorly educated foreigners occupied the most important posts. On rainy days public offices were closed, and when a minister failed to appear at his office, none of the employees reported for work. "General Caballero, Minister of Justice and Worship," Vasconcellos reported, "was intoxicated almost daily." The chargé was rudely shocked when some guests showed up in shirt sleeves at a ball given by the president.[45] No matter who became president, Paraguay faced a grim future:

Your Excellency will realize that in such a country where corruption marks all strata of society, composed in the most part of refugee adventurers; where the high offices of judges are held by incapable and venal men; where, finally, one may buy one of the authorities for a few pesos—in such a semi-barbarous country, I say, there can be no guarantee for diplomatic agents. . . . The Viscount Rio Branco and Baron Cotegipe could say if my description of this unfortunate country is exaggerated. Their excellencies had occasion to study it and also to realize that it is impossible to deal with such a people when ignorance is combined with the most highly developed bad taste. The Paraguayans, accustomed to the yoke of Francia and the López, can be handled only with an iron hand. No diplomacy can be used successfully except that of the gun. This they greatly respect because the lesson we gave them is still fresh and they fear another.[46]

Internal anarchy and rumors of invasion from Argentina preceded the 1878 election. In Barrero Grande and Caraguatay departments, Rivarola and various bandits, thieves, and deserters were said to be operating, using the extensive forests for cover. Rumors persisted that Benigno Ferreira and Rivarola were about to invade with a rebel force in an effort to overthrow the government. If this were to happen, Vasconcellos opined, it would mean the complete ruin of the country, the *coup de grâce*, but the government should be able to handle the menace. When Uriarte declared a state of siege for one month to permit extermination of the bandits, a lively debate occurred in Congress. Deputy Octaviano Rivarola warned against the declaration of martial law, under which personal liberties were endangered and horrible crimes committed. He reminded the chamber that in the five previous states of siege, numerous atrocities had occurred. Nevertheless, ignoring the ridicule of Liberals, Congress approved.[47] Defying all efforts to capture him, Rivarola remained at liberty. Finally, after Bareiro's inauguration, he committed the inevitable fatal mistake of appearing in Asunción on a safe conduct prior to going into exile. General Caballero, who was dining with friends when told of Rivarola's decision to accept amnesty, is said to have exclaimed jubilantly: "Ereimé poróngmacó, nde cambá afang!" This obscenity in Guaraní may be translated roughly as "Now we've got you for certain, you black bastard!"[48] Officials greeted Rivarola with apparent cordiality on December 24, and a week later their agents stabbed him to death near the police station while many observers ignored his pleas for aid.[49] Here was another murder to be charged to the Bareiro-Caballero circle.

The election of 1878 was only a formality. In the most astonishing political statement of the decade, *La Reforma* hailed the election of Bareiro and Saguier as a "victory of the *liberal party* of the Republic" and a resounding success for the Club Libertad.[50] But there was still turmoil in Barrero Grande and Caraguatay, where bandits committed their depredations so frequently that panic reigned in those departments.[51]

At last Cándido Bareiro had succeeded in winning the presidency. The road had been long and rough. Many times the office had appeared to be in his grasp, and each time Brazilian interference had denied him the prize. In 1870, he had been forced to allow Rivarola to become the first postwar constitutional president. In 1871, Gill and the Brazilians maneuvered Jovellanos into office; in 1874, the same combination prevented him from enjoying the victory won by revolution. Ferreira was gone but Jovellanos remained and the Brazilians imposed Gill as his successor. Bareiro refrained from heading a coup when Gill was murdered in 1877, permitted Uriarte to complete his term, and so entered office on November 25, 1878, as the constitutionally elected president of Paraguay.

Uriarte's brief administration, which had been marked by quarrels with Congress and general frustration, ended with rejoicing over the outcome of the Chaco arbitration. Paraguayan officials were confident that their country's title to the disputed area was unassailable. To prepare the case, President Gill had appointed José Falcón, Higinio Uriarte, and Dr. Benjamín Aceval. To present Paraguay's case in Washington, Gill selected Aceval, who had studied law in Buenos Aires, served on the Supreme Court, sat as a deputy in Congress, and held the position of minister of foreign affairs.[52] Well armed with documents, maps, and books, Aceval proceeded to Washington, where President Hayes received him on December 7, 1877. Probably the most important of the Paraguayan documents was an original *expediente* of 1782 that showed Paraguay's villas, forts, reductions, and other Chaco establishments. A description of the old Reducción Melodía, founded by Padre Amancio González Escobar, proved Paraguayan occupation of the site of Villa Occidental. After careful consideration of the evidence, President Hayes on November 12, 1878, awarded the disputed area to Paraguay.[53]

A hero's welcome greeted Dr. Aceval when he returned to Asunción on March 25, 1879. A bevy of girls gave him a crown of flowers, flags flew in his honor, and many orators hailed him as a great patriot. President Bareiro offered him the post of minister of foreign affairs, where his talents would serve Paraguay well in the Chaco negotiations with Bolivia, but Dr. Aceval preferred to head the newly founded Colegio Nacional, a position which he held until 1886.[54]

One more bit of drama remained. The formal transfer of sovereignty and the evacuation of Argentine troops was set for May 14, 1879. The Brazilians, in response to a request from President Bareiro, graciously provided the gunboat *Fernández Viera* to take the Paraguayan delegation upstream for the ceremony. Congress approved a series of decrees on May 13 that renamed the village Villa Hayes, designated Aceval, Uriarte, and Escobar to head the delegation, and appointed Col. Juan Alberto Meza as military and political commander of the Chaco.[55] A salvo of artillery and the ringing of bells in all the churches awakened

Paraguayans on May 14. The Paraguayan flag flew from all public buildings. President Bareiro was in the crowd that cheered as their delegation on the *Fernández Viera* and Argentines on the *Vigilante* steamed out of the harbor for the short run upstream.

In the small plaza of Villa Hayes, Argentine and Paraguayan troops stood at attention, the flagpole between them. There were speeches and a twenty-one gun salute as the Argentine flag came down. Another salute from twenty-one guns greeted the Paraguayan flag as it replaced the pale blue Argentine banner on the lanyards and slowly rose to fly over the little town.[56] This ceremony marked the recovery of Paraguayan sovereignty after a decade of occupation by Brazil and Argentina. Ahead lay a long dispute with Bolivia over the Chaco Boreal and efforts to attract foreign capital to develop the country's resources and immigrants to people the land.

The decade of occupation had left Paraguay very poorly prepared for democratic processes, and the Allies had done nothing to establish a sound government in Paraguay. Sensitive to charges that they planned to make the country a protectorate, Brazilian statesmen largely stayed clear of involvement in governmental processes. Whether, under the circumstances, a joint Allied commission could have done better is a moot question; but people like Mitre, Sarmiento, Rio Branco, and Cotegipe should have been able to devise a military government to ease the transition from dictatorship to some sort of democracy. Instead of aiding in creating governmental machinery, Brazil manipulated Paraguayan governments for its major purposes of gaining its own territorial objectives and restraining Argentina. This practice gave Argentina an opportunity to encourage dissident politicians in their plots to overthrow Brazilian-protected governments.

The quarreling Allies did practically nothing to start their defeated enemy on the way to economic recovery. Brazil had permitted Paraguay to float two ruinous loans in London and then had done nothing to prevent Paraguayan politicians from stealing the proceeds. For a few months the Allies played with the railway that was so justly the pride of Carlos Antonio López, then did very little to rehabilitate that major transportation artery. Domestic pressures and lack of statesmanship prevented Argentina from permitting Paraguayan products free access to its markets; internal turmoil and economic depression made large postwar loans as impossible as they would have been unwise. The outrageous theft of the London loans clearly demonstrated that no credits could be advanced to Paraguay without the closest supervision by the creditors.

Paraguay in 1878 appeared to be a cultural and economic wasteland, the hopeless remnant of a country where abject poverty and epidemic diseases combined with climatic disasters to threaten the republic's existence. Neither Argentina nor Brazil could have assumed the enormous task of rehabilitating the decimated nation. Thus it was to that purpose that Cándido Bareiro and his Colorado successors dedicated their efforts until the Liberals drove them from power in 1904.

15. Epilogue

The political, economic, and social problems that surfaced in Paraguay during the postwar decade continued dominant for the most part during the next sixty years. The Brazilian-Argentine rivalry receded as a major determinant of events once the Hayes Award had eliminated Argentine claims to the Chaco Boreal. Brazil, faced with serious domestic problems, made no significant effort to make an economic satellite of Paraguay, which could not escape its long-standing ties to Argentina. In the long dispute with Bolivia over the Chaco Boreal, Argentina generally favored Paraguay. Other diplomatic questions, such as revival of the Hopkins claim that originated under Carlos Antonio López, presented no serious difficulties. The war debts simply could not be paid, a fact that Argentina and Brazil finally recognized by cancelling them in the 1940s.

In domestic politics, the Colorados and Liberals continued their struggle, although formal party organization did not occur until 1887. In the postwar decade, as leader of the Lopiztas and conservatives, Bareiro had proved to be Paraguay's most astute politician, able to keep Generals Caballero and Escobar under control and to attract former Liberals, such as José Segundo Decoud, to his camp. Bareiro embodied Colorado principles and it is he, rather than Bernardino Caballero, who should be considered the founder of the Colorado Party. Bareiro's presidency, cut short by his death on September 4, 1880, saw the founding of the Colegio Nacional and the Seminario Conciliar de Asunción to train priests, but these institutions received little support from the bankrupt country, which still had no bank and had insufficient revenues for the ordinary expenses of government.

Bareiro's death offered Caballero the chance for which he had been waiting patiently. Encouraged by his supporters, Caballero seized control in a bloodless coup that a weak and groveling Congress promptly approved, leaving the mortified vice-president helpless and politically isolated. This blatant violation of the constitution was consistent with Colorado principles and could not be reconciled with democratic processes. Liberals, only slightly less cynical than their opponents, protested bitterly as Colorados won elections by forcefully driving them from the polls. Caballero maintained a semblance of internal peace by typical dictatorial methods and shrugged off the shrill criticisms from the few newspapers he allowed to exist. The Colorado caudillo held office until 1886 and chose his close and admiring friend, General Patricio Escobar, as his successor.

Electoral fraud and violence in the election of 1886 so enraged the Liberals that they organized the Centro Democrático on July 10, 1887. This group was the Liberal Party, although the name was not formally adopted until 1894. The Colorados countered this move with the formal organization of the Asociación Nacional Republicana on August 25, 1887. By these actions, Liberals and Colorados institutionalized their political affiliations. Not only did the two parties continue their political warfare, but they also split into numerous factions that prevented either from presenting a united front.

The administration of Juan Gualberto González (1890–1894) was beset with troubles, mostly economic, that had political overtones. The Colorados had split into factions, with González opposing Caballero. Liberals sought to take advantage of this factionalism by mounting a revolt on October 18, 1891, that failed miserably. Although Juan B. Egusquiza was selected as successor to González with the latter's support, he helped the enemies of González to remove him from office by a coup early in 1894. The next ten years were marked by struggles within the Colorado Party for control, resulting in such turmoil that the Liberals, led by Benigno Ferreira, successfully rebelled in 1904 and drove the Colorados from power. They did not return to office until another military leader, General Alfredo Stroessner, directed a successful coup in 1954 and began a dictatorship that promises to be the longest in Paraguayan history.

The argument with Bolivia over the Chaco Boreal continued to concern the two governments throughout the Colorado era and on into the Liberal regime, where it culminated in the Chaco War of 1932–1935 and contributed to the downfall of the Liberals in 1936. Although both countries granted concessions to exploiting companies, the Paraguayan grant to Carlos Casado of Argentina in 1885 of 5,000,000 hectares at a minimal price was by far the most important. Casado and other enterprisers penetrated the Chaco with narrow-gauge railways and unimproved roads, established ports on the upper Paraguay River, exploited timber resources, and established huge ranches. Paraguayan forces dislodged Bolivians from the Río Paraguay, but Bolivia pressed southeastward along the Pilcomayo River while both countries set up small *fortines,* or military outposts, in the interior. Meanwhile, diplomats from the two countries negotiated treaties in 1879, 1887, and 1894 that were never ratified. Paraguay in 1884 gave a Bolivian, Miguel Suárez Arana, permission to establish Puerto Pacheco just below Bahía Negra. Arana expected to build a road, then a railway, to Santa Cruz in eastern Bolivia. This enterprise aroused hostile comments in the Paraguayan Congress and in 1887 Paraguayan forces took possession of Puerto Pacheco. To Paraguay, the Chaco question was simply one of a boundary between the two countries; to Bolivia, the Chaco question was one of ownership of the entire Chaco Boreal.

The London loans of 1871 and 1872 had to be settled before Paraguay could expect its credit to be restored in international money markets. No Paraguayan government had any intention of repudiating the debt, nor did any president advocate buying up the depreciated bonds. When Caballero came to power in 1880, the principal and interest due on the two loans was over $15,000,000, or, more accurately, £3,005,400. The government also owed $42,589 to the Argentine Banco Nacional. These debts would be paid but not the war damages to private citizens, which by 1885 amounted to more than $17,000,000. After the rejection of the Bareiro agreement of 1876, the Council of Foreign Bondholders continued to press for a settlement and sent an agent to Asunción in 1880 while Bareiro was president. Although this mission failed, neither the council, headed by Edward P. Bouviere, nor Caballero when he took office, let the matter drop. After many proposals and counter-proposals, Caballero sent José Segundo Decoud to London in 1885 to negotiate with Bouviere. The result was an agreement to reduce the capital debt to £850,000 and to grant about 145 acres of public land for each £100 of unpaid interest. This meant that 500 square leagues in various departments and the island of Yacyretá, or 2,316,500 acres, would be set aside for the bondholders, who would select the land within five years. The bondholders organized the Anglo-Paraguay Land and Cattle Company and in 1887 sent Henry Valpy, an old Paraguayan hand, to select the land.

Unfortunately, although cession of the land went through without delay, Paraguay was unable to pay interest on the reduced principal. A new agreement in 1895 added £100,920 to the principal. This agreement was kept, and by 1908 the debt had been reduced to £831,850. The Anglo-Paraguay Land and Cattle Company became a major vehicle for additional British investment, but the settlement was no great boon to Paraguay. Those 500 leagues could have been sold for more than enough to buy up all of the bonds, which in 1885 were selling at 7 or 8.

The promotion of immigration was one concern of governments during the postwar decade. Unfortunately, the debacle of the "Lincolnshire farmers" in 1872–1873 made prospective immigrants wary of being caught in a similar disaster. The Paraguayans learned much from this episode and during the Colorado era made serious efforts to attract both individual immigrants and colonies to settle vacant lands. A General Department of Immigration and Colonization was created, consuls were charged with advertising Paraguay's attractions, and a General Office of Information published a monthly review intermittently. A law of June, 1881, offered aid in moving to an agricultural colony in Paraguay, free agricultural implements, sustenance for several months, land at very low prices and easy terms, and other advantages. Other laws, especially in 1903 and 1904, brought Colorado policies to maturity. These various laws resulted in the creation of several agricultural colonies, starting with a German colony at San Bernardino on Lake Ypacaraí in 1881. Undeterred by the failure of Nuevo Burdeos—later known as Villa Occidental and Villa Hayes—in 1854, a group of French farmers established another colony at this Chaco site in 1882. There were other notable efforts, such as Nueva Germania, Nueva Australia, Cosme, Presidente González, Yegros, and Trinacria, in which Germans, Italians, Paraguayans, Australians, Swiss, and a sprinkling of other nationalities participated.

While welcoming all immigrants except Negroes and Orientals, the government concentrated its efforts on promoting group immigration in the form of agricultural colonies. The modest results were a significant beginning. An official report shows 12,241 registered immigrants for the years 1881–1907, but many failed to be registered. The total number of immigrants, including those who settled in urban areas, probably was less than 23,000 for this period, while it is estimated that about 90,000 Paraguayans emigrated to neighboring Argentine and Brazilian provinces. Nevertheless, Paraguay's population increased significantly. Although all censuses were inaccurate, they may be taken as being relatively close approximations. The population grew from about 300,000 in 1879 to 535,000 in 1899, excluding Indians, whose numbers were guessed to be about 100,000.

Paralleling Colorado efforts to attract immigrants was the policy of selling off most of the country's 16,000 square leagues (about 74,000,-000 acres) of public domain. This sale, which began in 1885, was suspended for a short time to allow the Council of Foreign Bondholders to select the 500 leagues provided for in the Decoud agreement. When sales resumed, there was a wild orgy of speculation in which both foreigners and Paraguayans participated. Prices had tripled by 1890, but still Paraguayan land was cheap when compared with similar land in Argentina. Ultimately the purchasers created huge estancias and haciendas, and a few companies monopolized the yerbales. Theoretically, squatters were to have preemptive rights to buy the land they occupied. Unable to take advantage of this privilege, most of them became tenants or drifted away to urban areas and neighboring foreign provinces, or became virtual slaves in the yerbales, or took employment with such huge enterprises as Carlos Casado, Ltd. Income from land sales was insignificant after 1895 and in 1900 the sales were stopped. But it was too late. Instead of becoming a nation of small farmers, Paraguay had reestablished the old encomienda in a new form that perpetuated abject poverty in both urban and rural areas. Colorado apologists, defending the land sales of 1885–1900, argue that taxable property was created, large investments were attracted to the country, and the creation of major enterprises in the Chaco strengthened Paraguay's hand in the struggle with Bolivia. Ironically, to promote the policy of creating agricultural colonies, the government generally had to buy back land it had possessed but a short time before.

When Caballero seized the presidency in 1880, Luís Patri was still operating the Paraguay Central Railway and hoping for a chance to be rid of the enterprise. He succeeded in 1886 when Travassos, Patri & Co. accepted $1,200,000 in bonds from Paraguay for the railway and land grant. With the bonds as capital, Patri started the Banco de Comercio, and also became president of the board of directors for the railway and contractor to complete the line to Villa Rica, a stretch of 75 kilometers, for $18,220 gold per kilometer. Paraguay's finances were not equal to this endeavor, so Escobar's government in 1887 authorized sale of the railway to English capitalists for $2,100,000 gold. This would provide money to pay for the extension to Villa Rica, and the new company would build the line from Villa Rica to Encarnación. The English capitalists won much better terms. Paraguay agreed to accept one-half of the price in gold and 21,000 shares of preference stock for the other half, as well as guaranteeing a 6 percent return to the company on its investment, while the company was to pay 35 percent of the gross income to Paraguay. The government also guaranteed a 6 percent return on the extension to Encarnación at the rate of $30,000 gold per kilometer. The transaction was completed in 1889, with ample provision for the distribution of graft to key politicians and influential persons. The railway would have to be very profitable for Paraguay to benefit.

Prospects were bright for a while. Patri completed the line to Villa Rica in 1889 and was paid from the $1,050,000 received by the government from the English capitalists. By August, 1891, the new owners had completed 100 kilometers of track beyond Villa Rica, reaching nearly to Pirapó but less than half the distance to Encarnación. There the line stopped. Paraguay defaulted on its payments of the guarantee and the contractors went into bankruptcy. This development precipitated a long controversy between the government and the company that continued until 1907, when Paraguay surrendered its shares and both sides dropped their claims. This settlement was the result of Argentine aid to the Liberal revolt of 1904, which marked a new phase in the old Argentine-Brazilian struggle to control Paraguay. Throughout the Liberal regime, Argentine influence continued to be strong, and Anglo-Argentine capital dominated the country's economy. The Paraguay Central Railway was one of the major enterprises to fall under their control, but it yielded small profit to the new owners.

Banking and industry, two obvious needs of the Paraguayan economy, had their real beginnings during the Colorado era. The industries were almost entirely extractive and performed the first steps in processing. La Industrial Paraguaya, the Villa Mora tramway, and the Anglo-Paraguay Land and Cattle Company were all British. British capital in the country considerably exceeded Argentine investment, although the ties between Argentine and British investors were so close that it is difficult to distinguish between them.

Colorado presidents without exception promoted the formation of banks. The Banco Nacional del Paraguay had a checkered career. Started with public and private funds in January, 1884, it was bankrupt by 1890. Several other banks, both public and private, began operation during the Colorado era and provided much-needed credit. Foreign capital, gradually attracted to banking, dominated the business after 1900. In 1895, there were five banks, three of them private and free from government control. One, the Banco Agrícola, was entirely government owned and survived the economic troubles that caused so much havoc in South America in the 1890s. The Banco del Paraguay y Río de la Plata, started in 1889 with heavy government backing, was bankrupt by 1895. Lack of capital and poor management caused the failures, but when the Liberals took over at the end of 1904 there were enough healthy banks to meet the country's needs.

Paraguayan social problems were a direct outgrowth of the country's poverty. Although a few large enterprises, corporate and private, enjoyed comparative prosperity, the average income of the Paraguayan worker and tenant was extremely low. The country continued to be one of the poorest in the Americas. Even if the people had enjoyed much larger incomes, they could not have obtained adequate medical attention. The appointment of various councils, committees, and commissions by successive governments resulted in very little improvement in public health. The people were victims of venereal and parasitic diseases, leprosy, tuberculosis, and nearly every other ailment known to medical science. While the very small affluent class followed accepted nineteenth-century moral standards for the most part, family ties were very loose among the lower classes. The rate of illegitimacy, well over 50 percent, caused religious leaders to shrug off the problem as being insoluble.

The masses of people were largely functional illiterates throughout the Colorado era. Public schools outside of such cities as Asunción and Villa Rica offered very poor educational opportunities, and attendance requirements were never enforced. Private and parochial schools were far better, especially in Asunción. Those who could afford to do so generally sent their children abroad, to Argentina, England, France, and, less frequently, the United States to be educated. The result of this practice, together with the improvement of the National University, was seen in the emergence of a notable group of scholars and professional men in the 1890s who gave to Paraguay's intellectual life an impetus that has never been lost. Nevertheless, at the end of the Colorado era in 1904, Paraguay was far from having recovered from the social and economic disaster of the War of the Triple Alliance.

Notes

ABBREVIATIONS USED

AGN-BA	Archivo General de la Nación, Buenos Aires
AHI-RJ	Arquivo Histórico de Itamaraty, Rio de Janeiro
AN-A	Archivo Nacional, Asunción
AN-RJ	Arquivo Nacional, Rio de Janeiro
CBC	Coleção Barão de Cotegipe, Instituto Histórico e Geográfico Brasileiro, Rio de Janeiro. The notation 25/137, for example, means Lata (Box) 25, Document 137
Cen.	Central (in Brazilian despatches)
Conf.	Confidencial, confidential
CCAP	Colección de Carlos Alberto Pusineri Scala, Asunción
DA	Diplomatic Despatches from United States Ministers to Argentina, File Microcopies of Records in the National Archives, Washington, D.C., No. 69, Roll 18 (69/18)
DIPU	Diplomatic Instructions of the Department of State, 1801–1906. Paraguay and Uruguay, Oct. 6, 1858–July 26, 1906. File Microcopies of Records in the National Archives, Washington, D.C., No. 77, Roll 128 (77/128)
DPU	Diplomatic Despatches from United States Ministers to Paraguay and Uruguay, 1858–1906. File Microcopies of Records in the National Archives, Washington, D.C., No. 128, Rolls 1–19 (128/1, etc.)
GP-CCAP	Gill Papers, Colección de Carlos Alberto Pusineri Scala, Asunción
GP-DD	Guerra do Paraguay, Diversos Documentos de 1871–1872, Arquivo Nacional, Rio de Janeiro
HC	House of Commons
IAEA	*Inter-American Economic Affairs*
IHGB	Instituto Histórico e Geográfico Brasileiro, Rio de Janeiro
MDBA-DI	Missões Diplomáticas Brasileiras, Assumpção, Despachos, Instrucções, Arquivo Histórico de Itamaraty, Rio de Janeiro
MDBA-OR	Missões Diplomáticas Brasileiras, Assumpção, Oficios Recibidos, Arquivo Histórico de Itamaraty, Rio de Janeiro
NAUS	National Archives, United States

NPFO   Notes from the Paraguayan Foreign Office. Records of the
                United States Legation in Paraguay, 1861–1935. File Micro-
                copies of Records in the National Archives, Washington,
                D.C., T 693
NPL   Notes from the Paraguayan Legation in the United States to
                the Department of State. March 12, 1853–May 16, 1906.
                File Microcopies of Records in the National Archives,
                Washington, D.C., No. 350, Roll 1 (350/1)
PRO-C   Public Record Office, Chancery, London
PRO-FO   Public Record Office, Foreign Office, London (FO 6, Argentine
                Confederation; FO 13, Brazil; FO 59, Paraguay)
Res.   Reservado (in Brazilian despatches)
RIHGB   *Revista do Instituto Histórico e Geográfico Brasileiro*
Sec.   Seccão (in Brazilian despatches)

Chapter 1: End of the Paraguayan War

1. For the Yataity-Corá conference, see Juan Silvano Godoy, *La entrevista
de Yataity Corá entre los generales Mitre y López*; Adolfo J. Báez, *Yataity
Corá. Una conferencia histórica*; George Thompson, *The War in Paraguay.
With a Historical Sketch of the Country and its People and Notes upon the
Military Engineering of the War*, p. 174; and Efraím Cardozo, *Hace cién años.
Crónicas de la guerra de 1864–1870*, IV, 214–226.

2. Edward Thornton to Edmund Hammond, Rio de Janeiro, Oct. 23, 1867,
Hammond Papers, PRO-FO 391/16.

3. Memorandum of Sept. 18, 1867, *Archivo del General Mitre*, VI, 263–267;
Efraím Cardozo, *Paraguay independiente*, pp. 233–234. A modern polemicist
sees the war as an English conspiracy to open up Paraguay as a source of cheap
raw materials to replace England's lost colonies in North America! (Manual J.
Cibils, *Anarquía y revolución en el Paraguay*, p. 22). For a Marxist interpretation, see León Pomer, *La guerra del Paraguay. Gran negocio!*

4. In November, 1866, Caxias took command of the Brazilian army while
Admiral José Joaquim Inácio replaced Admiral Marquês Tamandaré in December. For Caxias, see Augusto Tasso Fragoso, *História da guerra entre a
tríplice aliança e o Paraguai*, III, 151 ff.

5. Cardozo, *Paraguay independiente*, pp. 229–241; Fragoso, *História*, III,
372–375.

6. Fragoso, *História*, III, 374–376; Charles Ames Washburn, *The History of
Paraguay, with Notes of Personal Observations, and Reminiscences of Diplomacy under Difficulties*, II, 228–235.

7. Cardozo, *Paraguay independiente*, p. 236, gives Feb. 22 as the date of
bombardment; other sources agree on Feb. 24. Fragoso, *História*, III, 373;
Washburn, *History of Paraguay*, II, 241; and George Frederick Masterman,
Seven Eventful Years in Paraguay, pp. 226–227, give eyewitness accounts.

8. Cardozo, *Paraguay independiente*, p. 242. See also Juan C. Centurión,
"La reorganización del ejército nacional en 1869," *Revista del Instituto Paraguayo*, Año II, Tomo III (1899): 29. .

9. Washburn, *History of Paraguay*, II, 125. For the conspiracy fabrication,
see Manuel Avila, "Apuntes sobre la conspiración de 1868," *Revista del Instituto Paraguayo*, Año II, Tomo III (1899): 215–228, and ibid. 4 (1900): 3–30;
Harris Gaylord Warren, *Paraguay, An Informal History*, pp. 251–257; Juan

Silvano Godoi, *Documentos históricos. El fusilamiento del Obispo Palacios y los tribunales de sangre de San Fernando*; A. Rebaudi, *Guerra del Paraguay —un episodio*, pp. 60 ff.; Charles J. Kolinski, *Independence or Death! The Story of the Paraguayan War*, pp. 157–162; Masterman, *Seven Eventful Years in Paraguay*, pp. 250–291. Gilbert Phelps, *Tragedy of Paraguay*, pp. 210–227, has a rehash.

10. Fragoso, *História*, III, 70–73, and IV, 69; Martin T. McMahon to William H.: Seward, on the *Wasp* off Angostura, Dec. 11, 1868, DPU-NAUS 128/3; Antonio Díaz, *Historia política y militar de las repúblicas del Plata desde el año de 1828 hasta el de 1866*, XIII, 113.

11. Fragoso, *História*, IV, 79–87; Kolinski, *Independence or Death!*, 166–168; Octaviano Pereira de Sousa, *História da guerra do Paraguai*, p. 346.

12. McMahon to Seward, No. 13, Piribebuy, Jan. 31, 1869, DPU-NAUS 128/3. Itá-Ybaté is spelled variously: Ytá-Ybaté, Itá-Ibaté, Itá-Ivaté, and Itá-Yvaté are all used.

13. McMahon to Seward, Rio de Janeiro, Oct. 26, 1868; id. to id., Off Angostura Batteries, Dec. 11, 1868; id. to id., Piribebuy, No. 13, Jan. 31, 1869, DPU-NAUS 128/3.

14. McMahon to Seward, Piribebuy, No. 13, Jan. 31, 1869, DPU-NAUS 128/3.

15. Ibid.

16. Under the will, McMahon was to be the guardian of the López children, but he never served in that capacity. A copy of the will is in Court of Probate, Will Book 1872, vol. 16, Somerset House, London. See also [Francisco Solano López], *Proclamas y cartas del Mariscal López*, pp. 182–183.

17. Statement of Francesca López de Leite Pereira, widow of the Brazilian consul, at Curuguatay, Dec. 31, 1869, *La Regeneración*, Jan. 14, 1870.

18. Marquês de Caxias to López, Lomas Valentinas, undated, encl. E, McMahon to Seward, No. 13, Piribebuy, Jan. 31, 1869, DPU-NAUS 128/3; López to Caxias et al., Pykysyry, Dec. 24, 1868, encl. F, ibid.; George Buckley Mathew to Lord Stanley, No. 3, Rio de Janeiro, Jan. 7, 1869, PRO-FO 13/46. Mathew was British minister to Brazil.

19. Fragoso, *História*, IV, 129–137; William Stewart to William Stewart, Sr., Buenos Aires, Jan. 20, 1869, PRO-FO 59/29; Mathew to Stanley, Rio de Janeiro, Jan. 7, 1869, PRO-FO 13/461; Testimony of Martin T. McMahon in Stewart v. Gelot, May 11, 1871, *The Scotsman* (Edinburgh), May 12, 1871; Thompson, *The War in Paraguay*, pp. 306–307. Most of the captured papers are in the Rio Branco Collection, Biblioteca Nacional, Rio de Janeiro.

20. McMahon to Seward, No. 13, Piribebuy, Jan. 31, 1869, DPU-NAUS 128/3; Thompson, *The War in Paraguay*, pp. 314–315; Fragoso, *História*, IV, 137–143.

21. McMahon to Seward, No. 13, Piribebuy, Jan. 31, 1869, DPU-NAUS 128/3.

22. Fragoso, *História*, IV, 146–149; Lorenzo Chapperon to McMahon, Asunción, July 11, 1869, encl., McMahon to Hamilton Fish, Asunción, Nov. 18, 1869, DPU-NAUS 128/3; Efraím Cardozo, *Efemérides de la historia del Paraguay*, pp. 18–19. By March 6, 1869, there were 23,570 Brazilian troops in and near Asunción. Francisco Ignacio Marcondes Homem de Mello, "Viagem ao Paraguay em fevereiro e março de 1869," *Revista Trimensal do Instituto Histórico, Geographico, e Ethnographico do Brasil* 36, part 2 (1873): 23, 31; Héc-

tor Francisco Decoud, *Sobre los escombros de la guerra—una década de vida nacional, 1869–1880*, p. 13.

23. Juansilvano Godoi, "El gobierno provisorio," *El Barón de Río Branco*, p. 228. The author at various times signed himself Juan Silvano Godoi, Juan Silvano Godoy, and Juansilvano Godoi.

24. [Manoel] Francisco Correia to Robert Clinton Wright, Rio de Janeiro, May 30, 1870, encl., Wright to Fish, No. 178, Rio de Janeiro, June 10, 1871, *Foreign Relations of the United States, 1871* (Washington, D.C., 1872), p. 48; Carte telegraphica, Buenos Ayres, Jan. 14, 1869, GP-DD 547/22, AN-RJ; Albert Amerlan, *Nights on the Rio Paraguay,* p. 144.

25. C. Villati to John Thompson, Asunción, Jan. 19, 1869, in George Thompson to Clarendon, London, April 6, 1869, PRO-FO 59/29.

26. Decoud, *Escombros*, p. 1; Arturo Bray, *Hombres y épocas del Paraguay*, II, 128; W. Stuart to Stanley, No. 16 Conf., Buenos Aires, Feb. 9, 1869, PRO-FO 6/282.

27. Mathew to Clarendon, No. 5, Rio de Janeiro, Feb. 8, 1869, PRO-FO 13/461; Godoi, "El gobierno provisorio," *El Barón de Río Branco*, p. 225; Decoud, *Escombros*, pp. 30–38; Gómes Freire Esteves, "Historia contemporánea de la república," in *El Paraguay constitucional, 1870–1920*, eds. Luis Freire Esteves and Juan C. González Peña, p. 3; Atilio García Mellid, *Proceso a los falsificadores de la historia del Paraguay*, II, 308–313; Juan Emiliano O'Leary, "El saqueo de la Asunción," *Patria*, Jan. 1, 1919; Carte telegraphica, Buenos Ayres, Jan. 14, 1869, GP-DD 547/22 AN-RJ; Godoi, "El gobierno provisorio," *El Barón de Río Branco*, pp. 224–227.

28. Manoel Francisco Correia, "Saque de Assumpção e Luque atribuido ao exercito brasileiro na guerra do Paraguay: Refutação," RIHGB 59: 376–391.

29. Quoted by Fragoso, *História*, IV, 157.

30. Decoud, *Escombros*, p. 13. Pedro II conferred the title of Duque de Caxias upon his victorious general on March 23 (Fragoso, *História*, IV, 158–159).

31. W. Stuart to Stanley, No. 16 Conf., Buenos Aires, Feb. 9, 1869, PRO-FO 6/282.

32. Ltr., Manuel Antonio de Mattos, *The Standard* (Buenos Aires), April 11, 1869, encl., W. Stuart to Clarendon, No. 47, Buenos Aires, April 26, 1869, ibid.

33. Bray, *Hombres y épocas del Paraguay*, II, 128.

34. McMahon to Fish, No. 23, Buenos Aires, July 19, 1869, DPU-NAUS 128/3.

35. P. A. Freund and W. F. Mulhall, *Letters from Paraguay—Extracted from "The Standard,"* p. 18. One British adventurer wrote a very amateurish novel in which he has his party find the treasure (Alexander F. Baillie, *A Paraguayan Treasure: The Search and the Discovery*).

36. Harris Gaylord Warren, "Litigation in English Courts and Claims Against Paraguay Resulting from the War of the Triple Alliance," IAEA 22 (Spring 1969): 32–35.

37. This cordillera campaign may be followed in Fragoso, *História*, IV, 266 ff. The battle of Piribebuy was on August 12; Campo Grande followed on August 16.

38. H. Fawkes to Rear Adm. G. Ramsay, HMS *Cracker*, Asunción, Jan. 22, 1869, PRO-FO 6/282.

39. William Eden's declaration in *The Weekly Standard* (Buenos Aires), Sept. 1, 1869; Juan C. Centurión, "La reorganización del ejército nacional en 1869," p. 32; Francisco Ysidoro Resquín, "Breves relaciones históricas de la guerra contra el gobierno de la República del Paraguay, por los gobiernos de la Triple Alianza, brasilero, argentino, y oriental–Estractado de documentos de la luz pública, y de los sucesos de armas, durante la guerra de más de cinco años, que sostiene el gobierno de la nación paraguaya, contra los poderes de la Triple Alianza. Asunción del Paraguay, año de 1875," AN-A. An edited version was published as *Datos históricos de la guerra del Paraguay con la Triple Alianza* (Buenos Aires, 1896). When the Brazilians finally occupied Caacupé on Aug. 15, 1869, they found 22 cannon in various stages of manufacture, and necessary forges, molds, and other equipment (*The Weekly Standard*, Sept. 7, 1869; Fragoso, *História*, IV, 280–281).

40. William Eden's declaration in *The Weekly Standard*, Sept. 1, 1869; Stuart to Clarendon, No. 102, Buenos Aires, Aug. 25, 1869, PRO-FO 6/284.

41. H. Fawkes to Ramsay, HMS *Cracker*, Asunción, Feb. 8, 1869, PRO-FO 59/29.

42. Ulrich Lopacher and Alfred Tobler, *Un suizo en la guerra del Paraguay*, p. 79.

43. Marcondes, "Viagem ao Paraguay," pp. 34–35.

44. McMahon to Secretary of State, No. 15, Piribebuy, April 21, 1869, DPU-NAUS 128/3.

45. Marcondes, "Viagem ao Paraguay," p. 34.

46. Barão do Rio-Branco, *Efemérides brasileiras*; Fragoso, *História*, IV; W. Stuart to Clarendon, No. 25, Buenos Aires, March 12, 1869, PRO-FO 6/282.

47. McMahon to Fish, No. 17, Asunción, May 12, 1869, DPU-NAUS 128/3; id. to id., No. 22, Buenos Aires, July 19, 1869, ibid.; *Documentos oficiales sobre cuestiones de límites entre la República del Paraguay y la Argentina* [Asunción, 1873], 22, NPL-NAUS 350/1, hereafter, *Documentos oficiales*; *La Nación* (Buenos Aires), Jan. 15, 1870; R. C. Kirk to Fish, No. 6, Buenos Aires, Aug. 6, 1869, DA-NAUS 69/18. Kirk, for a second time minister to Argentina and Uruguay, reported that McMahon said he had brought about $30,000 out of Paraguay.

48. Centurión, "La reorganización del ejército nacional en 1869," p. 35; Cirilo Antonio Rivarola, captured on May 25, was one prize of these forays. He and other prisoners gave valuable information about Paraguayan positions (Fragoso, *História*, IV, 220). The cordillera campaign is richly documented in "Guerra do Paraguay, 1870," 547/21, AN-RJ.

49. Fragoso, *História*, IV, 220–221.

50. Fragoso estimates the total Allied force in Paraguay at 33,507 men in August, 1869: 28,507 Brazilians, 4,000 Argentines, and 1,000 Uruguayans (ibid., IV, 254–255). See also George Buckley Mathew to Clarendon, No. 17, Petropolis, April 9, 1870, PRO-FO 13/469.

51. Fragoso, *História*, IV, 273.

52. Lima Figueiredo, *Grandes soldados do Brasil*, p. 158. Alfredo d'Escragnolle Taunay describes Madame Lynch's richly furnished house and "the great quantity of delicate wines and liqueurs" (*Diário do exército 1869–1870, a campanha da cordilheira de Campo Grande a Aquidaba*, p. 131).

53. Fragoso, *História*, IV, 280. William Eden, an armorer who was at Caa-

cupé, reported that López left some 700 wounded and a few soldiers as spies (*The Weekly Standard*, Sept. 1, 1869, and Jan. 10, 1870).

54. Francisco Pinheiro Guimarães, *Um voluntário da pátria*, pp. 175–176; Fragoso, *História*, IV, 283–293.

55. Cardozo, *Paraguay independiente*, pp. 252–253; Bray, *Hombres y épocas del Paraguay*, I, 73–80; Fragoso, *História*, V, 84–94.

56. H. G. MacDonnell to Clarendon, No. 8, Buenos Aires, Jan. 28, 1870, PRO-FO 6/29; José Antônio Correia da Câmara to Gastão de Orleans, March 13, 1870, encl., Gastão de Orleans to Barão de Muritiba, Villa de Rosario, March 15, 1870, Correspondencia sobre a guerra do Paraguay, Guerra do Paraguay, 1870, 547/21 AN-RJ, hereafter Guerra do Paraguay, 1870; Conde d'Eu to Minister of War, Jan. 14, 1870, in Fragoso, *História*, V, 128.

57. Paraguayan deserters Lt. Col. Cirilo Solalinde, Major Ignacio Segovia, Capt. Lozano Quevedo, and Lt. Roque Samaniego came to the Brazilian camp on Feb. 26, confirming that López was at Cerro Corá (Fragoso, *História*, V, 149 n. 140).

58. The end of López has been well documented. A contemporary account is in *The Standard*, March 17 and 24, 1870. Fragoso, *História*, V, 150–170, gives eyewitness reports, including that of General Câmara. For Câmara's various accounts, see Câmara to Gastão de Orleans, March 1 and 13, 1870, encls., Gastão de Orleans to Barão de Muritiba, Villa de Rosario, March 15, 1870, Guerra do Paraguay, 1870, 547/21 AN-RJ, and Visconde de Pelotas to Commander in Chief, Asunción, April 30, 1870, in Fragoso, *História*, V, 159–160. Secondary accounts are Charles J. Kolinski, "The Death of Francisco Solano López," *The Historian* 26, no. 1 (Nov. 1963): 75–91, and his *Independence or Death!*, pp. 185–190.

59. Issue of March 6, 1870.

60. Issue of March 9, 1870.

61. *The Standard*, March 9, 1870.

62. "The Fall of Lopez," ibid., March 10, 1870. The sarcasm is obvious.

Chapter 2: The Stricken Nation

1. Dr. João Nogueira Jaguaribe, "Quanto custou a guerra contra o Paraguay?" *Jornal do Comercio* (Rio de Janeiro), Aug. 25, 1912, in Fragoso, *História*, V, 232–252. General Dionísio Cerqueira estimated Brazilian dead at 100,000 (*Reminiscencias da campanha do Paraguai*, p. 401, cited by Kolinski, *Independence or Death!*, p. 194). In 1874, President Sarmiento reported that the war had left Argentina a debt of about 30,000,000 pesos which had been paid ("Mensaje del presidente de la república a las sesiones del congreso argentino. Mayo de 1874," in *Memoria del Ministerio de Relaciones Exteriores, presentada al congreso nacional en 1874*, p. 9).

2. Kirk to Fish, No. 20, Buenos Aires, Sept. 11, 1869, DA-NAUS 69/18.

3. Warren, "Litigation," pp. 32–35; *La Regeneración*, Aug. 5, 1870.

4. Stevens to Fish, Paraguay No. 2, Montevideo, Sept. 8, 1870, and No. 9, Montevideo, June 5, 1872, DPU-NAUS 128/3.

5. Jerry W. Cooney, "Abolition in the Republic of Paraguay: 1840–1870," *Jahrbuch für Geschichte von Staat, Wirtschaft und Gesellschaft* 11 (1974): 154.

6. "Hassan" in *La Regeneración*, July 31, 1870. For an excellent study of Paraguay's Indians, see Branislava Susnik, *El indio colonial del Paraguay.*

7. *Handbook of the River Plate Republics*, p. 385; *Manual de las repúblicas del Plata. Datos topográficos, históricos, y económicos* . . . , p. 324.

8. Petre to Granville, No. 4, Asunción, June 20, 1882, PRO-FO 59/39. The weight of reliable evidence leans strongly to a figure of less than 500,000 for the population of prewar Paraguay. See also *Diplomatic and Consular Reports on Trade and Finance, Paraguay, 1892*, p. 17, which states: "Before the war the population was reckoned at 300,000, and it is the opinion of writers and men of that period that this calculation was correct." The figure is much too small.

9. Cecilio Báez, *Le Paraguay. Son évolution historique et sa situation actuelle*, pp. 62–64.

10. Stevens to Fish, Paraguay No. 2, Montevideo, Sept. 8, 1870, DPU-NAUS 128/3.

11. Encl., MacDonnell to Granville, No. 7 Commercial, Buenos Aires, Aug. 2, 1872, PRO-FO 59/35.

12. Testimony of Alexander Francis Baillie, *Report from Select Committee on Loans to Foreign States* (HC 3770/113, London, 1875, p. 229). One laconic report states: "The city was invaded by Italians." (Carte telegraphica, Buenos Ayres, Jan. 14, 1869, GP-DD 547/22, AN-RJ.)

13. M. L. Forgues, "Le Paraguay. Fragments de journal et de correspondances, 1872–1873," *Le Tour du Monde: Nouvelle Journal des Voyages* 27, nos. 701–703: 385.

14. *La Regeneración*, Nov. 28, 1869.

15. This description is closely paraphrased from Forgues, "Le Paraguay," p. 386.

16. A capable cavalry commander, Andrade Neves was wounded at Lomas Valentinas on Dec. 28, 1868 (Barão do Rio-Branco, *Efemérides brasileiras*, pp. 17–18).

17. Marcondes, "Viagem ao Paraguay," pp. 22–23.

18. Ibid., pp. 24–25.

19. *La Regeneración*, Oct. 1, 3, 7, and 10, 1869, Jan. 21 and May 15, 1870.

20. *Registro oficial de la República del Paraguay correspondiente a los años 1869 á 1875*, p. 168. Since pagination is continuous, no volume reference will be made.

21. The complete list is in the monetary law of Jan. 20, 1875, NPFO-NAUS, 693/3. The decree of Oct. 6, 1876, and the law of Dec. 30, 1876, made slight adjustments (*Registro oficial*, 1876, pp. 121–142).

22. Carlos Alberto Pusineri Scala, "La moneda de 1870," *Historia paraguaya*, 8-9-10 (1963–1965): 128 ff.; Ramón Zubizarreta, "La cuestión de la moneda," *Revista del Instituto Paraguayo* 11 (1904): 133.

23. Forgues, "Le Paraguay," p. 400.

24. Ibid., p. 395.

25. *The Standard*, Aug. 1, 1872. John L. Stevens was certainly wrong in reporting no shortage of food a year earlier (Stevens to Fish, Montevideo, Aug. 18, 1871, DPU-NAUS 128/3).

26. *La Regeneración*, Feb. 13 and 16, 1870; Decoud, *Escombros*, pp. 76–77.

27. Ltr., "Cumbay," Asunción, Jan. 29, 1870, *La República* (Buenos Aires), Feb. 11, 1870; Stevens to Fish, Montevideo, Feb. 12, 1872, DPU-NAUS 128/3.

28. *La Regeneración*, Feb. 2, 1870.

29. *The Standard*, Feb. 13, 1870.

30. "Hassan," "Economía política," *La Regeneración*, July 31 and Sept. 16, 1870.

31. *El Progreso* (Asunción), April 14, 1873.

32. *La República* (Asunción), Jan. 20 and 22, 1874.

33. *The Weekly Standard*, Jan. 12, 1870.

34. Ltr., "M. G.," *La Nación* (Buenos Aires), Jan. 29, 1870.

35. Ltr., "W," Asunción, Feb. 19, 1870, *The Weekly Standard*, March 2, 1870.

36. *The Standard*, Aug. 1, 1872.

37. Forgues, "Le Paraguay," pp. 408, 415.

38. Unidentified clipping in Joaquim Maria Nascentes de Azambuja to Manoel Francisco Correia, 1ª Sec. No. 8, Asunción, Jan. 29, 1873, MDBA-OR 201/1/10, AHI-RJ.

39. Forgues, "Le Paraguay," pp. 394–395.

40. Ibid., p. 414.

41. Ibid.

42. Ibid., p. 402.

43. Ibid., p. 408.

44. Lopacher and Tobler, *Un suizo*, p. 77.

45. Forgues, "Le Paraguay," p. 391.

46. Azambuja to José Falcón, 1ª Sec. No. 8, Asunción, Sept. 25, 1872, encl. Azambuja to Correia, 1ª Sec. No. 15, Asunción, Sept. 25, 1872, MDBA-OR 201/1/10; Azambuja to Correia, 1ª Sec. No. 3, Asunción, Jan. 20, 1873, MDBA-OR 201/1/11, and clipping, encl. Azambuja to Correia, 1ª Sec. No. 8, Asunción, Jan. 29, 1873, MDBA-OR 201/1/10.

47. Lopacher and Tobler, *Un suizo*, p. 45.

48. For Stewart's early career in Paraguay, see Harris Gaylord Warren, "Dr. William Stewart in Paraguay, 1857–1869," *The Americas* 25 (Jan. 1969): 247–264.

49. Cdr. E. L. Parsons to Adm. George Ramsay, Buenos Aires, Nov. 15, 1868, encl. Ramsay to Lords Commissioner of the Admiralty, Montevideo, Nov. 28, 1868, and Memorandum on Paraguayan War, Detention of British Subjects, and Cruelties of President López. Foreign Office Memorandum, May 29, 1869, PRO-FO 59/29. The British *Beacon* and *Cracker*, French *Décidée*, Italian *Ardita*, and American *Wasp* frequently appeared in Asunción's harbor after Jan., 1869.

50. The French and Italian consuls, Aimé Paul de Cuverville and Lorenzo Chapperon, came in for bitter criticism, as their compatriots accused them of wholesale thefts. (C. Villata to John Thompson, Asunción, Jan. 19, 1869, in George Thompson to Clarendon, London, April 6, 1869, PRO-FO 59/29; Godoi, *El Barón de Río-Branco*, p. 283).

51. W. Stuart to Clarendon, No. 25, Buenos Aires, March 12, 1869, PRO-FO 6/282.

52. Alonzo Taylor to Clarendon, June 4, 1870, PRO-FO 59/30.

53. Fragoso, *História*, IV, 280. Fifty-six British subjects were rescued at Valenzuela and Caacupé. The list is in Henry Fawkes to Richard Purvis, encl. No. 2, Asunción, Aug. 21, 1869, Stuart to Clarendon, No. 102, Buenos Aires, Aug. 25, 1869, PRO-FO 6/284. Individual accounts are in *The Weekly Stand-*

ard, Sept. 1, 1869. Forty-one refugees arrived at Buenos Aires on the *Taraguí*, Aug. 31, 1869 (*The Standard*, Supplement, Sept. 8, 1869).

54. MacDonnell to Clarendon, No. 32, Buenos Aires, April 9, 1870, PRO-FO 6/291; *The Weekly Standard*, Sept. 15, 1869. Skinner stayed in Paraguay and died in a fall from his horse in Nov., 1872 (*The Weekly Standard*, Nov. 27, 1872).

55. Wm. Rhind to Clarendon, Jan. 4, 1869, and Edwin Holmes to Clarendon, Jan. 8, 1869, PRO-FO 59/29; MacDonnell to Clarendon, No. 73, Buenos Aires, June 13, 1870, PRO-FO 6/276; *La Regeneración*, Jan. 14, 1870; Marcondes, "Viagem ao Paraguay," p. 32. Wisner, born in 1800, had been in Paraguay for 24 years.

56. Héctor Francisco Decoud, *La convención nacional constituyente y la carta magna de la república*, p. 43; *La Regeneración*, Oct. 21, 1869; Carte telegraphica, Buenos Ayres, Jan. 14, 1869, GP-DD 547/22, AN-RJ.

57. Decoud, *Escombros*, pp. 77–78.

58. *The Weekly Standard*, Jan. 19, 1870.

59. Ltr., "S.S.S.," Asunción, Dec. 26, 1869, *La Nación* (Buenos Aires), Feb. 2, 1870.

60. *The Weekly Standard*, Jan. 19, 1870.

61. *La Regeneración*, Dec. 17 and 19, 1869, and Jan. 21 and July 31, 1870.

62. *Registro oficial, 1869–1875*, p. 340.

63. *The Weekly Standard*, Jan. 19, 1870.

64. Ibid., Feb. 13, 1870.

Chapter 3: Politics and Diplomacy, 1869–1870

1. Names of the original signers of the agreement of Dec. 19, 1864, which formalized the Association, are in Juan Bautista Gill Aguínaga, *La asociación paraguaya en la guerra de la triple alianza*, p. 28; Freire Esteves, "Historia contemporánea," p. 1; Higinio Arbo, *Política paraguaya*, pp. 4–6.

2. Gill Aguínaga, *Asociación paraguaya*, p. 31.

3. Visconde de Mamamu to Manoel Luis Osorio, Rio de Janeiro, April 22, 1865, ibid., p. 125.

4. Carlos Loizaga to Bartolomé Mitre, Buenos Aires, April 21, 1865, ibid., p. 123; Juan A. Gelly y Obes to Loizaga, Buenos Aires, April 22, 1865, ibid., p. 124.

5. Juan Francisco Decoud, his son José Segundo, Benigno Ferreira, and Jaime Sosa Escalada conferred with Estigarribia on Sept. 8 and urged his surrender (Cardozo, *Hace cién años*, II, 209–228; Rafael Calzada, *Rasgos biográficos de José Segundo Decoud*, pp. 15–16).

6. Iturburu set the figure at 795, somewhat optimistic (Iturburu to President of the Comisión Directiva, Paso de los Libres, Sept. 28, 1865, in Gill Aguínaga, *Asociación paraguaya*, pp. 149–150). By October, 1865, there were 144 in the ranks; six months later, there were only 225 (ibid., p. 59).

7. *Documentos oficiales relativos al abuso de la bandera nacional paraguaya por los gefes aliados* (Piribebui, [1869]), 10, AN-A; Fragoso, *História*, IV, 171–173.

8. Decoud, *Convención nacional*, p. 42.

9. Freire Esteves, "Historia contemporánea," p. 2; Arbo, *Política paraguaya*, p. 7; Godoi, "El gobierno provisorio," *El Barón de Río Branco*, p. 229.

10. Enrique D. Parodi called Bareiro "vain and presumptuous" and said that he passed as a wise man by keeping silent about thorny problems ("La Prensa," *Revista del Paraguay*, No. 9, Sept., 1891, p. 390); José Sienra Carranza, "Retrospecto del Paraguay," *Revista Histórica* 1, no. 1 (March 1899): 8; Godoi, "El gobierno provisorio," *El Barón de Río Branco*, pp. 230–231.

11. Sarmiento had not yet sent an envoy to check on Silva Paranhos (W. G. Stuart to Clarendon, No. 19, Buenos Aires, Feb. 12, 1869, PRO-FO 6/282); Stuart to Mathew, Buenos Aires, April 10, 1869, ibid.; Ernesto Quesada, *Historia diplomática nacional: La política argentina-paraguaya*, p. 31.

12. Mathew to Clarendon, No. 54, Rio de Janeiro, Aug. 24, 1869, PRO-FO 13/462.

13. Decoudistas were bitter about Egusquiza, whom they knew to be an Allied tool as well as a Bareirista (Eduarado Amarilla Fretes, *La liquidación de la guerra de la Triple Alianza contra el Paraguay*, pp. 33–34). Edward Augustus Hopkins claimed that he "wrote the petition asking for the same [the Provisional Government] to the allies" (Hopkins, "My Life-Record . . .," in Pablo Max Ynsfrán, *La expedición norteamericana contra El Paraguay, 1858–1859*, I, 254).

14. Memoranda exchanged by Silva Paranhos, Varela, and Dr. Adolfo Rodríguez are in *La República* (Buenos Aires), July 7 and 8, 1869, and Fragoso, *História*, V, 260–262.

15. Amarilla Fretes, *Liquidación de la guerra*, pp. 34–35; Godoi, "El gobierno provisorio," *El Barón de Río Branco*, pp. 231–232.

16. "Establishment of a Provisional Government in Paraguay," encl., Mathew to Clarendon, No. 143, Rio de Janeiro, July 4, 1869, PRO-FO 13/462; R. C. Kirk to Fish, No. 3, Buenos Aires, July 21, 1869, DA-NAUS 69/18; "Arrangement between the Argentine Republic, Brazil, and Uruguay relative to the Establishment of a Provisional Government in Paraguay.—Buenos Ayres, June 2, 1869," *State Papers*, London, 1870, vol. 63, p. 627); Fragoso, *História*, V. 279–302; Fragoso, *A paz com o Paraguai depois da guerra da Triplice Alianza*, pp. 47–48.

17. Freire Esteves, "Historia contemporánea," p. 6. García Mellid observes that Roque Pérez was a high-ranking Mason (*Proceso*, II, 412).

18. McMahon to Fish, No. 23, Buenos Aires, July 19, 1869, DPU-NAUS 128/3.

19. W. C. Stuart to Clarendon, Buenos Aires, June 23, 1869, PRO-FO 6/283; id. to id., No. 76 Conf., Buenos Aires, June 23, 1869, ibid.; id. to id., No. 87 Conf., Buenos Aires, July 20, 1869, ibid.

20. Benites to Clarendon, Paris, Sept. 17, 1869, PRO-FO 59/29; Clarendon to Benites, London, Sept. 25, 1869, ibid.; Benites to Secretary of State, Paris, Sept. 17, 1869, NPL-NAUS 350/1; Mathew to Clarendon, Rio de Janeiro, Nov. 22, 1869, PRO-FO 13/462.

21. Quesada, *Historia diplomática*, p. 33; Antonio Salúm-Fecha, *Historia diplomática del Paraguay de 1869 a 1938*, pp. 10 11; Capt. Henry Fawkes to Capt. Richard Purvis, Asunción, July 31, 1869, PRO-FO 59/29.

22. Wilfredo Valdez [Jaime Sosa Escalada], "La guerra futura. La guerra de Chile y Brasil con la República Argentina. Alianza—la causa común. Estudio de los hombres del Paraguay—el Triunvirato," *Revista del Paraguay* 2, nos. 3–9 (1892): 198 (hereafter, Valdez, "Estudio"); *Registro oficial, 1869–1875*, p. 4; Fragoso, *História*, V, 279–302; Justo Pastor Benítez, *La convención constitu-*

yente de 1870, p. 2; clipping in R. C. Kirk to Fish, No. 12, Buenos Aires, Aug. 12, 1869, DA-NAUS 69/18.

23. *Registro oficial, 1869–1875*, pp. 3–4; Fragoso, *História*, V, 267; Kirk to Fish, No. 5, Buenos Aires, Aug. 22, 1869, DA-NAUS 69/18; Godoi, "El gobierno provisorio," *El Barón de Río Branco*, pp. 244–249.

24. Valdez, "Estudio," pp. 257–260.

25. Godoi, "El gobierno provisorio," *El Barón de Río Branco*, pp. 237–238; Benítez, *La convención constituyente de 1870*, p. 65.

26. Godoi, "El gobierno provisorio," *El Barón de Río Branco*, pp. 241–242.

27. Cecilio Báez, *Cuadros históricos y descriptivos*, pp. 227–231.

28. Sienra Carranza, "Retrospecto del Paraguay," *Revista Histórica* 1, no. 1, p. 8. This is an extract taken from Sienra Carranza's *Retrospecto del Paraguay —Notas sobre el último deceno* (Montevideo, 1880).

29. Ltr., "M. G.," *La Nación* (Buenos Aires), Jan. 29, 1870.

30. *La Regeneración*, Feb. 13, 1870.

31. Ltr., Asunción, Jan. 9, 1870, *La República*, Buenos Aires, Jan. 15, 1870. Some of the unsigned letters in the porteño press probably came from Félix Amadeo Benites, the Argentine consul general in Asunción, whose exequatur was issued on Nov. 24, 1869 (Godoi, "El gobierno provisorio," *El Barón de Río Branco*, p. 274).

32. Antonio Coelho de Sá e Albuquerque to Marquês de Caxias, Rio de Janeiro, May 6, 1867, copy in Actas do Conselho de Estado (Act of Sept. 2, 1867), V, 1, AN-RJ. Albuquerque was minister of foreign affairs from July 27 to Dec. 9, 1867.

33. Fragoso, *História*, V, 2–7.

34. Ibid., II, 25; *Memoria del ministerio de relaciones exteriores presentada al congreso nacional en 1872*, pp. 1–10. Pagination is not continuous in this volume.

35. Actas do Conselho de Estado (Act of Sept. 2, 1867), V, 1–6, AN-RJ.

36. Ibid. (Act of April 26, 1870), VI, 44.

37. Sarmiento to the Congress, July 14, 1871, *Memoria del ministerio de relaciones exteriores presentada al congreso nacional en 1872*, p. 12; Kirk to Fish, No. 48, Buenos Aires, April 13, 1870, DA-NAUS, 69/18; Actas do Conselho de Estado (Act of April 26, 1870), VI, 44, AN-RJ.

38. Ibid., VI, 45–46a, 50a; Fragoso, *A paz com o Paraguai*, pp. 73–75.

39. MacDonnell to Clarendon, No. 90, Buenos Aires, July 12, 1870, PRO-FO 6/292; Sarmiento to the Congress, *The Standard*, July 6, 1870. Varela resigned while negotiations were in progress, and Sarmiento appointed General Julio de Vedia to represent Argentina. Silva Paranhos, apparently, had returned to Asunción on May 11 with a draft already signed by Varela and Rodríguez (MacDonnell to Clarendon, No. 61, Buenos Aires, May 14, 1870, PRO-FO 6/291).

40. "Preliminary Agreement of Peace between the Argentine Republic and Brazil and Paraguay . . . June 20, 1870," *State Papers*, 63 (London, 1872–1873), 322.

41. Sienra Carranza, "Retrospecto del Paraguay," *Revista Histórica* 1, no. 1, p. 7.

42. Issue of July 5, 1870.

43. Issue of July 6, 1870.

44. *La Nación*, Sept. 27, 1870. For Brazilian cabinet changes, see Max Fleuiss, *História administrativa do Brasil*, pp. 300, 303.

Chapter 4: The Provisional Government in Power

1. *Registro oficial, 1869–1875*, p. 5; Sienra Carranza, "Retrospecto del Paraguay," *Revista Histórica* 2, no. 2, p. 199. One of the Triumvirate's first acts was to create the *Registro oficial*, sometimes called the *Registro nacional*.

2. Encl., Kirk to Fish, No. 15, Buenos Aires, Aug. 22, 1869, DA-NAUS 68/10; Stuart to Clarendon, No. 101, Buenos Aires, Aug. 25, 1869, PRO-FO 6/284; Fragoso, *A paz com o Paraguai*, pp. 53 ff.

3. Godoi, "El gobierno provisorio," *El Barón de Río Branco*, p. 272.

4. This complicated tangle may be followed in Warren, "Litigation," pp. 31–46. See also Elisa A. Lynch, *Esposición y protesta que hace Elisa A. Lynch*. Madame Lynch married Xavier (or Zavier) Quatrefages at Folkstone, County of Kent, on June 3, 1850, under the name Elizabeth Alecia Lynch (Certified Copy of an Entry of Marriage, General Register Office, Somerset House, London, April 26, 1957). I am indebted to Mrs. Joseph Robinson, Oxford, England, and to the Rev. Mr. Raymond Harris, St. Barnabas' Vicarage, Swindon, England, for the copy.

5. Rio Branco to the Emperor, At Court, July 15, 1871, *Anuário do Museo Imperial* (1951), p. 50.

6. *La República* (Buenos Aires), Feb. 11, 1870; Forgues, "Le Paraguay," pp. 385–386.

7. *The Standard*, Aug. 1, 1872.

8. George Glynn Petre to Granville, No. 1, Asunción, June 9, 1882, PRO-FO 59/39.

9. Related to Jovellanos by marriage, Alcorta was a very capable and intelligent Argentine with long experience in Asunción. In Buenos Aires during the war, he returned to Asunción with the allies as a sutler (Godoi, "El gobierno provisorio," *El Barón de Río Branco*, pp. 264–266; Valdez, "Estudio," p. 200). Machaín's degree was from the University of Santiago, Chile, in 1868 (García Mellid, *Proceso*, II, 415).

10. *Revista Histórica* 1 (1899): 28–32; *Registro oficial, 1869–1875*, pp. 5–10; *La Regeneración*, Oct. 1, 1869. A copy of the original *Manifiesto del gobierno provisorio compuesto de los ciudadanos Cirilo Antonio Rivarola, Carlos Loizaga y José Díaz de Bedoya* is in the Museo Mitre, Buenos Aires. See also Godoi, "El gobierno provisorio," *El Barón de Río Branco*, pp. 251–260.

11. Decoud, *Convención nacional*, p. 104.

12. José Segundo Decoud became minister of interior, or secretary of state in charge of the ministry; Hacienda, which included treasury, agriculture, and commerce, went to Serapio Machaín (Decree of Aug. 29, 1869, *La Regeneración*, Oct. 10, 1869).

13. *Registro oficial, 1869–1875*, pp. 28, 38–39, 41–43.

14. Decree of Sept. 11, 1869, ibid., 9.

15. Decrees of Sept. 25, 27 and Dec. 16, 1869, Jan. 1 and March 4, 1870, ibid., 20–21, 37, 43, 56, 58.

16. Ibid., 29–30; Fragoso, *História*, V, 272; Lewis and Edward Hertslet et al., comps., *A Complete Collection of the Treaties and Conventions, and Re-*

ciprocal Regulations at Present Subsisting between Great Britain and Foreign Powers . . . , XIII, 676–677; *La Regeneración,* Oct. 7, 1869. For varying estimates of the number of slaves in Paraguay, see Efraím Cardozo, *Paraguay independiente,* p. 250; Josefina Pla, *Hermano negro: La esclavitud en el Paraguay;* and Cooney, "Abolition in the Republic of Paraguay: 1840–1870," p. 163 n. 4.

17. Decrees of Oct. 14, 1869, and Jan. 14, 1870, *Registro oficial, 1869–1875,* pp. 30, 53–55; *La Regeneración,* Feb. 9, 1870.

18. Ltr., *La Nación* (Buenos Aires), Jan. 29, 1870.

19. Worth 8 reales in Buenos Aires and Rio de Janeiro, it brought 10 reales in Asunción. To reduce this inflation, the Triumvirate decreed on March 15, 1870, that it should be worth only 8 reales (Freire Esteves, "Historia contemporánea," p. 10). There was also Brazilian paper money that fluctuated in value (Carlos Alberto Pusineri Scala, *Las monedas que circularon en el Paraguay durante la guerra,* reprint from *Historia paraguaya,* vol. 12, 1967–1968).

20. Teodosio González, *Infortunios del Paraguay,* p. 107.

21. *Registro oficial, 1869–1875,* pp. 24–27, 46.

22. In addition, it had spent $f240,502 for relief, all of which came from nine contributors. Gumercindo Coll gave $f138,958.31 (*La Regeneración,* Jan. 23, 1870), most of which probably was sent from Buenos Aires for Coll to distribute.

23. *La Regeneración,* Jan. 9 and March 11, 1870; MacDonnell to Clarendon, No. 3 Commercial, Buenos Aires, Jan. 16, 1869 [1870], PRO-FO 6/291.

24. *La República,* Jan. 15, 18, and Feb. 9, 1870.

25. *The Weekly Standard,* Jan. 19, 1870.

26. *La Regeneración,* Feb. 9 and March 11, 1870; Bedoya to the Provisional Government, Buenos Aires, May 4, 1870, ibid., May 13, 1870; MacDonnell to Clarendon, No. 59, Buenos Aires, May 14, 1870, PRO-FO 6/291. In August, the Buenos Aires house of Juan Thori Hermano y Rocca loaned Paraguay $f30,000 at 3% monthly interest, to be retired by customs receipts (*La Regeneración,* Aug. 14, 1870).

27. Issue of May 13, 1870. *La Regeneración* on Aug. 12, 1870, quoted the Buenos Aires *La Discusión* as reporting Bedoya's arrest for cattle stealing.

28. *La Regeneración,* Nov. 21, 1869.

29. Ibid., Dec. 10, 1869.

30. Ibid., Dec. 19, 1869. The terms Blues (Azules), Liberals, and Decoudistas refer to the same group, as do Reds (Colorados), Lopiztas, and Bareiristas.

31. This group was the first step toward formation of the Liberal Party in 1887, and met frequently (*La Regeneración,* Dec. 19, 1869, Jan. 26 and Feb. 11, 1870).

32. Ibid., March 13, 1870.

33. Ibid., March 25, 1870; Decoud, *Convención nacional,* pp. 108–109.

34. The three priests were identified closely with the Bareiro group: Becchis, Maíz, and Duarte, all of whom had been closely associated with López. Becchis edited *La Estrella* from March 1 to June 30, 1869 (Arsenio López Decoud, *Album gráfico de la República del Paraguay,* p. 257).

35. *La Regeneración,* April 13, 1870; *La República,* April 7, 1870.

36. A recent example is García Mellid, *Proceso.*

37. J. Natalicio González and Pablo M. Ynsfrán, *El Paraguay contemporáneo,* p. 36.

304 Notes to Page 72–80

38. *La Regeneración*, May 1, 1870. *Círculo* meant "gang" in this period, since neither "circle" nor "ring" conveys the sneer definitely intended by Decoud. *Círculo* has since lost its derogatory meaning.

39. *La Regeneración*, May 8, 1870.

40. Ibid. The Capitanía del Puerto, or Harbor Master's Office, was an important site, probably second only to police headquarters, or La Policía.

41. Ibid., May 26, 1870; Decoud, *Convención nacional*, p. 119.

42. *La Regeneración*, May 13, 1870.

43. Ibid.

44. Ibid., May 15, 1870.

45. Ibid., May 13, 1870. A meeting of the Gran Club, with all Paraguayans invited, was to be held on May 14 in the National Theater. *El Semanario* and *Cabichui* were official papers of the López.

46. *La Regeneración*, May 6, 11, and 13, 1870.

47. Ibid., May 31, 1870.

48. *El Paraguay*, May 21, 1870.

49. Forgues, "Le Paraguay," pp. 385–388.

50. Vedia to Martín de Gainza, Asunción, May 22, 1870, Gainza Papers, AGN-BA. Gainza was Argentine minister of war and marine. Rivarola had asked Vedia for 50 cavalrymen, who were sent on the *Gualeguay*.

Chapter 5: The Convention of 1870

1. Each of the three parishes in Asunción had two delegates, each department of nine districts in the country was to have one delegate, making a total of 56 delegates (*Registro oficial, 1869–1875*, pp. 68–72; *La Regeneración*, April 8, 1870; Carlos R. Centurión, *Los hombres de la convención de 70*, pp. 5–6).

2. H. G. MacDonnell to Clarendon, No. 94, Buenos Aires, July 23, 1870, PRO-FO 6/292 and 5/59.

3. *La Regeneración*, May 1, 1870.

4. Decoud, *Convención nacional*, pp. 125–126. The Liberals, or Decoudistas, were "not a party but a romantic circle" (Justo Pastor Benítez, "La convención paraguaya de 1870," *IIº Congreso Internacional de Historia de América*, IV, 66).

5. Names of 55 delegates were published in *La Regeneración*, Aug. 12, 1870.

6. Freire Esteves, "Historia contemporánea," p. 13.

7. The *quiguaberá* is the Spanish *peineta de oro*, or high comb, worn by upper-class women; the *placeras* were a mob of common women.

8. Perhaps the eyewitness, José Sienra Carranza, embellished his account in his "Retrospecto del Paraguay," *Revista Histórica* 1, no. 1, p. 8.

9. *La República* (Buenos Aires), July 25, 1870.

10. Jaime Sosa [Escalada], "Política brasilera en el Paraguay," *Revista del Paraguay* 2, no. 1 (1892): 14–15.

11. Issue of Aug. 12, 1870.

12. Summaries of the Convention's sessions from Aug. 15 to Dec. 10, 1870, are in *Actas de la convención nacional constituyente del año 1870*.

13. *La Regeneración*, Aug. 14, 1870, anticipated much of this florid address.

14. *Actas de la convención*, pp. 5–7.

15. Cayo Miltos and Pedro Recalde were leaders of the thirteen Bareiristas (ibid., p. 7).

16. Ibid., pp. 10–13. José del Rosario Miranda became vice-president of the convention.

17. Benítez, "La convención paraguaya de 1870," p. 69.

18. Freire Esteves, "Historia contemporánea," p. 15.

19. During the war it was reported that Mitre favored as president "a Machaín who frequently comes by coach from the capital city of Corrientes to visit President Mitre in his camp" (El Semanario, No. 615, Feb. 3, 1866).

20. Carlos R. Centurión, Historia de la cultura paraguaya, I, 323.

21. Ibid., I, 324–325.

22. Godoi, "El gobierno provisorio," El Barón de Río Branco, p. 264; Benítez, "La convención paraguaya de 1870," p. 68.

23. Sienra Carranza, "Retrospecto del Paraguay," Revista Histórica 1, no. 1, pp. 10–11; Freire Esteves, "Historia contemporánea," p. 15.

24. Benítez, "La convención paraguaya," p. 68.

25. Actas de la convención, pp. 26–27; José S. Decoud to Cirilo Rivarola, Asunción, Aug. 30 [31], 1870, encl., C. Bareiro to John L. Stevens, Asunción, Sept. 6, 1870, NPFO-NAUS 693/3; La Regeneración, Sept. 11, 1870.

26. Ibid.; García Mellid, Proceso, II, 415.

27. Decoud, Convención nacional, pp. 107–108; Cándido Bareiro to José Auto de Guimarães, Asunción, Sept. 2, 1870, La Voz del Pueblo, Sept. 8, 1870; Benítez, "La convención paraguaya de 1870," pp. 66–67.

28. "Proclama al pueblo," Asunción, Sept. 1, 1870, encl., Bareiro to Stevens, Asunción, Sept. 6, 1870, NPFO-NAUS 693/3.

29. Stevens to Fish, No. 3, Montevideo, Oct. 1, 1870, DPU-NAUS 128/3. Stevens was in Asunción from Aug. 26 to Sept. 4.

30. "M" in La Regeneración, Sept. 11, 1870.

31. Cándido Bareiro to Carlos Tejedor, Asunción, Sept. 6, 1870, Memoria presentada por el ministro de estado en el departamento de relaciones esteriores al congreso nacional en 1871, pp. 191–194.

32. Actas de la convención, p. 29.

33. "Historia contemporánea," p. 18.

34. García Mellid, Proceso, II, 411.

35. Miguel Palacios presided over the Convention from Sept. 20 to Nov. 18; Miranda served again from Nov. 19 to Dec. 10 (Actas de la convención, passim). Palacios, younger brother of Bishop Manuel Palacios, whom López had executed, was studying in Paris when the war began. He died in 1875 at the age of 32 (Benítez, "La convención paraguaya de 1870," p. 67).

36. Most notable among the new participants were the brothers Juan Bautista and Emilio Gill and Adolfo Saguier. Juan Bautista Gill was elected on Sept. 11 in Encarnación parish—no opposition was permitted (La Regeneración, Sept. 14, 1870; Actas de la convención, pp. 38–44).

37. Cardozo, Paraguay independiente, p. 269.

38. La Regeneración, Sept. 11 and 16, 1870.

39. Ibid., Sept. 4, 1870.

40. Ibid., Sept. 7 and 14, 1870.

41. This society obtained little publicity. Twenty-six members and officers are listed (La Regeneración, Sept. 7, 1870). Taboada denied that police had

306 Notes to Pages 87–91

attacked the office (Taboada to Bareiro, Asunción, Sept. 5, 1870, *La Voz del Pueblo*, Sept. 8, 1870).

42. Circular of Sept. 2, 1870, ibid.

43. Proclamation of Sept. 6, 1870, ibid.

44. *La Regeneración*, Sept. 16 and 21, 1870.

45. MacDonnell to Granville, No. 21, Buenos Aires, Oct. 9, 1870, PRO-FO 6/292, enclosed clipping from *The Standard*. On Oct 8, *La Nación* (Buenos Aires) reported that Taboada said he had arrested 148 Italians; on Oct. 18 the same paper reported that 100 to 500 Italians were in the attack and 30 or more were killed. This violence alarmed the foreigners, who met on Sept. 25 and named a committee of nine from as many countries (*La Nación*, Oct. 5, 1870). The committee accomplished nothing.

46. Carlos R. Centurión, *Historia de las letras paraguayas*, II, 47.

47. "S. A." in *La Regeneración*, July 31, 1870. Four committees did the work.

48. The never modest Edward Augustus Hopkins claimed to have had a hand in educating Paraguayans by collaborating with José Segundo Decoud in translating Joseph Alden's "school-book upon the Constitution" (Ynsfrán, *La expedición norteamericana contra el Paraguay, 1858–1859*, I, 251).

49. Washburn shows the Saguiers as anti-Lopiztas (Washburn, *History of Paraguay*, I, 535–537).

50. During the heated debate on Nov. 24, several deputies walked out and 15 of them signed a circular protesting that the election was unconstitutional (*El Pueblo*, Nov. 27, 1870; MacDonnell to Granville, No. 42, Buenos Aires, Dec. 7, 1870, PRO-FO 6/292; Miguel Palacios to Secretary of Foreign Affairs [of Great Britain], Asunción, Dec. 31, 1870, PRO-FO 59/30; *Actas de la convención*, pp. 128–131; Julio de Vedia to Carlos Tejedor, Asunción, Nov. 26, 1870, *Memoria presentada por el ministro de estado en el departamento de relaciones esteriores al congreso nacional en 1871*, pp. 195–196).

51. *Constitución de la República del Paraguay sancionada por la honorable convención constituyente en sesión del 18 de noviembre de 1870*. See also Juan Carlos Mendonça, ed., *Las constituciones paraguayas y los proyectos de constitución de los partidos políticos*, pp. 33–57.

52. Organization of government under the constitution is discussed in J. Natalico González and Pablo M. Ynsfrán, *El Paraguay contemporáneo*, pp. 33–41; the Constitution of 1870 is at pp. 41–53.

53. Ch. 14. The same chapter defined treason, set qualifications for judges, defined their responsibilities, and set up safeguards for citizens.

54. González and Ynsfrán, *El Paraguay contemporáneo*, pp. 37–41. There were also a Ministerio Público, or Attorney General's Office; a Ministerio de la Defensa Pública, or Public Defender's Office, to aid the poor, children, or absent offenders; and a Tribunal de Jurados, or Tribunal of Jurors, with jurisdiction over offenses of the press, political offenses, and crimes that could be punished with sentences in excess of three years.

55. Fernando Viera, *Colección legislativa de la República del Paraguay, 1842–1895*, pp. 43–53.

56. González, *Infortunios del Paraguay*, pp. 40–59; *Actas de la convención*, p. 87.

57. Sienra Carranza, "Retrospecto del Paraguay," *Revista Histórica* 1, no. 1, pp. 12–13.

58. García Mellid, *Proceso*, II, 413. Among other critics are Justo Pastor Benítez and Efraím Cardozo, two of Paraguay's greatest historians. See also the perceptive but anonymous *Panorama política del Paraguay: La postguerra del Chaco (1936–1946)*, pp. 8–11.

Chapter 6: Politics and Diplomacy, 1870–1871

1. *El Pueblo*, Oct. 18 and 29, Nov. 1, 10, 11, 15, and 19, 1870. The quotation is from Oct. 29.

2. Jaime Sosa [Escalada], *Negociaciones diplomáticas entre el Brasil, la República Argentina y el Paraguay*, p. 3.

3. MacDonnell to Granville, No. 42, Buenos Aires, Dec. 7, 1870, PRO-FO 6/292.

4. Issue of Nov. 27, 1870.

5. Cabinet and other changes may be followed in *Registro oficial, 1869–1875*, pp. 180–186, and MacDonnell to Granville, No. 42, Buenos Aires, Dec. 7, 1870, PRO-FO 6/292.

6. Proclamation to the People, Nov. 30, 1870, *Registro oficial, 1869–1875*, pp. 125–126.

7. *El Pueblo*, Dec. 10, 1870.

8. New elections were held on March 18 in Encarnación parish in Asunción, in Quiindi, and in four rural electoral districts. No elections had been held in Misiones, so two deputies and a senator were elected on June 2 (decrees of March 18 and June 12, 1871, *Registro oficial, 1869–1875*, pp. 175, 177, and 195).

9. One notable exception was the law of Feb. 9, 1871, which authorized the London loan. However, Máximo Terrero, chief architect of the loan, was appointed Paraguayan consul-general in London on May 10, 1871 (ibid., p. 192).

10. Gill to Guimarães, Asunción, Jan. 5 and 7, 1871, GP-DD, AN-RJ 547/22.

11. Cámara de Diputados, *Actas de las sesiones del período legislativo del año 1871*, pp. 64, 122, and 124; González, *Infortunios del Paraguay*, pp. 106–107.

12. MacDonnell to Granville, No. 34, Buenos Aires, Nov. 17, 1870, PRO-FO 6/292. Granville's notation on this despatch is dated Jan. 7, 1871.

13. Miguel Palacios to Secretary of Foreign Affairs, Asunción, Dec. 31, 1870, PRO-FO 59/30.

14. Foreign Office to Minister of Foreign Affairs of Paraguay, April 12, 1871, PRO-FO 59/31. The Foreign Office itself stated that this constituted recognition (Foreign Office to Chappell & Son, London, April 17, 1871, ibid.).

15. Palacios to Minister of Foreign Affairs, Asunción, March 4, 1871, ibid.; Stewart to Granville, London, April 28, 1871, ibid.; Granville to Stewart, London, May 5, 1871, ibid.; Foreign Office to Stewart, June 16, 1871, ibid.

16. Gregorio Benites, *Anales diplomático y militar de la Guerra del Paraguay*, II, 177. Athough the name is generally written "Benítez" at present, the forms "Benites" and "Benítes" were used in the postwar era, with "Benites" predominating.

17. E. A. Lynch to Granville, Upper Norwood, May 29, 1871, PRO-FO 59/

31; Certificate of John Burnet and William Mason, Edinburgh, July 12, 1871, encl., Emiliano López to Granville, London, Aug. 4, 1871, ibid.

18. Arsenio López Decoud, *Album gráfico de la República del Paraguay*, pp. 214–215.

19. Palacios to Minister of Foreign Affairs, Asunción, March 4, 1871, PRO-FO 59/31.

20. Stevens to Fish, Montevideo, Sept. 8, 1870, and Paraguay despatch No. 5, Montevideo, Aug. 8, 1871, DPU-NAUS 128/3; Fish to Stevens, No. 5, Washington, Oct. 5, 1871, DIPU-NAUS 77/128.

21. Stevens to Fish, Paraguay despatch No. 5, Montevideo, Aug. 8, 1871, DPU-NAUS 128/3.

22. Guimarães to Minister of War, No. 441, Asunción, March 23, 1871, GP-DD AN-RJ 547/22.

23. Many letters in the Cotegipe Collection support this observation. For example, see Brizuela to Cotegipe, Montevideo, June 27, 1873, CBC 25/137.

24. *The Weekly Standard*, May 24, 1871.

25. The various decrees are in *Registro oficial, 1869–1875*. Cabinet changes may be followed in López Decoud, *Album gráfico*, p. 214.

26. Guimarães to Cotegipe, Asunción, Aug. 1, 1871, CBC 29/26. The name is generally written "Guimarães," but the General frequently signed himself "Guimarens"; his intimates referred to him as "José Auto."

27. Guimarães to Cotegipe, Asunción, Oct. 2, 1871, CBC 29/7.

28. Id. to id., No. 678, Asunción, Oct. 19, 1871, CBC 29/8.

29. Id. to íd., Asunción, Oct. 2, 1871, CBC 29/7. Soon rumors were circulating that Caballero, Serrano, Godoy, Duarte, Maíz, and others were plotting a revolt, and Loizaga tried to persuade Rivarola to resign (id. to id., No. 678, Asunción, Oct. 19, 1871, CBC 29/8).

30. Guimarães to Cotegipe, Asunción, Aug. 29, 1871, CBC 29/3.

31. *Registro oficial, 1869–1875*, pp. 263–267; *La Prensa* (Buenos Aires), Oct. 24, 1871; *Boletín oficial*, Oct. 15, 1871, encl., Guimarães to Domingos José Nogueira Jaguaribe, No. 678, Asunción, Oct. 19, 1871, GP-DD AN-RJ 547/22. These events can also be followed in Freire Esteves, "Historia contemporánea," pp. 21 ff.; Sienra Carranza, "Retrospecto del Paraguay," *Revista histórica* 1, no. 1, pp. 33–40; Fragoso, *História*, V, 301–302; and Calzada, *Rasgos biográficos*, p. 35. Adolf N. Schuster, in his exceptionally fine *Paraguay: Land, Volk, Geschichte, Wirtschaftsleben und Kolonisation*, p. 254, dismisses these events with a very brief statement. See also Stevens to Fish, No. 7, Montevideo, Feb. 12, 1872, DPU-NAUS 128/3.

32. *El Pueblo*, Oct. 16, 1871; Decree of Oct. 21, 1871, *Registro oficial, 1869–1875*, pp. 269–270; *La Prensa* (Buenos Aires), Oct. 21, 1871; MacDonnell to Granville, No. 106, Buenos Aires, Oct. 25, 1871, PRO-FO 6/303.

33. Ramón J. Cárcano, *Guerra del Paraguay. Acción y reacción de la triple alianza*, II, 461.

34. Guimarães to Cotegipe, No. 753, Asunción, Dec. [Nov.] 21, 1871, CBC 29/10; Domingo A. Ortíz to Guimarães, Asunción, Nov. 26, 1871, GP-DD AN-RJ 547/22.

35. Wilfredo Valdez, that is, Jaime Sosa Escalada, charged Rivarola with coveting some land that Concha refused to sell to him and therefore used the revolt as an excuse to have him killed ("Estudio," p. 262).

36. The best accounts of these events are Cárcano, *Guerra—Acción y reac-*

ción, II, 459–470; Freire Esteves, "Historia contemporánea," pp. 24–26; Sïenra Carranza, "Retrospecto del Paraguay," *Revista Histórica* 2, no. 2, pp. 44–45; and Eduardo Aramburú, *Manifiesto al pueblo paraguayo*, pp. 15–16.

37. José Falcón to Minister of Foreign Affairs of Great Britain, Asunción, Dec. 13, 1871, PRO-FO 59/31. A previous effort to select a vice-president had met with Rivarola's veto (Guimarães to Nogueira Jaguaribe, No. 678, Asunción, Oct. 19, 1871, GP-DD AN-RJ 547/22).

38. Cirilo A. Rivarola, "Manifiesto a mis conciudadanos," Asunción, Sept. 5, 1872, encl., Azambuja to Correia, Asunción, Sept. 19, 1872, 1ª Sec., No. 21, MDBA-OR 201/1/10, AHI-RJ; *Registro oficial, 1869–1875*, pp. 278–280. Although the official title of Jovellanos was Vice-President in Exercise of the Executive Power, he was also called President.

39. Guimarães to Cotegipe, Asunción, Sept. 8, 1871, CBC 29/5; Sienra Carranza, "Retrospecto del Paraguay," *Revista Histórica* 2, no. 2, pp. 47–49.

40. Gill to Cotegipe, Asunción, Dec. 16, 1871, CBC, 25/137.

41. Cotegipe to Gill, Asunción, Dec. 16, 1871, ibid.; Rio Branco to Cotegipe, Rio de Janeiro, Jan. 16, 1872, CBC 53/36.

42. Vedia to Martín de Gainza, Asunción, Dec. 17, 1871, Gainza Papers, AGN-BA.

43. Rivarola to Cotegipe, Res., Barrero Grande, Dec. 26, 1871, CBC 60/212.

44. Visconde de São Vicente to Rio Branco, Rio de Janeiro, Oct. 12, 1870, in Joaquim Nabuco, *Um estadista do Imperio. Nabuco de Araujo, sua vida, suas opiniões, sua época*, III, 651–662. An unsigned draft of the instructions is in MDBA-DI, 201/4/8, AHI-RJ, and a misdated copy is in GP-DD AN-RJ 547/22. See also Fragoso, *A paz com o Paraguai*, pp. 81–84. The São Vicente cabinet held office from Sept. 29, 1870, to March 7, 1871 (Fleuiss, *História administrativa do Brasil*, p. 303).

45. Apparently Rio Branco took Caballero and Godoy with him from Rio de Janeiro and supported them. An outbreak of fever in Asunción kept them in Buenos Aires, then suffering a severe heat wave. Rio Branco expected to use them. Godoy was impatient and wanted to go to Asunción at once, but Rio Branco believed it would be inhuman to let him go and contrary to his purpose (Rio Branco to São Vicente, Buenos Aires, Jan. 9, 1871, *Anuário do Museu Imperial*, 1951, p. 38).

46. Actas do Conselho de Estado, Acta de 7 de dezembro de 1870, V, 58–60, AN-RJ; Silva Paranhos to São Vicente, Buenos Aires, Jan. 5, 1871, in Fragoso, *A paz com o Paraguai*, pp. 99–100.

47. Rio Branco to São Vicente, Buenos Aires, Jan. 9, 1871, *Anuário do Museu Imperial*, 1951, p. 37.

48. These conferences are summarized in *Memoria del ministerio de relaciones exteriores presentada al congreso nacional en 1872*, pp. 19–42, hereafter *Memoria Argentina, 1872*, and in Fragoso, *A paz com o Paraguai*, pp. 83–88. See also Amarilla Fretes, *Liquidación de la guerra*, pp. 61–62; Cecilio Báez, *Historia diplomática del Paraguay*, II, 217.

49. Rio Branco to São Vicente, Buenos Aires, Jan. 9, 1871, *Anuário do Museu Imperial*, 1951, p. 421; Rio Branco to Cotegipe, Buenos Aires, Feb. 7, 1871, CBC 53/19; Rio-Branco, *Efemérides brasileiras*, p. 126; Fleuiss, *História administrativa do Brasil*, p. 304.

50. Cárcano, *Guerra—Acción y reacción*, II, 437–443.

51. Decree of Oct. 5, 1871, *Memoria Argentina, 1872*, pp. 43–46.

52. Fragoso, *A paz com o Paraguai*, pp. 104–106.

53. Rio Branco to Cotegipe, Rio de Janeiro, Oct. 6, 1871, CBC 53/31.

54. Cárcano, *Guerra—Acción y reacción*, II, 456.

55. Message of July 14, 1871, *Memoria Argentina, 1872*, pp. 179–180.

56. Falcón to Cotegipe, Quintana, and Rodríguez, Asunción, Nov. 4, 1871, CBC 22/21; Fragoso, *A paz com o Paraguai*, p. 117.

57. "Proyecto de tratado definitivo de paz," GP-DD AN-RJ 547/22; Fragoso, *A paz com o Paraguai*, p. 117; *Memoria Argentina, 1872*, pp. 64–95; Cotegipe to Correia, Asunción, Nov. 15, 1871, in Fragoso, *A paz com o Paraguai*, p. 118.

58. Quintana to Tejedor, Asunción, Nov. 5, 1871, quoted by Cárcano, *Guerra—Acción y reacción*, II, 457–458; id. to id., Asunción, Nov. 9, 1871, ibid., II, 461; Tejedor to Quintana, Buenos Aires, Nov. 11, 1871, ibid., II, 462–463.

59. Quintana to Tejedor, Buenos Aires, Jan. 28, 1872, *Memoria Argentina, 1872*, pp. 46–51; Cárcano, *Guerra—Acción y reacción*, II, 482.

60. Ibid., II, 486–487.

61. Cotegipe to Correia, Asunción, Dec. 1, 1871, quoted by Fragoso, *A paz com o Paraguai*, pp. 126–127; Quintana to Tejedor, Buenos Aires, Jan. 28, 1872, *Memoria Argentina, 1872*, p. 50. Quintana's detailed account of the Asunción conference is his memorandum of Jan. 28, 1872, "La cuestión de límites en su relación con la alianza," pp. 95–136.

62. Gondim to Cotegipe, Montevideo, Dec. 27, 1871, CBC 142/154; Cárcano, *Guerra—Acción y reacción*, II, 502.

Chapter 7: Crises of 1872

1. Rio Branco to Cotegipe, Rio de Janeiro, Dec. 5, 1871, CBC 53/34. See also Alvaro Lins, *Rio-Branco (o Barão do Rio-Branco) 1845–1912*, I, 97.

2. Manoel Francisco Correia to the Conselho de Estado, Rio de Janeiro, Dec. 16, 1871, and Conferencia de Dec. 22, 1871, Actas do Conselho de Estado, IV, 111a–119, AN-RJ.

3. Correia to Cotegipe, Sec. Cen., Res. No. 14, Rio de Janeiro, Dec. 31, 1871, GP-DD AN-RJ 547/22.

4. Quintana to Domingo Ortíz, Asunción, Dec. 13, 1871, in Fragoso, *A paz com o Paraguai*, p. 129; Ortíz to Quintana, Asunción, Dec. 15, 1871, ibid., pp. 129–130; Ortíz to Cotegipe, Asunción, Dec. 16, 1871, ibid., p. 130; Cotegipe to Ortíz, Asunción, Dec. 17, 1871, ibid.

5. Cárcano, *Guerra—Acción y reacción*, II, 520; Sosa, "Política brasilera en el Paraguay," p. 18; Cardozo, *Paraguay independiente*, p. 272; Loizaga was named sole plenipotentiary on Jan. 5, 1872 (Falcón to Cotegipe, Asunción, Jan. 5, 1872, CBC 22/28).

6. *Archivo Mitre*, XXVIII, 22–25; Valdez, "Estudio," pp. 353–366; Fragoso, *A paz com o Paraguai*, pp. 133–142. The treaty of limits provided for a mixed commission to mark the boundary. This commission began its work in September, 1872, and completed the task two years later. Domingo Antonio Ortíz for Paraguay and Col. Rufino Enéas Gustavo Galvão for Brazil were the principals (Azambuja to Correia, no. 336, Asunción, Sept. 11, 1872, MDBA-OR 201/1/10; Galvão to Gondim, No. 434, Asunción, Oct. 29, 1874, ibid., 201/1/12).

7. Brizuela to Cotegipe, Asunción, Jan. 20, 1872, CBC 11/14; Báez, *Historia diplomática del Paraguay*, II, 217; González, *Infortunios del Paraguay*, p. 32;

Benítez, *Historia diplomática del Paraguay*, pp. 253–255; Loizaga to Cotegipe, Asunción, Jan. 19 and Feb. 6, 1872, CBC 34/121, 126.

8. Valdez, "Estudio," p. 297.

9. MacDonnell to Granville, No. 4, Buenos Aires, Jan. 15, 1872, PRO-FO 6/309.

10. Stevens to Fish, Paraguayan Affairs No. 9, Montevideo, June 5, 1872, DPU-NAUS 128/3. A copy of the treaty of Jan. 9, 1872, is enclosed.

11. Stevens to Fish, No. 7, Montevideo, Feb. 12, 1872, ibid.

12. Rio Branco to Cotegipe, Rio de Janeiro, Jan. 27, 1872, CBC 53/37.

13. Mitre to Cotegipe, Buenos Aires, Jan. 24, 1872, and Cotegipe to Mitre, Asunción, Feb. 4, 1872, *Archivo Mitre*, XXVIII, 11–19.

14. Dexter E. Lapp to Fish, Buenos Aires, Feb. 13, 1872, DA-NAUS, 69/18; Amarilla Fretes, *Liquidación de la guerra*, pp. 73–77; *Memoria Argentina, 1872*, pp. 136–137.

15. Vedia to Gainza, Asunción, March 7, 1872, Gainza Papers, AGN-BA.

16. Loizaga to Tejedor, Asunción, Feb. 16, 1872, encl., Loizaga to Cotegipe, Asunción, Feb. 16, 1872, CBC 34/130; Tejedor to Minister of Foreign Affairs of Paraguay, Buenos Aires, Feb. 29, 1872, *Memoria Argentina, 1872*, pp. 144–146.

17. Mitre to Rio Branco, Buenos Aires, Feb. 16, 1872, *Archivo Mitre*, XXVIII, 31–35; Tejedor to Correia, Buenos Aires, Jan. 31, 1872, *Apéndice á la memoria del ministerio de relaciones esteriores presentada al congreso nacional en el año de 1872*, pp. 3–4; *La Prensa* (Buenos Aires), Feb. 16, 17, and June 1, 1872; Cárcano, *Guerra—Acción y reacción*, II, 565; Tejedor to Correia, Buenos Aires, Feb. 15, 1872, *Memoria Argentina, 1872*, pp. 139–141.

18. Actas do conselho de Estado, Acta de 1 de março de 1872, VI, 120–135, AN-RJ.

19. Correia to Tejedor, Rio de Janeiro, March 22, 1872, GP-DD AN-RJ 547/22; *Apéndice, Memoria Argentina, 1872*, pp. 20–36.

20. Loizaga to Cotegipe, Asunción, Feb. 14, 1872, CBC 34/128; Fragoso, *A paz com o Paraguai*, p. 197.

21. MacDonnell to Granville, No. 33, Buenos Aires, May 14, 1872, PRO-FO 6/309.

22. Tejedor to Correia, Buenos Aires, April 27, 1872, *Apéndice, Memoria Argentina, 1872*, pp. 39–60. There were 3,001 Brazilian troops in Asunción as of Feb. 16, 1872, but 348 were hospitalized (Divisão brasileiro no Paraguay, GP-DD No. 60, AN-RJ 547/22).

23. Estanislao S. Zeballos, "Las fuerzas armadas y la posición internacional de la república," *Revista de Derecho, Historia y Letras* 30 (Buenos Aires, 1908): 526.

24. "Mensaje del presidente de la república al abrir las sesiones del congreso argentino," *Memoria del ministerio de relaciones esteriores presentada al congreso nacional en 1874*, p. 14.

25. Guimarães to Cotegipe, Res., Asunción, Feb. 16, 1872, CBC 29/16.

26. Act of Feb. 14, 1872, *Registro oficial, 1869–1875*, p. 401.

27. Freire Esteves, "Historia contemporánea," p. 27.

28. Julio de Vedia to Martín Gainza, Asunción, March 7, 1872, Gainza Papers, AGN-BA. Vedia began his letter on March 7 and added to it day by day.

29. Guimarães to Nogueira Jaguaribe, Asunción, March 16, 1872, GP-DD No. 68, AN-RJ 547/22.

30. Gill to Cotegipe, Rio de Janeiro, April 3, 1872, CBC 25/139. When he reached Rio de Janeiro, Gill did not see Cotegipe, who was on vacation.

31. República del Paraguay, Cámara de Senadores, *Actas de las sesiones del período legislativo del año 1872*, p. 26.

32. Gill to Cotegipe, Rio de Janeiro, April 3, 1872, CBC 25/139; Vedia to Gainza, Asunción, March 7, 1872, Gainza Papers, AGN-BA; Guimarães to Cotegipe, Asunción, March 11, 1872, CBC 29/20; Correia to Magalhães, Sec. Cen., Res. No. 5, Rio de Janeiro, March 27, 1872, MDBA-DI 201/4/8.

33. Vedia to Gainza, Asunción, March 7, 1872, Gainza Papers, AGN-BA.

34. Ltr., Asunción, March 9, 1872, *La Nación* (Buenos Aires), March 14, 1872; Báez, *Historia diplomática*, II, 217.

35. Senadores, *Actas, 1872*, pp. 27–28.

36. Guimarães to Cotegipe, Asunción, March 11, 1872, CBC 29/20; *La Nación*, March 24, 1872; López Decoud, *Album gráfico*, p. 215.

37. Gill to Cotegipe, Rio de Janeiro, April 3, 1872, CBC 25/139.

38. Jovellanos to Cotegipe, Asunción, March 22, 1872, CBC 30/140.

39. Guimarães to Cotegipe, Asunción, June 3, 1872, CBC 29/25.

40. For his defense, see Barão de Cotegipe, *As negociações com o Paraguay e a nota do governo argentino de 27 de abril. Carta ao Exmo. Senhor Conselheiro Manoel Francisco Correia, ministro e secretario d'estado dos negocios estrangeiros*. A copy is in CBC 85/10.

41. George Buckley Mathew to Granville, No. 8 Conf., Rio de Janeiro, June 22, 1872, PRO-FO 13/483; MacDonnell to Granville, No. 49, Buenos Aires, June 29, 1872, PRO-FO 6/309; Stevens to Fish, No. 37, Montevideo, July 8, 1872, DPU-NAUS 128/3. Jovellanos sent Loizaga to Buenos Aires "in response to friendly advances by President Sarmiento" (Stevens to Fish, No. 13, Montevideo, Sept. 3, 1872, ibid.). For the Mitre mission to Rio de Janeiro, see J. Paulo de Medeyros, *A missão do General Mitre no Brasil*; *Archivo del General Mitre, la misión al Brasil año 1872*, vol. 28; Cárcano, *Guerra—Acción y reacción*, II, 633–734; Fragoso, *A paz com o Paraguai*, pp. 265–285.

42. Fish to Stevens, No. 35, Washington, April 19, 1872, DIPU-NAUS 77/128; Stevens to Fish, No. 37, Montevideo, July 8, 1872, DPU-NAUS 128/3.

43. Stevens to Fish, No. 13, Montevideo, Sept. 3, 1872, ibid.

44. Azambuja to Correia, Asunción, Aug. 17, 1872, MDBA-OR 201/1/10; Guimarães to Cotegipe, Asunción, Aug. 4, 1872, CBC 29/29.

45. Elizalde to Mitre, Buenos Aires, Aug. 20, 1872, *Archivo Mitre*, XXVIII, 244–246.

46. Tejedor to Mitre, Buenos Aires, Oct. 12, 1872, ibid., XXVIII, 235–236.

47. Azambuja to Correia, Sec. Cen., Res. No. 2, Asunción, Sept. 18, 1872, and id. to id., Sec. Cen., Res. No. 12, Asunción, Sept. 20, 1872, MDBA-OR 201/1/10; Tejedor to Mitre, Buenos Aires, Sept. 25, 1872, *Archivo Mitre*, XXVIII, 234.

48. *La Nación* (Buenos Aires), Sept. 4 and 5, 1872; *Memoria del ministerio de relaciones esteriores presentada al congreso nacional en 1873*, pp. iii–viii.

49. Tejedor to Mitre, Buenos Aires, Nov. 12, 1872, *Archivo Mitre*, XXVIII, 237–238.

50. Tejedor to Mitre, Buenos Aires, June 27, 1872, ibid., XXVIII, 47–50; J. Paulo de Medeiros, "Mitre," in *Mitre. Homenaje de la Academia Nacional de la Historia en el cincuentenario de su muerte (1906–1956)*, p. 740.

51. Mitre to Argentine Minister of Foreign Affairs, Rio de Janeiro, July 7,

1872, *Archivo Mitre*, XXVIII, 69–70; id. to id., Rio de Janeiro, July 9, 1872, ibid., XXVIII, 70–74; id. to id., Rio de Janeiro, Sept. 11, 1872; ibid., XXVIII, 108–120; id. to id., Rio de Janeiro, Sept. 19, 1872, ibid., XXVIII, 130–134; Estanislao S. Zeballos, "Diplomacia desarmada, fracaso de las misiones Quintana y Mitre, en el Paraguay," *Revista de Derecho, Historia, y Letras* 31 (Buenos Aires, 1908): 116–117.

52. Mitre to Minister of Foreign Affairs, Rio de Janeiro, Sept. 26, 1872, *Archivo Mitre*, XXVIII, 148–152.

53. Elizalde to Mitre, Buenos Aires, Aug. 7, 1872, ibid., XXVIII, 239–243.

54. Elizalde to Mitre, Buenos Aires, Aug. 29, 1872, ibid., XXVIII, 247–248; id. to id., Buenos Aires, Sept. 11, 1872, ibid., XXVIII, 251–253; id. to id., Buenos Aires, Oct. 12, 1872, ibid., XXVIII, 260–261.

55. Mitre to Minister of Foreign Affairs, Rio de Janeiro, Oct. 3, 1872, ibid., XXVIII, 155–157.

56. Pedro Calmon, "Mitre y el Brasil," *Mitre, homenaje*, pp. 65–66.

57. Mitre to Tejedor, Rio de Janeiro, Oct. 28, 1872, *Memoria Argentina, 1873*, p. 148; id. to id., Rio de Janeiro, Nov. 5, 1872, ibid., 150–151.

58. Among the numerous sources for the Mitre-São Vicente treaty, the following are readily available: *Archivo Mitre*, XXVIII, 166–186; Báez, *Historia diplomática*, II, 218–220; *Memoria Argentina, 1873*, pp. 220–225; *La Nación* (Buenos Aires), Nov. 27, 1872; *La Tribuna* (Buenos Aires), Nov. 26, 1872.

59. Mitre to Rufino Varela, Rio de Janeiro, Nov. 20, 1872, *Correspondencia literaria, histórica y política del General Bartolomé Mitre*, II, 204.

Chapter 8: Rails, Loans, and Immigrants
1. Much of the following is taken from Harris Gaylord Warren, "The Paraguay Central Railway, 1856–1889," IAEA 20 (Spring 1967): 3–22.

2. Amerlan, *Nights on the Rio Paraguay*, p. 145; Fragoso, *História*, IV, 220.

3. *La Regeneración*, Oct. 14, Nov. 19, 1869, and March 6, 1870; *Memoria Argentina, 1877*, I, 530–531.

4. *The Weekly Standard*, March 2, 1870.

5. Forgues, "Le Paraguay," p. 401. Forgues made his journey to Paraguarí on Sept. 22, 1872. There are more than 100 patterns of the gorgeous *ñandutí* for which Itauguá has been the principal source for more than 200 years.

6. Freund and Mulhall, *Letters*, p. 6. The "29 years" is in error, since the first train ran in 1861 and Mulhall was writing in 1887. The *tipoi* is a loose-fitting, low-cut garment worn universally in Paraguay by women of the poorer classes and as a house garment by a great many more.

7. Ibid.

8. M. G. and E. T. Mulhall, *Handbook of the River Plate Republics* (1875), pp. 393–394.

9. Ltr., "W," Asunción, Feb. 19, 1870, *The Weekly Standard*, March 2, 1870; Henri Pitaud, *Les français au Paraguay*, p. 73.

10. *The Weekly Standard*, Aug. 25, 1869.

11. *La Regeneración*, Nov. 19, 1869, and March 6, 1870.

12. There were 9 stations: Asunción, Trinidad, Luque, Areguá, Patiño-cué, Tacuaral, Pirayú, Cerro León, and Paraguarí. Fares and tariffs were low. The Brazilians divested themselves of the railway late in March or early in April, 1870 (*La Regeneración*, April 17, 1870).

13. Cecil Gosling to Earl Grey, Asunción, April 29, 1908, PRO-FO 371–494. Gosling was the British consul. Wisner came to Paraguay in 1845, probably as an engineer with a Brazilian military mission, and remained as military adviser to the López.

14. Falcón to Azambuja, Asunción, Nov. 20, 1872, encl. no. 1, Azambuja to Correia, 4ª Sec. No. 16, Asunción, Nov. 20, 1872, MDBA-OR 201/1/10; id. to id., Asunción, Jan. 17, 1873, encl., Azambuja to Correia, 4ª Sec. No. 20, MDBA-OR 201/1/11.

15. Araguáia to Caravellas, Asunción, June 27, 1873, ibid. By January 1877, Paraguay owed $81,326.95 (Vasconcellos to Albuquerque, 4ª Sec. No. 12, Asunción, Jan. 25, 1877, MDBA-OR 201/1/14).

16. El Paraguay, June 14, 1870. Horrocks was appointed on April 16, 1870 (Registro oficial, 1869–1875, p. 74).

17. La Regeneración, Aug. 5 and 12, 1870.

18. El Pueblo, Dec. 2 and 17, 1870. Changes in administration are noted in Registro oficial, 1869–1875, pp. 47, 246.

19. Bedoya to MacDonnell, Buenos Aires, May 11, 1870, encl., MacDonnell to Clarendon, No. 59, Buenos Aires, May 14, 1870, PRO-FO 371/494.

20. Act of April 24, 1871, Registro oficial, 1869–1875, pp. 189–190; Diputados, Actas, 1871, pp. 62–63, 102, 134.

21. Senadores, Actas, 1872, p. 88; ibid., 1873, pp. 31–32, 36.

22. Terrero to Jovellanos, Conf., London, May 7, 1872, and id. to id., Conf., London, May 18, 1872, and Sept. 18, 1872, CCAP. Terrero had received, under date of Feb. 18, 1872, a copy of Alcorta's instructions (id. to id., London, Jan. 26, 1873, CCAP).

23. Warren, "The Paraguay Central Railway, 1856–1889," p. 12.

24. Registro oficial, 1869–1875, pp. 603–604; Cámara de Senadores, Actas de las sesiones de los períodos legislativos de los años 1874–75–76–77–78–79–80, pp. 7–9.

25. Mulhall, Handbook (1875), p. 394.

26. Warren, "The Paraguay Central Railway, 1856–1889," p. 14.

27. Cámara de Diputados, Actas de las sesiones de los períodos legislativos de los años 1873–74–75–76–77–78–79–80, pp. 180, 195; Senadores, Actas, 1874–1880, pp. 195–196; Registro oficial, 1876, pp. 183–184; González, Infortunios del Paraguay, p. 144; Vasconcellos to Albuquerque, Sec. Cen. No. 26, Asunción, Oct. 28, 1877, MDBA-OR 201/1/14. The land grant was 10 squares of 100 varas on each side for 40 miles. The Paraguayan vara is 34.09 inches. In later years, Patri held many prominent positions in commerce and society (López Decoud, Album gráfico, lxxvi; Freire Esteves, "Historia contemporánea," p. 179).

28. Senadores, Actas, 1874–1880, pp. 195–196; Diputados, Actas, 1873–1880, p. 302.

29. Vasconcellos to Gaspar de Silveira Martins, Sec. Cen. No. 40, Asunción, July 12, 1878, and Vasconcellos to Villa Bella, Sec. Cen. No. 43, Asunción, July 30, 1878, MDBA-OR 201/1/15; La Reforma, July 29, 1878.

30. Patri invested $f106,630 in repairs during the 1877–1881 period, all of which probably came from net receipts. Gross income for that period was about $237,000 gold; gross income for 1880–1885 was about $293,000 gold (Arthur G. Vansittart, "Paraguay. Report by Mr. [Arthur G.] Vansittart on

the Commerce, Finances &c. of Paraguay," HC, *Sessional Papers, Accounts and Papers, Commercial Reports,* LXXI, 144).

31. See Harris Gaylord Warren, "The Golden Fleecing: The Paraguayan Loans of 1871 and 1872," IAEA 26 (Summer 1972): 3–24.

32. Baillie, *Treasure,* p. 237.

33. *Registro oficial, 1869–1875,* p. 192; "The Paraguay Loan, 1871," *Special Report from the Select Committee on Loans to Foreign States,* HC, *Sessional Papers,* XI, reports on the Paraguayan loans at pp. xxxvi–xliv, testimony at pp. 174–230; hereafter, *Loans Report.*

34. MacDonnell to Granville, No. 34 Commercial, Buenos Aires, Dec. 13, 1871, PRO-FO 6/304.

35. Note from the Paraguayan to the Imperial Government, Ministry of Foreign Affairs, Asunción, May 21, 1871, encl. of translation in T. Clement Gabbold to Granville, No. 49, Rio de Janeiro, Aug. 19, 1871; Note of the Imperial Government to the Confidential Agent of Paraguay, Foreign Office, Rio de Janeiro, July 5, 1871, encl. Gabbold to Granville, No. 49, Rio de Janeiro, Aug. 19, 1871, PRO-FO 13/477. The Brazilian minister in London did lend his good offices in favor of the loan (Brizuela to Cotegipe, Asunción, July 6, 1873, CBC 11/27).

36. Profits were to be shared with 55% for the Warings, 25% to Grant, and 20% to Laing (*Loans Report,* p. 229).

37. Agreement of Nov. 21, 1871, between Terrero and Waring Brothers & Co., *Loans Report,* p. 175, and Appendix No. 32, pp. 192–193; see also Gregorio Benítes, *Las imposturas de Juan Bautista Gill y el informe del Comité del Parlamento de Inglaterra en la cuestión empréstitos del Paraguay,* p. 34.

38. *Loans Report,* Appendix No. 32, pp. 192–193; Benítes, *Imposturas,* pp. 15–31.

39. Act of Feb. 9, 1872, *Registro oficial, 1869–1875,* p. 404.

40. José Segundo Decoud, *La historia de una administración, o sea las dilapidaciones de Salvador Jovellanos . . . ;* Henry Cavendish Archibald Angelo to MacDonnell, Asunción, Nov. 23, 1872, encl., MacDonnell to Granville, No. 69, Buenos Aires, Nov. 29, 1872, PRO-FO 59-35; Rivarola, *Manifiesto del ciudadano Cirilo A. Rivarola al pueblo paraguayo,* pp. 6–11.

41. Valdez, "Estudio," pp. 266–267. Benítes told the Brazilians that Gill had stolen a large part of the first loan (Caravellas to Gondim, Sec. Cen. No. 11, Rio de Janeiro, Feb. 17, 1874, MDBA-DI 201/4/8).

42. Azumbuja to Correia, Sec. Cen. No. 8, Asunción, Aug. 21, 1872, MDBA-OR 201/1/10.

43. Terrero to Jovellanos, London, May 4, 1872, and Terrero to Rivarola, London, Jan. 11, 1872, CCAP. News of Rivarola's fall had not yet reached London. Ohlsen left for Paraguay on Jan. 13, 1872. For the law authorizing the second loan, see *Registro oficial, 1869–1875,* pp. 404–405, and *Loans Report,* p. 182.

44. Terrero to Jovellanos, Conf., London, May 18, 1872, and id. to id., London, May 22, 1872, CCAP.

45. Agreement between Máximo Terrero and Robinson, Fleming & Co., May 27, 1872, *Loans Report,* pp. 181–182.

46. Terrero to Jovellanos, Conf., London, June 8 and 19, 1872, CCAP.

47. Correia to Azumbuja, 1ª Sec. No. 1 Res., Rio de Janeiro, n. d. [June 1872], MDBA-DI 2014/8.

48. *Loans Report*, pp. 185, 189–190.

49. Terrero to Jovellanos, Conf., London, July 6, 1872, and id. to id., Conf., London, Aug. 6, 1872, CCAP. Apparently Alcorta, working with Dr. William Stewart, had peddled a concession for the export of yerba free of duty for six years. Terrero reprimanded Jovellanos sternly for having approved the concession (id. to id., London, Sept. 18, 1872, CCAP).

50. Benítes, *Imposturas*, pp. 46–47; Senadores, *Actas, 1874–1880*, p. 60; Correia to Azambuja, Sec. Cen. Res. No. 2, Rio de Janeiro, June 30, 1872, MDBA-DI 201/4/8. Also accredited to Brazil, Benítes was charged with settling the argument between Paraguay and Brazil over smuggling by sutlers (Jovellanos to Cotegipe, Asunción, July 19, 1872, CBC 30/142).

51. For details, see Warren, "Golden Fleecing," pp. 3–24.

52. Terrero to Jovellanos, Conf., London, Nov. 7, 1872, CCAP; Affidavit of Máximo Terrero, Dec. 31, 1872, Paraguay v. Fleming, P.-No. 205, No. 3374, PRO-C 31/2673; Benítes to Granville, London, Nov. 25, 1872, PRO-FO 59/32; Terrero to Jovellanos, London, Sept. 18, 1872, CCAP; Benítez, *Manifiesto de Gregorio Benítez . . .*, pp. 1–2. Just when the name was changed from "Benítes" to "Benítez" is hard to say.

53. Warren, "Litigation," pp. 31–46.

54. Terrero to Jovellanos, London, Nov. 23, 1872, and id. to id., Conf., London, Nov. 24, 1872, CCAP. Terrero's letters to Jovellanos on Dec. 6 and 21, 1872, and Jan. 26, 1873, CCAP, reveal an embittered agent who protested that he had done everything possible for Paraguayan credit.

55. *Loans Report*, p. 188; Benítes, *Imposturas*, p. 44; Robinson, Fleming & Co. to Terrero, London, July 13, 1874, CCAP. Benítes submitted accounts to show what happened to the £416,000, but the Gill administration was skeptical.

56. *Nación Paraguaya*, July 4, 1873. The gold was expected to arrive on the *Taragui*, but was held up for a few days by the consignee in Buenos Aires, who refused to deliver to an agent of the government, leaving many people with their mouths watering (*El Fénix*, June 6, 1873).

57. *Nación Paraguaya*, Aug. 20 and 21, 1873.

58. *El Paraguay*, May 21, 1870. This was the paper's first issue.

59. *La Prensa* (Buenos Aires), April 24, 1872, citing *La Voz del Pueblo*.

60. Diputados, *Actas, 1869–1875*, p. 37.

61. *The Times* (London), Aug. 25, 1871.

62. For a detailed account, see Harris Gaylord Warren, "The 'Lincolnshire Farmers' in Paraguay: An Abortive Emigration Scheme of 1872–1873," *The Americas* 21 (Jan. 1965): 243–269; *Nación Paraguaya*, Jan. 21, 1874; Terrero to Jovellanos, Conf., London, June 19, 1872, CCAP.

63. "Concessions," June 6, 1872, encl., R. H. Meade to E. Hammond, London, Aug. 30, 1873, PRO-FO 59/35; "Emigration to Paraguay (South America). Terms and Concessions granted by the Government of Paraguay to the English Colony in Charge of J. W. Billiatt, with a few remarks upon the natural productions, soil, and climate of Paraguay," encl., Meade to Hammond, London, Sept. 9, 1873, ibid.

64. Terrero to Jovellanos, London, Sept. 27, 1872, and id. to id., London, Oct. 18, 1872, CCAP.

65. Warren, "Lincolnshire Farmers," pp. 252–253.

66. Terrero to Jovellanos, Conf., London, June 19, 1872, CCAP. Terrero

had informed Jovellanos that the second contingent would sail on Oct. 20 (Terrero to Jovellanos, London, Sept. 18, 1872, CCAP).

67. Warren, "Lincolnshire Farmers," pp. 255–259.

68. Vasconcellos to Franklin Americo de Menges Doria, 1ª Sec. No. 17, Asunción, Dec. 6, 1881, MDBA-OR 201/1/16; Vasconcellos to Villa Bella, 1ª Sec. No. 45, Asunción, Dec. 10, 1875, MDBA-OR 201/1/13. The claim was paid for $6,643.50 in 1885 (*Registro oficial*, 1885, p. 255).

69. Lionel S. Sackville West, "Report on the present political, financial, and social state of the Republic of Paraguay," encl., West to Derby, No. 109, Conf., Buenos Aires, Oct. 30, 1875, PRO-FO 6/328; hereafter, West, "Report 1875."

70. Law of May 8, 1876, *Registro oficial*, 1876, pp. 80–81; *La Reforma*, May 10, 1876. This grant was the fruition of a year's effort by Stewart, who obtained Senate approval in 1875 (Senadores, *Actas, 1874–1880*, p. 128); Saguier to Gill, Buenos Aires, Sept. 25, 1876, CCAP. We have no further information on the Alston enterprise.

71. Law of June 27, 1876, *Registro oficial*, 1876, p. 121.

72. *Los Debates*, Aug. 11, 1876.

73. Congress in 1879 issued a ten-year patent to Balanza covering his process (Act of Aug. 25, 1879, *Registro oficial*, 1879, pp. 45–46). The enterprising botanist left Paraguay on May 2, 1887, and died in Hanoi on Nov. 22, 1891. A son, Ernest, married Jeanne Boissière in 1886, moved to Villa Rica in 1895, and became the founder of a numerous and wealthy family (Pitaud, *Les français au Paraguay*, pp. 82–85).

74. Centurión, *Historia de las letras paraguayas*, II, 35–40, 55. Chacón later was Bolivian consul.

Chapter 9: Paraguayan Society in the Postwar Decade

1. *La Regeneración*, Oct. 17, 1869.

2. Ltr., Asunción, Dec. 26, 1870, *The Weekly Standard*, Jan. 11, 1871.

3. *The Standard*, Jan. 13, 1871; *La Prensa*, Feb. 11, 1871; T. E. Ash, *The Plague of 1871*, pp. 5 ff. At Villa Occidental, 15 deaths in the Argentine garrison caused General Vedia to move the Military Legion to Corrientes (Guimarães to Minister of War [Raymundo Terra de Araújo Lima], No. 352, Asunción, Jan. 24, 1871, GP-DD AN-RJ 547/22).

4. Alfredo Sérgio Teixeira de Macedo [Brazilian chargé] to Caravellas, 2ª Sec. No. 4, Asunción, Feb. 18, 1873, MDBA-OR 201/1/11.

5. *The Weekly Standard*, Sept. 15, 1869.

6. Police Chief Juan Francisco Decoud and Angel D. Peña cooperated in 1869 in vain efforts to clean up the city (*La Regeneración*, Oct. 1, Nov. 21, 24, 28, 1869, and Feb. 18, 1870).

7. *El Paraguay*, May 24, 1870; *The Standard*, Jan. 28, 1871.

8. Decree of July 7, 1870, *Registro oficial, 1869–1875*, p. 98; Minister of Interior to José Falcón, Asunción, Nov. 4, 1871, CBC 22/22; Cotegipe to Guimarães, Asunción, Nov. 6, 1871, encl., Guimarães to Jaguaribe, No. 755, Asunción, Dec. 29, 1871, GP-DD AN-RJ 547/22; Decree of May 8, 1876, *Registro oficial*, 1876, p. 78; [Higinio Uriarte], *Mensaje presentado por el poder ejecutivo al congreso de la nación en la apertura de sus sesiones del octavo período legislativo*.

9. See issues of *La Regeneración* in 1869 and 1870 for physician's notices.

10. *La Regeneración*, April 13, 1870.

11. Order of Chief of Police Francisco Santos, Sept. 16, 1873, *Nación Paraguaya*, Sept. 19, 1873.

12. Lawyers' announcements are numerous in issues of *La Regeneración*, especially from Nov. 21, 1869, to June 8, 1870.

13. *The Weekly Standard*, Jan. 12, 1870.

14. Ltr., "M. G." [Miguel Gallegos?], *La Nación*, Jan. 29, 1870.

15. Ibid., Nov. 24, 1869.

16. *La Regeneración*, Sept. 16, 1870.

17. Ibid., Nov. 10, 12, and 19, 1869.

18. Decoud, *Escombros*, p. 76.

19. *La Regeneración*, Dec. 12, 1869.

20. Ibid., Jan. 5, 1870.

21. *La República* (Buenos Aires), Jan. 9 and 28, 1870; *La Regeneración* (Aug. 5, 1870) urged completion of the theater, which was being turned into a big latrine and from which thieves were taking bricks.

22. *La República*, Jan. 15, 1870.

23. Order of Francisco Santos, Sept. 16, 1873, *Nación Paraguaya*, Sept. 19, 1873.

24. Pitaud, *Les français au Paraguay*, p. 82.

25. Forgues, "Le Paraguay," p. 391.

26. *The Weekly Standard*, Jan. 12, 1872.

27. *Nación Paraguaya*, Sept. 19, 1873.

28. Eduardo Callado to Cotegipe, Sec. Cen. No. 28, Asunción, July 29, 1876, MDBA-OR 201/1/14.

29. Issue of Sept. 13, 1876; see also West, "Report, 1875."

30. Callado to Cotegipe, 1ª Sec. No. 6, Asunción, Oct. 31, 1876, MDBA-OR 201/1/14.

31. *El Fénix*, May 30, 1873.

32. Decree of Feb. 29, 1876, *Registro oficial*, 1876, pp. 39, 122; ibid., 1877, pp. 250–260.

33. See Josefina Pla, *Hermano negro*, pp. 159–166; Cooney, "Abolition in the Republic of Paraguay," p. 161. Justo Pastor Benítez minimizes the negroid strain added during Allied occupation (*Formación social del pueblo paraguayo*, p. 81).

34. The Triays were among Paraguay's wealthiest families; the Yegros name is one of the proudest in Paraguayan history. For more on this, see Freund and Mulhall, *Letters*, p. 20.

35. Forgues, "Le Paraguay," p. 391.

36. Azambuja to Correia, Sec. Cen. No. 26, Asunción, Dec. 3, 1872, MDBA-OR 201/1/10; Amaral Valente to Caravellas, Sec. Cen. No. 7, Asunción, Dec. 2, 1873, ibid., 201/1/11; *El Orden*, Dec. 6, 1872; *La República* (Buenos Aires), Dec. 8, 1872; Pitaud, *Les français au Paraguay*, pp. 71–72; Vasconcellos to Pedro Luiz Pereira de Souza, Sec. Cen. No. 40, Asunción, Sept. 7, 1880, MDBA-OR 201/1/16.

37. Azambuja to Correia, 1ª Sec. Res. No. 7, Asunción, Nov. 23, 1872, ibid., 201/1/10; id. to id., 1ª Sec. No. 4, Asunción, Jan. 20, 1874, ibid., 201/1/11.

38. Jorge Lopes da Costa Moreira to Azambuja, Villa Rica, Aug. 30, 1872, encl., Azambuja to Correia, Sec. Cen. No. 16, Asunción, Sept. 16, 1872, ibid.

39. Azambuja to Correia, 1ª Sec. No. 8, Asunción, Jan. 29, 1873, MDBA-OR 201/1/12; Susnik, *El indio colonial del Paraguay*, III.

40. João Lima in Trinidad and Manoel Ferreira lost all of their animals (Antonio S. Daltro to Gondim, No. 2, Asunción, Jan. 7, 1874, encl., Gondim to Caravellas, 1ª Sec. No. 4, Asunción, Jan. 12, 1874, MDBA-OR, 201/1/13).

41. Pereira Leal to Cotegipe, Sec. Cen. No. 25, Asunción, Dec. 1, 1875, ibid., 201/1/14; Mendes Totta to Azambuja, Asunción, Nov. 30, 1872, encl., Azambuja to Correia, Sec. Cen. No. 52, Dec. 8, 1872, ibid.; Pereira Leal to Caravellas, 1ª Sec. No. 8 Conf., Asunción, June 7, 1875, ibid.

42. Marcondes, "Viagem ao Paraguay," p. 38; *El Progreso*, April 30, 1873. Despite the revolution then going on, Araguáia gave a sumptuous ball on June 4, 1873 (*El Fénix*, June 6, 1873). Although private social groups were formed, we have little information about them. There are fugitive references to the Italian Mutual Aid Society in 1873 (*El Fénix*, May 11, 1873) and to Los Compañeros and La Esperanza Society in 1870 (*La Voz del Pueblo*, Sept. 8, 1870).

43. *La Regeneración*, Nov. 7, Dec. 1, 10, and 15, 1869, and Sept. 21, 1870.

44. Forgues, "Le Paraguay," p. 399.

45. Ibid., p. 397.

46. *El Fénix*, May 14, 1873.

47. Forgues, "Le Paraguay," pp. 412–413.

48. Centurión, *Historia de las letras paraguayas*, I, 291–296; E[nrique] B. P[arodi], "La prensa," *Revista del Paraguay* 1 (Aug. 1891): 341.

49. Parodi, "La prensa," pp. 443–444.

50. Ibid., p. 347.

51. Juan José Decoud died in 1871 at the age of 24 (Centurión, *Historia de las letras paraguayas*, II, 25–26).

52. *La Regeneración*, Jan. 7, 1870.

53. Ibid., Oct. 1, 1869.

54. Ibid., Oct. 7, 1869.

55. *El Paraguay*, May 21, 1870.

56. Parodi, "La prensa," p. 396.

57. Ibid., p. 443.

58. *La Regeneración*, April 6, 1870.

59. Parodi, "La prensa," p. 443.

60. Decree of Nov. 17, 1870, *El Pueblo*, Nov. 18, 1870. Neither *La Situación* nor *La Ley* lasted more than a month.

61. *El Pueblo*, Nov. 22, 1870.

62. Guimarães to Cotegipe, Asunción, June 3 and 23, 1872, CBC 20/25, 27.

63. *Nación Paraguaya*, July 25, 1873. The paper showed no indication of dying in its issue of Jan. 23, 1874, the last in the collection of the Biblioteca Nacional, Asunción. Another paper, *El Orden*, appeared briefly in 1872.

64. *Nación Paraguaya*, Oct. 19, 1873. The Argentines published *El Chaco* at Villa Occidental.

65. Centurión, *Historia de la cultura paraguaya*, I, 352–353. More exact data about *El Derecho* are lacking. We have had to depend upon scattered issues in private collections, particularly CCAP, a few short runs in various libraries, and copies included in diplomatic despatches.

66. No. 9 is dated Feb. 22, 1874. *Nación Paraguaya* (Jan. 14, 1874) wel-

comed its appearance with a warning to observe requirements of the state of siege.

67. The issue of March 11, 1875, is No. 16 and is enclosed in Gondim to Caravellas, 1ª Sec. No. 4 Conf., Asunción, March 12, 1875, MDBA-OR 201/1/13.

68. *El Fénix*, June 8, 1873.

69. *El Imparcial*, Aug. 24, 1873.

70. Its beginning was noted in Callado to Cotegipe, 1ª Sec. No. 2 Conf., Asunción, July 7, 1876, MDBA-OR 201/1/14. Scattered copies are in CCAP.

71. *Los Debates*, Aug. 13, 1876. Another venture in 1874 was *La Patria*, which endured until its editor, the Spaniard Francisco Martínez, was killed in the Molas revolt of 1875. Martínez had been associated with *El Pueblo*.

72. Miranda to Albuquerque, 1ª Sec. No. 46, Asunción, Aug. 16, 1877, MDBA-OR 201/1/14.

73. Marcondes, "Viagem ao Paraguay," p. 30.

74. *La Regeneración*, Nov. 10, 1869. The Escuela Central de Niñas opened Nov. 1 under the direction of Doña Asunción Escalada, wife of Jaime Sosa (*La Regeneración*, Oct. 14, 1869). She remained with the Escuela Central a short time, then opened a private school, which she conducted until 1875. Doña Asunción shared her husband's exile in Buenos Aires and died there on Dec. 11, 1894 (Centurión, *Historia de las letras paraguayas*, II, 42); Luís G. Benítez, *Historia cultural, reseña de su evolución en el Paraguay*, p. 208.

75. *La Regeneración*, Oct. 28 and Nov. 10, 1869.

76. Ibid., Nov. 10, 1869.

77. Ibid., Nov. 28, 1869.

78. Decree of March 7, 1870, *Registro oficial, 1869–1875*, pp. 58–60; *La Regeneración*, April 1, 1870.

79. Benítez, *Historia cultural*, pp. 253–255.

80. *La Regeneración*, April 13 and Sept. 16, 1870.

81. Act of Aug. 13, 1872, *Registro oficial, 1869–1875*, p. 335.

82. Ibid., pp. 316–317, 376–386.

83. "Memoria del ministerio de justicia, culto e instrucción pública," June 26, 1876, *Los Debates*, Aug. 2, 1876.

84. *Mensaje presentada por el poder ejecutivo al congreso de la nación en la apertura de sus sesiones del octavo periodo legislativo.*

85. *El Pueblo*, Dec. 1 and 7, 1870.

86. Tenure as director was brief. Changes may be followed in *Registro oficial, 1869–1875*, p. 517, and Centurión, *Historia de las letras paraguayas*, II, 69–70. A normal school became part of the colegio in 1874 (Decree of Oct. 31, 1874), *Registro oficial, 1869–1875*, p. 602).

87. The funding was provided by the act of Jan. 4, 1877 (*Registro oficial*, 1877, pp. 192, 210, 216).

88. Cecilio Báez, *Cuadros históricos y descriptivos*, p. 237; Diputados, *Actas*, May 30, 1879, p. 451.

89. Centurión, *Historia de las letras paraguayas*, II, 91–92. The law of Aug. 21, 1879, authorized paying the expenses of four young men to study at the Colegio Pio Latino Americano de Roma (*Registro oficial*, 1879, pp. 541–542).

90. *La Regeneración*, Nov. 26, 1869.

91. Centurión, *Historia de las letras paraguayas*, II, 14.

92. Decree of Jan. 17, 1875, *Registro oficial, 1869–1875*, pp. 686–694.

93. Forgues, "Le Paraguay," p. 399.

94. *La Regeneración*, Oct. 7 and Nov. 10, 1869, Feb. 9, 11, and 15, 1870.

95. *El Paraguay*, May 24 and 28, 1870.

96. *La Regeneración*, Aug. 10, 1870; italics in original.

97. *Registro oficial, 1869–1875*, pp. 424–428. These decrees were written in-to law on Feb. 27, 1873.

98. Maíz, *Etapas de mi vida. Contestación a las imposturas de Juan Silvano Godoy*, p. 11.

99. Ibid., pp. 1–74. Maíz returned to Asunción on Dec. 5, 1870.

100. Ibid., p. 80. Duarte was also acting outside of ecclesiastical authority, since he was not restored to priestly functions until April, 1873 (*El Progreso*, April 9, 1873).

101. *El Pueblo*, March 19, 1871.

102. Rio Branco to the Emperor, At Court, July 15, 1871, *Anuário do Museu Imperial* 12 (1951): 50.

103. M. M., "Paraguay, 25 de noviembre de 1882, *Revista del Paraguay* 2 (1892): 425; *Nación Paraguaya*, Aug. 15, 1873. Moreno took office on Sept. 22, 1873, and was recognized by presidential decree on Oct. 28 (*Registro oficial, 1869–1875*, pp. 483–484; Maíz, *Etapas de mi vida*, p. 84). He had been appointed priest of the parish of Barrero Grande, Caraguatay, and Piribebuy on Sept. 22, 1869 (*Registro oficial, 1869–1875*, p. 48).

104. Maíz made Becchis his secretary (Maíz, *Etapas de mi vida*, pp. 88–89); *Boletin oficial*, June 11, 1874, pp. 96–97; Miguel Ferrini to Maíz, Rio de Janeiro, Nov. 16, 1874, Maíz, *Etapas de mi vida*, p. 110.

105. Gondim to Caravellas, 1ª Sec. No. 6, Asunción, June 14, 1874, MDBA-OR 201/1/12; Caravellas to Gondim, 1ª Sec. No. 2 Conf., Rio de Janeiro, June 30, 1874, MDBA-DI 201/4/8.

106. Uriarte to Gill, London, Dec. 24, 1874, GP-CCAP.

107. Gondim to Caravellas, 1ª Sec. No. 1 Conf., Asunción, Jan. 28, 1875, MDBA-OR 201/1/13. Caravellas was pleased to see Becchis go, for the priest had been a center of opposition among the clergy (Caravellas to Gondim, 1ª Sec. No. 2 Conf., Rio de Janeiro, Feb. 22, 1875, MDBA-DI 201/4/8).

108. Maíz, *Etapas de mi vida*, pp. 139–142; Riveros, appointed on Dec. 13, 1877, was parish priest of San Lorenzo de Campo Grande. See also *Memoria del ministerio de relaciones exteriores presentada al congreso legislativo en el año de 1879*, p. 3; Vasconcellos to Albuquerque, Sec. Cen. No. 38, Asunción, Dec. 26, 1877, MDBA-OR 201/1/14.

109. *La Reforma*, May 1, 1879. The Senate approved Aponte's nomination on May 3 (*Registro oficial*, 1879, p. 49); Vasconcellos to Moreira de Barros, Sec. Cen. No. 46, Asunción, Oct. 19, 1879, MDBA-OR 201/1/15; *La Reforma*, Oct. 12, 1879; Maíz, *Etapas de mi vida*, p. 144.

Chapter 10: Jovellanos and the Plots of 1872–1873

1. H[ipólito] Sánchez Quell, *Proyección del General Caballero en la ruta de la patria*, p. 28.

2. M. M., "Paraguay, 25 de noviembre de 1882," *Revista del Paraguay*, 2 (1892): 275.

3. García Mellid, *Proceso*, II, 360.

4. M. M., "Paraguay, 25 de noviembre de 1882," *Revista del Paraguay* 2 (1892): 311.

5. Caballero died on Feb. 26, 1912. A good sketch of Caballero and summary of Coloradismo in action is Bray, *Hombres y épocas del Paraguay*, I, 93–107. A very scathing characterization is in M. M., "Paraguay, 25 de noviembre de 1882," *Revista del Paraguay* 2 (1892) and 3 (1893). See also Efraím Cardozo, *Efemérides de la historia del Paraguay*, pp. 84–85.

6. Walter R. Seymour to F. R. St. John, Asunción, July 8, 1873, encl., St. John to Granville, No. 46, Buenos Aires, July 18, 1873, PRO-FO 6/314.

7. Godoi, "El gobierno provisorio," *El Barón de Río Branco*, p. 262; Bray, *Hombres y épocas del Paraguay*, II, 125–162.

8. Seymour to St. John, Asunción, July 8, 1873, encl., St. John to Granville, No. 46, Buenos Aires, July 18, 1873, PRO-FO 6/314.

9. Ricardo Brugada, *Política paraguaya. Benigno Ferreira*, p. 7.

10. It was Bareiro who had hired Alberto Hans, Felix Aucaigne, and Charles Expilly as propagandists. Benites paid them off in 1872.

11. Seymour to St. John, Asunción, July 8, 1873, encl., St. John to Granville, No. 46, Buenos Aires, July 18, 1873, PRO-FO 6/314.

12. Benítez, "La convención paraguaya de 1870," in *IIº Congreso Internacional de Historia de América*, IV, 67.

13. M. M., "Paraguay, 25 de noviembre de 1882," *Revista del Paraguay* 3 (1893): 35.

14. Guimarães to Cotegipe, Asunción, Feb. 21, 1872, CBC 29/17; Guimarães to Rio Branco, March 6, 1872, CBC 53/40; Cotegipe to Guimarães, Rio de Janeiro, March 21, 1872, CBC 29/22.

15. Brizuela to Cotegipe, Montevideo, April 2, 1872, CBC 11/15.

16. Guimarães to Cotegipe, Asunción, April 23, 1872, CBC 29/23; Cotegipe to Jovellanos, Bahia, June 14, 1872, CBC 30/140.

17. Brizuela to Cotegipe, Asunción, June 1, 1872, CBC 11/16; Guimarães to Cotegipe, Asunción, May [28?], 1872, CBC 29/24.

18. Brizuela to Cotegipe, Asunción, June 1, 1872, CBC 11/16.

19. Id. to id., Asunción, June 5 and 6, 1872, CBC 11/16 and 11/17.

20. Id. to id., Asunción, June 21, 1872, CBC 11/19; Guimarães to Cotegipe, Asunción, June 23, 1872, CBC 29/27.

21. Azambuja to Correia, Buenos Aires, July 25, 1872, MDBA-OR 201/1/10; Correia to Azambuja, 1ª Sec. No. 9, Rio de Janeiro, July 30, 1872, MDBA-DI 201/4/7.

22. Azambuja to Correia, Buenos Aires, July 25, 1872, MDBA-OR 201/1/10.

23. Azambuja to Correia, 1ª Sec. No. 3, Asunción, Aug. 3, 1872, ibid. The Boundary Commission (Commissão Mixta de Limites entre Brasil e o Paraguai) began its work on Sept. 13, 1872, with Brazil's Col. Rufino Enéas Gustavo Galvão as chairman, and completed its task in October 1874 (Falcón to Azambuja, No. 336, Asunción, Sept. 11, 1872, encl., Azambuja to Correia, 1ª Sec. No. 13, Asunción, Sept. 11, 1872, ibid.; Galvão to Gondim, No. 434, Asunción, Oct. 29, 1874, MDBA-OR 201/1/12.

24. Azambuja to Correia, 1ª Sec. No. 1 Conf., Asunción, Aug. 16, 1872, MDBA-OR 201/1/10.

25. Ibid.

26. Azambuja to Correia, 1ª Sec. No. 3, Asunción, Sept. 5, 1872, ibid. Unfortunately, Azambuja tried to interfere in internal affairs. He wanted, for

example, to name justices for the Superior Tribunal, but Jovellanos avoided this effort (Guimarães to Cotegipe, Asunción, Sept. 27, 1872, CBA 29/32).

27. Azambuja to Correia, 1ª Sec. No. 18, Asunción, Sept. 18, 1872, MDBA-OR 201/1/10; id. to id., 1ª Sec. Res. No. 4, Asunción, Sept. 18, 1872, and encl., Gill to Azambuja, Montevideo, Sept. 9, 1872, ibid.

28. Correia to Azambuja, Sec. Cen. No. 3 Conf., Rio de Janeiro, Sept. 20, 1872, MDBA-DI 201/4/8.

29. Azambuja to Correia, Sec. Cen. Res. No. 5, Asunción, Sept. 25, 1872, MDBA-OR 201/1/10.

30. Azambuja to Correia, 1ª Sec. No. ,21, Sept. 19, 1872, ibid.; Rivarola, "Manifiesto a mis conciudadanos," Asunción, Sept. 5, 1872, encl., ibid.

31. Gill to Azambuja, Montevideo, Oct. 1 and 5, 1872, encls., Azambuja to Correia, Sec. Cen. Res. No. 15, Asunción, Oct. 14, 1872, ibid.; Gill to Cotegipe, Montevideo, Oct. 1, 1872, CBC 25/140.

32. Azambuja to Correia, Sec. Cen. Res. No. 11, Asunción, Sept. 24, 1872; Sec. Cen. Res. No. 15, Asunción, Oct. 14, 1872, and Sec. Cen. Conf. No. 3, Asunción, Oct. 18, 1872, MDBA-OR 201/1/10. Argentina had 200 troops in Asunción; the Paraguayan "army" had 400 men.

33. Correia to Azambuja, 1ª Sec. No. 9 Res., Rio de Janeiro, Oct. 23, 1872, MDBA-DI 201/4/7.

34. Azambuja to Correia, Sec. Cen. Conf. No. 5, Asunción, Oct. 18, 1872, MDBA-OR 201/1/10; id. to id., Sec. Cen. Conf. No. 6, Asunción, Oct. 18, 1872, ibid. Guimarães complained that Azambuja, by meddling in internal affairs, was endangering Brazil's policy and that the editor of *Nación Paraguaya*, an enemy of Brazil, was a friend of Azambuja (Guimarães to Rio Branco, Asunción, Oct. 23, 1872, encl., Guimarães to Cotegipe, Asunción, Oct. 23, 1872, CBA 29/33).

35. Azambuja to Correia, Sec. Cen. Conf. No. 7, Asunción, Oct. 23, 1872, MDBA-OR 201/1/10. Rio Branco had authorized this subsidy in 1869 (Correia to Azambuja, 4ª Sec. No. 1, Rio de Janeiro, Sept. 25, 1872, MDBA-DI 201/4/8). *Nación Paraguaya*, Oct. 20, 1872, asserted that *El Derecho* was a Brazilian organ.

36. Decree of Oct. 28, 1872, *Registro oficial, 1869–1875*, pp. 367–368.

37. Azambuja to Correia, Sec. Cen. Res. No. 19, Asunción, Nov. 20, 1872, MDBA-OR 201/1/10; id. to id., 1ª Sec. Conf. No. 5, Asunción, Nov. 23, 1872, ibid.

38. Brizuela to Cotegipe, Montevideo, Dec. 5, 1872, CBC 11/22; id. to id., Asunción, Jan. 2, 1873, CBC 11/23; id. to id., Montevideo, Jan. 27, 1873, CBC 11/25. Brizuela left Asunción on Jan. 19, 1873.

39. Gill to Cotegipe, Montevideo, Jan. 2, 1872 [1873], CBC 23/138.

40. Guimarães to Cotegipe, Asunción, Jan. 15 and 25, 1873, CBC 29/38, 39; Jovellanos to Cotegipe, Asunción, Jan. 28, 1873, CBC 30/144.

41. Azambuja to Correia, 1ª Sec. Res. No. 3, Asunción, Feb. 9, 1873, MDBA-OR 201/1/11; Guimarães to Cotegipe, Asunción, Feb. 12, 1873, CBC 29/40; *Nación Paraguaya*, Feb. 2 and 4, 1873. Falcón had written a piece entitled "De la conquista del Paraguay por el tratado de alianza," which *Nación Paraguaya* planned to serialize.

42. Azambuja to Correia, Sec. Cen. No. 3 Res., Asunción, Feb. 19, 1873, MDBA-OR 201/1/11.

43. Rivarola, *Manifiesto del ciudadano Cirilo A. Rivarola al pueblo paraguayo*; hereafter, Rivarola, *Manifiesto, 1873.*

44. Teixeira de Macedo to Caravellas, 1ª Sec. No. 18, Asunción, March 9, 1873, MDBA-OR 201/1/11.

45. Rivarola, *Manifiesto, 1873*, pp. 12, 17.

Chapter 11: The Triumph of Juan Bautista Gill

1. This interpretation is strongly supported by Teixeira de Macedo to Caravellas, 1ª Sec. No. 19, Asunción, March 16, 1873, MDBA-OR 201/1/11.

2. Teixeira de Macedo to Caravellas, 1ª Sec. No. 26, Asunción, April 2, 1873, ibid.; *The Weekly Standard*, April 9, 1873.

3. Teixeira de Macedo to Caravellas, 1ª Sec. No. 4 Res., Asunción, March 25, 1873, MDBA-OR 201/1/11; Guimarães to Cotegipe, Asunción, March 27, 1873, CBC 29/43.

4. Encl. No. 6, Macedo de Teixeira to Caravellas, 1ª Sec. No. 4 Res., Asunción, March 25, 1873, MDBA-OR 201/1/11. *El Progreso*, a critical paper edited by Dr. Ramos Ferreira, equated the Gran Partido Nacional with Lopiztas (issue of March 30, 1873).

5. Teixeira de Macedo to Caravellas, 1ª Sec. No. 4 Res., Asunción, March 25, 1873, MDBA-OR 201/1/11.

6. M. M., "Paraguay, 25 de noviembre," *Revista del Paraguay* 2 (1892): 426–427; Teixeira de Macedo to Caravellas, 1ª Sec. No. 26, Asunción, April 2, 1873, MDBA-OR 201/1/11.

7. Mitre to Tejedor, Asunción, April 16, 1873, *La Nación* (Buenos Aires), May 16, 1873; Guimarães to Cotegipe, Conf., Asunción, April 12, 1873, CBC 29/44; Jovellanos to Cotegipe, Asunción, May 15, 1873, CBC 30/145; Rio Branco to the Emperor, at Court, April 22, 1873, *Anuário do Museu Imperial*, XII, 180.

8. Issues of April 2, 6, 9, 16, 27, 30 and May 4, 1873.

9. Guimarães to Cotegipe, Asunción, May 3, 1873, CBC 29/45.

10. Mitre accepted the appointment on March 5, 1873 (*Mensaje del presidente de la república al abrir las sesiones del congreso argentino. Mayo de 1873*, p. 25; Mitre to Tejedor, Asunción, April 16, 1873, *La Nación*, May 16, 1874).

11. Magalhães, later Visconde de Araguáia, was born in Rio de Janeiro on Aug. 13, 1811. He held diplomatic posts, including Turin and Rome, where he died on July 10, 1882 (Rio-Branco, *Efemérides brasileiras*).

12. St. John to Granville, No. 9 Conf., Buenos Aires, April 2, 1873, PRO-FO 59/35.

13. *El Progreso*, April 6, 9, and 16, 1873; *La Nación*, April 10, 1873; Guimarães to Cotegipe, Conf., April 12, 1873, CBC 29/44. Mitre's mission to Asunción is discussed in Zeballos, "Diplomacia desarmada, fracaso de las misiones Quintana y Mitre, en el Paraguay," pp. 107–134, 248–283.

14. Cárcano, *Guerra—Acción y reacción*, II, 740.

15. The protocol of May 7, 1873, as amended on June 4, carried these stipulations. All of the negotiations are reviewed in *Documentos oficiales sobre cuestiones de límites entre la República del Paraguay y la Argentina.* A copy is in NPL-NAUS 350/1.

16. Cárcano, *Guerra—Acción y reacción*, II, 750, 755; Fragoso, *A paz com o*

Paraguai, p. 294; *Documentos oficiales*. Mitre's correspondence with Tejedor and his memorandum on Argentine claims are in *La Nación*, May 17, 21, 23, and 27, 1874.

17. Araguáia to Mitre, Asunción, Sept. 5, 1873, *La Nación*, May 27, 1874.
18. Amaral Valente to Caravellas, Sec. Cen. No. 2 Conf., Asunción, Oct. 31, 1873, MDBA-OR 201/1/11; id. to id., Sec. Cen. No. 2 Res., Nov. 15, 1873, ibid. Both Mitre and Araguáia left Asunción during the first week of September. When Araguáia left, Amaral Valente was chargé until the arrival of Luiz Augusto de Padua Fleury on Sept. 19, 1873, who remained until Oct. 29, 1873, and Valente again became chargé (Padua Fleury to Caravellas, Sec. Cen. No. 1, Asunción, Sept. 23, 1873, ibid.; Valente to Caravellas, 1ª Sec. No. 8, Asunción, Dec. 5, 1873, ibid.).
19. West to Granville, No. 24, Buenos Aires, Dec. 16, 1873, PRO-FO 6/314; Mathew to Derby, No. 35 Conf., Rio de Janeiro, May 5, 1874, PRO-FO 13/497; Sarmiento's message to Congress, May 14, 1874, *The Standard*, May 15, 1874; *Nación Paraguaya*, Dec. 17, 1873; Gondim to Caravellas, 1ª Sec. No. 10, Asunción, Dec. 17, 1873, MDBA-OR 201/1/11; Caravellas to Gondim, 1ª Sec. No. 3, Rio de Janeiro, Jan. 7, 1874, MDBA-DI 201/4/8.
20. St. John to Granville, No. 15 Conf., Buenos Aires, April 28, 1873, PRO-FO 59/35.
21. *El Fénix*, May 14, 18, and 21, 1873.
22. Ibid., May 28 and June 6, 1873.
23. The English chargé in Buenos Aires gloomily predicted that no matter who won, English investors would never receive a penny of their money (Frederick R. St. John to Granville, No. 45, Buenos Aires, July 7, 1873, PRO-FO 6/314).
24. Rio Branco to the Emperor, At Court, May 27, 1873, *Anuário do Museu Imperial*, XII, 186. Apparently the munitions were to go on the *Taraguí*.
25. *El Fénix*, June 8, 1873; Mitre to Tejedor, Asunción, June 22, 1873, *La Nación*, July 5, 1873; *The Standard*, July 5, 1873.
26. Bareiro and Caballero to Mitre, Recoleta, June 17, 1873, encl., Mitre to Tejedor, Asunción, June 22, 1873, *La Nación*, July 5, 1873.
27. Casualties were light, the rebels losing 10 killed to the government's 4. Details are in Mitre to Tejedor, Asunción, June 22, 1873, *La Nación*, July 5, 1873; *The Standard*, July 7, 1873; M. M., "Paraguay, 25 de noviembre de 1882," *Revista del Paraguay* 2 (1892): 506–507. Francisco Soteras, Capt. Miguel Alfaro, Jaime Sosa Escalada, and Fulgencio Coronel defended the city with 200 men.
28. Decree of June 21, 1873, *Registro oficial, 1869–1875*, p. 444. One of the captives was Juan Silvano Godoy, who remained in prison until August 23, 1873 (*El Imparcial*, Aug. 24, 1873).
29. *Nación Paraguaya*, July 17 and 18, 1873. The captain of the port, José M. Centurión, reported Caballero's movements (Centurión to José del Rosario Miranda, Encarnación [on the Paraná], July 4, 1873, ibid.).
30. *The Weekly Standard*, July 9, 1873.
31. Ltr., Asunción, July 58 [28], 1873, ibid., Aug. 6, 1873. Jovellanos ended martial law on July 18 (*Nación Paraguaya*, July 20, 1873).
32. General Order of the Day, Quyindy, July 14, 1873, ibid., July 27, 1873. Brizuela, who arrived in Asunción on June 29, denounced the government as

corrupt and grossly incompetent (Brizuela to Cotegipe, Asunción, July 6, 1873, CBC 11/27).

33. *El Imparcial*, July 20, 1873.

34. See especially Cardozo, *Paraguay independiente*, pp. 275–276, and Freire Esteves, "Historia contemporánea," pp. 30 ff.

35. *La Pampa* (Buenos Aires), Oct. 9, 1873; *Nación Paraguaya*, Oct. 29, 1873.

36. Gill to Cotegipe, Montevideo, Oct. 1, 1873, CBC 25/143; Cotegipe to Gill, Bahia, Oct. 20, 1873, ibid.; Gill to Rio Branco, Montevideo, Oct. 30, 1873, MDBA-DI 201/4/7; Rio Branco to Gill, Rio de Janeiro, Nov. 13, 1873, ibid., 201/4/8.

37. Rio Branco to Cotegipe, Rio de Janeiro, Nov. 12, 1873, CBC 53/50.

38. Carlos Carneiro de Campos, third Viscount Caravelas, had taken office in 1871. Despatches carry the name as "Caravellas."

39. Caravellas to Amaral Valente, Sec. Cen. No. 5 Res., Rio de Janeiro, Oct. 21, 1873, MDBA-DI 201/4/8; Valente to Caravellas, Sec. Cen. No. 3 Res., Asunción, Nov. 29, 1873, MDBA-OR 201/1/11; Rivarola, Bareiro, Caballero, and Serrano to Gill, Nov. 17, 1873, GP-CCAP.

40. Valente to Caravellas, Sec. Cen. No. 4 Res., Asunción, Nov. 28, 1873, MDBA-OR 201/1/11; Caballero to Gill, Corrientes, Sept. 29 and Dec. 8 [?], 1873, GP-CCAP. Soteras left the cabinet on Dec. 9, 1873; Jaime Sosa followed him as Minister of Hacienda (*Nación Paraguaya*, Dec. 17, 1873).

41. Gondim to Caravellas, Sec. Cen. No. 4, Asunción, Jan. 14, 1874, MDBA-OR 201/1/12; Manoel Araújo Cortez to José da Costa Azevedo, Asunción, Jan. 26, 1874, encl., Gondim to Caravellas, 1ª Sec. No. 9, Asunción, Jan. 29, 1874, ibid.

42. Caravellas to Gondim, Sec. Cen. No. 11 Res., Rio de Janeiro, Dec. 17, 1873, MDBA-DI 201/4/8; Gondim to Caravellas, Sec. Cen. No. 9, Asunción, Dec. 9, 1873, MDBA-OR 201/1/11. Nevertheless, Caravellas continued to warn Jovellanos about the impending attack (Caravellas to Gondim, 1ª Sec. No. 41, Rio de Janeiro, Dec. 10, 1873, MDBA-DI 201/4/8).

43. Rio Branco to Caravellas, n. d., Rio de Janeiro, MDBA-DI 201/4/7; Caravellas to Gondim, Sec. Cen. No. 11 Res., Rio de Janeiro, Dec. 17, 1873, MDBA-DI 201/4/8.

44. Gondim to Caravellas, Sec. Cen. No. 6 Res., Asunción, Dec. 31, 1873, MDBA-OR 201/1/11; Escobar to Gill, Corrientes, Dec. 25, 1873, GP-CCAP.

45. Caballero's manifesto, "A bordo de la cañonera nacional Tebicuari, en las aguas de la Villa del Pilar. 31 Diciembre de 1873," encl., Gondim to Caravellas, Sec. Cen. Res. No. 4, Asunción, Jan. 14, 1874, MDBA-OR 201/1/12.

46. Gondim to Caravellas, 1ª Sec. No. 1, Asunción, Jan. 2, 1874, ibid.; Senadores, *Actas, 1874*, pp. 3–4; *Registro oficial, 1869–1875*, pp. 497–499; *Nación Paraguaya*, Jan. 6, 1874; Gondim to Caravellas, Sec. Cen. No. 5 Res., Asunción, Jan. 15, 1874, MDBA-OR 201/1/12, and Sec. Cen. No. 4, Asunción, Jan. 14, 1874, Sec. Cen. No. 1 Conf., Asunción, Jan. 28, 1874, 1ª Sec. No. 9, Asunción, Jan. 29, 1874, ibid.

47. Gondim to Caravellas, 1ª Sec. No. 5, Asunción, Jan. 15, 1874, ibid. The government had spent $f155,388.98 in June, 1873, as "war expenses" (*Nación Paraguaya*, July 4, 1873); Caravellas to Gondim, Sec. Cen. No. 4 Res., Rio de Janeiro, Jan. 25, 1874, MDBA-DI 201/4/8; Mathew to West, Petropolis, Feb. 10, 1874, PRO-FO 13/497.

48. The contrary view is ably expressed by Eduardo Aramburú, *Manifiesto al pueblo paraguayo*, p. 15.

49. Guimarães to Cotegipe, Conf., Asunción, Feb. 18, 1874, CBC 29/50.

50. Gondim to Caravellas, 1ª Sec. Conf. No. 2, Asunción, Feb. 19, 1874, MDBA-OR 201/1/12.

51. Caravellas to Gondim, Sec. Cen. No. 8 Conf., Rio de Janeiro, March 3, 1874, MDBA-DI 201/4/9, and Sec. Cen. No. 2 Conf., Rio de Janeiro, March 10, 1874, MDBA-DI 201/4/8.

52. Ltr., Asunción, Feb. 18, 1874, *La Nación* (Buenos Aires), Feb. 28, 1874; Harris Gaylord Warren, "Brazil's Paraguayan Policy, 1869–1876," *The Americas* 28 (April 1972): 388–406.

53. Gondim to Caravellas, 1ª Sec. No. 3 Conf., Asunción, March 3, 1874, MDBA-OR 201/1/12; *La Nación*, March 13, 1874; Gill to Cotegipe, Asunción, March 23, 1874, CBC 25/145.

54. Gondim to Caravellas, Sec. Cen. No. 4 Conf., Asunción, March 16, 1874, Sec. Cen. No. 7, Asunción, April 9, 1874, MDBA-OR 201/1/12; Barão de Jaguarão to Cotegipe, Asunción, April 16, 1874, CBC 29/52. Serrano became minister of interior, Caballero was demoted to justice, and Escobar became minister of war. To Emilio Gill went the post of jefe político de Asunción (Gill to Cotegipe, Asunción, April 8, 1874, CBC 25/146); *Boletín oficial de la nación*, April 9, 1874; Manuel Ávila, "La contra revolución de Molas en 1874: Remeniscencias," *Revista del Instituto Paraguayo*, Año III, Tomo I (1900): 114–128; Gondim to Cotegipe, Sec. Cen. No. 17 Res., Asunción, April 14, 1874, MDBA-OR 201/1/12; Jaguarão to Cotegipe, Conf., Asunción, May 21, 1874, CBC 29/53.

55. This move was completed on April 23, and Gondim reported that Sarmiento ordered it "in order to leave Paraguay the master of its own destiny" (Gondim to Caravellas, 1ª Sec. No. 24, Asunción, June 2, 1874, MDBA-OR 201/1/12).

56. *The Weekly Standard*, May 13, 1874, from *Courier de la Plata*.

57. *La Patria*, May 1, 1874.

58. Gondim to Caravellas, 1ª Sec. No. 21, Asunción, May 22, 1874, 1ª Sec. No. 25, Asunción, June 3, 1874, 1ª Sec. No. 30, Asunción, July 4, 1874, and 1ª Sec. No. 34, Asunción, Sept. 30, 1874, MDBA-OR 201/1/12; Jaguarão to Cotegipe, Asunción, July 3, 1874, CBC 29/55; Machaín to U.S. Secretary of State, Asunción, Nov. 27, 1874, NPL-NAUS 350/1.

Chapter 12: In the Toils of the Past

1. *Discurso pronunciado por el presidente electo en el acto de la jura ante el congreso legislativo de la nación*, Asunción, Nov. 25, 1874; *Boletín oficial de la nación*, Nov. 25, 1874; Gondim to Caravellas, 1ª Sec. No. 40, Asunción, Nov. 28, 1874, MDBA-OR 201/1/12.

2. *Boletín oficial de la nación*, Nov. 25, 1874; Bareiro replaced Emilio Gill in Hacienda on Oct. 14, 1875; José Urdapilleta replaced Serrano in Interior on Oct. 16, and Bernardo Valente became director of customs (*Registro oficial, 1869–1875*, p. 811).

3. The Saguier-Gill correspondence makes up the bulk of the Gill Papers.

4. Gondim to Caravellas, 1ª Sec. No. 11 Conf., Asunción, Dec. 14, 1874, MDBA-OR 201/1/12.

5. Message of Higinio Uriarte to Congress, *La Reforma*, April 30, 1876. Uriarte was acting president during Gill's tour of the interior.

6. Caldwell to Fish, Montevideo, Jan. 12, 1875, DPU-NAUS 128/4. Caldwell left Montevideo on the *Wasp* on Dec. 3, 1874, and was back in Montevideo on Dec. 23, having spent less than a week in Asunción.

7. Id. to id., Montevideo, March 16, 1875, ibid.

8. Gondim to Caravellas, Sec. Cen. No. 21 Res., Asunción, Aug. 23, 1874, and 1ª Sec. No. 11 Conf., Asunción, Dec. 14, 1874, MDBA-OR 201/1/12.

9. Gondim to Cotegipe, Sec. Cen. No. 4 Res., Asunción, Jan. 5, 1876, MDBA-OR 201/1/14. Neither paper appeared regularly. *Cabrión* began publication in 1874; *A Gazeta Brazileira* appeared early in 1875—No. 16 is dated March 11, 1875.

10. Gondim to Caravellas, 1ª Sec. No. 11 Conf., Asunción, Dec. 14, 1874, MDBA-OR 201/1/12.

11. Id. to id., Sec. Cen. No. 1 Conf., Asunción, March 12, 1875, MDBA-OR 201/1/13.

12. Gondim to Caravellas, 1ª Sec. No. 4 Conf., Asunción, March 12, 1875, ibid. Gondim was ordered to await the arrival of his successor.

13. Gondim to Caravellas, 1ª Sec. No. 5 Conf., Asunción, March 28, 1875, ibid.

14. *La Patria*, April 2, 1875.

15. Gondim to Caravellas, 1ª Sec. No. 7 Conf., Asunción, April 2, 1875, and Sec. Cen. No. 7, April 28, 1875, ibid.; Pereira Leal to Caravellas, 1ª Sec. No. 7, Asunción, May 25, 1875, ibid.

16. Pereira Leal to Caravellas, Sec. Cen. No. 2 Conf., Asunción, April 30, 1875, Sec. Cen. No. 4 Res., Asunción, May 15, 1875, and Sec. Cen. No. 5 Res., Asunción, June 7, 1875, ibid.; Saguier to Gill, Buenos Aires, April 20, May 26 and 27, and July 29, 1875, GP-CCAP; Gondim to Cotegipe, Sec. Cen. No. 1 Res., Asunción, Jan. 5, 1876, MDBA-OR 201/1/14. Gondim had returned to Paraguay on Dec. 31, 1875, to replace Pereira Leal.

17. Pereira Leal to Cotegipe, Asunción, Aug. 23 and 30, 1875, CBC 32/75, 76.

18. Ramón Zubizarreta, "La cuestión de la moneda," *Revista del Instituto Paraguayo* 11 (1904): 125.

19. West, "Report, 1875"; "Memoria sobre la hacienda pública de la república del Paraguay durante el año de 1876," *La Reforma*, Sept. 8, 1876; Saguier to Gill, Buenos Aires, July 25, 1875, GP-CCAP.

20. One may assume that this loan was in the new Argentine pesos authorized in 1875.

21. Carlos Pastore, *La lucha por la tierra en el Paraguay*, pp. 168 ff.

22. The yearly figures are 1870, $100,000; 1871, $180,000; 1872, $265,000; and 1873, $385,000 (West, "Report, 1875"). The internal debt in 1872 was about $924,275. See also Azambuja to Correia, 2ª Sec. No. 2, Asunción, Oct. 29, 1872, MDBA-OR 201/1/10; *Registro oficial, 1869–1875*, pp. 276–286.

23. Two irreconcilable figures are available. West reported revenues of about $285,560 and expenditures of $767,430 in 1873 ("Report, 1875"), while *La Nación* (Aug. 19, 1874) listed receipts as $514,106. Neither West nor *La Nación* included the £125,000 in gold received in June 1873, nor did Jovellanos ever give an acceptable accounting of its disposition.

24. *La Nación*, Aug. 18, 1874, gives total customs receipts as $430,000, a fig-

ure higher than that reported by West. The June 1873 duties were $f34,875 and fell to $f32,419 in Dec. (*Nación Paraguaya*, July 4, 1873, and Jan. 6, 1874). Statistics for the postwar decade are incomplete and unreliable.

25. *La Nación*, Aug. 18, 1874. In addition to other measures against Benites, the government seized and sold his personal library (ibid., Sept. 2, 1874).

26. *Registro oficial, 1869–1875*, p. 584; Zubizarreta, "La cuestión de la moneda," pp. 129–131.

27. Pereira Leal to Cotegipe, 1ª Sec. No. 9, Asunción, July 28, 1875, MDBA-OR 201/1/13. Gonçalves was a beneficiary of the London loans, having received £10,000 in payment for weapons he never delivered. Segovia's advances to the "Lincolnshire farmers" were repaid in Caballero's regime.

28. *Registro oficial, 1869–1875*, pp. 621–632. Senators and deputies were to receive $f200 monthly, ministers $f400, and the President $f1,000.

29. *El Nacional* (Buenos Aires), May 7, 1875. The bonds were to be retired at the rate of $f37,500 annually, with interest and principal to be paid in metal in Paraguay and in gold abroad. (*Registro oficial, 1869–1875*, pp. 690–692; *Estrato del Boletín oficial. Leyes de finanzas sancionadas por el honorable congreso en las sesiones estraordinarias*, pp. 1–3, hereafter, *Boletín oficial, finanzas, 1875*).

30. *Registro oficial, 1869–1875*, pp. 725–726; *Boletín oficial, finanzas, 1875*, pp. 4–5.

31. Acts of Jan. 20 and 21, 1875, ibid., pp. 3–4.

32. Gondim to Caravellas, 1ª Sec. No. 1, Asunción, Jan. 13, 1875, MDBA-OR 201/1/13.

33. Id. to id., 1ª Sec. No. 3, Asunción, Jan. 30, 1875, ibid.

34. Saguier to Gill, Buenos Aires, March 11, 1875, GP-CCAP; *El Nacional* (Buenos Aires), May 7, 1875; *La Nación* (Buenos Aires), March 31, 1875.

35. *Registro oficial, 1869–1875*, pp. 750–752; West, "Report, 1875"; Pereira Leal to Cotegipe, 1ª Sec. No. 9, Asunción, July 28, 1875, MDBA-OR 201/1/13. The paper money law authorized fractional paper currency of 5¢, 10¢, and 20¢ as well as peso notes of various denominations. Pedro Gill was appointed Paraguayan agent in Buenos Aires to dispose of the tobacco, and three government officials were to liquidate the Asociación (Decree of May 29, 1875, *Registro oficial, 1869–1875*, p. 767).

36. Caldwell to Fish, Montevideo, March 16, 1876, DPU-NAUS 128/4; *El Nacional*, May 7, 1875; Saguier to Gill, Buenos Aires, May 11 and 12, 1875, GP-CCAP; Pereira Leal to Cotegipe, Asunción, Oct. 2, 1875, CBC 32/79.

37. *La Nación*, July 8 and Aug. 11, 1875; *Registro oficial, 1869–1875*, pp. 792, 798. The modifying decree was dated Sept. 4, 1875.

38. Saguier to Gill, Buenos Aires, Aug. 13, 21, 25, and 29, 1875, GP-CCAP.

39. Gill's message of Oct. 5, 1875, is encl. Pereira Leal to Cotegipe, Sec. Cen. No. 12, Asunción, Oct. 6, 1875, MDBA-OR 201/1/13; cabinet changes are detailed in López Decoud, *Album gráfico*, p. 216.

40. The act of Oct. 21, 1875, formally repealed the monopolies (*Registro oficial, 1869–1875*, p. 816); the January laws were repealed on Oct. 27; the land sales act was dated Nov. 3, 1875.

41. West, "Report, 1875"; Calzada, *Rasgos biográficos*, pp. 36–37; *La República* (Buenos Aires), Dec. 17, 1875.

42. Azambuja to Correia, 1ª Sec. No. 8, Asunción, Aug. 27, 1872, MDBA-OR 201/1/10.

43. Caravellas to Gondim, Sec. Cen. No. 6 Res., Rio de Janeiro, Feb. 6, 1874, and Sec. Cen. No. 11 Res., Rio de Janeiro, Feb. 17, 1874, MDBA-DI 201/4/9. Benites sailed for Montevideo on the *Bonifacio*.

44. Gondim to Caravellas, 1ª Sec. No. 5, Asunción, May 22, 1874, MDBA-OR 201/1/12; *Boletín oficial de la nación*, May 21, 1874; *La Libertad*, May 4 and 5, 1874. Burrell and Valpy claimed damages and back pay from the López era.

45. Gondim to Caravellas, 1ª Sec. No. 5, Asunción, May 22, 1874, MDBA-OR 201/1/12; Benites, *Las imposturas de Juan Bautista Gill*; Benítez, *Manifiesto*.

46. Gondim to Caravellas, 1ª Sec. No. 5, Asunción, May 22, 1874, MDBA-OR 201/1/12. The confession of May 18 is enclosed.

47. Id. to id., 1ª Sec. No. 29, Asunción, July 4, 1874, ibid.

48. Vedia to Gainza, Villa Occidental, May 29, 1874, Gainza Papers, AGN-BA.

49. Gondim to Caravellas, Sec. Cen. No. 1 Conf., Asunción, March 12, 1875, MDBA-OR 201/1/13; Caravellas to Gondim, Sec. Cen. No. 10 Conf., Rio de Janeiro, Feb. 24, 1875, MDBA-DI 201/4/9; Pereira Leal to Cotegipe, Sec. Cen. No. 10, Asunción, July 30, 1875, MDBA-OR 201/1/13.

50. The Senate authorized the mission on July 7, 1874 (Senadores, *Actas, 1874*, pp. 24–25). The three men left Asunción on July 13, 1874, stopped over in Rio de Janeiro from July 29 to Sept. 23, and reached London in October. Although anxious to leave much sooner, they did not return until Dec. 18, 1875 (Uriarte to Gill, July 13, 21, 23, 29, Aug. 2, Sept. 23, 1874, and Dec. 18, 1875, GP-CCAP). Gill gave them a letter of introduction to Cotegipe, stating that Caballero wanted to express personally his sympathies for Brazil (Gill to Cotegipe, Asunción, July 3, 1874, CBC 25/147).

51. Terrero to Gill, London, July 11 and 14, 1874, GP-CCAP.

52. Uriarte to Gill, London, Nov. 9, 1874, ibid.

53. Terrero to Gill, London, Nov. 22, 1874, ibid.

54. Uriarte to Gill, London, Nov. 24, 1874, ibid.

55. Id. to id., London, April 8, 1875, ibid.

56. Id. to id., London, May 8, 1875, ibid. This would be an order placed with the Stewarts of Galashiels before the Paraguayan War began.

57. Uriarte to Gill, London, Dec. 9 and 24, 1874, Jan. 25, Feb. 9 and 24, March 9 and 16, April 8 and 23, and May 8, 1875, ibid. Uriarte returned from Paris on April 3. He asked Gill to obtain the needed documents from Benites, but that was the end of the Paris matter.

58. Uriarte sued Luis Mons, seeking to recover excessive legal fees paid by Benites, but he made no progress. He refers to a favorable award against Terrero but gives no details (Uriarte to Gill, London, April 8 and 23, and May 8, 1875, GP-CCAP).

59. Caballero to Gill, London, April 23 and June 8, 1875, ibid.

60. Uriarte to Gill, London, June 8 and 23, July 8 and 23, 1875, ibid.

61. This agent could have been John Morris, who had been in Paraguay as early as 1852 (Juan F. Pérez Acosta, *Carlos Antonio López*, p. 368). See also Uriarte to Gill, London, July 10[?], 1875, and Caballero to Gill, London, Oct. 2, 1875, GP-CCAP.

62. Saguier to Gill, Buenos Aires, Dec. 9, 1875, ibid.

63. Decree of March 19, 1870, *Registro oficial, 1869–1875*, pp. 63–64.

64. Carlos Loizaga to Silva Paranhos, Asunción, March 28, 1870, and Silva Paranhos to Loizaga, Asunción, March 31, 1870, *La Regeneración*, April 3, 1870; Elisa A. Lynch, *Esposición y protesta que hace Elisa A. Lynch*, pp. 9–11; E. A. Lynch to editor of *La Regeneración*, Vapor Princesa, April 10, 1870, *La Regeneración*, April 13, 1870; Lynch, *Esposición*, pp. 11–12.

65. Quoted in *La Nación*, March 31, 1870. The charges are wildly exaggerated.

66. *La Regeneración*, May 11, 1870; *Registro oficial, 1869–1875*, pp. 76–78; Lynch, *Esposición*, pp. 14–15; MacDonnell to Clarendon, No. 48 Conf., Buenos Aires, April 29, 1870, and id. to id., Buenos Aires, April 30, 1870, PRO-FO 6/291. The Brazilians reported that Madame Lynch had $25,000 worth of jewels, $8,000 in gold, and £13,000 on deposit in the Bank of England. Shortly after her capture, Cotegipe, in answering a query of Pedro II, reported that Madame Lynch had been treated with the courtesy due her sex, but he would have preferred that she be set free in Montevideo (Wanderley Pinho, *Cartas do Imperador D. Pedro II ao Barão de Cotegipe*, p. 233); see also Lynch to Cotegipe, On board the "City of Limerick," Rio de Janeiro, June 22, 1870, CBC 26/1.

67. Lynch, *Esposición*, pp. 15–21.

68. The attack occurred on July 21, 1872. A Brazilian, João Mendisco, was also killed (Azambuja to Correia, Sec. Cen. No. 9, Asunción, Aug. 28, 1872, and id. to id., Sec. Cen. No. 22, Asunción, Sept. 24, 1872, MDBA-OR 201/1/11; *La Regeneración*, May 15, 1870; St. John to Granville, No. 3 Conf., Buenos Aires, Jan. 22, 1873, PRO-FO 6/314); *Registro oficial, 1869–1875*, pp. 390–391. Forgues, "Le Paraguay," p. 386, calls Berchon a usurer.

69. Lynch, *Esposición*, p. 5.

70. Gill to Lynch, Montevideo, Aug. 29, 1872, ibid., p. 26; Gill to Elisa A. Lynch López, Asunción, March 23, 1874, ibid., pp. 26–27. Madame Lynch never signed herself "Lynch López."

71. Gill to Lynch, Asunción, July 11, 1874, ibid., pp. 27–28; italics in source.

72. West to Mrs. Lynch, Buenos Aires, July 22, 1875, encl., West to Derby, No. 115, Buenos Aires, Nov. 8, 1875, PRO-FO 6/328.

73. Gill to Elisa A. Lynch López, Asunción, July 22, 1875, Lynch, *Esposición*, pp. 28–29.

74. Id. to id., Asunción, Aug. 17, 1875, ibid., pp. 29–30.

75. Saguier to Gill, Buenos Aires, July 29, 1875, GP-CCAP.

76. West to Derby, No. 115, Buenos Aires, Nov. 8, 1875, PRO-FO 6/328; *La Nación*, Oct. 21, 1875; Lynch, *Esposición*, p. 36.

77. *La Nación*, Oct. 28, 1875.

78. The tramway began to operate on Jan. 19, 1873 (Guimarães to Cotegipe, Asunción, Jan. 15, 1873, CBC 29/38). Guimarães often included in a letter events that occurred after the letter's date.

79. Lynch, *Esposición*, p. 37.

80. Ibid., p. 39.

81. For the petition, see ibid., p. 47; *La Nación*, Oct. 30, 1875; encl., Pereira Leal to Cotegipe, 1ª Sec. No. 12, Asunción, Oct. 26, 1875, MDBA-OR 201/1/13. Authorship of the petition has not been determined.

82. Pereira Leal to Cotegipe, 1ª Sec. No. 12, Asunción, Oct. 26, 1875, MDBA-OR 201/1/13; Lynch, *Esposición*, pp. 38–43; West to Derby, No. 115, Buenos Aires, Nov. 8, 1875, PRO-FO 6/328.

83. Lynch, *Esposición*, pp. 49–51.
84. Saguier to Gill, Buenos Aires, Nov. 6, 1875, GP-CCAP.
85. Bray, *Hombres y épocas del Paraguay*, II, 121–122.

Chapter 13: Diplomacy and Revolution, 1875–1876

1. Acta de 24 de Janeiro de 1874, Actas do Conselho de Estado, 107/7, pp. 32–37a, AN-RJ; *Memoria del ministerio de relaciones exteriores presentada al congreso nacional en 1874*, pp. v–vii; Caravellas to Gondim, Sec. Cen. No. 19 Res., Rio de Janeiro, June 19, 1874, MDBA-DI 201/4/8.
2. Gondim to Caravellas, Sec. Cen. No. 19 Res., Asunción, Aug. 21, 1874, MDBA-OR 201/1/12.
3. Uriarte to Gill, Rio de Janeiro, Sept. 23, 1874, GP-CCAP.
4. Gondim to Caravellas, Sec. Cen. No. 18 Res., Asunción, July 19, 1874, MDBA-OR 201/1/12. Caravellas instructed Gondim to impress upon Gill the need for negotiating a definitive treaty with Argentina (Caravellas to Gondim, Sec. Cen. No. 20 Res., Rio de Janeiro, July 27, 1874, MDBA-DI 201/4/8).
5. Gondim thought that this was proof that Serrano was not, as rumor insisted, "a confirmed and irreconcilable enemy of the Empire." (Gondim to Caravellas, Sec. Cen. No. 19 Res., Asunción, Aug. 21, 1874, MDBA-OR 201/1/12). Gondim sent Sosa to Rio de Janeiro on the Brazilian transport *Madeira*, departing Asunción on Aug. 12. In Rio de Janeiro, Sosa had little to do while waiting for Tejedor (Caravellas to Gondim, Sec. Cen. No. 28 Res., Rio de Janeiro, Nov. 7, 1874, MDBA-DI 201/4/8).
6. Sinforiano Alcorta, *Antecedentes históricos sobre los tratados con el Paraguay*, p. 11.
7. Gondim to Luiz Augusto de Padua Fleury, Asunción, Aug. 21, 1874, encl., Gondim to Caravellas, Sec. Cen. No. 19 Res., Asunción, Aug. 21, 1874, MDBA-OR 201/1/12; Tejedor to Padua Fleury, Buenos Aires, Sept. 24, 1874, Félix Farías Papers, AGN-BA; Gondim to Caravellas, Sec. Cen. No. 23 Res., Asunción, Aug. 22, 1874, MDBA-OR 201/1/12.
8. Uriarte to Gill, Rio de Janeiro, Sept. 23, 1874, GP-CCAP.
9. See Gill's instructions to Higinio Uriarte, Asunción, July 31, 1874, in Jaime Sosa, *Negociaciones diplomáticas entre el Brasil, la República Argentina y el Paraguay. Misión del ciudadano paraguayo Jaime Sosa á Rio [de] Janeiro*, pp. 6–7; Fragoso, *A paz com o Paraguai*, pp. 311 ff.
10. Quoted by Sosa, *Negociaciones*, p. 8. Brizuela assured Cotegipe that Jovellanos's letter was written later in Buenos Aires by request (Brizuela to Cotegipe, Montevideo, Dec. 27, 1875, CBC 11/31).
11. Sosa, *Negociaciones*. Sosa's mission is described in Ernesto Quesada, *Historia diplomática nacional: La política argentina-paraguaya*; Joaquim Nabuco, *Um estadista do imperio*, III, 349 ff.; and Cárcano, *Guerra—Acción y reacción*, II, 781–795.
12. Rio Branco to the Emperor, At Court, May 11, 1875, *Anuário do Museu Imperial*, XII, 142–143. Rio Branco suspected that terms of the treaty had been agreed to in Buenos Aires before Sosa and Tejedor arrived in Brazil (id. to id., At Court, June 1, 1875, ibid., XII, 151).
13. The area assigned to Villa Occidental was a strip four leagues in depth running south from the Arroyo Verde, a small stream that flows into the Paraguay about five miles north of Villa Occidental, to the Pilcomayo. Atajo, or

Cerrito Island, was to be Argentine; the islands of Apipé and Yacyretá in the Paraná west of Encarnación went to Paraguay. Argentina surrendered any claims to war indemnities; individuals had one year in which to submit claims to a mixed commission (Benítez, *Historia diplomática del Paraguay*, pp. 265–266; Amarilla Fretes, *Liquidación*, pp. 107–109; Báez, *Cuadros históricos y descriptivos*, pp. 234–235).

14. Rio Branco to the Emperor, At Court, May 28, 1875, *Anuário do Museu Imperial*, XII, 147–148.

15. Sosa to Minister of Foreign Affairs, Rio de Janeiro, May 30, 1875, Sosa, *Negociaciones*, pp. 83–93.

16. Amarilla Fretes, *Liquidación*, 109.

17. Rio Branco to the Emperor, At Court, May 28, 1875, *Anuário do Museu Imperial*, XII, 147–148; id. to id., At Court, May 31, 1875, ibid., XII, 150.

18. Caravellas to Legation in Paraguay, Sec. Cen. No. 8 Res., Rio de Janeiro, June 1, 1875, MDBA-DI 201/4/8; Cotegipe to Gondim, Sec. Cen. No. 13 Res., Rio de Janeiro, June 9, 1875, MDBA-DI 201/4/9; Francisco Xavier da Costa Aguiar de Andrade to Pereira Leal, Conf., Montevideo, June 7, 1875, encl. No. 1, Pereira Leal to Caravellas, Sec. Cen. No. 7, Asunción, June 7, 1875, MDBA-OR 201/1/13; Actas Reservadas do Conselho de Estado, June 11, 1875, pp. 1–14a, AN-RJ. A copy of Caravellas's memorandum of May 31 to the Council describing the Sosa-Tejedor negotiations is in GP-DD, Doc. 55, 547/22 AN-RJ.

19. Pereira Leal to Caravellas, Sec. Cen. No. 7 Res., Asunción, June 19, 1875, MDBA-OR 201/1/13; *Registro oficial, 1869–1875*, pp. 773–774. The Chamber of Deputies expelled Sosa and branded him a traitor on June 28 (Diputados, *Actas, 1875*, p. 165).

20. Pereira Leal to Caravellas, Sec. Cen. No. 7 Res., Asunción, June 19, 1875, MDBA-OR 201/1/13. Machaín left on the *Braconnot* on June 21, and Emilio Gill took over as minister of foreign affairs ad interim (id. to id., 4ª Sec. No. 35, Asunción, June 21, 1875, ibid.). Several months earlier, Gill had expressed to Cotegipe his hope that Paraguay would benefit from Brazil's protection in negotiations with Argentina (Gill to Cotegipe, Conf., Asunción, Jan. 23, 1875, CBC 25/149).

21. Pereira Leal to Caravellas, Sec. Cen. Res. No. 6, Asunción, June 19, 1875, MDBA-OR 201/1/13. After consulting with the naval commander, Barão da Passagem, and General Mesquita, Pereira Leal sent the *Jaurú* to Corumbá for the artillery battalion (id. to id., Sec. Cen. Res. No. 8, Asunción, June 23, 1875, ibid.). The *Jaurú* belonged to the Companhia de Navegação do Alto Paraguay.

22. Rocha to Avellaneda, Buenos Aires, June 14, 1875, cited by Cárcano, *Guerra—Acción y reacción*, II, 798–805.

23. Pereira Leal to Caravellas, Sec. Cen. No. 9 Res., Asunción, June 30, 1875, MDBA-OR 201/1/13; Cotegipe to Pereira Leal, Sec. Cen. No. 18 Res., Rio de Janeiro, Aug. 27, 1875, MDBA-OR 201/4/9.

24. Alcorta, *Antecedentes*, p. 146; Gondim to Cotegipe, Sec. Cen. No. 1 Res., Asunción, Jan. 5, 1876, MDBA-OR 201/1/14.

25. Machaín to Gill, Rio de Janiero, Oct. 1, 1875, GP-CCAP.

26. *Memoria del ministerio de relaciones exteriores presentada al congreso nacional en el año de 1876*, p. iv; Quesada, *Historia diplomática*, pp. 130–132.

334 Notes to Pages 250–255

27. Cárcano, *Guerra—Acción y reacción*, II, 816.

28. Ibid., II, 816–820 (Brazil's envoy was the minister in Montevideo, Francisco Javier da Costa Aguiar d'Andrada); Pereira Leal to Cotegipe, Asunción, Oct. 4, 1875, CBC 32/78; id. to id., Sec. Cen. No. 16 Conf., Asunción, Nov. 3, 1875, and Sec. Cen. No. 17 Conf., Asunción, Nov. 26, 1875, MDBA-OR 201/1/13.

29. Quesada, *Historia diplomática*, p. 2, calls it a "peregrino en bola, que desorientó a las cancellerías y precipitó la solución de la crisis."

30. Fleuiss, *História administrativa do Brasil*, p. 313. Caxias remained in power until Jan. 5, 1878 (Rio-Branco, *Efemérides brasileiras*, p. 300).

31. *El Nacional*, June 16, 1875; *La Nación*, July 8, 1875.

32. Pereira Leal to Cotegipe, 1ª Sec. No. 1 Res., Asunción, July 30, 1875, MDBA-OR 201/1/13.

33. West to Derby, No. 89 Conf., HMS *Cracker*, Asunción, Sept. 14, 1875, PRO-FO 6/327.

34. Saguier to Gill, Buenos Aires, May 11, June 9, 19, 25, 28, July 13, 25, and Sept. 10, 1875, GP-CCAP.

35. Pereira Leal to Cotegipe, Sec. Cen. No. 16 Conf., Asunción, Nov. 3, 1876, MDBA-OR 201/1/13; Brizuela to Cotegipe, Montevideo, Oct. 26, 1875, CBC 11/28.

36. Pereira Leal to Cotegipe, Sec. Cen. No. 13 Res., Asunción, Oct. 22, 1875, and Sec. Cen. No. 15 Conf., Asunción, Oct. 20, 1875, MDBA-OR 201/1/13.

37. Id. to id., Asunción, Nov. 14, 1875, CBC 32/83. Cotegipe, too, trusted none of the Paraguayans, "all of whom, more or less, have the same vices." Only Brazil's "interference had kept Paraguay from throwing itself into the arms of its ambitious neighbors" (Cotegipe to Pereira Leal, Conf., Rio de Janeiro, Nov. 12, 1875, ibid.).

38. Pereira Leal to Cotegipe, Asunción, Nov. 20, 1875, CBC 32/81.

39. Saguier to Gill, Buenos Aires, Oct. 27, 1875, GP-CCAP; Pereira Leal to Cotegipe, 1ª Sec. No. 14, Asunción, Oct. 28, 1875, MDBA-OR 201/1/13; *La Reforma*, Oct. 28, 1875.

40. Rivarola to a friend, Corrientes, June 27, 1875, encl., Pereira Leal to Cotegipe, Sec. Cen. No. 10, Asunción, July 8, 1875, MDBA-OR 201/1/13.

41. Rivarola saw Pereira Leal on Nov. 25, 1875 (id. to id., 1ª Sec. No. 17, Asunción, Nov. 24, 1875, and Sec. Cen. Conf. No. 18, Asunción, Nov. 24, 1875, ibid.).

42. Saguier to Gill, Buenos Aires, Nov. 9, 1875, GP-CCAP.

43. Pereira Leal to Cotegipe, 1ª Sec. No. 15, Asunción, Oct. 28, 1875, MDBA-OR 201/1/13; Brizuela to Cotegipe, Montevideo, Dec. 27, 1875, CBC 11/31; Saguier to Gill, Buenos Aires, Nov. 12, 1875, GP-CCAP. José Machaín received the appointment and sailed in March 1876 for the United States (Caldwell to Fish, No. 4, Montevideo, March 16, 1876, DPU-NAUS 128/4).

44. Pereira Leal to Cotegipe, 1ª Sec. No. 16, Asunción, Nov. 6, 1875, MDBA-OR 201/1/13; *La Reforma*, Nov. 6, 1875; *El Nacional*, Dec. 18, 1875; *Boletin oficial de la nación*, Dec. 9, 1875; Pereira Leal to Cotegipe, 1ª Sec. No. 2, Res., Asunción, Dec. 12, 1875, MDBA-OR 201/1/13; *Registro oficial, 1869–1875*, pp. 841–842; *La República*, Dec. 22, 1875; *La Reforma*, Dec. 10, 12, 14, and 17, 1875; *La Nación*, Dec. 21, 1875; *El Nacional*, Dec. 21, 1875; Gondim to Cotegipe, Sec. Cen. No. 2 Res., Asunción, Jan. 13, 1876, MDBA-OR 201/1/14.,

After Serrano's defeat, Argentina offered to send 500 Remington rifles, ammunition, and sabers if Gill needed them (Saguier to Gill, Buenos Aires, Jan. 12, 1876, GP-CCAP).

45. Brizuela to Cotegipe, Montevideo, Dec. 24, 1875, CBC 11/30; Uriarte to Gill, Buenos Aires, Dec. 13, 1875, GP-CCAP; Pereira Leal to Cotegipe, Sec. Cen. No. 3 Res., Asunción, Jan. 19, 1876, MDBA-OR 201/1/14; Caldwell to Fish, No. 2, Montevideo, March 16, 1876, DPU-NAUS 128/4.

46. Saguier to Gill, Buenos Aires, Aug. 4 and Nov. 7, 1875, GP-CCAP.

47. Cotegipe to Gondim, Sec. Cen. No. 18 Res., Rio de Janeiro, Nov. 13, 1875, MDBA-DI 201/4/9.

48. Ibid.

49. Cotegipe to Gondim, Rio de Janeiro, Nov. 13, 1875, CBC 24/157.

50. West to Derby, No. 8, Buenos Aires, Oct. 30, 1875, and No. 721 Conf., Buenos Aires, Nov. 22, 1875, PRO-FO 6/328.

51. Gondim to Cotegipe, Sec. Cen. No. 1 Res., Asunción, Jan. 5, 1876, MDBA-OR 201/1/14; Gill to Cotegipe, Asunción, Jan. 6, 1876, CBC 25/152. Pereira Leal took his leave on Dec. 31, 1875, the same day that Gondim arrived. Aceval had hurried back to Asunción a few days ahead of Gondim (Brizuela to Cotegipe, Montevideo, Dec. 27, 1875, CBC 11/31).

52. Gondim to Cotegipe, Sec. Cen. No. 1 Res., Asunción, Jan. 5, 1876, and Sec. Cen. No. 3 Res., Asunción, Jan. 19, 1876, MDBA-OR 201/1/14.

53. Freire Esteves, "Historia contemporánea," pp. 37–38.

54. Saguier to Gill, Buenos Aires, Jan. 4 and 12, 1876, DP-CCAP.

55. *La República* (Buenos Aires), March 28, 1885; Alcorta, *Antecedentes*, p. xl.

56. This went far beyond Saguier's assurance that Argentina would grant free importation of tobacco for ten years if Paraguay would submit all of the Chaco to arbitration (Saguier to Gill, Buenos Aires, Jan. 12, 1876, GP-CCAP).

57. The Machaín-Irigoyen treaties are available in *Colección de tratados celebrados por la República Argentina con las naciones extrangeras*, I, 69–88; *Memoria del ministerio de relaciones esteriores presentada al congreso nacional en el año 1877*, I, 69–89; hereafter *Memoria Argentina, 1877*; Senadores, *Actas 1874–1880*, pp. 124–155; West to Derby, No. 14, Buenos Aires, Feb. 9, 1876, PRO-FO 6/333; Amarilla Fretes, *El Paraguay en el primer cincuentenario del fallo arbitral del Presidente Hayes*, pp. 45–49. The Treaty of Friendship, Commerce and Navigation, also signed on Feb. 3, contained nothing exceptional (encl., St. John to Derby, Buenos Aires, Aug. 23, 1876, PRO-FO 6/335). The islands of Atajo and Apipé went to Argentina, Yacyretá to Paraguay.

58. *El Nacional*, Feb. 7, 1876; *La Reforma*, Dec. 7, 1875.

59. "Mensaje del presidente de la república al abrir las sesiones del congreso argentino, mayo de 1876," *Memoria Argentina, 1876*, pp. 15–16.

60. *La Reforma*, Feb. 7 and 8, 1876; *El Nacional*, Feb. 7, 1876.

61. Caldwell to Fish, Montevideo, March 16, 1876, DPU-NAUS 128/4.

62. Saguier to Gill, Buenos Aires, Feb. 15, 1876, GP-CCAP; Senadores, *Actas, 1874–1880*, pp. 124–125; *La Reforma*, Feb. 23, 1876.

63. Gondim to Cotegipe, Sec. Cen. No. 5 Res., Asunción, Feb. 13, 1876, MDBA-OR 201/1/14; Gill to Cotegipe, Asunción, Feb. 14, 1876, CBC 25/153; Cotegipe to Gondim, Conf., Rio de Janeiro, March 4, 1876, CBC 25/158.

64. *Memoria Argentina, 1876*, pp. vi–xi. Argentine ratification was com-

pleted on July 1 and exchange of ratifications occurred on Sept. 13, 1876 (*Memoria Argentina, 1877,* I, xxxiii).

65. José de Almeida e Vasconcellos to Albuquerque, Sec. Cen. No. 15, Asunción, Aug. 30, 1877, MDBA-OR 201/1/14; *Memoria de relaciones esteriores presentada al congreso nacional en el año 1878,* pp. 3–4. Vasconcellos had become chargé on Aug. 21, 1877.

Chapter 14: End of an Era

1. Saguier to Gill, Buenos Aires, July 29 and Aug. 4, 1875, GP-CCAP.

2. Robinson, Fleming & Co. to Gill, London, Oct. 8, 1875, GP-CCAP; Bareiro to Adolfo Saguier, Montevideo, May 7, 1876, *La Reforma,* May 17, 1876; *Memoria Argentina, 1877,* I, 586–594.

3. *Registro oficial, 1876,* pp. 97–98; Bareiro to Saguier, Montevideo, May 7, 1876, *La Reforma,* May 17, 1876.

4. Ibid.

5. Anon. to Gill, London, Feb. 24, 1876, GP-CCAP; *La Reforma,* May 17, 18, and 19, 1876; Callado to Cotegipe, 1ª Sec. No. 4, Asunción, May 17, 1876, MDBA-OR 201/1/14; Saguier to Gill, Buenos Aires, May 12, 1876, GP-CCAP; Brizuela to Cotegipe, Montevideo, May 24, 1876, CBC 11/33; Saguier to Gill, Buenos Aires, June 10 and 16, 1876, GP-CCAP.

6. Gondim to Cotegipe, Sec. Cen. No. 4, Feb. 26, 1876, MDBA-OR 201/1/14; Uriarte to Gill, Asunción, March 29, April 2 and 9, 1876, GP-CCAP.

7. Brizuela to Cotegipe, Montevideo, April 2, 1876, CBC 11/35.

8. Id. to id., Montevideo, May 24, 1876, CBC 11/33.

9. Gondim to Cotegipe, Sec. Cen. No. 16, Asunción, May 6, 1876, MDBA-OR 201/1/14; Callado to Cotegipe, Sec. Cen. No. 19, Asunción, May 11, 1876, ibid.; Cotegipe to Gondim, Conf., Rio de Janeiro, May 30, 1876, CBC 27/161.

10. Juan B. Gill, "Manifiesto," Asunción, May 13, 1866, encl., Callado to Cotegipe, Sec. Cen. No. 20, Asunción, May 14, 1876, MDBA-OR 201/1/14; *La Reforma,* May 17, 1876; Cardozo, *Efemérides,* pp. 236–237.

11. Gill to Cotegipe, Conf., Asunción, May 11, 1876, CBC 25/154.

12. Cotegipe to Gill, Rio de Janeiro, June 7, 1876, CBC 25/155.

13. Cotegipe to Callado, 1ª Sec. No. 2, Rio de Janeiro, June 9, 1876, MDBA-DI 201/4/9.

14. Callado to Cotegipe, Sec. Cen. No. 27, Asunción, June 23, 1876, MDBA-OR 201/1/14; Mesquita to Callado, Asunción, June 24, 1876, encl., Callado to Cotegipe, Sec. Cen. No. 28, Asunción, July 2, 1876, ibid.; *La Reforma,* July 7, 1876.

15. *El Nacional,* May 19, 1876; Saguier to Gill, Buenos Aires, May 25, 27, and July 3, 1876, GP-CCAP.

16. Callado to Cotegipe, 1ª Sec. No. 8 Res., Asunción, May 19, 1876, MDBA-OR 201/1/14.

17. Callado to Cotegipe, 1ª Sec. No. 1 Conf., MDBA-OR 201/1/14; *Registro oficial, 1876,* pp. 97–98; laws of June 30, 1876, ibid., pp. 102–103.

18. Cotegipe to Facundo Machaín, Rio de Janeiro, July 15, 1876, encl., Mathew to Derby, No. 66, Rio de Janeiro, July 19, 1876, PRO-FO 13/518.

19. St. John to Derby, No. 81, Buenos Aires, July 31, 1876, ibid., 6/334; Saguier to Gill, Buenos Aires, Oct. 3, 1876, GP-CCAP; Brizuela to Cotegipe, Montevideo, Sept. 5, 1876, CBC 11/36.

20. Macháin to Cotegipe, Asunción, Aug. 23, 1876, encl., Mathew to Derby, No. 84, Rio de Janeiro, Sept. 12, 1876, PRO-FO 13/518.

21. Cotegipe to Macháin, Rio de Janeiro, Oct. 9, 1876, encl., Mathew to Derby, No. 94, Rio de Janeiro, Oct. 23, 1876, ibid.; Cotegipe to Macháin, Rio de Janeiro, Oct. 18, 1876, *Memoria Argentina, 1877*, I, 615–635; Callado to Cotegipe, 1ª Sec. No. 5 Conf., Asunción, Oct. 18, 1876, MDBA-OR 201/1/14; *La Reforma*, Oct. 21, 1876; *Los Debates*, Oct. 22, 1876.

22. *Los Debates*, Aug. 16 and 18, 1876.

23. Callado to Cotegipe, 1ª Sec. Nos. 2 and 3, Asunción, Aug. 19, 1876, MDBA-OR 201/1/14; *La Reforma*, Aug. 19, 1876; *La Nación*, Aug. 20, 1876; Mathew to Derby, No. 89, Rio de Janeiro, Sept. 12, 1876, PRO-FO 13/518; Saguier to Gill, Buenos Aires, Oct. 10, 1876, GP-CCAP.

24. Callado to Cotegipe, 1ª Sec. No. 6 Conf., Asunción, Oct. 28, 1876, MDBA-OR 201/1/14.

25. *La Reforma*, Jan. 31, 1877; Callado to Cotegipe, 1ª Sec. No. 55, Asunción, Nov. 30, 1886, MDBA-OR 201/1/14.

26. Callado to Cotegipe, 1ª Sec. No. 2 Conf., Asunción, Jan. 8, 1877, ibid.

27. *Registro oficial, 1876*, pp. 153 ff; Zubizarreta, "La cuestión de la moneda," pp. 136–139; *La Reforma*, Dec. 1, 1876; Callado to Cotegipe, 1ª Séc. No. 56, Asunción, Dec. 2, 1876, MDBA-OR 201/1/14; Saguier to Gill, Buenos Aires, Feb. 6 and 20, 1877, GP-CCAP; *La Nación*, Dec. 14, 1876.

28. Bareiro and Alexander J. Baillie negotiated another agreement on behalf of the Council that the Brazilians opposed, and the Paraguayan Senate dutifully rejected the proposal on August 23, 1877 (Henrique de Miranda to Albuquerque, 1ª Sec. No. 41 Conf., Asunción, Aug. 16, 1877, MDBA-OR 201/1/14; Vasconcellos to Albuquerque, Sec. Cen. No. 13, Asunción, Aug. 21, 1877, and 1ª Sec. No. 13 Conf., Asunción, Aug. 24, 1877, ibid.). Miranda became Brazilian chargé on Aug. 4, 1877 (Miranda to Albuquerque, 1ª Sec. No. 42, Asunción, Aug. 7, 1877, ibid.). Diogo Velho Cavalcanti de Albuquerque became Brazilian Minister of Foreign Affairs on Feb. 15, 1877 (Fleiuss, *História administrativa do Brasil*, p. 313).

29. Centurión, *Historia de las letras paraguayas*, II, 21–22.

30. Cardozo, *Efemérides*, pp. 144–145, names Nicanor Godoy as the assassin; *La Reforma*, which has a detailed account April 13, 1877, charges Molas with the deed. See also Callado to Albuquerque, 1ª Sec. No. 22, Asunción, April 15, 1877, MDBA-OR 201/1/14; Caldwell to Wm. M. Evarts, Paraguayan Series No. 4, Montevideo, April 24, 1877, DPU-NAUS 128/4; West to Derby, No. 35, Buenos Aires, April 23, 1877, PRO-FO 6/340.

31. Brizuela to Cotegipe, Montevideo, April 24, 1877, CBC 11/40.

32. Callado to Albuquerque, 1ª Sec. No. 23, Asunción, April 17, 1877, MDBA-OR 201/1/14; *La Reforma*, April 24, 1877.

33. Vasconcellos to Albuquerque, Sec. Cen. No. 30, Asunción, Dec. 12, 1877, and 1ª Sec. No. 16 Conf., Asunción, Dec. 26, 1877, MDBA-OR 201/1/14.

34. Vasconcellos to Villa Bella, 1ª Sec. No. 3 Conf., Asunción, April 10, 1878, MDBA-OR 201/1/15.

35. Harriss-Gastrell to Salisbury, No. 34, Buenos Aires, May 18, 1878, PRO-FO 6/347; Foreign Office to Committee of Foreign Bondholders, London, July 8, 1878, PRO-FO 59/37; Harriss-Gastrell to Salisbury, No. 35, Buenos Aires, Sept. 28, 1878, PRO-FO 6/347.

36. Benítez, "La convención paraguaya de 1870," p. 69; Vasconcellos to

Cabo Frio, Privado & Conf., Asunción, April 30, 1877, MDBA-OR 201/1/14; Brizuela to Cotegipe, Montevideo, April 26 and May 8, 1877, CBC 11/41, 42.

37. *El Comercio,* May 18, 1877.

38. This cabinet shakeup came on August 12–14, 1877, and left Caballero, Saguier, Bareiro, Jara, and Escobar in office (López Decoud, *Album gráfico,* p. 216).

39. Vasconcellos to Albuquerque, 1ª Sec. No. 1 Res., Asunción, Oct. 19, 1877, MDBA-OR 201/1/14.

40. *La Reforma,* Oct. 29, 1877; West to Derby, No. 94, Buenos Aires, Nov. 10, 1877, PRO-FO 6/340; Caldwell to Evarts, Paraguayan Series No. 5, Montevideo, Nov. 15, 1877, DPU-NAUS 128/4.

41. Vasconcellos to Albuquerque, 1ª Sec. No. 52, Asunción, Nov. 10, 1877, MDBA-OR 201/1/14.

42. Id. to id., 1ª Sec. No. 1 Res., Asunción, Oct. 19, 1877, ibid.

43. *La Reforma,* Feb. 26, 1878.

44. Rio Branco had written: "Caballero está dando preciosos apontamientos para uma Memoria que meo filho lhe vae escrever, *porque elle não o sabe fazer,* que nos será muito util." (Caballero is giving valuable data for a Memoir that my son is going to write for him, because he [Caballero] does not know how to do it, which will be very useful for us.) (Rio Branco to Visconde de São Vicente, Buenos Aires, Jan. 9, 1871, *Anuário do Museu Imperial,* XII, 38, italics added.) The passage may mean that Caballero did not know how to write the memoir, not that he did not know how to write.

45. Vasconcellos to Carvalho, 1ª Sec. No. 2 Conf., Asunción, March 12, 1878, MDBA-OR 201/1/15.

46. Vasconcellos to Albuquerque, 1ª Sec. Conf., Asunción, May 3, 1878, ibid.

47. Vasconcellos to Villa Bella, 1ª Sec. No. 23, Asunción, June 21, 1878, and 1ª Sec. No. 25, Asunción, July 7, 1878, ibid.; *La Reforma,* June 22, 1878; Act of June 28, 1878, Diputados, *Actas, 1878,* pp. 387–392.

48. Valdez, "Estudio," p. 256.

49. Vasconcellos to Villa Bella, Sec. Cen. No. 1 Res., Asunción, Jan. 3, 1879, MDBA-OR 201/1/15; M. M., "Paraguay, 25 de noviembre de 1882," *Revista del Paraguay* 3 (1893): 12–15; Cardozo, *Efemérides,* pp. 299–300.

50. *La Reforma,* Oct. 9, 1878; italics added. Bareiro and Saguier resigned their cabinet positions in August and were replaced by Juan Antonio Jara and Agustín Cañete (Vasconcellos to Villa Bella, 1ª Sec. No. 24, Asunción, Aug. 14, 1878, MDBA-OR 201/1/15).

51. *La Reforma,* Oct. 22, 1878.

52. Callado to Cotegipe, 1ª Sec. Conf. No. 7, Asunción, Feb. 13, 1877, MDBA-OR 201/1/14; *El Liberal,* Nov. 12, 1878. In his last letter to Cotegipe, Gill asked for Brazil's support in the forthcoming arbitration (Gill to Cotegipe, Asunción, Feb. 12, 1877, CBC 25/156).

53. *Memoria del ministerio de relaciones exteriores presentada al congreso legislativo en el año de 1878,* pp. 50–51; *Memoria del ministerio de relaciones exteriores presentada al congreso legislativo en el año de 1879,* p. 25. A list of the documents submitted by Aceval is in Aceval to Evarts, Washington, March 27, 1878, NPL-NAUS 350/1. See also Benjamín Aceval, *Appendix and Documents Annexed to the Memoir Filed by the Minister of Paraguay on the Question Submitted to Arbitration,* and Aceval, *Chaco paraguayo. Cuestión de límites entre el Paraguay y la Argentina. Memoria presentada al árbitro Mr.*

Rutherford B. Hayes. Documentos anexos y fallo arbitral, which cover the matter adequately. For the Argentine case, see *Memoria Argentina, 1877,* pp. 682–746. The Argentine representative was Dr. Manuel R. García, who presented the weak case prepared by Dr. Ángel J. Carranza (Amarilla Fretes, *Liquidación,* p. 113). See also *La Reforma,* Jan. 21, 1879, and *Colección de tratados celebrados por la República Argentina con las naciones extrangeras,* I, 85–88.

54. Báez, *Cuadros históricos y descriptivos,* p. 238.

55. Bareiro to Vasconcellos, Asunción, May 12, 1879, MDBA-OR 201/1/15; *La Reforma,* May 16, 1879.

56. Carlos Alberto Pusineri Scala, "La moneda de 1870," *Historia Paraguaya* 8–9–10 (1963–1965): 143–144; Freire Esteves, "Historia contemporánea," p. 51.

Bibliography

Manuscripts and Printed Documents
Argentina
Archivo de Martín Gainza, MSS., Archivo General de la Nación, Buenos Aires; hereafter AGN-BA.
Félix Frías, Correspondencia confidencial de la legación Argentina, 1869–1871. MSS., AGN-BA.
Mensaje del presidente de la república al abrir las sesiones del congreso argentino. Mayo de 1873. Buenos Aires, 1873.
Mensaje del presidente de la república al abrir las sesiones del congreso argentino. Mayo de 1874. Buenos Aires, 1874.
Mensaje del presidente al abrir las sesiones del congreso argentino en mayo de 1876. Buenos Aires, 1876.
Ministerio de Relaciones Exteriores, *Colección de tratados celebrados por la República Argentina con las naciones extrangeras.* 3 vols. Buenos Aires, 1884.
———, *Memoria presentada por el ministro de estado en el departamento de relaciones esteriores al congreso nacional en 1871.* Buenos Aires, 1871. The spellings "esteriores" and "exteriores" were used indiscriminately.
———, *Memoria del ministerio de relaciones exteriores presentada al congreso nacional en 1872.* Buenos Aires, 1872. *Apéndice á la memoria del ministerio de relaciones esteriores presentada al congreso nacional en el año de 1872.* Buenos Aires, 1872.
———, *Memoria del ministerio de relaciones esteriores presentada al congreso nacional en 1873.* Buenos Aires, 1873.
———, *Memoria del ministerio de relaciones exteriores presentada al congreso nacional en 1874.* Buenos Aires, 1874.
———, *Memoria del ministerio de relaciones exteriores presentada al congreso nacional en el año 1876.* Buenos Aires, 1876.
———, *Memoria del ministerio de relaciones esteriores presentada al congreso nacional en el año 1877.* 3 vols. Buenos Aires, 1877.
———, *Memoria del ministerio de relaciones esteriores presentada al congreso nacional en el año 1878.* Buenos Aires, 1878.
———, *Memoria del ministerio de relaciones exteriores presentada al congreso nacional en 1880.* Buenos Aires, 1880.
Mitre, Bartolomé, *Archivo del General Mitre.* 28 vols. Buenos Aires, 1911–1914.

————, *Correspondencia literaria, histórica y política del General Bartolomé Mitre.* 3 vols. Buenos Aires, 1912.

Brazil

Actas do Conselho d'Estado. MSS., Arquivo Nacional, Rio de Janeiro, Cod. 307, IV–VI.

"Cartas do Visconde do Rio Branco," *Anuário do Museu Imperial*, XII (Petropolis, 1951), 37–202.

Correspondencia sobre a guerra do Paraguay. Guerra do Paraguay. Diversos documentos de 1871–1872. MSS., Arquivo Nacional, Rio de Janeiro, Cod. 547, 1–22.

Correspondencia trocada entre o governo imperial e o da República Argentina relativa aos tratados celebrados entre o Brasil e a República do Paraguay, e á desocupacão da ilha do Atajo. Rio de Janeiro, 1872. Published in English as *Correspondence between the Brazilian and Argentine Governments Respecting the Treaties Concluded between Brazil and the Republic of Paraguay and the Withdrawal of Troops from the Island of Atajo.* London, 1872.

Missões diplomáticas brasileiras, Assumpção. Despachos, Instrucções, 1859–1877, 201/4/7-10. MSS., Arquivo Histórico, Ministério das Relações Exteriores, Itamaraty, Rio de Janeiro.

Missões diplomáticas brasileiras, Assumpção. Oficios recibidos, 1864–1881, 201/1/10-16. MSS., Arquivo Histórico, Ministério das Relações Exteriores, Itamaraty, Rio de Janeiro.

Pinho, Wanderley, ed., *Cartas do Imperador D. Pedro II ao Barão de Cotegipe.* Bibliotheca Pedagógica Brasileira, Series V, Volume XII, São Paulo, 1933.

Great Britain

Affidavit of Máximo Terrero, Dec. 31, 1872, Paraguay v. Fleming, P.-No. 205, No. 3374, Public Record Office, Chancery, 31/2673.

"Arrangements between the Argentine Republic, Brazil, and Uruguay relative to the Establishment of a Provisional Government in Paraguay.—Buenos Ayres, June 2, 1869," *State Papers*, v. 63. London, 1872–1873.

Diplomatic and Consular Despatches and Reports, Public Record Office, Foreign Office:

Argentine Confederation, 1869–1881. F. O. 6/282–284, 291–293, 302–304, 308–310, 313–315, 320–322, 327, 328, 332–335, 339–341, 347, 349, 353–355, 357, 364.

Brazil, 1869–1880. F. O. 13/461, 462, 469, 477, 483, 484, 489, 497, 498, 508, 517, 518, 529, 530, 539, 547, 548, 562.

Paraguay, 1872–1881. F. O. 59/32–38.

Paraguay. Consular. Domestic. Señor Benites and Various. January to December 1872, F. O. 59/32.

Paraguay. Consular. Domestic. Señor Benites and Various. January to December 1873. F. O. 59/33.

Paraguay. Consular. Domestic. Señor Uriarte. Domestic Various. January to December 1874. F. O. 59/34.

Paraguay. British Emigration 1872–1874. F. O. 59/35.

Paraguay. Domestic. Señor Uriarte. Domestic Various. January to December 1875. F. O. 59/36.

Paraguay. Domestic Various. 1876 and 1878. F.O. 59/37.

Paraguay. Domestic. Various. Commercial Domestic Various, 1879 to 1881. F. O. 59/38.

"Emigration to Paraguay (South America). Terms and concessions granted by the Government of Paraguay to the English colony in Charge of J. W. Billiatt, with a few remarks upon the natural productions, soil, and climate of Paraguay," encl., R. H. Meade to E. Hammond, London, Sept. 9, 1873, PRO-FO 59/35.

Hammond Papers, PRO-FO 391/16.

Hertslet, Lewis and Edward Hertslet, et al., comps. *A Complete Collection of the Treaties and Conventions, and Reciprocal Regulations at Present Subsisting between Great Britain and Foreign Powers; and of the Laws, Decrees, Orders in Council, &c, concerning the Same; so far as they Relate to Commerce and Navigation, the Slave Trade, Post-Office Communications, Copyright, &c.; and to the Privileges and Interests of the subjects of the High Contracting Parties.* 31 vols. London, 1827–1925.

López, Francisco Solano, "Last Will and Testament," Court of Probate, Will Book 1872, vol. 16, Somerset House, London.

"Memorandum on Paraguayan War, Detention of British Subjects, and Cruelties of President López," Foreign Office, May 29, 1869, PRO-FO 59/29.

"Preliminary Agreement of Peace between the Argentine Republic and Brazil and Paraguay . . . June 20, 1870," *State Papers*, v. 63, London, 1872–1873.

"The Paraguay Loan, 1871," *Special Report from the Select Committee on Loans to Foreign States*, House of Commons, *Sessional Papers*, XI (London, 1875), xxxvi–xliv, 174–230.

Vansittart, Arthur G., "Paraguay. Report by Mr. Vansittart on the Commerce, Finances &c. of Paraguay," *Sessional Papers, Accounts and Papers, Commercial Reports*, LXXI (London, 1883), 77–154. This report is encl. No. 2, George G. Petre to Granville, Buenos Aires, Nov. 20, 1882, PRO-FO 6/368.

West, Lionel S. Sackville, "Report on the Present Political, Financial and Social State of the Republic of Paraguay," encl., West to Derby, No. 109 Confidential, Buenos Aires, Oct. 30, 1875, PRO-FO 6/328.

Paraguay

Aceval, Benjamín, *Appendix and Documents Annexed to the Memoir Filed by the Minister of Paraguay, on the Question Submitted to Arbitration.* New York, 1878. English and Spanish texts.

———, *Chaco paraguayo. Cuestión de límites entre el Paraguay y la Argentina. Memoria presentada al árbitro Mr. Rutherford B. Hayes. Documentos anexos y fallo arbitral.* Asunción, 1896.

Actas de la convención nacional constituyente del año 1870. Asunción, 1897.

Boletín oficial de la nación. Asunción, 1871–

Cámara de Diputados, *Actas de las sesiones del periodo legislativo del año 1871*. Asunción, 1908.

———, *Actas de las sesiones del periodo legislativo del año 1872*. Asunción, 1908.

———, *Actas de las sesiones de los periodos legislativos de los años 1873–74–75–76–77–78–79–80*. Asunción, 1910.

Cámara de Senadores, *Actas de las sesiones del periodo legislativo del año 1872*. Asunción, 1908.

———, *Actas de las sesiones del periodo legislativo del año 1873*. Asunción, 1908.

———, *Actas de las sesiones de los periodos legislativos de los años 1874–75–76–77–78–79–80*. Asunción, 1908.

Colección de leyes sancionadas por el congreso de la nación en sus sesiones extraordinarias de 1876. Decreto del P.E. reglamentando las mismas. Asunción, 1877.

Constitución de la República del Paraguay sancionada por la honorable convención constituyente en sesión del 18 de noviembre de 1870. Asunción, 1871.

Documentos oficiales relativos al abuso de la bandera nacional paraguaya por los gefes aliados. Piribebui, 1869.

Documentos oficiales sobre cuestiones de límites entre la República del Paraguay y la Argentina. [Asunción, 1873.]

Estrato del boletín oficial, leyes de finanzas sancionadas por el honorable congreso en las sesiones estraordinarias. Asunción, 1875.

[Gill, Juan Bautista], *Discurso pronunciado por el presidente electo en el acto de la jura ante el congreso legislativo de la nación*. Asunción, Nov. 25, 1874.

Gill Papers, Colección de Carlos Alberto Pusineri Scala, Asunción.

[López, Francisco Solano], *Proclamas y cartas del Mariscal López*. Buenos Aires, 1957.

Manifiesto del gobierno provisorio compuesto de los ciudadanos Cirilo Antonio Rivarola, Carlos Loizaga, y José Díaz de Bedoya. Asunción, 1869.

Memoria del ministerio de hacienda presentada al congreso legislativo de la República del 1º de abril de 1873. Asunción, 1873.

"Memoria del ministerio de justicia, culto e instrucción pública," *Los Debates*, Aug. 2, 1876.

Memoria del ministerio de relaciones exteriores presentada al congreso legislativo en el año 1878. Asunción. 1878.

Memoria del ministerio de relaciones exteriores presentada al congreso legislativo en el año de 1879. Asunción, 1879.

Memoria del ministerio de relaciones exteriores presentada al honorable congreso nacional en 1880. Asunción, 1881.

"Memoria sobre la hacienda pública de la república durante el año de 1876," *La Reforma*, Sept. 8, 1876.

Mendonça, Juan Carlos, ed., *Las constituciones paraguayas y los proyectos de constitución de los partidos políticos* (Colección Cultura Paraguaya). Asunción, 1967.

Mensaje del presidente de la República del Paraguay al abrir las sesiones del congreso en abril de 1880. Asunción, 1880.

Mensaje del presidente provisorio de la República del Paraguay al abrir las sesiones del congreso nacional en abril de 1881. Asunción, 1881.

Mensaje del vice-presidente de la república en ejercicio del P.E. al congreso legislativo de la nación. Asunción, 1873.

Mensaje presentada por el poder ejecutivo al congreso de la nación en la apertura de sus sesiones del octavo período legislativo. Asunción, 1878.

Registro oficial de la República del Paraguay correspondiente á los años 1869 á 1875. Asunción, 1887.

Registro oficial de la República del Paraguay correspondiente á los años 1876 á 1885. Asunción, 1887.

Reglamento para las aduanas de la República del Paraguay para el año de 1873. Asunción, 1873.

Resquín, Francisco Ysidoro, "Breves relaciones históricas de la guerra contra el gobierno de la República del Paraguay, por los gobiernos de la Triple Alianza, brasilero, argentino, y oriental—estractado de documentos de la luz pública, y de los sucesos de armas, durante la guerra de más de cinco años, que sostiene el gobierno de la nación paraguaya, contra los poderes de la Triple Alianza. Asunción del Paraguay, año de 1875." Archivo Nacional, Asunción.

Viera, Fernando, *Colección legislativa de la República del Paraguay 1842–1895.* Asunción, 1896.

United States

Despatches from United States Ministers to Argentina. File Microcopies of Records in the National Archives: No. 69, 47 vols., Aug. 2, 1823–Aug. 3, 1906.

Despatches from United States Ministers to Paraguay and Uruguay. File Microcopies of Records in the National Archives: No. 128, 19 vols., Oct. 11, 1858–July 17, 1906.

Diplomatic Instructions of the Department of State, 1801–1906. Paraguay and Uruguay, Oct. 6, 1858–July 26, 1906. File Microcopies of Records in the National Archives: No. 77, Roll 128.

Foreign Relations of the United States, 1871, 1st Session, 42d Congress. Washington, 1872.

Foreign Relations of the United States, 1871–1872, 2nd Session, 42d Congress. Washington, 1872.

Notes from the Paraguayan Legation in the United States to the Department of State, March 12, 1853–May 16, 1906. National Archives Microfilm Publications, Microcopy T 350, Rolls 1–2.

Records of the United States Legation in Paraguay, 1861–1935. Copies of notes sent to the Paraguayan Foreign Office, Nov. 23, 1861–May 10, 1873 and Sept. 22, 1882–May 14, 1907. National Archives Microfilm Publications, Microcopy T 693, Roll 4.

Records of the United States Legation in Paraguay, 1861–1935. Notes from the Paraguayan Foreign Office, Nov. 18, 1865–June 4, 1885. National Archives Microfilm Publications, Microcopy T 693, Roll 3.

Books, Pamphlets, and Articles

Academia Nacional de la Historia, *Mitre: Homenaje de la Academia Nacional de la Historia en el cinquentenario de su muerte (1906–1956).* Buenos Aires, 1957.

Alcorta, Sinforiano, *Antecedentes históricos sobre los tratados con el Paraguay*. Buenos Aires, 1885. First published as articles in *La Libertad* (Buenos Aires); a file of these articles is in Archivo del Dr. Victorino de la Plaza, AGN-BA.

Amarilla Fretes, Eduardo, *La liquidación de la guerra de la triple alianza contra el Paraguay (negociaciones diplómaticas)*. Asunción, 1941.

————, *El Paraguay en el primer cincuentenario del fallo arbitral del Presidente Hayes*, Asunción, 1932.

Amerlan, Albert, *Nights on the Rio Paraguay. Scenes of War and Character Scetches* [*sic*] (tr. from the German by Henry F. Suksdorf). Buenos Aires, 1902.

Aramburú, Eduardo, *Manifiesto al pueblo paraguayo*. Montevideo, 1876.

Arbo, Higinio. *Política paraguaya*. Buenos Aires, 1947.

Ash, T. E., *The Plague of 1871*. Buenos Aires, 1871.

Ávila, Manuel, "Apuntes sobre la conspiración de 1868. Pequeña contribución a la historia de la guerra con la triple alianza y de la tiranía de López." *Revista del Instituto Paraguayo*, Año II, Tomo III (Asunción, 1899): 215–228; Año III, Tomo I (Asunción, 1900): 3–30.

————, "La contra revolución de Molas en 1874: reminiscencias." *Revista del Instituto Paraguayo*, Año III, Tomo I (Asunción, 1900): 114–128, 207–224.

————, *La contra revolución de Molas en 1874—reminiscencias*. Asunción, 1900.

Báez, Adolfo J., *Yataity Corá. Una conferencia histórica*. Buenos Aires, 1929.

Báez, Cecilio, *Cuadros históricos y descriptivos*. Asunción, 1906.

————, *Historia diplomática del Paraguay, precidida de un estudio sociológico de los pueblos mediterráneos que concurrieron a la formación de la nación española*. 2 vols., Asunción, 1932.

————, *Le Paraguay. Son évolution historique et sa situation actuelle*. Paris, 1927.

————, *La tiranía en el Paraguay. Sus causas, caracteres y resultados*. Asunción, 1903. A collection of articles published in *El Cívico*.

Baillie, Alexander F., *A Paraguayan Treasure. The Search and the Discovery*. London, 1887.

[Barman, Jean and Roderick James Barman], "Arquivo do Barão de Cotegipe." *Revista do Instituto Histórico e Geográfico Brasileiro* 290 (Rio de Janeiro, 1971): 163–402. Description and catalog of the Coleção Barão de Cotegipe.

Benites, Gregorio, *Anales diplomático y militar de la guerra del Paraguay*. Asunción, 1906.

————, *Las imposturas de Juan Bautista Gill y el informe del comité del parlamento de Inglaterra en la cuestión empréstitos del Paraguay*. Montevideo, 1876. A copy of this rare pamphlet is in PRO-FO 6/448.

Benítez, Gregorio, *Manifiesto de Gregorio Benítez, ex-ministro plenipotenciario del Paraguay cerca de los gobiernos del Brasil, Inglaterra, Francia, Italia, etc., etc. al pueblo paraguayo y a sus amigos en el estrangero*. Montevideo, 1876. Benítez and Benites are the same person.

Benítez, Justo Pastor, *Carlos Antonio López (estructuración del estado paraguayo)*. Prólogo de Julio César Chaves. Buenos Aires, 1949.

———, *Formación social del pueblo paraguayo*. Buenos Aires, 1955.

———, *La convención constituyente de 1870*. Asunción, 1928.

———, "La convención paraguaya de 1870." In *II° Congreso Internacional de Historia de América*. 4 vols. Buenos Aires, 1938. IV, 65–71.

Benítez, Luís G., *Historia cultural—Reseña de su evolución en el Paraguay*. Asunción, 1966. This and the following item are basically textbooks.

———, *Historia diplomática del Paraguay*. Asunción, 1972.

Bray, Arturo, *Hombres y épocas del Paraguay*. 2 vols. Buenos Aires, 1957. The first edition of vol. 1 was published in 1943, the second edition in 1957.

Brugada, Ricardo, *Política paraguaya. 'Benigno Ferreira*. Asunción, 1906. Reprinted from *La Democracia*, Aug. 29, 1904; bound with other pamphlets in *Folletos*, Museo Mitre, Buenos Aires.

Calmon, Pedro, "Mitre y el Brasil." In *Mitre. Homenaje de la Academia Nacional de la Historia en el cincuentenario de su muerte (1906–1956)*, pp. 63–67. Buenos Aires, 1957.

Calzada, Rafael, *Rasgos biográficos de José Segundo Decoud. Homenaje en el 4° aniversario de su fallecimiento, 4 de marzo de 1909*. Buenos Aires, 1913.

Cárcano, Ramón J., *Guerra del Paraguay. Acción y reacción de la triple alianza*. 2 vols. Buenos Aires, 1941. Sometimes listed in 3 vols., vol. 1 being *Guerra del Paraguay. Orígines y causas*. Buenos Aires, 1939.

Cardozo, Efraím, *Efemérides de la historia del Paraguay*. Asunción and Buenos Aires, 1967.

———, *Hace cién años. Crónicas de la guerra de 1864–1870*. 8 vols. Asunción, 1967–1976.

———, *Paraguay independiente*. Vol. 21 of *Historia de América y de los pueblos americanos*, edited by Antonio Ballesteros y Beretta. Barcelona, 1949.

Centurión, Carlos R., *Historia de la cultura paraguaya*. 2 vols. Asunción, 1961. A revision of the next item.

———, *Historia de las letras paraguayas*. 3 vols. Buenos Aires, 1948.

———, *Los hombres de la convención de 70*. Asunción, 1938.

Centurión, Juan C., "La reorganización del ejército nacional en 1869." *Revista del Instituto Paraguayo*, Año II, Tomo III (Asunción, 1899): 23–35.

Chaves, Julio César, *El Presidente López, vida y gobierno de Don Carlos*. Buenos Aires, 1955.

Cibils, Manuel J., *Anarquía y revolución en el Paraguay*. Buenos Aires, 1957.

Cooney, Jerry W., "Abolition in the Republic of Paraguay: 1840–1870." In *Jahrbuch für Geschichte von Staat, Wirtschaft und Gesellschaft Lateinamerikas*, 11 (Cologne and Vienna, 1974): 149–166.

Correia, Manoel Francisco, "Saque de Assumpção e Luque atribuido ao exército brazileiro na guerra do Paraguay: Refutação." *Revista do Instituto Histórico e Geographico Brazileiro* 59 (Rio de Janeiro, 1896): 369–393.

Cotegipe, Barão de, *As negociações com o Paraguay e a nota do governo argentino de 27 de abril. Carta ao Exmo. Senhor conselheiro, ministro e secretario d'estado dos negocios estrangeiros*. Bahia, 1872.

Decoud, Héctor Francisco, *La convención nacional constituyente y la carta magna de la república*. Buenos Aires, 1934.
————, *La revolución del comandante Molas*. Buenos Aires, 1930.
————, *Sobre los escombros de la guerra—una decada de vida nacional, 1869–1880*. Asunción, 1925.
Decoud, José Segundo, *Cuestiones políticas y económicas*. Asunción, 1877.
————, *La historia de una administración o sea las dilapidaciones de Salvador Jovellanos, vicepresidente de la República del Paraguay en el ejercicio del P[oder] E[jecutivo]*. Asunción, 1877. Collection of articles published in *La Reforma*.
Díaz, Antonio, *Historia política y militar de las repúblicas del Plata desde el año de 1828 hasta el de 1866*. 13 vols. in 12. Montevideo, 1877–1879.
Figueirêdo, Lima, *Grandes soldados do Brasil*. 4th ed. Rio de Janeiro, 1944.
Fleuiss, Max, *História administrativa do Brasil*. Rio de Janeiro, 1923.
Forgues, M. L., "Le Paraguay. Fragments de journal et de correspondances, 1872–1873." *Le Tour du monde: Nouvelle journal des voyages*, 27, nos. 701, 702, 703 (Paris, 1874): 369–416.
Fragoso, Augusto Tasso, *História da guerra entre a tríplice aliança e o Paraguai*. 2d ed., 5 vols. Rio de Janeiro, 1956–1960.
————, *A paz com o Paraguai depois da guerra da tríplice aliança*. Rio de Janeiro, 1941.
Freire Esteves, Gómes, "Historia contemporánea de la república." In Luis Freire Esteves and Juan C. González Peña, eds., *El Paraguay constitucional, 1870–1920*. Buenos Aires, 1921.
————, *Historia contemporánea del Paraguay. Lucha de cancillerías en el Río de la Plata*. Buenos Aires, 1921. Separate printing of above entry.
Freund, P. A., and W. F. Mulhall, *Letters from Paraguay extracted from "The Standard."* Buenos Aires, 1888.
García Mellid, Atilio, *Proceso a los falsificadores de la historia del Paraguay*. 2 vols. Buenos Aires, 1963–1964.
Gill Aguínaga, Juan Bautista, *La asociación paraguaya en la guerra de la triple alianza*. Buenos Aires, 1959.
Godoi, Juansilvano, *Documentos históricos. El fusilamiento del Obispo Palacios y los tribunales de sangre de San Fernando*. Asunción, 1916.
————, *El Barón de Río Branco. La muerte del Mariscal López. El concepto de la patria*. Asunción, 1912.
————, *La entrevista de Yataity Corá entre los generales Mitre y López*. Buenos Aires, 1890. Here the author's name is spelled Juan Silvano Godoy.
————, *Mi misión a Río de Janeiro*. Buenos Aires, 1897. Here the author's name is spelled Juan Silvano Godoi, as it is in the next items.
————, *Monografías históricas* (primera serie). Buenos Aires, 1893.
————, *Monographias históricas com um appendice contendo o capitulo VIII do livro de Benjamin Mossé sobre a campanha do Paraguay e o depoimento do General D. Francisco Isidoro Resquin*. Rio Grande, 1895.
Guimarães, Francisco Pinheiro, *Um voluntário da pátria: Folha dos serviços prestados pelo General Dr. Francisco Pinheiro Guimarães as classes armadas*. (Coleção documentos brasileiros 94.) 2d ed. Rio de Janeiro, 1958.
González, Natalicio, and Pablo Max Ynsfrán, *El Paraguay contemporáneo*. Paris, 1926.

González, Teodosio, *Infortunios del Paraguay*. Buenos Aires, 1931.

Kolinski, Charles J., "The Death of Francisco Solano López." *The Historian* 26, no. 1 (Nov. 1963): 75–91.

———, *Independence or Death! The Story of the Paraguayan War.* Gainesville, 1965.

Lins, Alvaro, *Rio-Branco (o Barão do Rio-Branco) 1845–1912.* (Coleção documentos brasileiros 50.) 2 vols. Rio de Janeiro and São Paulo, 1945. Title of the second edition, São Paulo, 1965, is *Rio-Branco (o Barão do Rio-Branco). Biografia pessoal e história política.*

Lopacher, Ulrich, and Alfred Tobler, *Un suizo en la guerra del Paraguay.* Trans. and with a preliminary note by Arturo Nagy and Francisco Pérez-Maricevich. Asunción, 1960.

López Decoud, Arsenio, *Album gráfico de la República del Paraguay.* Buenos Aires, 1911.

Lynch, Elisa A[licia], *Esposición y protesta que hace Elisa A. Lynch.* Buenos Aires, 1875.

Maíz, Fidel, *Etapas de mi vida: Contestación a las imposturas de Juan Silvano Godoy.* Asunción, 1919.

Marcondes Homem de Mello, Francisco Ignacio, "Viagem ao Paraguay em fevereiro e março de 1869." *Revista Trimensal do Instituto Histórico, Geographico e Ethnographico do Brasil* 36, part 2 (1873): 3–53.

Maresma, Gladis Fois, "El periodismo paraguayo y su actitud frente a la Guerra de la Triple Alianza y Francisco S. López." M.A. Thesis, University of New Mexico, Albuquerque, January, 1970.

Masterman, George Frederick, *Seven Eventful Years in Paraguay: A Narrative of Personal Experience amongst the Paraguayans.* London, 1869.

Medeiros, J. Paulo de, "Mitre." In *Mitre. Homenaje de la Academia Nacional de la Historia en el cincuentenario de su muerte (1906–1956).* Buenos Aires, 1957, pp. 69–78.

Medeyros, J. Paulo de, *A missão do General Mitre no Brasil.* Rio de Janeiro, 1941.

M. M. [Miguel Macías?], "Paraguay, 25 de noviembre de 1882." *Revista del Paraguay* 2 (Buenos Aires, 1892): 207–313, 422–427, 506–511; 3 (1893): 9–15, 33–53. The title refers to Bernardino Caballero's inauguration.

Mulhall, M[ichael] G[eorge], and E[dward] T[homas] Mulhall. *Handbook of the River Plate; Comprising Buenos Ayres, the Upper Provinces, Banda Oriental and Paraguay.* London and Buenos Aires, 1875.

———, *Handbook of the River Plate Republics, Comprising Buenos Ayres and the Provinces of the Argentine Republic and the Republics of Uruguay and Paraguay.* London and Buenos Aires, 1875.

———, *Handbook of the River Plate, Comprising the Argentine Republic, Uruguay, and Paraguay.* 5th ed. Buenos Aires and London, 1885.

———, *Manual de las repúblicas del Plata. Datos topográficos, históricos, y económicos (sobre los productos, colonias, empresas, comercio, rentas nacionales, etc.).* Buenos Aires, 1876.

Nabuco, Joaquim, *Um estadista do Imperio. Nabuco de Araújo, sua vida, suas opiniões, sua época.* 3 vols. Rio de Janeiro and Paris, [1897–1899]. Life of José Thomas Nabuco de Araújo, 1813–1878.

O'Leary, Juan Emiliano, "El saqueo de la Asunción." *Patria* (Asunción), Jan. 1, 1919.

Panorama política del Paraguay: La postguerra del Chaco (1936–1946). [Asunción, 1946.] Obviously written by Liberals.

Parodi, Enrique D., "La prensa." *Revista del Paraguay* 1 (1891): 341–348, 389–396, 441–453.

———. "Ferro-carril de la Asunción á Santos." *Revista del Paraguay* 1 (1891): 533–559, 613–628.

Pastore, Carlos, *La lucha por la tierra en el Paraguay*. 2d. ed. Montevideo, 1972.

Peña, Enrique, "Monedas y medallas paraguayas." *Revista del Instituto Paraguayo* 3 (1900): 51–99.

Pereira de Sousa, Octaviano, *História da guerra do Paraguai* (Boletim, *Revista do Instituto Histórico e Geographico Brasileiro*). Rio de Janeiro, 1930.

Pérez Acosta, Juan F., *Carlos Antonio López, obrero máximo, labor administrativo y constructivo*. Asunción, 1948.

Phelps, Gilbert, *Tragedy of Paraguay*. New York, 1975.

Pitaud, Henri, *Les français au Paraguay*. Bordeaux and Paris, 1955.

Pla, Josefina, *Hermano negro: La esclavitud en el Paraguay*. Madrid, 1972.

Pomer, León, *La guerra del Paraguay. Gran negocio!* Buenos Aires, 1968.

Pusineri Scala, Carlos Alberto, "La moneda de 1870." *Historia Paraguaya* 8–9–10 (Asunción, 1963–1965): 128–150.

———, "Las monedas que circularon en el Paraguay durante la guerra de la triple alianza." *Historia Paraguaya* 12 (1967–1968): 3–20.

Quesada, Ernesto, *Historia diplomática nacional: La política argentina-paraguaya*. Buenos Aires, 1902.

Rebaudi, A., *Guerra del Paraguay—un episodio*. Buenos Aires, 1918.

Rio-Branco, Barão de, *Efemérides brasileiras*. Rio de Janeiro, 1946.

Rivarola, Cirilo A., *Manifiesto del ciudadano Cirilo A. Rivarola al pueblo paraguayo*. Buenos Aires, 1873. Bound with other pamphlets in *Folletos*, Museo Mitre, Buenos Aires.

Salum-Flecha, Antonio, *Historia diplomática del Paraguay de 1869 a 1938*. Asunción, 1972.

Sánchez Quell, H[ipólito], *Proyección del General Caballero en la ruta de la patria*. 2d ed. Asunción, 1970.

Schuster, Adolph N., *Paraguay: Land, Volk, Geschichte, Wirtschaftsleben und Kolonisation*. Stuttgart, 1929.

Sienra Carranza, José, "Retrospecto del Paraguay: Notas sobre el último decenio." *Revista Histórico* 1, no. 1 (Asunción, March 1, 1899): 5–19; 2, no. 2 (Asunción, March 16, 1899): 33–57.

Sosa Escalada, Jaime, *Negociaciones diplomáticas entre el Brasil, la República Argentina y el Paraguay*. Buenos Aires, 1875.

———, "Política brasilera en el Paraguay." *Revista del Paraguay* 2, no. 1 (1892): 1–23.

Susnik, Branislava, *El indio colonial del Paraguay*. 3 vols. Asunción, 1965–1971.

Talavera, Natalicio, *La guerra del Paraguay: Correspondencias publicadas en El Semanario*. Buenos Aires, 1958.

Taunay, Alfredo d'Escragnolle, *Diário do exército 1869—1870: A campanha da cordilheira de Campo Grande a Aquidabá* (Obras do Visconde de Taunay, III), 2d ed. São Paulo, 1958.

[Terrero, Máximo, and Francisco Wisner von Morgenstern], *Paraguay: A Note as to its Position and Prospects*. [London], 1871.

Thompson, George, *The War in Paraguay. With a Historical Sketch of the Country and its People and Notes upon the Military Engineering of the War*. London, 1869.

Valdez, Wilfredo [pseud. of Jaime Sosa Escalada], "La guerra futura. La guerra de Chile y Brasil con la República Argentina—alianza—la causa común. Estudio de los hombres del Paraguay—el triunvirato." *Revista del Paraguay* 2, nos. 3–9 (1892): 137–144, 197–200, 256–269, 289–306, 353–366, 398–409.

Valle, Florentino del, *Cartilla cívica: Proceso político del Paraguay 1870–1950. El partido Liberal y la Asociación Nacional Republicana (partido Colorado) en la balanza de la verdad histórica*. Buenos Aires, 1951.

Warren, Harris Gaylord, "Brazil's Paraguayan Policy, 1869–1876." *The Americas* 28 (April 1972): 388–406.

―――, "Dr. William Stewart in Paraguay, 1857–1869." *The Americas* 25 (Jan. 1969): 247–264.

―――, "The Golden Fleecing: the Paraguayan Loans of 1871 and 1872." *Inter-American Economic Affairs* 26 (Summer 1972): 3–24.

―――, "The 'Lincolnshire Farmers' in Paraguay: An Abortive Emigration Scheme of 1872–1873." *The Americas* 21 (Jan. 1965): 243–269.

―――, "Litigation in English Courts and Claims against Paraguay Resulting from the War of the Triple Alliance." *Inter-American Economic Affairs* 22 (Spring 1969) 31–46.

―――, *Paraguay, An Informal History*. Norman, Okla., 1959.

―――, "The Paraguay Central Railway, 1856–1889." *Inter-American Economic Affairs* 20 (Spring 1967): 3–22.

W., C. de, *La verdad sobre las cuestiones entre el Brasil y la República Argentina originadas por los tratados con el Paraguay*. Buenos Aires, 1872. Bound with other pamphlets in *Folletos*, Museo Mitre, Buenos Aires.

Washburn, Charles A[mes], *The History of Paraguay, with Notes of Personal Observations, and Reminiscences of Diplomacy under Difficulties*. 2 vols. Boston, 1871.

Wisner de Morgenstern, Francisco, "El Paraguay de 1871, según Wisner." *Revista del Instituto Paraguayo* 8 (Asunción, 1903): 763–772.

Ynsfrán, Pablo Max, *La expedición norteamericana contra El Paraguay, 1858–1859* (Biblioteca de Historia y Arqueología Americanas). 2 vols. Mexico City and Buenos Aires, 1954–1958.

Zeballos, Estanislao S., "Diplomacia desarmada, fracaso de las misiones Quintana y Mitre, en el Paraguay." *Revista de Derecho, Historia y Letras* 31 (Buenos Aires, 1908): 107–134, 248–283.

―――, "Las fuerzas armadas y la posición internacional de la república." *Revista de Derecho, Historia y Letras* 30 (Buenos Aires, 1908): 517–542.

Zubizarreta, Ramón, "La cuestión de la moneda." *Revista del Instituto Paraguayo* 11 (1904): 113–164.

Newspapers

El Comercio, Asunción, 1877.
Los Debates, Asunción, 1876.
El Derecho, Asunción, 1874.

El Fénix, Asunción, 1873.
A Gazeta Brazileira, Asunción, 1875.
El Imparcial, Asunción, 1875.
La Nación, Buenos Aires, 1870–1876.
El Nacional, Buenos Aires, 1872–1876.
Nación Paraguaya, Asunción, 1873–1874.
La Opinión, Buenos Aires, 1872.
La Opinión Pública, Asunción, 1870.
El Orden, Asunción, 1872.
El Paraguay, Asunción, 1870.
La Patria, Asunción, 1874–1875, 1919.
La Patria, Buenos Aires, 1876.
La Prensa, Buenos Aires, 1871–1878.
El Progreso, Asunción, 1873.
El Pueblo, Asunción, 1870–1871.
La Reforma, Asunción, 1875–1878.
La Regeneración, Asunción, 1869–1870.
La República, Asunción, 1872–1873.
La República, Buenos Aires, 1869–1885.
The Scotsman, Edinburgh, 1871.
El Semanario, Asunción, 1866.
La Situación, Asunción, 1870.
The Standard, Buenos Aires, 1869–1872.
The Times, London, 1871.
La Tribuna, Buenos Aires, 1872.
La Voz del Pueblo, Asunción, 1870.
The Weekly Standard, Buenos Aires, 1869–1878.

Index

rendered to, 143; rejects Bareiro's agreement, 270; urges renewed negotiations, 275
Council of Medicine and Public Hygiene, 151
Council of Public Instruction, 168
Coups d'etat: of 1870, 82–85; of 1871, 103; of 1874, 213; of 1878, 283; of 1894, 284
Courts, 155, 217, 272, 277. *See also* Judiciary
HMS *Cracker*, 237, 257
Crime, 152, 154–155, 157–158
Croskey, Joseph Rodney, 264, 269
Curupaity, battle of, 10, 275
Customs duties. *See* Tariffs
Cuverville, Aimé Paul de, 18, 298 n. 50
Cuyabá, 219

Daltro, Antônio da Silva, 220, 226, 252
Los Debates, 155, 271
Debt, foreign. *See* Foreign debt; London loans
Debt, internal, 142
Decoud, Adolfo, 29, 162; asks end of political agitation, 74; captured at Paraguarí, 198; characterizes Paraguayan factions, 72; denies Decoud control of provisional government, 70; in plot of 1872, 189; originates slogan "Manos a la obra!" 162; quarrels with Jovellanos and Ferreira, 254
Decoud, André, 269
Decoud, Antonio, 34
Decoud, Diógenes, 162
Decoud, Héctor Francisco, 162
Decoud, José Segundo, 50, 65, 74, 94, 162; attacks Bareiro editorially, 87; Caballero's political mentor, 179; cabinet positions of, 100, 302 n. 12; career of, 181–182; condemns Bareiro agreement, 266; condemns Jovellanos clique, 139; contributions to Constitutional Convention of 1870, 79–81, 85; converted to conservatism, 181, 283; editor of

La Opinión, La Reforma, and *La Regeneración,* 86, 165, 181; editorial attacks against Brazil, 259, 260, 271; favors Adolfo Saguier as president, 275; in Tacuaral revolt, 103; officer in Paraguayan Legion, 49; on Council of Public Instruction, 168; opposes Brazilian occupation of Paraguay, 227; opposes Rivarola's candidates in 1871 election, 161; philosopher of Colorado Party, 178, 181; presidential choice of Club del Pueblo, 55; role in plot of 1870, 82; role in revolt of 1873, 181, 203; secretary to Rivarola, 64; supports Caballero and Bareiristas, 101, 123, 178
Decoud, Juan Francisco, 84, 65; as police chief in Asunción, 65; captured at Paraguarí, 198; center of Decoudista faction 50; finances *La Regeneración,* 70, 161; in plot of 1872, 189; nominated as triumvir, 55; protests attack on *La Voz del Pueblo,* 79; resigns from Paraguayan Legion, 49; sons of, 162; under house arrest, 84
Decoud. Juan José, 55, 72, 162; condemns immorality, 152–153; death of, 319 n. 51; dismissed as attorney general, 84; editor of *La Regeneración,* 70; "father" of the Paraguayan Constitution, 89; in Godoy plot of 1870, 82; publishes articles on constitution, 70, 78
Decoudistas: attack Bedoya, 69; begin *La Regeneración,* 70; Club del Pueblo begun by, 55; leaders of, 50; opponents of, 52; oppose Egusquiza, 300 n. 13; origin of, 49
El Derecho, 79, 164, 190, 319 n. 65
Derqui, Manuel, 250, 257
d'Eu, Conde. *See* Conde d'Eu
El Diario, 187
Díaz, Isidora, 238
Díaz, José Eduvigis, 10